AF361279

MERCHANT WRITERS

Florentine Memoirs from the
Middle Ages and Renaissance

MERCHANT WRITERS

Florentine Memoirs from the Middle Ages and Renaissance

VITTORE BRANCA

Translated by Murtha Baca
With a Biographical Essay by Cesare De Michelis

UNIVERSITY OF TORONTO PRESS
Toronto Buffalo London

ISBN 978-1-4426-3714-6

Library and Archives Canada Cataloguing in Publication

Mercanti scrittori. English
Merchant writers : Florentine memoirs from the Middle Ages and
Renaissance / Vittore Branca ; translated by Murtha Baca ; with a
biographical essay by Cesare De Michelis.

(Lorenzo Da Ponte Italian library series)
Translation of: Mercanti scrittori.
Includes bibliographical references and index.
ISBN 978-1-4426-3714-6 (bound)

1. Florence (Italy)–Social life and customs.   2. Commerce–History–
Medieval, 500–1500.   3. Merchants–Italy–Florence–Biography.
4. Florence (Italy)–Commerce–History.   5. Florence (Italy)–Biography.
I. Branca, Vittore, editor   II. Baca, Murtha, translator   III. Title.
IV. Series: Lorenzo Da Ponte Italian library

DG735.6.M4713 2015   C813'.6   C2015-904445-6

Publication of this book has been assisted by the
Istituto Italiano di Cultura, Toronto.
This book has been published under the aegis and with
financial assistance of:
Fondazione Cassamarca, Treviso; Ministero degli Affari Esteri,
Direzione Generale per la Promozione e la Cooperazione Culturale;
Ministero degli Affari Esteri, Direzione Generale per i Beni e le Attività
Culturali, Direzione Generale per i Beni Librari e gli Istituti Culturali,
Servizio per la Promozione del Libro e della Lettura.
University of Toronto Press acknowledges the financial assistance to its
publishing program of the Canada Council for the Arts and the
Ontario Arts Council.

Funded by the   Financé par le
Government   gouvernement
of Canada   du Canada

Canadä

Contents

Contents

Translator's Note

When my friend and colleague Luigi Ballerini[1] approached me about doing an English translation of Vittore Branca's monumental anthology of texts by Italian merchant writers of the late Middle Ages and Renaissance, I asked him who he imagined our ideal reader to be, so that I could keep this in mind as I deciphered the texts by the various authors selected by Branca. Luigi mentioned a recently deceased mutual friend, Joseph Perloff – an eminent cardiologist and man of culture – as the kind of reader he imagined for an English translation of Branca's *Mercanti scrittori*. Our friend was a widely read man, whose widow is a prominent humanistic scholar; he was highly intelligent and curious about everything, but had no in-depth knowledge of Italian history, language, or literature. With this kind of reader in mind, I set about translating the texts by the nine men represented in this anthology, none of whom had any literary

---

1 I have worked for Luigi on previous translation projects for the Lorenzo Da Ponte Italian Library: Pellegrino Artusi's time-honoured late nineteenth-century cookbook, *Science in the Kitchen and the Art of Eating Well* (2003), which I did with Stephen Sartarelli, and the anthology edited by Lauro Martines, *A Renaissance Sextet: Six Tales in Historical Context* (2004). In the late 1990s, we worked together on a sort of "sampler," entitled *Merchant Writers of the Italian Renaissance*, published in 1999 by Marsilio New York. That was a different and much briefer (about 160 pages) anthology of texts selected and annotated by Vittore Branca. The current book is based directly on Branca's classic *Mercanti Scrittori: ricordi nella Firenze tra Medioevo e Rinancimento*, published in 1986 by Rusconi, which is 603 pages long. For the 1999 English-language edition, Branca chose brief excerpts of texts by Domenico Lenzi, Paolo da Certaldo, Giovanni di Paolo Morelli, Bonaccorso Pitti, Donato Velluti, Goro Dati, Francesco Datini, and Lapo di Giovanni Niccolini de' Sirigatti. He also added texts by Giovanni Boccaccio, Lorenzo de' Medici, and Niccolò Machiavelli, which were not included in the original 1986 Italian publication, and are not included here.

aspirations, as well as the introduction by Branca, so rich in cultural and literary references and imbued with Branca's deep humanistic sense.

Unlike their fellow merchant Boccaccio, the men who wrote the texts included here were not "authors." They were traders, manufacturers, businessmen of the middle and upper classes, who wrote in a very Tuscan version of Italian and some of whom knew a smattering of Latin. It should always be kept in mind that the documents these men wrote were never meant to be "published" in any sense. Thus the texts are often quite unpolished, and even "telegraphic." The exceptions are Giovanni di Paolo Morelli and Bonaccorso Pitti, who expended a considerable amount of effort in constructing what they hoped would be well-structured, compelling narratives. But for all of the merchant writers, the intended audience were family members, descendants, and themselves – they never dreamed that they would be read in a language other than their own, by readers in far-flung places, hundreds of years after their death.

The translation of such highly personal and idiosyncratic documents (which sometimes include passages that approach "stream of consciousness," and on other occasions include rather tedious lists of people, dates, merchandise, prices, and so on) involves particular challenges. On many occasions as I was toiling over these texts, it occurred to me that it is easier to translate something written by a good writer than a bad one.[2] While Morelli and Pitti had some skill with language, and were both quite gripping storytellers, Franceso Datini's last will and testament is so poorly written, garbled, and fraught with legal bombast as to be fairly incomprehensible in places. Accounts of fluctuations in grain prices such as we find in the journal of Domenico Lenzi can be almost stultifying in their detail (except in Lenzi's dramatic descriptions of the misery and violence that frequently occurred when grain was scarce), yet they reflect the reality of the writers' lives and times. While I attempted to make the English translations as clear and comprehensible as possible, and to avoid outright grammatical errors, I did not attempt to "prettify" the writers' texts, or to make them appear more cultured or eloquent than they really were. At times the very clumsiness of the language makes their accounts more dramatic, or even heart-wrenching – as in Morelli's account of the death of his son, his own profound existential crisis, and his strange dream, fraught with symbols and spiritual references.

---

2 I *have* translated works by "real" authors, from Boccaccio and Machiavelli to Pier Maria Pasinetti and Remo Bodei.

Another challenge in translating historic texts is the context of the language and society of the time. Many expressions, such as *notaio delle Riformagioni* (Morelli), do not exist in modern Italian (this notary was one of the highest officials in the chancery of the Florentine republic, who registered all new laws and decisions of the assemblies). I translated all of Branca's own footnotes, with the exception of those that dealt with linguistic forms and other issues that would be incomprehensible to the contemporary English-language reader. On several occasions, I provided additional footnotes to explain Italian words for which there is no English equivalent, such as *zara* or *coderone* (two games mentioned by Morelli). I also provided footnotes explaining English words that may not be known to all readers, such as *malmsey* and *theriac* (the former a fortified wine, the latter a mixture of honey and medicaments, mentioned by Morelli as remedies for particular ailments). For some words that are known to contemporary speakers of Italian, but have no exact English equivalent, such as *popolo minuto* (denoting specifically at the time of the merchant writers the craftsmen, shopkeepers, and labourers who were not permitted to organize into guilds, and more generally "the working classes"), I left the term in Italian and provided a footnote. I also added some footnotes and bibliographic references to help explain and provide additional information on historical or political situations that would not necessarily be common knowledge for modern English-language readers. I modernized place names or indicated the modern name whenever the writers used outdated spellings or appellations, and provided some notes on geography where I deemed they would be helpful to the modern reader.

Every translation is, of course, an act of interpretation and negotiation.[3] The translator's task is to render as accurately as possible the meaning and intent of the original text while retaining as much as possible of its style (good or bad) and "flavour," and at the same time producing a comprehensible, readable, non-anachronistic text in the target language. But as good as a translation may be, it is always an act of "mediation," which inevitably puts the reader at a certain remove from the original text. It is well known that two translations of the same work can be dramatically different. A stunning example is provided by two English translations of Thomas Mann's legendary novella *Death in Venice* – what was considered the "classic" English translation for decades, published

---

3 See Umberto Eco, *Mouse or Rat? Translation as Negotiation* (London: Phoenix, 2004).

by H.T. Lowe-Porter in 1930, is so different from (and "out of date" compared to) the translation done by Michael Henry Heim in 2004 as to seem to be a different novella.[4]

I met Vittore Branca on several occasions during the latter part of his life, including a brief encounter in 1986 when he was at the Getty Research Institute (where I now work) as a residential scholar. Of course his *Bocciaccio medievale* had been a sort of Bible for us when I was a graduate student in the Department of Italian at UCLA, where I was fortunate to attend a seminar taught by him during one of his visits to Los Angeles. On those distant occasions, neither he nor I imagined that one day I would have the honour of translating his seminal anthology of texts by the merchant writers of Renaissance Tuscany into my own native language.

Branca's knowledge of the language, history, and literature of the Italian Middle Ages and Renaissance (as well as other periods) is legendary. He carefully selected, and in many cases transcribed from the original manuscripts, the texts that are included in *Merchant Writers*. His linguistic, cultural, and historical knowledge is reflected in his many footnotes, which enable readers who are non-experts to grasp the complex political, social, and financial institutions and relationships described in the texts. Translating *Merchant Writers* was for me like taking a journey into a period of Italian and Western European history when commerce and "international relations" were transforming the world, and political, economic, and social power in Italy was being hotly contested in various arenas both inside and outside the country. It was a pleasure that I hope my English translation will allow me to share with readers whom Branca never knew he would reach – including historians and students of historiography, cultural anthropologists, scholars of cultural studies, students of literature, and the international community of admirers of Boccaccio who are eager to learn more about the cultural milieu in which that giant of Italian literature was formed.

Murtha Baca

---

4 See Michael Cunningham's introduction to the first edition of the Heim translation of *Death in Venice* (New York: Ecco, 2004).

MERCHANT WRITERS

Introduction

In the *Decameron*, Boccaccio recounted the epic of the Italian merchants of the thirteenth and fourteenth centuries in Europe, and even on the African and Asian shores of the Mediterranean.[1]

In the thriving civilization of the late Middle Ages in Italy, Florence was one of the main centres of the new power that was encroaching on the power of the military and that of the Catholic Church, and was a prime mover of the "economic revolution" (as Robert S. Lopez defined it)[2] that characterized the age straddling the thirteenth and fourteenth centuries. It was economic power that conditioned both the political and military power of kings and lords and the religious power of popes and bishops. Merchants and bankers could "make and break" kings, as one of them, Niccolò Acciaiuoli[3] (who had done so with the king of Naples) said. They could start and stop wars at the drop of a hat (as the Bardi and

---

1 *Note from the translator:* The introduction to the present translation of the full 1986 Rusconi edition of Vittore Branca's *Mercanti Scrittori: Ricordi nella Firenza tra Medioevo e Rinascimento* is a sort of hybrid that I devised between the introduction to that edition and a somewhat different introduction that Branca wrote for the 1999 "sampler" published by Marsilio New York, also translated by me, which was aimed at a broader, English-speaking readership; the 1986 introduction was written primarily for Italian-speaking scholars of the late Middle Ages and early Renaissance. As in the anthology itself, I retain most of Branca's original footnotes, eliminating only a few that deal with linguistic and other issues that would not be meaningful to readers of the English translation. I also expand upon some of his footnotes, and add some of my own, particularly in the introduction, to enable readers to better understand Branca's numerous cultural and especially literary references, which he assumed would be common knowledge to the intended audience of the 1986 Italian edition.

2 In *The Birth of Europe*, see the Bibliographic Note at the end of this essay.

3 Niccolò Acciaiuoli (1310–1365) was the scion of a powerful Florentine family of bankers. He was grand seneschal of the Kingdom of Naples and count of Melfi, Malta, and Gozo.

Peruzzi families did with France and England);[4] they could get popes elected, and have prelates and lords excommunicated, as Acciaiuoli and Frescobaldi did. Merchants had truly become the "fifth element" of the universe, along with air, water, earth, and fire. They were the "pillars of Christianity" – that is, of Christian civilization – as the famous historian of the time, Giovanni Villani, characterized them.[5] Florence was the great centre of banking and commerce in continental Europe and, via the Angevin dynasty in Naples, the Byzantine world as well; it dominated the first true economic-commercial dealings, based on the invention of double-entry accounting, on the letter of exchange that made it possible to move huge sums of money beyond any border, and on the stability and internationality of money. During the late Middle Ages, the Florentine florin played the same role that the dollar did in the twentieth century.

Boccaccio himself had gone back and forth between France and Italy, Greece and Asia Minor between about 1330 and 1340, when he was working for the powerful Bardi trading company of Angevin Naples. Thus he was able to appreciate the annotations, diaries, and first-hand accounts written by the busy men of action who worked for the banking-commercial-industrial "companies." Boccaccio made these often exceptional people the protagonists – be they heroes or victims – of several tales in his masterwork, the *Decameron*. He captured the uninhibited, bold, adventurous character of these men who travelled throughout Europe and from one side of the Mediterranean to the other. He portrayed their commitment, their culture, and their pioneering spirit, thus indirectly giving his seal of approval to their writings, in which those talents and that adventurous, exciting life were reflected.[6]

It was no accident that among the first merchants to take up the pen were two men who worked in the circle of the Boccaccio family; in fact,

---

4 The Bardi and the Peruzzi were two of the leading banking families in Florence. See Ephraim Russell, "The Societies of the Bardi and the Peruzzi and Their Dealings with Edward III," in George Unwin, ed., *Finance and Trade under Edward III: The London Lay Subsidy of 1332* (Manchester: Manchester University Press, 1918), 93–135; and Edwin S. Hunt, *The Medieval Super-Companies: A Study of the Peruzzi Company of Florence* (Cambridge: Cambridge University Press, 1994).

5 Giovanni Villani (circa 1276–1348) was a Florentine banker and statesman. His *New Chronicles* are a seminal account of the history of his native city.

6 I will not dwell on Boccaccio here, as I have done in my numerous writings on the *Decameron*. In *Boccaccio: The Man and His Works*, the English translation by Richard Monges of my *Boccaccio Medievale* (New York: New York University Press, 1976), in the chapter entitled "The Mercantile Epic" (276–307), I analysed the *Decameron* tales that have merchant protagonists, also alluding to the works of the merchant writers.

one of them, Paolo da Certaldo, was from Boccaccio's home town. And it is no coincidence that precisely in the wake of certain pages by Boccaccio, the first-hand accounts of Italian merchants in later years took the form of a fascinating, original literature that characterized the most advanced stage of the civilization of the Italian city-states of the late Middle Ages and Renaissance, from Boccaccio to Niccolò Machiavelli, Francesco Guicciardini, and Benvenuto Cellini all the way to the Italian diarists of the seventeenth century. This was a genre of writing that flourished in hundreds of examples and different experiences, a genre that is now studied side by side with the Petrarchan genre of lyric poetry, the narrative genre begun by Boccaccio, and the romantic-chivalric genre, as one of the most typical reflections of Italian society and culture between the fourteenth and seventeenth centuries – and as the richest source of private diaries before the French diarists from the late Renaissance onward.

This was a genre that might proudly proclaim the fourteenth-century motto: "No enterprise, no matter how small, can begin or end without these three things: power, knowledge, and love."[7] And the revival of interest in it seems in some way natural in our own times – an interest in writers not merely of words but of facts and concrete realities, in writings that are not literary, but rather colloquial, personal accounts of the everyday realities and problems of ordinary men concerned with goods and money, home and family, private and public affairs; men with the urge to possess and dominate and the awareness of how fleeting it all is, man's pride and his inadequacies, his aggressive materialism and his irrefutable need for God.

The middle-class merchants of the late Middle Ages and early Renaissance felt and lived and took for granted these eternal realities of man and existence – not in an intellectual or literary way, but in the most ordinary way, in their own everyday activities. They recorded their memoirs in the direct, concrete tone of entrepreneurs who left room for emotions, imagination, and fantasy alongside accounts, calculations, and profit margins. They wrote about things and events and people involved in production; they were writers who were a part of history, like Edison, Ford, Krupp, Gualino, Pirelli, Mattioli, and Rusca, or like Iacocca, Agnelli, Floriani, Travaglia, Renault, and Pompidou in the more recent past. The merchant writers were experiencing those realities at a time – like

---

7 See Armando Sapori, *Studi di storia economica: secoli XIII, XIV, XV*, II (Florence: Sansoni, 1955–67), 1:533.

ours – when the ideals and powers and institutions (Church and Empire) that had ruled society for centuries were in a state of crisis, and the ones that would dominate society in the centuries to come (supra-national economic institutions, large nations and their national agendas) were coming into being.

Most of these merchants were writing in the tempestuous atmosphere of the decline of the Florentine city-state and its guilds: the time between the brief, doomed, populistic Ciompi[8] revolt in 1378 and the Seignory[9] of the most powerful Florentine family at the time, the Medici, who had already been cunningly working behind the scenes in the person of Salvestro de' Medici at the time of the Ciompi uprising. This was also the time of Florence's most intense, dogged, aggressive campaign for supremacy not only in Tuscany, but in all of Italy.

Corresponding to the turbulently evolving political situation, on the economic level there was the early ascendancy of Florence during the thirteenth century (the florin was first coined in 1253) and the beginning of the fourteenth century, and then the economic depression during the mid-fourteenth century, with the dramatic failures of the banking houses of Bardi and Peruzzi and the devaluation of the florin, followed finally by the economic recovery of the late fourteenth century, which continued throughout the fifteenth century. This was an economic-mercantile revolution, or rather an evolution less turbulent than the concomitant political upheaval but no less profound and decisive – and it had already been perspicaciously envisioned and foretold by Boccaccio in the mercantile epic of his *Decameron*.

A transformation of Florentine economic and social life took place starting at the time of the greatest European and Mediterranean expansion under the regime of the guilds and "companies" (there were about two hundred guilds in Florence in the early fourteenth century), at the time of the most cautious, albeit fortunate, form of capitalism, after the

---

8 The *ciompi* were property-less workers in the wool industry. See Gene Brucker, "The Revolt of the Ciompi," in Nicolai Rubenstein, ed., *Florentine Studies: Politics and Society in Renaissance Florence* (London: Faber, 1968).

9 The Seignory (*Signoria*), the governing body of medieval and Renaissance Florence, was made up of nine Priors (*Priori*). The Priors were chosen by drawing lots from the members of the guilds of the city: six from the major guilds, and two from the minor guilds. The ninth Prior was the Standard-bearer of Justice (*Gonfaloniere di Giustizia*), who in addition to having the voting rights of the other Priors, was in charge of security and public order.

depression mentioned above, under the oligarchic domination of the wealthy and according to the directives, no longer of the guilds, but of the banks and "holding companies," which had their most extreme example in the Medici. The pioneering spirit of the adventurous merchants who had set out to conquer the Occident and the Orient, the discovery of new lands (Boccaccio himself recounted the discovery of the Canary Islands) out of a thirst for wealth and power but also with a spirit of adventure and of human generosity, came to be supplanted by a systematic, cautious exploitation of those conquests through the accumulation of wealth. The powerful, explosive, expansive age of the Wool Guild, the Exchange, and the "companies" – the age of the Mozzi, the Frescobaldi, the Bardi, the Peruzzi, and the Acciaiuoli dynasties – was succeeded by the age of the highly calculating, almost inordinate cautiousness of the Datini, Albizzi, Strozzi, Ricasoli, Capponi, Pitti, Niccolini, Alberti, and Medici families. These families were also concerned with controlling the political situation above all in order to profit from the *monti* (public funds), to be able to obtain reductions on taxes and forced loans, to establish international relationships of privilege, or even to set up monopolies via official missions and with the backing of popes and kings.

This audacious, mad dash for wealth, the building up of capital via the most open, ruthless economic cycle (from usury to exploitative production to the dumping of assets), the conquest of the European and Mediterranean markets even at the cost of violence, gave way to a cautious, deliberate quest for solid property investments, farming, or easy shortcuts to wealth (gambling, diplomatic posts as a source of "insider trading," manipulation of currency values). The motto of these new merchants seems to have been the one expressed by Giovanni di Paolo Morelli: "Do less at first, and you shall be safe." Little by little, the various "companies" that had operated as far away as the distant lands of the Orient were replaced by banks that concentrated their operations on money – often public monies – in Florence, the rest of Italy, and Western Europe. In spite of a pathetic effort to create a "broad florin" in 1422, the Florentine florin, the veritable "dollar" of the late Middle Ages, was losing its position as the prevailing currency of Europe and the Mediterranean to the Venetian ducat.[10]

---

10 The *fiorino largo* (broad florin or galley florin), issued in 1422, was a coin of the same size, weight, and value as the Venetian ducat. See Pasquale Villari, *The Two First Centuries of Florentine History: The Republic and Parties at the Time of Dante*, translated by Linda Villari (New York: Charles Scribner's Sons, 1901), 328.

The finest books of memoirs, the richest in humanity and narrative spirit – including those of Velluti, Morelli, and Pitti in this anthology – accurately reflect this tempestuous political and social background, rhetorically dominated by the values and myths of the *libertas* of the Florentine city-state: justice, peace, civic unity. But later these myths came to be disturbed by blinding flashes of light and sinister shadows, shot through with great nostalgia and anguished shudders, by intractable hatreds and ambitions run wild, by appalling greed and headstrong enthusiasm, leading up to Lorenzo de' Medici's humanistic myths of a Florentine primacy in Italy and Europe[11] and the prophetic illusions and upheavals instigated by Savonarola.[12]

These writings by merchants and traders had already begun to appear in Florence during the thirteenth century, in the margins of ledgers and account books, where merchants recorded the acquisition of lands or the leasing of farmland to sharecroppers (as in the diaries of the Guicciardini family). These notations were also family histories and *ricordanze*.[13] The awareness of the natural convergence of economic prosperity and power and the growing fortunes of the family was always the inspiration for these books, which were often written by several members of successive generations of a family: as with the Medici, from Foligno di Conte in 1360 to Lorenzo the Magnificent in 1472. They were usually called *ricordi* or *ricordanze* or "book of ..." with the name of the writer or of the family.

Of course Florence also produced the kind of technical or geographic-statistical documentation that was prevalent in other commercial centres and especially in Venice; suffice it to recall the famous "handbook" written in the mid-fourteenth century by Francesco Balducci Pegolotti.[14]

---

11 Lorenzo de' Medici (1449–1492), known as "Lorenzo the Magnificent," magnate, statesman, and patron of Renaissance artists such as Verrocchio, Botticelli, Signorelli, and Michelangelo, was leader of the Florentine Republic. See Lauro Martines, *April Blood: Florence and the Plot against the Medici* (New York and Oxford: Oxford University Press, 2003).

12 Girolamo Savonarola (1452–1498), the Dominican preacher and reformer whose zealous attempts to end corruption in Florence ended in his excommunication and execution as a heretic. See Lauro Martines, *Fire in the City: Savonarola and the Struggle for Renaissance Florence* (New York and Oxford: Oxford University Press, 2006).

13 *Ricordanza* (plural *ricordanze*) is word of Provençal origin used in Tuscany in the late thirteenth century to indicate a record of a commercial transaction.

14 Francesco Balducci Pegolotti, a Florentine merchant and politician, composed his *Libro di divisamenti di paesi e di misuri di mercatanzie e d'altre cose bisognevoli di sapere a mercatanti*, commonly known as the *Pratica della mercatura*, between 1335 and 1343. See Allan Evans, *Francesco Balducci Pegolotti: La Pratica della mercatura. A Study of the Man and His Work* (Cambridge, MA: Mediaeval Academy of America, 1936); reissued by Kraus Reprint in 1970.

But the seemingly "marginal" annotations found in account books and ledgers almost always had the character of histories of family life (births, marriages, deaths, above all in their economic implications such as wills and divisions of property, dowries, contracts of sale, construction of houses, and so on); or even insights of a psychological nature about people with whom the merchants had business dealings, or with whom they corresponded, reflections on family, social, or political situations or on moral and religious implications, always noted in a colloquial tone, only for the eyes of other family members. In the early fourteenth century, as we shall see, Domenico Lenzi interspersed the monotonous columns of grain prices at the Orsanmichele market with apocalyptic notes about famine and plague, which affected the oscillation of prices. These distant roots in personal account books are reflected in the more elaborate writings of the fifteenth century, in the form of accounting abbreviations and in certain syntactical expressions or stylistic features, and even in the writers' habit of "making an accounting" of the most diverse operations or events.

Thus, while they were keeping track of their activities (loans, sales, purchases, letters of exchange, the management of artisans and labourers), these "sons of Mercury" were also acquiring the habit of evaluating and characterizing their times and the things and people of those times. As Jacques Le Goff pointed out, they replaced "the eternally renewed, perpetually unpredictable time of the natural world with a new, measurable time, focused and foreseeable."[15] And they established a literary tradition that traced its origins to the Roman *paterfamilias* but also fused life and economic substance with life and family substance, like body and soul, like the circulation of the blood and spiritual activity. For these merchants, the family was the basic, fundamental cell of civic and political life, as in Morelli, and as theorized by the greatest humanists of those years, from Leonardo Bruni[16] ("nor can anything be perfect where the family does not exist," *Life of Dante*) to Marsilio Ficino[17] ("by leading your family you educate yourselves, you become experts, honoured in the earthly republic and worthy of the heavenly," *Letter to Pelotto*).

---

15 Jacques Le Goff, *Tempo della Chiesa e tempo del mercante* (Turin: Einaudi, 1977), 13.
16 Leonardo Bruni (circa 1370–1444), a Tuscan humanist and statesmen, has been called the first modern historian.
17 Marsilio Ficino (1433–1499) was a prominent humanist and philosopher of the early Renaissance.

Ragion di mercatura (merchant interests) and *ragion di famiglia* (family interests) – the two dominant themes of the diaries of three centuries (albeit with notable variants, as we shall see) – are clear and relevant from the very first attempts at this kind of writing.

The merchant writer was fully aware of the decisive value of his writings for both his economic activity and the life of his family, which were inextricably linked. It was no coincidence that when a merchant wanted to have his portrait made, he usually had himself depicted in the act of writing. Nor was it by chance that Dino Compagni, in his survey of the various professions in his *Canzone morale del pregio*, characterized the *pregio* (merit) of the merchant as "fine writing."[18]

For financial and political reasons, these annotations and accounts, both mercantile and domestic, became even more necessary at the beginning of the fifteenth century. The merchant's commercial activity had always been closely interwoven with his domestic life. But the growing impact of the public sphere on the private (and vice versa) during the early fifteenth century heightened the need for annotations that served both commercial and family interests. The establishment of the Florentine *catasto* or tax assessment in 1427,[19] the creation of the *Monte delle doti* in 1425,[20] and the increasing number of *prestanze* due to continual wars[21] all made it necessary to keep precise accounts of both financial and domestic affairs. For that matter, at this same time the increasingly oligarchic structure of the Florentine government and the strengthening of the increasingly conservative Guelph party provided incentives to men of a certain rank to reconstruct the histories of their families and to gather evidence and facts about their own past and present and those of their families.

Both for economic activity and for family and public life, it was necessary to have all the elements and all the documents relating to a family's estate, past and present, clear and ready to hand. This was the only way to defend one's estate from the often aggressive intervention of the state

---

18 Compagni was an important Florentine civic figure and historical writer. His *Chronicle* relates events that he witnessed in Florence between 1280 and 1312.

19 The *catasto* was a sort of declaration of income with a list of the members of the household and their status.

20 The *Monte delle doti* (Dowry Bank) was where money was deposited to create dowries for women of marriageable age.

21 *Prestanze* were forced loans made to the state by private citizens depending upon the size of their estate.

and whoever dominated it at the moment. This also enabled men to aspire to become part of the oligarchy of the government, whose members were selected for primarily economic and commercial motives.

These conditions are reflected and even recommended in the insistent teaching, more practical than humanistic, that often led the diarists into long digressions, from the past of their parents to the future they hoped to build for their children and grandchildren.

Luca Pitti, who had been given his start on the commercial scene in 1423 by his father Bonaccorso, and who through luck, brains, and vigilance became the proverbial progenitor of the economic and political greatness of his family, decided in 1459 to lay the foundations of his splendid *palazzo* located in the area of Florence where his forefathers had lived – a *palazzo* that would perpetuate the Pitti name for centuries; the artist and early art historian Giorgio Vasari wrote that "so much grandeur and magnificence have never been seen." Luca Pitti went from playing a leading role in the oligarchy of the wealthy middle class under the Medici regime to having his praises sung by poets like Ugolino Verino and Benedetto Dei, to being considered one of the four most powerful citizens of Florence at the time of Cosimo de' Medici's death in 1464. Indeed, he can be considered an emblematic figure in the sociopolitical situation reflected in the most characteristic writings of the merchants of the fourteenth and fifteenth centuries.

In the writings of the Florentine merchants, the preponderant convergence of commercial interests and family interests, over which the more ruthless state interests began to cast a shadow during the mid-fifteenth century, is depicted in various situations and in continual evolution, enlivened by the most diverse human temperaments. Underlying the most systematic and successful of these writings we usually find moral reflection and debate; attention to and preoccupation with spiritual and domestic matters; and political and familial commitments and aspirations that also had a public, civic aspect. During the fifteenth century, family and political considerations came to be overshadowed by the personality of the individual writer, so that sometimes these writings constituted, at least in part, a kind of autobiography (e.g., in Bonaccorso Pitti's writings or in private diaries like those of Dati and Morelli), although they are a far cry from autobiographical writings in the truly modern, intimistic sense.

Throughout the fourteenth century and during the early fifteenth century, Europe was still feeling the effects of the heated moral debates about the legality of the lending and trading that had begun to flourish during the second half of the thirteenth century. In response to the absolute, traditional opponents of exchanging currency, charging interest, and large profits (on the basis of the Old and New Testaments, but also of Aristotle) – that is, the primary activities of the merchants – there began to emerge new theologians and moralists (especially Franciscans) who were more indulgent toward banks and commerce, albeit within certain limits and under specific conditions. In any case, the early form of capitalism that followed the almost exclusively rural feudal economy of the medieval courts was seen in a bad light and kept on the margins of Christian life. Commercial interests and authentic evangelical ethics seemed difficult to reconcile, as the Dominican friar Giordano da Pisa preached at the beginning of the fourteenth century.

For this reason, the writings of the merchants are pervaded by moral concerns, often expressed impersonally and in a categorical way through aphorisms and proverbs and reinforced by insistent moral and religious precepts. Two particularly exemplary, singularly effective writers – Domenico Lenzi and Paolo da Certaldo – stand out in this group.

Between 1320 and 1335, Domenico Lenzi,[22] better known as *il Biadaiolo* (i.e., a seller of *biade*, fodder), made long lists of grain prices on the Florentine market of Orsanmichele; completing them with lists for the period of 1309 to 1319, Lenzi collected them in a splendid illuminated manuscript (today designated as Tempi 3 in the Laurentian Library in Florence) under the highly religious, moralistic title of *Specchio umano* (Mirror of Humanity). Lenzi unscrupulously profited from the ups and downs of the basic products necessary for human subsistence. But he also saw a providential occurrence in those fluctuations, as other merchants such as Giovanni Villani, Boccaccio, and Paolo da Certaldo were writing at the same time: "All the plagues and battles, ruins and floods ... occur by the permission of divine justice, to punish men's sins" (Villani, XI, 2); "the deadly plague ... was sent upon mortals by the righteous ire of God to punish us for our evil deeds" (*Decameron*, Introduction, 8); "those tribulations of yours and your affairs are permitted by God on account of your sins, or the sins of your father or mother"

---

22 There is little documentation on Domenico Lenzi, who wrote his *Mirror of Humanity* during the mid-fourteenth century, with an obvious literary and stylistic commitment, and intended for a wider audience than those of most of the other merchant writers. Unlike many of the merchant writings, his was not a modestly secret, private book intended only for his family.

(Paolo da Certaldo, precept 339). Lenzi, the humble grain trader, observed this divine design with moral and religious reflections, often in proverbs and verses written by himself and others, interspersed among the lists of prices and financial-agrarian annotations that occupy most of the manuscript (and are extremely valuable documents for the history of economy, particularly the agrarian economy, as Charles de la Roncière[23] and Giuliano Pinto[24] clearly demonstrated).

Although Lenzi called himself a "crude, ignorant" writer, not only is his work a "merchant classic," as it has repeatedly been defined; he was also a lively, effective writer, guided by a keen awareness of the dignity of his work. He was a Christian who was well aware of the danger of considering financial gain to be a *raison d'être*, and of the need for human moderation. Lenzi was highly sensitive to the needs of "God's poor," and very conscious of the supernatural destiny of man.

It is precisely because of this heartfelt awareness on the part of the writer, along with his commitment as a citizen – which at times attained the level of a sort of civic poetry – that Lenzi's *Mirror of Humanity* takes its place alongside Boccaccio's *Decameron* at the beginning of that evocative genre of mercantile narrative writing and in the history of private diaries and practical, social teachings that would lead to Francesco Guicciardini's melancholy, very human *Ricordi* in 1530.[25]

Like no other writings of the time, the narratives of these merchant writers offered a harsh, tragic chronicle of poverty and hunger, describing how the poor periodically went wild from privation, from the desperate recourse to eating "plant roots and fruits of trees, and meats disgusting not only to the mouth but to the nose as well." In this sad, eternal epic of the struggle of the disinherited with hunger, always crushed and swept along by civic or economic tragedies, Lenzi singles out desperate scenes of poverty and violence with the figurative power of painters like Ambrogio Lorenzetti and Francesco Traini,

---

23 Charles de la Roncière, *Prix et salaires à Florence au XIVe siècle (1280–1380)* (Rome: École française de Rome, 1982).

24 Giuliano Pinto, ed., *Il libro del biadaiolo: carestie e annona a Firenze dalla metà del '200 al 1348 / [di Domenico Lenzi]* (Florence: L.S. Olschki, 1978).

25 Niccolò Machiavelli's friend Francesco Guicciardini (1483–1540) was one of the most important political writers of the Italian Renaissance. His *Ricordi*, translated by Mario Domandi as *Maxims and Reflections of a Renaissance Statesman* (Philadelphia: University of Pennsylvania Press, 1972), is both a personal and a political memoir.

using a turgid, vehement language reminiscent of the descriptions of the lower circles of Dante's *Inferno*.

Lenzi echoes Dante as he concludes his magnificent, moving description of the poor forced out of Siena in 1329 with a flourish of disdain (also ignited by Florence's inexorable hatred for her rival city-state). These are harsh, dramatic pages that in the first warmth of hope and charity focus on sweeping images of generosity reminiscent of Boccaccio's Nathan.[26] But then suddenly the rhythm changes, becoming fast and agitated, as Lenzi describes the city of Siena's decision to drive out the poor ("all those to whom God alone is a brother should be allowed to die of hunger"), in their desperate delusion of a return to the hospice that had once generously taken them in ("there arose infinite cries and sounds of hands striking, shouts and crying, and people clawing their faces"), in their anguished madness, which explodes in a storm of tumult followed by merciless repression:

> ... the poor ran desperately in infinite numbers toward the public palace whence those orders had emanated, crying out "Have mercy!" or "Fire!" or "Die!" All this noise brought the people of the city running, armed with whatever they could find. Armed guards emerged from the public palace to put down the uprising, but to little avail; for the poor, striking with stones and sticks, stormed the palace, driving back the guards, who were fearful of greater injury.
>
> ...
>
> Several days after the uprising had quieted down, there began an intense search for whoever had incited or consented to so much violence and turmoil. In one night, no fewer than 60 men were taken from their beds, and as many were tortured as were executed by hanging ...

At the height of this tragedy of poverty and hunger, when "at a public council it was voted at last that the poor should be driven out of Siena and that no succour for the love of God was to be given them," Lenzi's antipathy erupts in the Dantesque cry:

> Oh! Cruel earth, why did you not open up? (*Inferno* XXXIII, 66)

Perhaps while he was still alive and certainly shortly after his death, Dante was considered a teacher of both moral and religious faith as well

---

26 *Decameron* X, tale 3.

as of noble poetry in the modest spiritual world of this "crude, ignorant" grain merchant.

The class that would dominate late Gothic Florentine culture, and that would ultimately be painted in lively colours in Boccaccio's *Decameron*, could certainly not fail to be part of the new public which, having first been won over to literature by Dante's *Divine Comedy*, developed tastes for the kind of art and literature that flourished in Florence during the second half of the fourteenth century. But already in these writings from the beginning of the century, the merchant class was asserting its deeply felt moral, social, and religious conscience and its talent for down-to-earth writing sustained by expressive power and some degree of literary and cultural experience.

These men, as Christian Bec demonstrated in his memorable studies of the fifteenth-century merchant writers,[27] were in fact quite sensitive to the moral message of the great writers, ancient and modern, from Cicero and Virgil and Seneca to Dante and Petrarch and Boccaccio; they were passionate readers and owners of those books. As we shall see, they even took up the Ciceronian and Petrarchan topos of the free, fruitful "dialogue" between the reader and exemplary texts, in a meditative, pedagogical sense. They not only had "ink-stained fingers" on account of the annotations necessitated by their profession; they also often had the ambition and the talent to write in order to communicate the human implications of their most routine activities, albeit only to those who were close to them. As Domenico De Robertis showed in his history of fifteenth-century Italian literature, this was the sign "of a social and economic condition that had been achieved not by individuals but by an entire class of people: it was even a moral condition ... a true literary *koiné* for the most part devoid of personal artistic aspirations, but one that established a level of communication higher than that of spoken language."[28]

This moral and cultural situation of the mid-fourteenth century was vividly portrayed by another grain merchant, Paolo da Certaldo, who had been designated to provide bread for the Florentine militias in

---

27 *Les marchands écrivains* and *Les livres des florentins*; see the Bibliographic Note at the end of this essay.
28 Domenico De Robertis, *Storia della letteratura italiana: Il Quattrocento* (Milan: Garzanti, 1966), 377.

1362–4.[29] Paolo, a compatriot and friend of Boccaccio (to whom he sold some land in 1360), the son of a prominent notary who worked on behalf of merchants, had a certain degree of culture, as revealed by the literary echoes and allusions to Dante in his writings. He was a wise, active administrator, and above all a meditative moral observer in his *Book of Good Practices,* which is the masterwork of the moralistic, pedagogic merchant writings. Paolo's continual references to his own experiences and his disenchanted human realism seem in some way to prefigure the concrete, bitter style of Francesco Guicciardini. "It is better to act in vain than to do nothing in vain," concluded Paolo, as did Guicciardini many years later: "The true praise is to be able to say: I did, I said" (*Ricordi,* 129). Indeed, there are many prefigurations of Guicciardini in Paolo da Certaldo's writing; he was continually correcting and updating, mingling memories of family and society with mercantile admonitions and scenes and tales (precept 378) and amorous stories reminiscent of the *Decameron* (Boccaccio's tale of Andreuccio, II, 5, can be seen as an illustration of Paolo da Certaldo's precept 86).

Paolo's 388 precepts or proverbs have an entirely merchant-like character in the tone in which they are written or transcribed, in spite of the fact that almost half of them clearly derive from earlier sources and that they appear to have been thrown together almost without rhyme or reason. Indeed, in terms of the glimpse of the merchant's everyday life, these precepts offer, as Salomone Morpurgo noted, "a tiny, shimmering mirror that in rapid but clear flashes reflects many of the most ordinary and therefore rarely recorded customs [of the day]."[30] When Paolo with his perspicacious eye observes the most ordinary aspects of his own everyday life, as Alfredo Schiaffini observed, "his writing is at its richest and most lively; he reveals the straightforward nature of a Florentine man of business, rich in experience, sharp and astute, ceremonious yet invincibly diffident, innately disposed to traffic in both goods and

---

29 Little is known about Paolo da Certaldo. His father was Messer Pace, a notary and man of the law, ambassador to Siena in 1318 and to Bologna in 1320, a member of the Priors in 1323, of the Good Men in 1331 and 1336, standard-bearer of his guild in 1338, a man who could be trusted among merchants. Other than the two documents cited in the text, we know nothing about Paolo except that he was unable to fulfil the terms of the contract for provisions for the Florentine troops and was fined, but obtained a pardon in 1370.

30 Paolo da Certaldo, *Il libro di buoni costumi,* ed. Salomone Morpurgo (Florence: Le Monnier, 1921).

currency, and happy if he succeeds in saving his soul from eternal damnation as well as filling his purse with lovely clinking florins and acquiring more lands."[31] In Paolo's list of proverbs, the family is closely linked
to earning money and managing property:

> So that the members of your household will be solicitous and useful, al-
> ways instruct them not to return home empty-handed. They should bring
> something with them when they return home, and especially when you are
> staying in the country. For it is well to bring all good things to a household.
> (Precept 89)

For Paolo, the only wealth that counted was wealth created by one's
own toil; even inherited wealth was seen as uncertain and unpredictable
(precepts 81, 352, and 385). But he also believed that moral and religious
ends should take precedence over the demands of business and family:

> Be careful not to be deceived by your conscience ... (precept 250) ... There
> is nothing that the Devil strives to do more than to make us steal, saying:
> "Take from others, and I will make sure that you won't have to give back"
> (precept 128) ... if you ever hope to go to Heaven, it will do you no good
> not to do evil, if you don't do good deeds as well (precept 388).

Thus a condemnation of usury and fraud is always present (e.g., in
precepts 115, 128, 321), even in the most venal of Paolo's precepts, those
that almost seem to condone deceit (precept 152). And the exhortation
to charity and compassion is explained by the Catholic moral principle:

> If you do not have compassion for those who are in trouble, you shall not
> find mercy yourself; therefore always have compassion for your fellow man,
> so that you can in good faith ask God for his compassion. (Precept 33)

This is a kind of charity that derives in a certain sense from a mercantile, contractual view of things, from the notion of a pact with God
(see also precepts 335 and 338). It is closely analogous to the famous
bequests left "to Messire the Lord God" – that is, alms – recorded in the
account books of the Florentine guilds.[32] This was a practice that in the

---

31 See Schiaffini's introduction to Paolo da Certaldo, *Il libro di buoni costumi* (Florence:
   Le Monnier, 1945).
32 Sapori, *Studi di storia economica*, 2:839 ff.

Gospels was always related to God, to a supernatural conception of life, impulses of sincere piety and religiosity (and this in spite of these merchants' open antipathy to the pope, indeed their outright anti-clerical attitude), devout to the point of daily visits to church and examinations of conscience. But while Paolo da Certaldo clung to the Christian vision of the Gospels as a renunciation of earthly things and as a preparation for heaven, he also remained faithful to the ethics and the practice of the merchants – to make the greatest profit possible – and to the economic and social success of the individual and of the family. As Christian Bec observed, "Paolo da Certaldo was neither altogether forgetful of Christian morals, nor perfectly imbued with the merchant ethic."[33] And yet Paolo's precepts often indicate a totally earthbound, middle-class ethic, in spite of frequent religious references, persistent thoughts of death and supernatural destiny, and faith in God and his providence (see for example precepts 335, 338, and 372).

This was a stretching, or rather a balancing act that went on continually between the end of the fourteenth century and the beginning of the fifteenth century in the works of several of the merchant writers, including Goro Dati and Francesco Datini, who was the most powerful, enterprising merchant of his time ("In the name of God and of gain" was his motto). This kind of dichotomy provoked heated debates on the destiny of the soul, and, for Datini, it resulted in the establishment of the Ceppo or Hospice, a famous charitable institution that is still operating today, almost as a sort of "ransom" or redemption for an entire life devoted to commercial trading and financial gain.

Along with the history of his family and the recording of his company's accounts and the sad recitals of financial crashes, in his *Libro segreto* (Secret Book), Gregorio Dati[34] makes statements clearly analogous to those of Paolo da Certaldo, even to the point of verbal echoes. For example, Paolo begins his book with the words "In the name of God amen"; Dati's book opens with the words "In the name of God and the

---

33 Christian Bec, *Les marchands écrivains: affaires et humanisme à Florence, 1375–1434* (Paris: Mouton et Cie, 1967).

34 Gregorio or Goro di Stagio Dati (1362–1435), a silk trader, member of the Guild of Por Santa Maria, an active merchant, was Standard-bearer of Justice in 1428. He had bad luck in business. In 1348 he bought into a company for the first time, for 300 florins, and also traded with Spain. Perhaps on account of his unfortunate dealings with Spain, by 1412 he was on the verge of bankruptcy; he was saved by his brother Leonardo, a general in the Dominican order, and by Cosimo de' Medici.

Virgin and all of the saints in heaven, I shall begin this book." But when this balancing act was at its most difficult, it waved the banner of "tribulations of the soul" (perhaps also on account of commercial disasters), first in a moral crisis that led to a resolute examination of conscience, a personal "confession" with firm resolutions to reform ("I realize that I have already passed the age of 40 with little obedience to God's commandments ... I resolve ..."). At moments like this, Dati proposed subjugating the most ironclad motives of business and political success to the religious imperatives of piety and charity. However, these are exceptions, perhaps caused also by Dati's entrance into public life and his serious financial difficulties, even the threat of bankruptcy (1404–12). But they are not unique, if we think of certain pages from the debate between the notary Lapo Mazzei and the merchant Francesco Datini.[35] They were natural in a traditional temperament – a temperament that reflected the past more than the future, a temperament with inclinations to mysticism – like that of Dati, the brother of a Dominican vicar general who corresponded with Vallombrosan monks, the author of a *History of Florence* with a decidedly conservative, religious bent.

This balancing act between predominantly domestic economic and social imperatives and Christian ethics, between the various merchant traditions – civic, religious, and humanistic – is reflected in what is rightly considered to be the masterpiece of the merchant writers: Giovanni di Paolo Morelli's *Ricordi*. Morelli interwove the history of his family and of his city with realistic portraits of individuals and narrative episodes as well as long moralistic and pedagogical digressions, financial precepts of a prevalently domestic nature, religious and emotional outpourings and

---

35 The extremely interesting correspondence between Mazzei and Datini was published in two volumes, *Lettere di un notaro a un mercante del secolo XIV*, edited by Cesare Guasti (Florence: Le Monnier, 1880; available as an Elibron Classics replica edition, 2006). Guasti tells us that Mazzei (circa 1347–1412) was a prominent, cultured notary, a friend and counsellor of Niccolò da Uzzano, Guido del Palagio, and other eminent Florentines; he was a colleague of Datini, whose will he drew up in 1410. On Datini (circa 1333–1410), one of the most famous merchants of the time, see the general studies of Federigo Melis, *Aspetti della vita economica medievale* (Siena: Monte dei Paschi di Siena, 1962), and the enjoyable biography by Iris Origo, *The Merchant of Prato: Francesco di Marco Datini, 1135–1410* (Boston: Nonpareil Books, 1986; first published in 1957). The correspondence between Mazzei and Datini reveals a continuous debate between the speculative, mystic notary and the merchant, a practical, down-to-earth man of business.

self-analyses (of an almost psychological nature – Morelli had a complex about being an orphan), mystical reflections and visions, all pervaded by a deep-seated pessimism about man and by a wholehearted if tormented faith in God and his providence.[36]

Morelli evoked the wars for the rights of the Italian city-states against the feudal lords who still dominated the countryside in his frightening descriptions of the continuous struggles against the Ubaldini clan, whom he characterized as "iniquitous tyrants, robbers, and destroyers of the people, and especially enemies of the Ghibellines"; and in his recounting of the siege of Montaccianico, which he epically protracted like a sort of new *Iliad* (he wrote that "the siege lasted seventeen years" – instead of the four months it actually lasted). Indeed, Morelli transformed the siege into a sort of fabulous exploit of heroes on winged horses ("it was like waging war against one of the stars in the sky"). He portrayed the fierce clashes between Florentine factions in similar dark, violent tones: they "fought house to house with crossbows. And for this reason many high, strong towers were built, many of which you can still see today within the first circle of city walls."

Even more immediate and direct was Morelli's awestruck evocation of the merchants who had made Florence into a world power through their group solidarity – men like his ancestor Paolo di Bartolomeo Morelli, who achieved political and financial status "not through the power of money, but through his own reason and diligence."

Morelli's evocation of the city-state of Florence in its early days and its first flourishing is liberally sprinkled with lively, robust portraits, which later evolved into profiles of wary, circumspect speculators or savers, especially in his insistent examples of diffident cautiousness. It seems that by this time the the distant lands to which his ancestors had travelled were too far away to be attractive; the adventurous wool trade and the daring art of money exchange had lost their fascination for Morelli. "Do less at first and you shall be safe" seems to have been the motto of this kind of calculating, pessimistic common sense, of this mode of behaviour which, as in Paolo da Certaldo and Dati, has "the right way" as its supreme rule.

The uninhibited temerity of the creators of the great Florentine fortunes had given way to the guarded acquisitiveness of men who were

---

36 The *Ricordi* were written between 1393 and the early months of 1411; Morelli returned
     to them in 1421 only to record the death of his son Antoniotto.

looking for safe, fat investments, and who worried about the state intervening in their business affairs. This is why, in Morelli's account, the
oligarchy that had an ironclad hold on the Florentine seignory – and
hence financial domination of the city – during those years is depicted
in its mercilessness in a series of rapid, impressionistic glimpses, lively
portraits that are dramatic but not exhaustive. But first he paints a dark,
deprecatory picture of the Ciompi rebellion, a short-lived revolt of the
Florentine working classes:

> Then a labourer named Michele di Lando rose up, and ruled Florence for
> three days, sending roving bands of men all around the city. During this
> time, leaders of the guilds were made members of the Seignory; a third of
> the members were workers and minor artisans and members of the guilds.
> And the Standard-bearer of Justice, Michele di Lando,[37] was a wool carder.
> All this time, the workers kept looting and burning houses. The entrances
> to houses were blocked, and at night lamps burned in every window.

After this sad glimpse of the poor masses run amok, but quickly squelched
and scattered, comes the end of the brief tyranny of one of the leaders of
the Ciompi, Giorgio Scali:

> He was arrested at the door of his home and taken before the Captain.
> When Antonio di Bese [the *gonfaloniere* or chief magistrate of Florence at
> that time] heard about this, he began to make a great fuss and said that he
> had been betrayed, but … that he was going to bring out the standard,[38] be-
> cause he didn't want a hair of Messer Giorgio's head to be touched. Filippo
> di Ser Giovanni was sitting on the keys, and said: "Yes, if you can!" When
> Antonio saw that the game was up and that all of his carrying on was ridicu-
> lous, he unwillingly agreed to what the others wanted. Messer Giorgio was
> beheaded, and Messer Tomaso di Marco fled, and Messer Donato de' Rico's
> head was chopped off …

Morelli's depictions of the continuous fighting and plotting among
the Florentines are even more passionate and violent, imbued with
dramatic tension. The sly shadow of Gian Galeazzo Visconti of Milan

---

37 The wool carder Michele di Lando was the first leader of the Ciompi Rebellion.
38 The *gonfalone* was a banner or ensign, frequently composed of or ending in several
    tails or streamers suspended from a crossbar, used by various Italian city-states.

("he dressed like a Franciscan monk, carried a rosary, and acted very benevolent") preyed on the fears of Morelli, who saw the Visconti dynasty closing in on his native city – until the triumphal march when the nightmare mysteriously disappeared.

Even more heated and implacable is the hatred for the Pisans that runs throughout Morelli's pages. For centuries, the Pisans were a thorn in the side of the Florentines' pride; the Florentines repeatedly defeated the Pisans, but never succeeded in dominating them. Morelli's hatred of the Pisans, like that of the popular Florentine poet Antonio Pucci,[39] swells to epic dimensions of contempt. After the victory of the Florentines over the Pisans in 1363, Morelli gleefully dwelt on the humiliation of Florence's enemies:

> The Pisans ... were bound with their own ropes and loaded onto fifty of their own carts; and in the first cart their eagle was hung, but not so that it would die, because its feet could reach the cart, and it was struggling violently. Their captain went in front, a prisoner, disgraced ... At the gate at San Frediano, through which the captain entered, there was a little live lion cub,[40] and all the Pisan prisoners were forced to kiss its arse.

Even during the twilight of the free Florentine city-state, Morelli remained strongly convinced of the providential function of the Florentine republic, which would surface during the tumult inspired by Savonarola, in the political mysticism of the *piagnoni*,[41] in the desperate heroism of the siege of Florence in 1530. "The holy, good City" and "the honour, state, greatness of the City" were always uppermost in Morelli's mind as a higher reality mandated by God, as a point of comparison and distinction between good and evil. But alongside the traditional, almost Dantesque nostalgia for "the upstanding, established men of the Florence of old, Guelphs loyal to the city-state," Morelli sensed the rising tide against the tight-fisted oligarchy of the Ricci and the Albizzi (families that only Morelli among the historians of his time dared to criticize). In spite of his natural diffidence as a middle-class Guelph, Morelli was aware of the need to revamp the politics of Florence in a way that was more open to the common people.

---

39 Antonio Pucci (circa 1310–1388) was a bell founder and self-taught poet whose works include a verse version of Giovanni Villani's *Chronicles*.

40 The heraldic lion known as the *marzocco* is a symbol of Florence.

41 The "lamenters," the nickname given to Savonarola's followers.

In this solid faith, this love for the Florentine state that reached Manichean proportions, the state did not represent an absolute, beyond any moral or principle, as a hundred years later it would for Niccolò Machiavelli represent the concrete realization, mandated by God, of a social and political order necessary for man to fully realize himself. As Hans Baron showed in his time,[42] and later Leonida Pandimiglio,[43] this was a continuation of the most authoritative medieval, Dantesque line of thought, albeit filtered and interpreted through the sensibility of the early Florentine humanists – the ideal arc that inscribes very different writers, from a strict humanist like Poggio Bracciolini[44] ("If human life were deprived of the homeland, our virtue would undoubtedly be left frozen, isolated, sterile …") to a Christian Platonist like Matteo Palmieri[45] ("no work among men can be more excellent than providing for the health of the homeland and preserving the state …").

Palmieri, who of all the Florentine moralists had the most affinity to Morelli, seemed to be defining the core of Morelli's memoirs when he wrote: "No other love touches us more than the love of our homeland and of our own children." The great dominating passion of the cautious, diffident merchant Giovanni Morelli was the family in all its aspects.

The family was constantly at the centre of Morelli's emotional, imaginative, and political life; it was the most consistent point of reference in his account of the history of Florence. It was the motive behind his most generous, human impulses and his most moving, limpid descriptions. It was the secret, supreme measure by which he judged, calculated, and acted. It was the dominating idea that somehow justified and redeemed even his moments of base slyness, his subtle moments of vulgarity, his completely utilitarian matrimonial strategies. If during the preceding era the Florentine seignory had been recognized as a *ragion di mercatura*, and in the following era it became a *ragion di stato*, for Morelli we can speak of a *ragion di famiglia* – which could be more merciless and

---

42 *The Crisis of the Early Italian Renaissance: Civic Humanism and Republican Liberty in an Age of Classicism and Tyranny* (Princeton: Princeton University Press, 1955).

43 Leonida Pandimiglio, "Giovanni di Pagolo Morelli e le strutture familiari," *Archivio Storico Italiano* 136 (1978).

44 The Florentine scholar Gian Francesco Poggio Bracciolini (1380–1458), considered one of the earliest humanists of the Italian Renaissance, discovered and disseminated numerous classical Latin manuscripts.

45 The Florentine historian Matteo di Marco Palmieri (1406–1475), whose best-known work is *Della vita civile* (On Civic Life), published in 1528, advocated civic humanism.

inhuman the more it was driven by family motives and the most generous of natural laws.

The power of Morelli's *ragion di famiglia* can be seen in the most sensitive, delicate component of his *Ricordi*: their linguistic fabric.[46] If this is
the ultimate demonstration of the centrality of the family – descriptions,
spiritual and economic reflections, pedagogical, moral, and health precepts (which recall Paolo da Certaldo), public and private memories – it
all converges in "love of one's own flesh and blood." The only time that
Morelli deviated from this approach was in his extravagant description
of his birthplace, the Mugello,[47] "the most beautiful place in the Tuscan
countryside," painted with the freshness of an artist like Fra Angelico
or Paolo Uccello, with a sense of love and reverence for one's ancestors and with a significant convergence of beauty and utility. Morelli's
most vivid portraits are of the "heroes" of the Morelli family – men and
women (Calandro, Bartolomeo, Paolo, Mea, Sandra) who, as Morelli
puts forth in the first part of his memoirs, set the stage for destiny of the
Morelli family – a modest family from the Mugello that rose to wealth
and great honours by hard work, honesty, and unshakeable devotion to
the "Catholic Guelph party." These are affectionately portrayed figures,
with an eloquent immediacy, especially when they are captured in moments of domestic *pietas*. One example is Gualberto di Giovanni ("He
was well educated; I believe he also studied law"), who as a young man
during the plague of 1374 took care of more than twenty of his relatives
who had fled to Bologna. Morelli also presented these figures in scenes
of domestic happiness, in courteous attitudes and gestures that were the
natural reflection of their joyful inner civility. Thus we see Mea di Paolo,
luminously alive in Morelli's description of her brother, like a figure in a
painting by a late Gothic master.

Alongside Mea is a whole gracious series of serene, prudent women,
sweet in character and housewifely – the foundation of their families'
fortune and strength and the embodiment of an intelligent, human approach to domestic economy. Morelli also sketched an amiable series of
young boys and girls in all their vulnerable timidity.

The most intense, moving moment in Morelli's diary occurs when he
recounts the anguished moment of the death of Alberto, his first-born

---

46 See my *Con amore volere: narrar di mercatanti fra Boccaccio e Machiavelli* (Venice: Marsilio,
    1996).
47 An area north of Florence, between the Apennine ridge and the Arno Valley.

son: the painful memories of all the sweetest, most tender moments, even "when he moved inside his mother's womb and … I would carefully place my hand on her belly, awaiting his birth with the greatest desire." Morelli initially gave himself over to the all-too-human abandon of an image that pursued him continuously, bringing back the pain hour by hour. From this sorrowful, disconsolate tenderness arose Morelli's grand, almost epic evocation of his dead son, and his inconsolable realization of the vanity of his own life: vain because he let the most intimate tenderness, the most cherished values, the most basic affections slip through his fingers:

> The best news you ever had was when your wife had your first child, and this was turned into the greatest sorrow and the greatest torment you ever had. Your first child was a son, so that his death would really break your heart. You saw him intelligent and healthy, so when you lost him you would suffer more; you loved him and yet you never gave him any of your wealth. You didn't treat him like a son, but like a stranger; you never gave him a moment's rest; you never looked on him kindly; you never kissed him once; you worked him to death in your shop …

Against the backdrop of Morelli's regret for the joys he had lost forever, the diarist looks back in anguish at his own life, almost as a sort of "everyman" story with the added depth of a father's love discovered precisely at the moment when it has become futile.

One might almost say that this vision, or rather this moment of meditation in which human events are strongly associated with eternal values – often with devotional references to St Catherine, the Blessed Dominici,[48] and St Antoninus, to whom Morelli was particularly devoted – brings to a close the diary that Morelli had written precisely to communicate to his family the meaning and the truth of life.

The "everyman story" that brings Morelli's diary to an ideal conclusion would not be as effective and dramatic if the stage hadn't been set for it by his natural capacity for moralistic reflection. Such a perspective would be inconceivable in the lively, fascinating diaries of Donato Velluti and Bonaccorso Pitti, although their works, too, contain a wealth of human observation.

---

48 Giovanni Dominici, a Dominican friar and orator, founder of the monastery at
   Fiesole.

In Morelli, instead, accounts of family and civic life, private and public lessons learned, quick or studied portraits of people, descriptions of landscapes or events, are all enlivened and given greater depth by a constant moral pondering. Even in Morelli's presentation of historical events, which he usually narrated with great precision, we find him always striving to discover an element of providence and to relate the outcomes of individual actions to the moral commitment of those who carried them out.

It is upon this tireless quest for a moral interpretation of life's experiences, which is at the core of Morelli's *Ricordi*, that his ample supply of precepts is naturally and coherently built – not as an episodic excursus or an oratorical pause, but rather as an essential element of the architecture of the work.

Even classical culture is inscribed within the central motifs of Christian ethics in Morelli's work; because, as Leonardo Bruni stated in a letter to Pope Eugenius IV, "the philosophy that deals with manners, the governance of states, and the best way to live one's life is almost equal in the pagan philosophers to our own."

For Morelli, as for Bruni and later for his friend Giovanni Dominici, the study of antiquity had an essentially moral value, constituting an awareness of man's dignity:

> … when you come of age and your intellect begins to savour the reason for things and the sweetness of knowledge, you shall derive as much pleasure out of it, as much delight, as much consolation as you do out of anything in the world. You shall not prize so much wealth, children, status or any great or honourable preeminence, once you have knowledge and can repute yourself a man and not a beast.

He then adds, in a more realistic, practical tone, already prefiguring the final moment of pride and vain hope that springs from a bitter lack of faith that seems to foreshadow Guicciardini, who exclaimed "How those who bring in the Romans at every word deceive themselves! There should be a whole city set aside just for them":

> … you can take as an example a valiant Roman or some other valorous man whom you have studied. But it is not possible to imitate men like these as you can men whom you see with your own eyes, and especially in the things with which we have to deal, which are more material than those of the great events of Rome.

Thus for Morelli the eternal moral truths were already the precious patrimony of the ancients, before they were accommodated and affirmed with new strength within the Christian message. Consequently, for Morelli the study of the classics, both ancient and modern (up to Dante and Boccaccio, whom Morelli mentioned repeatedly), had a privileged place in everyday life, along with prayer, as a source of the truest wisdom and the deepest humanity.

For this Florentine merchant, study and meditation provided not only consolation and comfort, but also – beyond the Ciceronian topos of a dialogue between man and book – rules of life, wellsprings of action, as a hundred years later for Machiavelli they would be "that food which is mine alone, and for which I was born." A solid middle-class merchant like Morelli, more realistic than the great political theorist and scholar Machiavelli, placed the great texts of contemporary wisdom alongside "the ancient courts of men of antiquity" so revered by Machiavelli.[49] Above all, he valued direct, real-life experience, because, as Guicciardini would later write, "It is a great mistake to speak of the things of the world indistinctly ... discernment and restraint are not found written in books; they must be taught by discretion."

In that silent daily conversation with divine voices and the greatest human voices, felt as the expression of the word of God, in that meditative space reserved every day for the peaceful pondering of one's own life experiences, lies the secret of the intensity of perspectives and nuances that adds greater depth to Morelli's accounts of domestic and historical events, spiritual and financial episodes, realistic portraits of men and things.

Some of the merchant writings dating from the time of Morelli to the fifteenth century have a more personalistic, more "Machiavellian" outlook.

In the diary he kept between 1367 and 1370, Donato Velluti[50] focused strictly on personal matters, above all the characters of individuals and

---

49 The passage about communing with the great men of the past is from Niccolò Machiavelli's famous letter to the Florentine diplomat and writer Francesco Vettori. See Niccolò Machiavelli, "Letter to Francesco Vettori," in Vittore Branca, ed., *Merchant Writers of the Italian Renaissance from Boccaccio to Machiavelli*, translated by Murtha Baca (New York: Marsilio Publishers, 1999), 159–63.

50 Donato Velluti (1313–1370), a judge, jurist, and merchant, was the son of Lamberto di Filippo Velluti. After holding various public offices, he was named Standard-bearer of Justice in 1370.

their "virtues"; his goal was clearly to glorify his own family. He too, at times, had conflicting moralistic preoccupations – he denounced usury, but admired it in one of his ancestors; and clearly for him love of his homeland and the passion for business both sprang from family interests. Activities other than those of the merchant were viewed with diffidence by this jurist who saw everything from the perspective of business.

But Velluti felicitously expressed family interests in a sort of "saga," especially in certain descriptions of his enterprising ancestors, unscrupulous relatives, and friends, both good and bad. These are often stylized portraits that take the form of quick sketches and impressions, richer in characteristic gestures than in inner life (such as those of Madonna Diana and Bonaccorso di Piero). Velluti's work took on a resolutely self-celebratory tone when he became more openly autobiographical in the last part of his book, although he repeatedly declared that what he was writing was not to praise himself, but out of love for his family.

Indeed, in the last portion of his account Velluti clearly intended to promote himself in the political arena; hence a great deal of space was given to the actions of the narrator himself, including swashbuckling adventures and escapades. Velluti's descriptions of himself in the act of carrying out public offices or missions, even in battles and episodes involving the emperor, had a certain exemplary significance, but this kind of account also acted as a sort of "advertisement" for his family. As Christian Bec hypothesized, when his family's fortunes seemed to be coming to an end and they could no longer aspire to political power, Velluti's reason for writing "to perpetuate the memory of the Velluti family" also seemed to dwindle away.

In 1379, shortly after the sad end of Velluti's story, Lapo di Giovanni Niccolini de' Sirigatti[51] began to write his "Book of Family Affairs." Unlike Velluti, Lapo became a rich, powerful representative of the Florentine oligarchy. A respected member of the powerful Wool Guild, during the span of time when he was writing his book (1379–1427) Lapo constantly increased both his wealth and his political power. While obviously superior to Velluti in practical matters and success in life, Lapo

---

51 Lapo di Giovanni Niccolini de' Sirigatti (circa 1360–1430), a prosperous merchant, had great success in the Wool Guild; he held numerous public offices and was Standard-bearer of Justice five times (in 1401, 1406, 1412, 1421, and 1425). He died on 24 December 1430 in the service of the Florentine state, as Vicegerent of the town of Vico Pisano.

was clearly Velluti's inferior as a writer. After the usual invocations, Lapo immediately starts to boast about how old his family was; with their roots in Florence for at least seven generations, always living in the same area of Florence near the palace of the *podestà*, as he himself did; always victorious over the threatened loss or damage to their ancestral home. Investments and purchases of real estate generally have a consortial-familial motif in Lapo's writings: to maintain the authoritative presence of the Niccolini family in their original quarter of Florence, to enhance their credit and their "good name" with their real-estate holdings, also with an eye to obtaining public offices.

Bonaccorso Pitti[52] must have been familiar with Velluti's book, which he would certainly have included among the "earliest writings" that interested him so much; he was a relative of Velluti and a colleague of Lapo, and, like Morelli, related by marriage to the Alberti and Acciaiuoli families. Bonaccorso was a merchant and a politician, a skilful negotiator and ambassador, a good writer who produced poetry that revealed a deep knowledge of Dante; he was not insensible to late Gothic and early humanistic culture, and was a friend of the famous humanist Coluccio Salutati, whom he supplied with books.

Bonaccorso explicitly stated that he began to write in order to assert the legitimacy – indeed, the right – of his family to participate in running the state, during a period in which the Pitti family's position in the Florentine ruling class was being strongly contested, especially by the Ricasoli family. As Leonida Pandimiglio clearly demonstrated,[53] Bonaccorso's book began "with the intention of being a sort of political manifesto of the Pitti family." "Apart from specific single scenes, there are two threads that are particularly worthy of note: financial affairs, and especially intra-familial transactions; and the gradual emergence of

---

52 Bonaccorso di Neri di Bonaccorso Pitti (1354–1432) came from a wealthy, solid family of merchants; he himself was a merchant and carried out numerous missions throughout Europe, was elected to several important offices and was Standard-bearer of Justice in 1417 and 1422. He was certainly the most active and adventurous of the Florentine diarists, and, along with Lapo, the most prominent politically. Because his cousin Ciore had unconscionably destroyed the family documents, Bonaccorso had to reconstruct the family history by perusing his grandfather's papers, official documents such as lists of Priors, and above all the family's own accounts. For the composition and structure of Bonaccorso's manuscript, see my article "Per il testo dei ricordi di Bonaccorso Pitti," in *Filologia e critica* 10 (1985).

53 In her article "Casa e famiglia: ricordanze fiorentine," *La cultura* (1985).

Bonaccorso as a point of reference not only for his own family, but for the families of his brothers as well." Thus a book that was written for political and family reasons, to instruct and admonish the younger members of the clan, so that "you, our sons and descendants ... see and learn from what happens when one attempts to stand firm against those who are more powerful, no matter how rightfully," concludes with an account of the family's reconciliation with the Ricasoli family. This passionate interest in strengthening one's own clan – also through purchases of property and ecclesiastical benefices – was always present and predominant for Bonaccorso, even during the long years when he was away from Florence, having adventures all over Europe.

Bonaccorso's diary, clearly intended to exalt his own family and to promote its position within the oligarchy of the great Florentine families, goes beyond the canonical lines of this type of literature, at times providing new perspectives with considerable narrative felicity. Like the composition and structure of the diary itself, these episodes revolve around two broad themes that occasionally intersect: the ancient origins and honourable ancestry of the Pitti family, and Bonaccorso's autobiographical account of his commercial and political adventures.

The particular charm of Bonaccorso Pitti's writings can be seen especially in certain lively episodes from his early life; in the quality of his writing and his insights, Pitti is second only to Morelli in these passages, which have a strongly autobiographical nature that is more energetic and enterprising than analytical or meditative.

Bonaccorso's ties with his home in Florence – but not with his family – were somewhat loosened in his early years by the death of his father and by financial difficulties that led the twenty-year-old, "young [and] inexperienced," to roam the world "and seek my fortune." This decision was contrary to the sedentary, cautious, Florence-centric tendencies of the merchants of that period (as seen in the writings of Dati, Lapo, and Morelli). Added to this spirit of adventure was Bonaccorso's rejection of the populism of the Ciompi and the artisan class. So, unlike many other members of the Florentine merchant class, Bonaccorso began his wanderings through Europe.

Bonaccorso is also distinguished from the other diarists of this time by his aristocratic consciousness of his family and indeed of life itself, which made him adverse to a certain mentality and to a certain middle-class narrow-mindedness that predominate in many merchant diaries. He had a strong sense of pride in the Guelph "aristocracy," including the Buondelmonti and Frescobaldi families, which had already risen to the heights of power during the last quarter of the thirteenth century, taking an active role in credit transactions, banking, and the wool trade. Even when he was wheeling and dealing, or outright gambling, Bonaccorso felt himself to be the rightful heir to his chivalrous, mysterious ancestor, Bonsignore dei Pitti, who had departed for the Holy Land around 1202 and disappeared without a trace. Bonaccorso always showed a conservative spirit, disdainful of "upstarts and the very young" and their deleterious effect on the state.

Bonaccorso was a genial "merchant of fortune" in the society of the late Middle Ages. He could just as well have been a soldier of fortune, as he could have been a bold knight-errant centuries before. He roamed through the world of European merchants, had encounters with Germans and Frenchmen, with Jews and Levantines, with Genoese and Venetians, cleverly competing with them like a military commander or a knight in a joust. Even his love life had a gallant, chivalrous bent to it – a far cry from the homely middle-class tone of the other merchant writers. He fell in love with a lady named Gemma, a widow; at her command he took off for Rome through the war-torn countryside, as his ancestor Bonsignore had departed for the Holy Land, like a knight taking up a challenge for his lady-love, who in this case mocked him for undertaking such a foolish escapade.

On one occasion, after a night of gambling and losing disastrously, Bonaccorso consoled himself by dancing with a pretty young stranger, who said to him: "Come and dance, Lombard; don't fret over your losses, for God will surely help you." He never felt inferior to the nobles with whom he consorted at the courts of France and Burgundy. After being insulted by the Viscount of Meaux, a relative of the king, Bonaccorso challenged him to a duel, finally obtaining satisfaction from the king himself. Unlike Dati and Morelli, who were cautiously penurious, Bonaccorso loved to wear beautiful clothes, ride fine horses, carry splendid weapons, boast of his wealth and lordly homes, spend and lend money generously – all with a late Gothic sensibility and a subtle nostalgia for the gallant days of chivalry.

Although Bonaccorso's behaviour did not conform to that of the other merchants of his time, for all its temerity and differentness it was still inspired by the *ragion di mercatura*, which was also, as we have seen, the *ragion di famiglia*. The young Bonaccorso realized that because of the precarious situation of his family, which at the time of his father's death had been left without a leader, he had to act with extraordinary personal commitment and in new ways, as demanded by the new times: the time of a Europe composed of nations, of an Italy torn asunder by hegemonic ambitions, of a capitalistic regime in Florence dominated by a few powerful families. Bonaccorso sensed that he needed to act quickly and unscrupulously, using systematic gambling as well as commerce and trading, and exploiting political power for economic gain. Then, when he had achieved a certain level of credit and financial and social stability, he could also invest heavily in real estate and in public funds; he could return to farming and manufacturing, in which his father had made considerable sums, and could become part of the new oligarchic system in Florence by holding public offices.

After sixteen years away from Florence, Bonaccorso returned with a wife and children in 1396 to settle down in his native city and become a fixture in the ruling class. Finally, after the republic was restored in 1382 when the Guelphs overthrew the short-lived Ciompi government, there was again a ruling class in Florence, now made up of upper middle-class merchants who were friends and associates of the Pitti family. Indeed, between 1395 and 1396, the political group led by Maso degli Albizzi (Bonaccorso's wife, Francesca, was a member of the Albizzi family) gained more and more power in the Florentine state, effecting a foreign policy favourable to France, where Bonaccorso could be very useful on account of his many connections.

But whether he was rambling around Europe or rooted in his native Florence, Bonaccorso's commitment was always fundamentally to his business and to his family. "A daring gambler" is how an anonymous diarist described him in 1386, at the time when Bonaccorso was already carrying out an important early commission in the Piazza della Signoria.[54] But as a gambler, Bonaccorso was never dangerous or maniacal, casual or frivolous. He was a systematic, technical gambler, professional and organized. Here, too, he was a "merchant" – a sort of precursor of the entrepreneurs of today's gambling casinos. For Bonaccorso, gambling was a commercial enterprise, like lending or exchanging money, in which one had to win through skill and caution, without complaining when one lost, because one deserved to lose.

Gambling was clearly Bonaccorso's ruling passion from the time of his first big European *quête* in Slavonia and Hungary in 1379. His narratives of this period are perhaps his most lively, animated pages, dominated

---

54 Alessandro Gherardi, ed., *Diario d'anonimo fiorentino dall'anno 1358 al 1389* (Florence: M. Cellini, 1876), 466.

by the reckless, exuberant character of Bonaccorso the protagonist –
reminiscent of the swashbuckling Benvenuto Cellini, it has been said.
Against the squalid, ruthless backdrop of speculators and moneylenders
reminiscent of Boccaccio's Ser Ciappelletto, we see Bonaccorso and his
Florentine friends amid exotic sights and sounds, constantly gambling
on the market and on life itself.

For Bonaccorso Pitti, gambling gradually became not only a source of
fresh money for investments and business deals, from saffron to horses
to wool to wine and foodstuffs, from precious metals and fabrics to jewels and even loans and usury; it also became a way to make connections
on an increasingly high social level, especially with the members of the
courts of Charles VI of France and Louis II of Anjou. Bonaccorso played
the role of the organizer of gambling sessions in various princely settings.
After 1396, having acted as the agent for several other big gambling entrepreneurs, and having taken some big risks himself, Bonaccorso refused to become directly entangled in such matters except on the very
highest level and in truly exceptional cases involving princes and other
royals who could be of advantage in his strategy of public relations in
favour of himself and the Florentine state. This was the new road down
which Bonaccorso had started in order to move the art of being a merchant toward new successes in the rapidly changing situation in Italy in
particular and Europe in general.

Activities that had been seen in a negative light by Paolo da Certaldo
and Boccaccio at the beginning of the fourteenth century – that is, gambling and consorting with powerful people for one's own personal gain –
were now chosen by Bonaccorso within the context of the new
sociopolitical reality as the best ways to establish himself quickly and
solidly; Morelli was still against this. Along with money from gambling,
Bonaccorso also received gifts and prebends from popes and cardinals,
kings and princes, often for political motives or as compensation for services rendered (middleman, informer, lobbyist for the interests of Florence at the papal court, and so on). Money also flowed in as a result of
special privileges that more or less gave Bonaccorso a monopoly on certain things. Another way up the ladder to the Florentine oligarchy was
through diplomatic activity; and this political advancement was now necessary for acquiring financial power in Florence, as Lorenzo de' Medici
("Lorenzo the Magnificent") would realize years later.

Gambling, a position of favour with the great and powerful, diplomatic
missions and government appointments all required an exquisitely personal touch, an activity – or rather, an eminently individualistic kind of

activism. Acting on behalf of one's family or of one's company (be it in banking, trading, or production) could perhaps even be counterproductive and certainly unnecessary in the context of this new political and economic strategy for gaining power.

Bonaccorso's activities, indeed his entire life and hence his writings, which mirror his life, can thus not help being of a highly personal nature: they were all focused on and emanated from his strong personality; hence his writing has an obsessively egocentric quality. Bonaccorso's narrative "I" dominates uncontested, starting from the insistent, sonorous formula "I, Bonaccorso" – an almost canonical invocation that begins both parts of his memoirs and punctuates the crucial moments of the narration. This "I" is also present in the structure and language of Bonaccorso's writings, which are admittedly very mercantile in character, as are the other writings in this anthology, but the persistent egotistical slant that is so characteristic of Bonaccorso's text distinguishes him from most of his fellow merchant writers. The powerful, implacable presence of Bonaccorso's own personality, his arrogant will to lord it over everyone and everything, his constant perception of himself as the architect of his own success (to the point of ostentatious boasting) were certainly the strongest and most efficacious stimuli for him as a writer. They have even led some critics to see in Bonaccorso's autobiographical writings a foreshadowing of the heroic self-projection of Benvenuto Cellini a century and a half later.

Whether he was Buda, Paris, Avignon, London, or Rotterdam, what Bonaccorso saw amid the crowds of people (at least when he was narrating the story) was principally himself, or whatever interested him directly. He focused on the "frightening, cruel" sight (akin to Manzoni's depiction of the plague in Milan) of a mother and her three sons burned alive in a house to which soldiers set fire in the Hundred Years' War, in order to emphasize his own presence and his own sufferings and the risks he ran during the British invasion of Picardy in 1383. He recounted his first important public office (as a member of the Eight on Security)[55] as a pretext for pointing out his own courage when the Public Palace was struck by lightning and he was injured. He wrote enthusiastically only about himself and what directly concerned him, although he generally wrote about historical events with a degree of precision, as

---

55 The *Otto di Guardia* (Eight Magistrates on Security) was the Florentine commission for state security.

Léon Mirot[56] and Gene Brucker have shown. The only times that Bonaccorso erred in making historical or political assessments were precisely on account of the distorting effect of his own interests and personal reactions.

In every place and every circumstance, Bonaccorso lived and acted, as Christian Bec observed, not to *see*, but to *do* – to do things himself and to write about himself and what interested him above all as a merchant, increasing his own wealth. The whole series of wanderings and extraordinary adventures that Bonaccorso had in the most diverse countries of Europe, alongside powerful figures (emperors and kings, princes and dukes, popes and cardinals, soldiers of fortune and government ministers) over a long span of years concludes with his return to Florence, seen in a totally financial light: "I found that I had 10,000 gold francs in wool, my house and furnishings and horses and equipment and cash, not counting the great deal of money that was owed to me, nor the money that the Count of Savoy owed me, nor a great deal of money that was owed to me by several people; so much so, that this amounted to around 5,000 francs."

For a writer with such an egocentric perspective, it is natural that the most lively, expressive moments are self-portraits or self-descriptions in the course of Bonaccorso's most varied adventures and circumstances, always resolutely in action, always realistically energetic. At times Bonaccorso depicts himself boastfully; other times his tone is disenchanted and even self-ironic. The two perspectives alternate quite effectively.

Bonaccorso was a hero who, when he wrote about himself, wanted not only always to be the centre of attention but also to be seen as indefatigably in action, provoking actions and reactions, bringing things rapidly to a conclusion. Proud of his ability to move swiftly – and therefore profitably – throughout Europe, Bonaccorso saw swiftness of decision and of action as a *sine qua non* of success. "Long before Machiavelli," noted Christian Bec, "Bonaccorso was reproaching his fellow Florentines, as well as the French, for their procrastinations. A man totally bent on action, Bonaccorso stressed feats rather than words." Like Machiavelli, Bonaccorso wrote in short, incisive sentences, with no paraphrases or discursive flourishes, going straight to the facts, indeed often cutting explanations short with brief or allusive sayings, or even with inelegant

---

56 "Bonaccorso Pitti, aventurier, joueur, diplomate et mémorialiste," *Annuaire Bulletin de la Société d'Histoire de France* 67 (1930): 183–252.

but expeditious expressions such as *etc., etc.,* or by referring to preceding words or actions.

This is how Bonaccorso lived his life: with no pauses for reflection or doubts or debate. The time of his narration is the time of the action, an action that always takes place with strict, inexorable logic. Without action, the account itself becomes feeble and vague.

Even in the work of a writer as exhibitionistic as Bonaccorso, autobiography was still a more or less important element – albeit the most lively and efficacious from an expressive point of view – of the *ragion di mercatura* and *ragion di famiglia.* For Bonaccorso, in spite of his egocentricity and his cosmopolitanism, the family and its patrimony – and the city of Florence, as the "family of families" – remained the overarching, constantly recurring points of reference in the midst of all his personal escapades and all the complex situations of the Europe of his day.

Several diaries from the fifteenth and early sixteenth centuries were written with the traditional approach, in which the vocation of the merchant and his devotion to his family were pursued under the protection of divine providence. The families in these cases are exemplary: Palmieri, Rucellai, Landucci, Masi, Corsini, Capponi, Machiavelli, Medici, Guicciardini.

Thanks to their activities as merchants and their land holdings in the Val di Pesa, the Machiavelli family also participated in the regime of the moneyed middle class. Bernardo Machiavelli,[57] although he had studied law and participated in public office, spent most of his energies as a good, parsimonious steward of his own not extensive property, attempting not only to buy and sell products of the land and fabrics, but also to profit from the very newest objects of commerce: books. Bernardo had the tight-fisted, hair-splitting nature of the second generation of Florentine merchants, who were more deeply rooted in their native city than the first generation; but he was open to the new art of printing, in which he also participated professionally by compiling indices. His wholly Florentine spirit, which took pleasure in local gossip and scandals – like

---

57 Bernardo di Niccolò di Buoninsegna Machiavelli (1428–1500), the father of Niccolò Machiavelli, the famous author of *The Prince,* was a doctor of jurisprudence and jurisconsult. In 1458 he married Bartolomea Nelli, the widow of Niccolò Benizzi, and had two daughters with her, Primavera and Margherita, and two sons, Niccolò (born 3 May 1469) and Totto. He occupied himself chiefly with managing the estate he had inherited from his uncle Totto, operating as an agrarian merchant.

Sacchetti, Velluti, and later Poliziano in the *Detti* – is expressed in the novelistic slant of the story of the affair with the servant girl that is included in the present anthology. In the end, Bernardo's story of his relative's affair with the maidservant takes on a financial dimension when he describes the indemnifications and investments in the Dowry Fund made on behalf of the pregnant girl. For Bernardo, the traditional attention to his children's education as a guarantee of the family's continued prosperity focused on the selection of good teachers and good texts; but he was also careful to note them in his ledger of expenditures. It is particularly interesting to observe how closely Bernardo followed his son Niccolò's progress not only in his studies but also in his first small commercial assignments. Like one of the gaily garbed, courtly young boys who make their appearance in the works of the Florentine painters Domenico Ghirlandaio and Benozzo Gozzoli, the seven-year-old Niccolò appears for the first time in his father's diary in an elegant little tunic and cloak; he is like one of the capable, serious boys described by Giovanni di Paolo Morelli.

Bernardo wrote that he paid for the binding of Livy's *Decades* with three flasks of red wine and a flask of vinegar; his punctilious notes seem inevitably to place his son Niccolò amid agrarian and commercial dealings: lambs and cheeses, asses and oxen, piglets and capons, grains and wine, olive oil and vinegar, textile manufacturing on a modest scale. Bernardo's world was one of small-scale financial investments – in public funds and private loans, and purchases of legal, historical, and literary texts (he bought all of Livy, in fact), which he completed with indices, had bound, and then resold. Ancient and modern books are mentioned in the same breath with red wine, cheeses, and fabrics to be woven or cut and sewn into various articles of clothing. Bernardo's reflections on the great classical texts and historical events and on the vicissitudes of the Florentine state are interspersed with observations on the humble, realistic necessities and experiences of everyday life – eating and drinking, growing crops and caring for livestock, trying to avoid taxes and forced loans, keeping precise records of debits and credits.

Earlier in the century, Giovanni di Paolo Morelli had admonished his son to "study Virgil, Boethius, Seneca, or other authors for at least an hour every day"; and he quoted from the scriptures, Dante, and even Boccaccio. Study and meditation were not merely a source of consolation and spiritual comfort for the Florentine merchants; they were also a guide for living, a source of action beyond the Ciceronian topos of man's "relationship" with books. Niccolò Machiavelli wrote about "that food which is mine alone" (i.e., the classics of ancient literature) at the time he was writing *The Prince*, while he also mentioned his humble occupations in the country, and the hours he spent at the local tavern. But, as already noted, for a solid merchant like Morelli, what realistically mattered more than the example of classical literature was above all the direct experience of material things as embodied in the political and commercial dealings of his day. More than eighty years later, this is what Niccolò Machiavelli echoed in his introduction to *The Prince*.

In spite of the different commercial and banking situations more than half a century after Bernardo Machiavelli's time, and in spite of the fact that Niccolò Machiavelli claimed that he knew nothing about financial matters, the author of *The Prince* was always aware of the practical domestic and commercial issues that had accompanied the political and economic upheaval in Florence since the mid-fourteenth century. Those tumultuous events were recounted not only by the historians who came after Villani,[58] but also in the homely diaries of the Florentine middle class of the fourteenth and fifteenth centuries, as they were in Bernardo's writings. As Morelli eloquently reveals, they were inspired above all by the most ordinary, everyday political, economic, and social experiences rather than by intellectual or abstract reflections.

In the Florentine diaries of the early Medici period, divine providence and its minister, Fortune, still predominated over "virtue" – in an anti-Machiavellian way. "By the fortune and grace of God" was an insistent formula in the writings of Bonaccorso Pitti and the diarists who came after him. (In his *Canzone morale* Bonaccorso wrote that "With the free will granted by God, man can take the good path ... fortune is good or bad, depending upon what Providence does ...") Christian Bec rightly pointed out that even Pitti's activism was regulated by the rule of never tempting fate or acting against divine providence.

In the diaries of the Florentine High Renaissance, even in the ones written by the strongest personalities up to and including Guicciardini, annotations and narrations usually had as their point of departure domestic and professional records rooted in practical, everyday realities. Like the diaries of the two preceding centuries, they were inspired by the most ordinary experiences.

---

58 These historians have been studied by Andrea Matucci in relation to Machiavelli. See his *Machiavelli nella storiografia fiorentina: per la storia di un genere letterario* (Florence: Olschki, 1991).

It was precisely on account of this immediate realism that the *ragion di stato* theorized by Giovanni Botero[59] began to make inroads on the *ragion di mercatura* and *ragion di famiglia* that had dominated Florentine diaries until the early fifteenth century. But the *ragion di stato* had already clearly manifested itself in the writings of Bonaccorso Pitti and Giovanni Rucellai.[60] As we have seen, merchants were becoming increasingly involved in politics, upon which depended public funds, forced loans, taxes, and contributions that could lead to European relationships and business deals as well as to monopolies and special privileges. Economic power and political power were becoming intertwined. "The State was governed more from behind the merchants' counters than from the Public Palace," observed the fifteenth-century chronicler Giovanni Cavalcanti.[61] The Florentine state had been put into a situation of crisis by the powerful families and their princes – including Lorenzo de' Medici, who began his own diary with considerations of a wholly politico-economic nature. By this time, the state had taken the place of the large clans from the politically engaged middle class that had run Florence in former times. This new driving force – the State – converging with the impulse to make money, would soon spring into the foreground and impose itself in a more absolute way, like a true Machiavellian prince. And the figure of the prince became increasingly dominant as an example – not in an abstract or heroic way, but based on a direct experience of civic life, notwithstanding the obligatory references to classical antiquity: "if you should reach the highest level [of the State], then I would advise you to strive to resemble our Roman forefathers, for as we are descended from them in essence, we should show this in virtue as well as in substance," Morelli had admonished his son a century earlier.

It is true that the middle-class Florentine merchants of the late fourteenth and fifteenth centuries no longer had the generous, adventurous

---

59 Giovanni Botero (circa 1544–1617) was an Italian thinker, priest, poet, and diplomat, best known for his 1589 work *Della ragione di Stato* (*The Reason of State*). See Botero, *The Reason of State*, translated by P.J. Waley and D.P. Waley (New Haven: Yale University Press, 1956).

60 Giovanni di Paolo Rucellai (1403–1481) was a wealthy Florentine wool merchant known for his *Zibaldone* (Hodgepodge Book). See Jennifer E. Simmons, *A Translation with Critical Commentary of Giovanni Rucellai's Zibaldone Quaresimale* (Clayton, Victoria: Monash University, 1983).

61 In his *Istorie fiorentine* II, 1. See Giovanni Cavalcanti, *Istorie fiorentine*, critical edition by G. Di Pino (Milan: Martello, 1944).

élan of their forefathers. But they were nourished by a spiritual and cultural experience, by a pondered human knowledge which, if it did not permit them to act with the temerity of their fathers, did make them aware of the values of history and the constant misery of man. If the aggressive merchant paladins had been the protagonists of the young, audacious civilization of writers like Dante and Boccaccio and artists like Arnolfo di Cambio and Giotto, then the merchants of the following period, with their books of thoughtful moral and civic memoirs, were the exemplars of the more reflective, mature civilization of fifteenth-century Florence. Their writings were harbingers of the concrete, discriminating, overarching cautiousness and the melancholy, deeply human moral discourse of Francesco Guicciardini in the sixteenth century.

Bibliographic Note

The foregoing introduction, as well as the selection of texts and the compilation of the footnotes, are the result of my studies of the "merchant writers" over a period of almost fifty years, beginning with those that first sparked my interest in this genre: "Per il testo del *Decameron*," in *Studi di filologia italiana* 8 (1950); my edition of Giovanni Morelli's *Ricordi* (Florence: Le Monnier, 1956); and "L'epopea dei mercanti," in *Lettere italiane* 8 (1956). I was stimulated above all by the pioneering studies of Christian Bec suggested by Fernand Braudel (*Les marchands écrivains: affaires et humanisme à Florence, 1375–1434* [Paris: Mouton & Cie, 1967]), and *Les livres des florentins* (Florence: Olschki, 1984), as well as several other fundamental studies: Gene Brucker's *Florentine Politics and Society, 1343–1378* (Princeton: Princeton University Press, 1962) and his edition of *Two Memoirs of Renaissance Florence: The Diaries of Buonaccorso Pitti and Gregorio Dati* (New York: Harper and Row, 1967; English translation by Julia Martines); Leonida Pandimiglio's study suggested by Arsenio Frugoni, "Casa e famiglia: ricordanze fiorentine" in *La cultura* (1985) and various studies on Morelli in *Studi sul Medioevo cristiano* (Rome: Istituto Storico Italiano per il Medio Evo, 1974) and *Studi medievali* series 3, vol. 22 (1981), and many other fundamental writings.

These pages also derive from some of my later, more systematic works, including *Con amore volere: narrar di mercatanti fra Boccaccio e Machiavelli* (Venice: Marsilio, 1996).

There are several works that provide a general background (especially ones written in or translated into English) that I would like to indicate to readers of the present anthology: Amintore Fanfani, *Le origini dello spirito capitalistico in Italia* (Milan: Società editrice "Vita e pensiero," 1933); Max Weber, *The Protestant Ethic and the Spirit of Capitalism,* edited, translated from the German, and with an introduction by Peter Baehr and Gordon C. Wells (New York: Penguin Books, 2002); Yves Renouard, *Les hommes d'affaires italiens du Moyen Age,* new edition by Bernard Guillemain from the author's notes (Paris: A. Colin, 1968); Michael M. Postan and Edwin E. Rich, eds., *Trade and Industry in the Middle Ages,* second edition (Cambridge: Cambridge University Press, 1987); Lauro Martines, *The Social World of the Florentine Humanists, 1390–1460* (Princeton: Princeton University Press, 1963) and *Power and Imagination: City-States in Renaissance Italy* (New York: Knopf, 1979); Armando Sapori, *Studi di storia economica: secoli XIII, XIV, XV* (Florence: Sansoni, 1955–67), *La mercatura medievale* (Florence: Sansoni, 1972), and *The Italian Merchant in the Middle Ages,* translated from the Italian by Patricia Ann Kennen (New York: Norton, 1970); Robert Sabatino Lopez, *The Birth of Europe* (New York: M. Evans, 1967); Vittore Branca, "The Mercantile Epic," in *Boccaccio: The Man and His Works,* translated by Richard Monges (New York: New York University Press, 1976); Alberto Tenenti, "Les marchands et la culture à Florence (1375–1434)," in *Annales ESC* 23 (1968); Georges Duby and Jacques Le Goff, eds., *Famille et parenté dans l'Occident* (Paris: École française de Rome, 1977); David Herlihy and Christiane Klapisch-Zuber, *Tuscans and Their Families: A Study of the Florentine Catasto of 1427* (New Haven: Yale University Press, 1985); Carlo M. Cipolla, *Il fiorino e il quattrino: la politica monetaria a Firenze nel Trecento* (Bologna: Il Mulino, 1982); Angelo Cicchetti and Raul Mordenti, *I libri di famiglia in Italia* (Rome: Edizioni di Storia e Letteratura, 1985); and Anthony Molho, *Marriage Alliance in Late Medieval Florence* (Cambridge, MA: Harvard University Press, 1994).

Vittore Branca

Book of Good Practices

Paolo da Certaldo

In the Name of God Amen

1. In this book we shall write many good examples, practices, proverbs, and admonitions. Therefore, my son, brother, my good friend, neighbour, or comrade, or whoever you may be who read this book, listen well and understand what you shall find written here, and put it into action. Much good and honour will come to you, in body and in soul.

2. We read that there are five keys to wisdom. Therefore, you who read and wish to learn the lessons of this book and of others, keep in mind five things – that is, the aforementioned five keys to wisdom – because without them or without one of them you will never attain understanding nor perfect knowledge of the things that you wish to know. Those five things are: fear God; honour your teacher; read continually; continually ask about those things that you do not know; absorb well into your mind what you read and learn and are taught by your teachers. By teacher is meant anyone who teaches you something that you do not know. Even a book that you read, when you understand it, is your teacher for the thing that you learn by reading.

The first key to wisdom is to always fear our Lord Jesus Christ, because he is all powerful; so he must be feared, revered, and honoured. He should be feared because he is powerful above all other powers; revered, because he is Lord of lords; honoured, because he is full of grace. Who could describe the grace of our Lord Jesus Christ with human speech? No tongue is powerful enough to thank him worthily. Oh how much grace he has granted us, when we think that he let us be born Christians! And I could speak of many other graces he has granted to us. So, always have the fear of our Lord Jesus Christ in your heart.

The second key to wisdom is to always honour your teachers – that is, whoever teaches you something. It is a great thing to honour one's teacher, for without teachers you cannot have perfect wisdom, and without wisdom you cannot be virtuous; and a man who lives without virtue is worse than dead. A teacher endures great hardships in teaching his pupil; so always honour your teachers, and you shall be considered the wiser for it.

The third key to wisdom is to continually read many books with great studiousness, because continual reading helps you to learn many things. And whoever reads many books discovers many new things, and by asking questions, learns a great deal. Thus always read and study with great attention.

The fourth key to wisdom is to question continually those you believe know more than you do about things that you do not know. Do not be ashamed to ask about those things that you do not know and that you wish to learn. Thus you must ask about that which you do not know – and when you ask someone about something in order to learn, be humble, and observe the time and place of the question that you ask.

The fifth key to wisdom is to keep well in mind what you read and what is taught to you, because not retaining what you read and are taught and learn is a waste of time. Thus, if you do not wish to read in vain, or cause wasted effort for your teacher, make every effort to retain what is taught to you. And likewise retain the lessons and practices that you shall read in this book and in others, putting the good into action and leaving aside the bad. And you shall become wise and respectable.

3. "Restraint will triumph." Have restraint in all of your dealings so that you shall not err, for he who is restrained shall conquer every vice. There is only one thing in which you should have no restraint, and that is in loving God, for the more you love him with all your heart, the more pleasing you shall be to him. And you must also fear him; and the more you fear him, the more careful you should be not to go against his commandments. And those commandments are these: Do not adore any other god except Our Lord Jesus Christ; observe Sunday as the Lord's day; honour your father and mother; do not commit murder; do not commit adultery; do not steal; do not bear false witness; do not covet your neighbour's wife; do not take the name of God in vain; do not covet your neighbour's goods.

4. These are the seven sacraments of the Church: baptism, confirmation, communion, ordination, extreme unction, matrimony.[1]

---

1 Paolo fails to mention one of the seven sacraments – confession. The Lateran Council of 1215 had made confession obligatory at least once a year.

5. Go frequently to church, and every morning before you do anything else, hear Mass, and pray to God for yourself and your father and mother, for those who wish you well, and for the souls of your loved ones who have passed on, and likewise for all the other dead.

6. Keep your mouth shut and your eyes open.

7. He who hears and sees and does not speak, truly wishes to live in peace.

8. He who begins to do good is promised Paradise, but Paradise is given to the one who perseveres in doing good.

9. Think of every hour as if it were the last you shall live – and always think about death.

10. It is a just thing that he who does not want to repent when he can, cannot repent when he wants to.

11. The closer one gets to temporal goods, the further he gets from spiritual goods.

12. Who is the wisest of wise men? The one who is most humble.

13. A penny with the fear of God lasts longer than a pound without the fear of God.

14. Just as all good is found in God, so in a humble man are found all the virtues.

15. It is better for you to be castigated by God than ruined by the world.

16. I have read and re-read, and I don't remember ever reading that a merciful man died a bad death, said St Augustine. Therefore, be merciful.

17. Do not stand beneath the banner of "I shall do good," for too many men have followed it to Hell. Rather, do good without procrastinating.

18. Humility is the vessel of wisdom.

19. Consider that whatever time is given to you, you shall be called to account for how you have spent it.

20. If we would be righteous, following the example of the saints, we should give honour to God, compassion to the dead, love to our fellow men, discipline to ourselves, hatred to sin, and to the devil we should give continual battle.

21. It is better to stand up straight before a good man with your legs aching than to sit on a bench with a bad man.

22. Ungratefulness dries up the source of mercy.

23. He who sees himself will not see others without utility.

24. The most reckless and the most insane thing a man can do is to be in a state of mortal sin – so take great care to avoid it.

25. Innocence – that is, not to injure others – is the safest weapon there is.

26. You shall never deprecate another if you take a good look at yourself.

27. He who is silent is wiser than he who speaks so obscurely that he cannot be understood by those who hear him.

28. Only mortal sin wounds the soul; thus it is much better to let your body be killed than to injure your soul.

29. Always strive to be hated by evil men and liked by good men.

30. Honour every virtuous man, and despise – that is, avoid – every immoral man.

31. Kind words increase the number of your friends and decrease the number of your enemies; harsh words – that is, evil words – do the opposite.

32. Just as the body has two corporal eyes, so the soul must have two spiritual eyes, one open to the glory of Heaven and the other to the sufferings of Hell. If you do this, you will never offend the blessed Jesus Christ, because you will fear the torment of Hell and aspire to the riches of eternal life.

33. If you do not have compassion for those who are in trouble, you shall not find mercy yourself; therefore always have compassion for your fellow man, so that you can in good faith ask God for his compassion.

34. The end of a cruel life is Hell; the end of a compassionate life is Heaven.

35. If you don't approach virtue when you are young, you will never succeed in leaving behind vice when you are old. So always follow virtue and avoid vice.

36. Crazy is he who lives in a state in which he would not want to die; therefore always be prepared for death, for you do not know the day that it shall come.

37. He who conquers himself in everything is strong against everything.

38. You cannot be in harmony with Christ if you are in disharmony with your fellow man; so always love your fellow man, and honour him as much as you can.

39. There are two doors to justice; by one man leaves evil behind, and by the other man enters to do good.

40. Do not be ashamed to ask for that for which you have a right.

41. Although Fortune has the power to take away your worldly riches, it does not have the power to take away your virtues; thus always be sure to be virtuous.

42. Never tire of the company of wise men.

43. The only medicine for misery and toil is to forget.

44. It is a useful thing to forget the injuries that have been done to you.

45. He who does not participate with you in your adversities is not a faithful friend.

46. A man without a friend is like a body without a soul.

47. He who does not correct his sins is doomed to sin again.

48. Whatever you want to say with your mouth, you should first paint it in your heart.

49. It is not appropriate for you to adorn yourself with clothing that is like a costume.

50. If you do not know what to say, be silent, and you shall be considered wiser.

51. Take care not to bestow love on anyone whom you do not already know by experience or by his actions or by keeping company with him or by his behaviour.

52. The only sin that does not deserve forgiveness is despair.

53. Give alms secretly so that it does not appear that you are glorying in the misery of others.

54. The manners of gentlefolk are often judged by the behaviour and manners of their companions.

55. Do not take on a burden that you cannot bear.

56. Anything that is not clear to one's hearers becomes a danger to the speaker. Therefore, whenever you say anything in a place where you can be heard, say it openly so that you may be understood.

57. The effects of a beginning are not praised, but rather the ending is praised according to how it unfolds. St Paul began badly and ended well, and Judas began well and ended badly. Therefore always persevere in the good, because if you leave off doing good you will begin to do evil.

58. Let the other man's affliction be your guard.

59. A reputation for chastity in a woman is a delicate thing, like a beautiful flower. Therefore, woman, always take care not to acquire a bad reputation on account of your evil acts and behaviour, for it will be very difficult for you to counteract it.

60. When you have good company among your own acquaintance, do not leave it for the company of strangers.

61. Always demonstrate by example that which you speak about, and you shall be deemed the wiser for it.

62. Let us take away the occasions of sin, so that sin may disappear along with them.

63. Envy always follows in the wake of virtue; therefore make sure that you are always envied, but do not envy others, for you cannot envy your fellow man without injury to yourself.

64. It often happens that he who does not correct himself after being chastised ends up mending his ways out of shame and injury. Therefore do not take it ill when someone reproaches you for errors you commit.

65. It is very difficult to know how to act in every kind of situation, but it is a wonderful thing to be able to do so. Therefore always make sure to be able to consort and converse with all kinds of people. As Dante said, you must consort with revellers in the tavern, with the saints in church, and with the demons in Hell – that is, you must know how to behave with all manner of people as necessary, and in the proper way. As the saying goes, "Whoever the man may be, take delight in his company."

66. A word uttered is like a stone thrown. Therefore, before you speak, always think and think again about what you are going to say, and the good or evil that may come of it.

67. He who forgives evil men harms good men.

68. When you become angry and are cruel to your servants, you clearly show others that you are weak. Therefore when you are in your home, act in a gracious, cheerful, humble, gentle manner.

69. It is a praiseworthy thing and a great grace for a poor man to know how to bear his poverty patiently in this world.

70. He who does not believe he has any friends is a friend to no one.

71. Poverty that is born of greed is an ugly thing; and the greed of a poor man is a very ugly thing.

72. The saying goes, "Deal with others' affairs in such a way as not to do harm to your own." Likewise, conduct your own affairs well, and do not do harm to others.

73. They say that "a hidden sin is half forgiven," but you should not set a bad example to others – therefore, do not sin.

74. You will repent speaking more often than you will repent remaining silent; therefore remain silent ten times for every single time you speak.

75. If you want to be loved, love.

76. When you teach, you shall learn.

77. Live as if God were watching you; and speak with God as if men could always hear you.

78. The way to goodness is to desire to be good, and to put that desire into action.

79. Always strive to be as you would wish to appear to those with whom you associate and those who know you.

80. Always exert yourself first for yourself rather than for others.

81. Knowing how to make money is wonderful and a great thing, but it is even greater to know how to spend money with moderation and in an appropriate way. And to know how to hold on to what has been bequeathed to you by your father or by other relatives is the greatest virtue, for that which a man does not earn is easier to spend than that which he earns through his own toil and sweat and diligence.

82. Courtesy is nothing more than restraint, and "restraint will triumph." Moderation is nothing more than keeping order in your affairs. Therefore whatever you do, do it with order and for a good end, and you shall not fail.

83. It is better for a man to have a good name in this world than to have a great treasure. Therefore strive to live honestly in this world so that you may gain a good name, for he who dies with a good name lives on forever. You can gain a good name in this world by practising virtues and shunning vices.

84. The thing that man should love above all is the right, for he who loves what is right loves God and his own soul and his fellow man. Therefore always love and defend and fight for what is right. Strive to have the love of your fellow men rather than their worldly goods, for he who has people's love will also have their goods. Take care never to abandon what is right, neither for money nor out of fear nor love of your relatives or friends or anything else. Rather, always sustain and defend what is right with all your power.

85. Take great care neither to consort with nor to befriend anyone who has the reputation of being a traitor or a heretic or a forger of money, or a murderer or assassin or glutton, or gossip or sodomite. Likewise, avoid men who are well known for other evil vices.

86. Take care not to leave your home at night, if you can help it. And if you must go out, take with you some trusted company and a good, strong light. Never go to the house of any worldly woman or anyone similar at night, even if she sends for you. And even if she sends for you repeatedly, tell her to come to your house, if she wishes to come; if she does not wish to come, she should remain at home, for much mischief has been seen to result from this kind of situation, especially in seaports and in foreign lands.

87. Never trust anyone who is not of your faith, that is, anyone who does not believe in Our Lord Jesus Christ, because he will never be loyal and will deceive you if he can.

88. Be very careful to never tell any lies, because he who becomes accustomed to lying can never leave off. And he who continues to tell lies

is quickly discovered to be a liar, because lies have short tails. And when a man or woman is discovered to be a liar, they are not believed even when they tell the truth, unless it is something that is already well known to many people.

89. So that the members of your household will be solicitous and useful, always instruct them not to return home empty-handed. They should bring something with them when they return home, and especially when you are staying in the country. For it is well to bring all good things to a household.

90. Always keep in your house a dozen or so large sacks: they are good for carrying things out in the event of a fire in your neighbourhood or near to you or to your house. Also keep a rope that can reach from the roof to the ground, so that you can slide down it from any window in your house, if there should be a fire. But keep in mind that you should keep it locked in a trunk, so that no servant or other member of your household can use it without you or your permission, so that they cannot use it for evil ends.

91. When you take a wife, take good care that she be born of a good father and mother, and that her grandmother was a woman of good reputation. For rarely is a girl bad when her mother and grandmother are good. Also take care that the woman that you take for your wife does not come from a family of diseased people or consumptives or scrofulous people or madmen or mangy people or people who suffer from gout, for it often happens that some or all of the children that she shall bear will suffer from some of the same vices and physical defects. And take care that she be wise and have a comely face, so that you shall have comely children from her; and if she be wise, she shall also be good.

92. Do not entrust your wealth nor your affairs to anyone who does not care about his own soul, for he who does not care about his own soul will not care about your affairs and will not act on your behalf in good faith. Indeed, he will always try to take advantage of you and not to help you, for he does not care about you even though he pretends to – he cares about your possessions, and your money. And this happens with all usurers and avaricious people more than with other people.

93. The saying goes, "Always help others no matter who they are, and always beware of those to whom you have done wrong." If it should happen that you do wrong to someone and later you make peace with him or become related to him through a member of your family, never trust him completely, and always pay close attention to what he does and says in your dealings with him.

94. Take care not to enter into undertakings that require you to hire armed men, because this is the cause of great enmity and hatred; therefore try very hard to avoid this.

95. Always make it a habit every evening to make sure that the lights have been extinguished and the fire covered in your home. And always make sure that you are the last one in your house to go to bed, and carefully check the whole house to make sure that the lights are out and the fire extinguished and that the doors are securely locked, and likewise the windows. Also check the cellar to make sure that the wine casks are well sealed and the doors and windows locked and the fire covered and the lights extinguished, and then you can go to bed and sleep to your heart's content.

96. If you have to go to any perilous place, go without telling anyone where you are going. Indeed, if you go to Siena, say that you are going to Lucca, and you shall be safe from bad people. And if while you are on the road you should encounter brigands or other bad people or become aware of any evil doings, do not remain there, but rather hasten to ride faster so that for all that they may try to catch up with you, they will not be able to overtake you until you have reached your lodging or some other safe place. And always try to appear to be as poor as possible.

97. Do not reveal your secrets to anyone of whom you are not sure, because as soon as you have told him of your affairs, you shall become enslaved to him. Do not be desirous of learning the secrets of others, for others like you may learn them, and will reveal them – and your friend will blame you, because he will not remember that he revealed his secrets to someone other than you. In this way, your friend can become your enemy through no fault of your own. And if you should learn or hear about the affairs of your neighbours or friends, do not speak or gossip about them to others – pretend not to know anything about them, for "man should not eat what he has, nor say what he knows, in one day," and "the tongue has no bones, but it often breaks bones."

98. When you need a favour from anyone, go to his home, for he will not refuse you in his own home as he would do outside of it.

99. Wherever you go or wherever you stay, always speak well of those who govern the city; and don't speak ill of those who are not in power, because they could come to power later and they won't consider you a friend of theirs nor of their rank.

100. Big loans and big debts and big credits are what ruin both society and individuals; therefore never incur them. And if someone should ask you to enter into such a transaction, say: "I have a partner, and I cannot

do what you wish without his consent." And if you have no partner, say: "I have an obligation with such and such a relative of mine, and he with me, and I would have to pay him a fine; therefore forgive me, for I cannot oblige you without great injury to myself. And you should not wish me to do something on account of which I would incur great damage."

101. When you hear or see noise or brawling in a place where you are, leave immediately, and do not return, for nothing but evil can come to you there. You shall be called upon to testify, and then, if you tell the truth, you shall gain enemies for it. Therefore flee from such disturbances whenever you can.

102. If you purchase lands or vineyards, keep in mind to buy a small, good field rather than a large, bad one, for in the good field you will always find workers. And if you want to recoup your money, you will always find a buyer for good land without losing. And for bad land you will not be able to get a price high enough to recoup your money when you decide to sell.

103. "The country produces good animals and bad men," as the saying goes, therefore go rarely to the country. Stay in the city, and become a tradesman or a merchant, and you shall come out well. And if you have to frequent the countryside, be careful not to be there on feast days, nor go to the public square where the labourers congregate, because they all drink and become heated with wine, and carry weapons, and go completely out of their heads. Indeed, each one thinks he is a king, and they want to be the only ones to talk, because all week long they have been in the fields, not speaking except to their beasts. And when they are heated with wine, they don't spare anyone, even if he is their superior. If you had words with them, they wouldn't show you any mercy at all; and if they laid hands on you or drew their weapons, you would never be able to avenge yourself, no matter what you did. Therefore avoid country folk on feast days. If you must have anything to do with these labourers, go to them while they are working in the fields, and you will find them humble and meek, thanks to the plough or hoe or spade. If you have to discuss accounts with them, never do it in the countryside; make them come to the city, and do it there. For if you do it in the country, many other labourers will gather, taking their side against you. And you will always come out the loser, and always be in the wrong.

104. Always appreciate any small service that you receive, and always try to return it doubly, so that you do not seem ungrateful. Any great service that you do for a friend or neighbour will always be poorly appreciated, but don't ever reproach him or remind him of what you

have done for him, so that he won't resent it; for then you will have wasted the favour that you've done for him. Man is more grateful for a favour when he is poor than willing to do a favour when he is prosperous.

105. Never lend your weapons to anyone who asks you to, for two reasons: one, because you don't know what he wants to do with them, and the other because you don't know if you will need them yourself in the meantime.

106. If anyone should say to you: "Come with me," do not go if you don't know where he wishes to take you, because it could happen that he is taking you to do you some harm. Therefore ask him where he wishes to go, so that when you've asked him and he says to you: "I am going to such and such a place for such and such a reason," and it turns out that he is going there to do harm or villainy to someone else, you will have the right at the appropriate moment to leave him and not to follow him or go with him, for he did not tell you the truth in the first place. .

107. The saying goes, "He who wants to eat on time, must think about it beforehand." Likewise, when you have something to do, you must not procrastinate until the last minute, when it will be too late for you to act.

108. A man who wishes to conduct his affairs well must have six qualities, which are these: foresight, steadiness, loyalty, thoughtfulness, orderliness, and humility. Therefore always take care to practise these things, and you shall never fail.

109. Do as much as you can to be loved by your fellow citizens and neighbours. Ask them for as few favours as possible, for he who asks his friends for favours must also do favours. Therefore only ask for help when you are in great need. And try as much as you can not to receive many invitations to dine or other courtesies, for he who receives courtesies must also render them.

110. Be very careful to avoid frequenting taverns; do not do it. Go to church on feast days. And go to church on the other days, when you can decently leave your shop or warehouse.

111. Always try to consort with good people and with men who are older than you and whom you believe to be wiser than you, and more honest. And always consort with men who are richer than you and higher in rank and of good breeding.

112. Try as much as you can not to speak ill of your friends or companions or neighbours, or of your city. For when you speak ill of those with whom you consort, you speak ill of yourself. As I said to you above, you should not consort with bad or dissolute people.

112. When you go to a strange or foreign place, endeavour to have as many friends there as you can, and especially a priest or friar who lives an honest and good life, and a doctor, and also a judge. Also strive to gain the friendship of one or more of the leading men of the place, but without spending money excessively on them. A kind and wise man, for the little honour that you, a stranger, render to him, will love you and support you. Learn some little things that he likes that you can get easily from your country, and make a gift of them once or twice a year – for example, a fine sword, or a knife, or bells for a falcon or some other smaller bird, or hoods or leather straps or thongs for falcons, or similar little things, or rings or belts or money bags or silk purses that would be good for him or for his wife or children.

114. If you are in the service of some master, love and serve him loyally and honestly and humbly and with great consideration and reverence, and protect his belongings well. And if he becomes upset with you for some reason, do not become upset yourself, but rather make sure that another time you do not commit the same act on account of which he has become upset with you, so that he will no longer have any reason to do so.

115. If you want to make sure that you never lack enough money to live on, have a shop where you can practise some trade or other. And never take out bills with interest – rather, get by on the little that you have rather than the much of others. For you must know that no trade can thrive if interest must be paid. Therefore never borrow money, as stated above.

116. Go often to church and to hear sermons, for you will learn many good examples and moral precepts there; for a man becomes wiser and more prudent, more companionable, and a better speaker because in church he hears all the good and the bad that have ever been done – the good, so that you shall imitate it, and the bad so that you shall avoid it. And make it a habit to visit the sick, to relieve and comfort them, and likewise to see them die; thus you shall take their example. And also make it a habit to go to see men being punished, not for the amusement of seeing their punishment, but so that it may be an example to you. Also make it a habit to accompany the dead to burial, for it is a great act of charity and very pleasing to God. And it is an even greater act of mercy to bury the poor and abandoned. Have masses said often for the souls of your departed ones, and also for the abandoned souls who have passed from this life. Think, if you were in prison and abandoned by your relatives and friends and no one ever came to visit you, and someone whom

you didn't know came to visit you and got you out of prison, what you would feel. That is how the abandoned souls feel about those who pray to God for them, or have prayers said for them.

117. Three things are necessary for the salvation of the soul: confession, contrition, and satisfaction. Satisfaction is understood in two ways: one is to absolve one's debts to others; the other is to do penance for one's own sins, as imposed on you by your confessor.

118. Always have your last will and testament ready; and if you should decide to add or remove something in it, have another will drawn up, and revoke the earlier one.

119. Never take revenge nor have revenge taken for you, for revenge injures one's soul and body and belongings. If someone injures you, help yourself by means of reason, and you will conquer every disdainful man.

120. A man who has sufficient means is insane to torment himself for more.

121. A man should not desire to live to eat and drink, but should eat and drink reasonably in order to live.

122. It is great folly to love or desire war, either for civic reasons or for private ones. For he who loves war does not love peace; and he who does not love peace does not love God; and he who does not love God does not love his own soul or body; and he who does not love himself – can you see how he gets along? Clearly, he gets along very ill. Therefore avoid as much as you can war on behalf of your city as well as against your own private enmities.

123. Do not take pleasure in legal battles; avoid legal disputes as much as you can. Indeed, it is better to gain less by avoiding a legal battle than to gain more by entering into one.

124. If you have many sons, place them in different trades, not all in a single trade, for they cannot all be of a single mind. Ask each one of them what craft or trade he would like to do, and then start him in that one, and he will turn out to be more skilled at it than if you had chosen for him. And never make any of your sons take a wife against his will.

125. There is almost no one in this world who is content. But he who is less content should think about those who are worse off than he, who are many, and should accept his lot in life.

126. Women are very vain and flighty; so when a woman doesn't have a husband, she is in great peril. Therefore if you have women in your house, keep them as close to you as you can, and don't stay away from home too much. Watch out for your own interests, and keep your women always in fear and trembling. Always make sure that they have tasks to do

in the home, and are never idle. For it is very dangerous for a woman or a man to be idle, but it is more dangerous for a woman.

127. If you wish to be free and not a servant, make yourself a servant of virtue, and not of vice or sin.

128. If you wish to save your soul, take great care not to take anything from anyone, neither by lending money at interest, nor by stealing, nor through deceit. Indeed, if you find something on the ground, you should return it, if you know to whom it belongs. And if you don't know, give it away in the name of God, on behalf of whomever it belonged to. There is nothing that the Devil strives to do more than to make us steal, saying: "Take from others, and I will make sure that you won't have to give back." It's too sweet a thing to take from others and too difficult and arduous to give back something that you have taken. And know that of all the other sins that you can confess, and having repented be forgiven for them by doing penance, you will not be forgiven for stealing if you do not return what you have taken. So be careful not to take anything so that you won't have to give anything back, for you will find it too troublesome.

129. Also take care not to defame your fellow man, for giving another man a bad name is one of the greatest sins. Remember that if you take away a man's good name, you'll have to restore it to him if you wish to be forgiven – and how can you restore it to him? For you will have spoken ill of him to twenty people, and those twenty people will each speak ill of him to a hundred people, and those hundred people will each speak ill of him to thousands of people. This is how a bad reputation spreads. And if you decide "I will now speak well of him," the good you speak of him will not reach the ears of all of the people who have heard ill of him; so it is never possible to make amends nor to undo the sin of slander. Therefore strive as much as you can not to speak ill of anyone, for you will not be able to make amends for it later. And especially if you sully the good name of a woman to a thousand people, and those thousand to more than ten thousand, how will you ever restore it? Certainly, you never will.

130. Make it a habit to fast on Saturdays in honour of the Blessed Virgin Mary, and on that day try as much as you can to avoid sinning. For one should not only fast from food – that is, avoid the sin of gluttony; one should also avoid all seven of the deadly sins: pride, greed, gluttony, lust, sloth, wrath, and envy. By avoiding these sins, you shall make a good fast that is pleasing to God, and you shall without fail reap great rewards from the Virgin Mary in this world and in the next.

131. Always remember, when you have to give a judgment, to do so in an honest, trustworthy, and just manner. Never stray from this course, neither for love nor fear nor family nor friendship nor social ties. For if you are just in giving a judgment, those against whom you make it will not reproach you for it in their hearts. And if you make a false judgment, he against whom you make it shall become your enemy, and he for whom you do it as a favour will know that you are neither loyal nor honest; indeed, he shall always be wary of you, and shall vituperate you always. And you shall be held to make up for the damage that you do to him against whom you have made a false judgment. So you see what a good thing it is to be an honest, trustworthy judge.

132. Never do anything to another that you would not wish to be done to you, and you cannot fail.

133. "Gifts obscure the mind and impede reason." Therefore, when you have to judge between two men, do not accept any gifts that may be sent to you by either of the parties. But on the other hand, I say to you that if in any dispute or other affair of yours you should need the friendship of an official or magistrate, it is easy to ingratiate yourself with gifts. Find out who among his retinue is closest to the man, and first strike up a friendship with that person, and give him some gift. Then ask him for help and advice, and he will teach you how to ingratiate yourself with his master and what gift you can give him that would please him most.

134. Be very careful to avoid the following perils, which are great, and cause great risk: storms at sea, fire, floods, riots, stampedes of horses, the tongue of an evil woman, having to govern peasants, pirates, and assassins.

135. Take care not to fall in love with a woman who is not your wife. Remember, all women are alike; therefore don't love one more than another, for the danger is too great. All great dishonours, shame, sins, and expenditure of money are incurred on account of women. Great enmities arise on account of women, and great friendships are lost because of them. Therefore have nothing to do with other men's wives; consort only with women whom you find without causing any problems or displeasure to anyone.

136. If you wish to be conscientious and precise in your affairs, in the purse where you keep your money always carry a paper on which you note what you have to do. And then, every time you open the purse, you will read the note, both during the day when you are out and about, and at night when you are at home.

137. If anyone should ask to buy your house or some other possession of yours, do not fret about it; take your time and respond to him that if such and such a thing would be to your advantage you would be happy to do it. Likewise, if any man, whoever he might be, should ask for your daughter's hand in marriage on his own behalf or on behalf of some friend of his, or should wish to give his own daughter in marriage to you or to your son, do not take it ill; rather, tell him: "I wish to consult with my relatives about this," and say that if it were to your advantage, you would be happy to accept. And always be desirous of entering into a family relationship with those who ask for your daughters or for you, rather than having to ask him to marry your daughter, or to ask for one of his.

138. Always make sure that the entrance to your house is locked at night, so that no one can leave or enter without you knowing it. For it is too great a danger to leave a house unlocked, especially if you have a dispute with anyone. At night, keep the keys to the street door of your house in your own room, and always lock it day or night whenever you go to sleep.

139. Foresight is a wonderful thing; therefore always be forward-looking in all of your affairs – in those at home, and in your work, and in all of your other affairs. I want you to know that there are certain years in which there is great famine and dearth of things necessary for living; therefore always take care if you can that your house be supplied with enough grain for two years, and if you cannot get grain, then obtain some other type of fodder that can be eaten. And if you cannot get a two years' supply, at least get enough for a year and a half, if you can; and always buy ahead of time. And I tell you the same about olive oil; so that if a famine should occur, you won't find yourself without these two things in the house – for the other things, you shall do the best you can. And be sure to have a cask of vinegar.

140. Never believe anyone who tells fortunes or teaches you spells, nor anyone who advises you to do alchemy, because they are all deceivers and swindlers. And whatever they say or do, they say it to get money out of your purse. Therefore in these matters, be very wise and cautious and take care never to believe anyone. Also, be as careful as you can above all not to let any evil person speak to you or show you or teach you how to forge money or to make money from scratch – if you love your life and soul and body, do not attend to or agree to anything like this. For if you should do so, whatever you might gain would be evilly gotten and thievery. Whoever does such things, no matter how great and wise and clever and ingenious he might be, in a very short time he will be discovered,

arrested, and burned at the stake; he will lose both his possessions and his life.

141. Getting together once a year to feast with your neighbours and friends is nothing but good. Therefore, according to your means, invite them to dine with you, and do them honour, and they shall do the same to you. Thus the love between you and them will grow.

142. Be very careful not to spend beyond your means. Each year, strive to save a quarter of what you make. Never fail to take into account extraordinary expenses that you might incur, and for those expenses save a quarter of what you make every year, so that when they come you will be able to meet those expenses without touching any of your land or patrimony or movable property that has been left to you. These extraordinary expenses, which do not occur regularly, are the following: legal expenses and disputes, and illnesses; and also daughters to be married. Also, because one's family is always growing, you should save as much as you can in the proper way. Be very careful about small expenditures outside the home, which are the thing that empties your purse and eats away at your wealth, because they are continual. Therefore stay away from taverns; and don't buy all the good merchandise you see, for "a house is like a she-wolf: the more she gets, the more she eats."

143. Cook once a day, in the morning, and keep something cooked for the evening; and eat sparingly in the evening, and you will remain healthy. If guests arrive unexpectedly, you can offer them a chicken or some other small thing; that is sufficient. You can say: "I had this prepared for me; tomorrow we shall take better refreshment." And perhaps they will leave in the morning, and you shall have done yourself honour with little expenditure.

144. Every morning when you get up, wash your hands and face before you leave the house; likewise when you are about to sit down for dinner, a small repast, or supper, always wash your hands before you eat. Likewise when you get up from the table, wash your hands and mouth and teeth, and you shall be clean. This is also good manners.

145. Always comport yourself in a decorous manner in your own chamber where there is no one else but you, as if you were in a room with your family or out among your neighbours. For he who does not behave well by himself cannot behave well with others.

146. Try as much as you can not to mix different types of wine at a single meal. If several wines are offered to you, find out which is a good one, and stick to it as long as it lasts. And drink it diluted with water, so that when you dine with a friend to do him honour and good to yourself,

you don't bring shame to him and harm to yourself. That is what would happen if you drank so much that you became drunk; and by becoming drunk you waste the wine and harm yourself.

147. Take care never to let your body suffer cold if you can help it. Especially at night when you are sleeping, stay well covered, both in summer and winter, and you shall remain very healthy.

148. Always rise early in the morning, before dawn if you can, and attend to your tasks at home. It is better to rise early in the morning than to stay up late at night. Even though you rise very early, do not leave the house until you hear that your neighbours and the shopkeepers have opened their homes and shops. Make the sign of the cross and take yourself off to church, and always say these words in your doorway before you leave home: "*Iesus autem transies per imedium illorum ibant.* Christ before all, peace on the way, may the Holy Spirit always be with us." If you say these verses, nothing but good shall come to you for the whole day, and you shall come to no harm.

149. If you can, make it a habit to eat only twice a day: dinner and supper. And only drink at meals, and you shall be much more healthy. This is how a man should live – eating at all hours is how an animal lives.

150. If you have a son who you believe is not behaving well at home, place him immediately with a merchant who will send him somewhere else, or send him to a respected friend of yours. Your son will leave off the way he has been behaving at home and learn new ways, and perhaps he will mend his ways and behave well. For if he stays with you, he will never change his ways.

151. If you want to do business in your own land or in some other place, always take care to set yourself up in the best area of the place or rather the best place for that particular business, if you can. Likewise, make sure always to have the best stewards and the most skilled in the business in which you wish to engage. And don't worry about the cost, for "neither rent for a good place nor a salary for good stewards was ever too costly." Bad ones cost dear.

152. When you buy grain, take care that they don't fill up the measure all at once, for two or three percent will always spill out. When you sell grain, fill the measure all at once and you will get more grain out of it. But the middle course, the course of reason, is always the best; stick to that in all of your dealings, and you shall end well.

153. If you live off the income from your land and you aren't good at managing money (and one out of six men is not), don't sell your crops all at one time. For if you should invest the money in something else,

and then not have money to live on, you might have to mortgage or sell off some of your land or chattels in order to live. In fact, you should calculate just how much money you need every month. If you are good at managing money, you still shouldn't sell all your crops at one time, to avoid going bankrupt. Sell them in four batches – in October, January, March, and May, always at the beginning of the month. Each time, sell a fourth, and you will get what you need out of your crops. Do the same for olive oil and wine and the other things produced on your land. Olive oil sells well during Lent, and in September; wine sells well from Lent until the end of August, if it is a wine that lasts. If it is a wine that should be drunk young, sell a portion of the must,[2] and keep the rest until the beginning of Lent.

154. Great care must be taken so that a pregnant woman will carry her child well to term, for it is quite perilous. Therefore she should not work too hard or drink unadulterated wine, which is the most deleterious thing for her. And she should be very careful not to sit or lie on the ground, neither in summer nor in winter, so that she does not take cold, for it is very perilous for a pregnant woman to take cold. When she gets a craving for a particular thing to eat, she should partake of it temperately and reasonably, and when she gives birth, she should be attended by good midwives and women who are experienced in childbirth.

155. An infant should be kept nice and clean and warm, and should be examined frequently all over his body. For the first year, he should be given only mother's milk, and then you can begin little by little to give him breast milk along with other things to eat. Later, at six or seven years of age, teach him to read; and then either have him study or have him work in whatever profession pleases him the most; and he will turn out to be a master of it. A female child should be taught to sew and not to read, for it is not well for a female to know how to read, unless you want her to become a nun. If you want to have her become a nun, put her in the convent before she can experience the vanities of the world; she will learn to read once she is in the convent. Feed a male child well, and clothe him in a fitting, decorous way, so that he will be strong and attractive. If you clothe him well, he will consort with the right sort of people. Dress a girl well; how you feed her doesn't matter, as long as she has sufficient nourishment to live; don't let her get too fat. And teach her to do all of the household tasks – to make bread, clean poultry, sift and cook and

---

2 The juice of grapes before it has fermented to produce wine.

wash clothes, and make the bed, and spin, and weave French purses or embroider silk with a needle, and cut cloth of linen and wool, and mend stockings, and all similar things, so that when you marry her off she won't seem to be a fool and they won't call her a country bumpkin. And you who have raised her won't be cursed.

156. There are four main types of love: the first is love of your own soul, the second is love of your children, the third is love of your good wife, and the fourth is love given by one friend to another. Protect and nurture these loves, for a man who does not have these four types of love is neither perfect nor upright. You should love your soul above all else; you should love your children above any other living creature, along with your father and mother and yourself; you should love your wife above all other women, for a good wife is the crown of her husband and brings him honour and status; you should love your good friend, because he who does not love a friend who loves him is not a loyal or upstanding man; indeed, he is a traitor and dishonest and worthy of every evil.

157. Openly praise a friend who reproaches you in secret.

158. If you tell your friend's vices, you tell your own.

159. He who renders service quickly serves twice.

160. He who accepts a service from man surrenders his own liberty.

161. He who pays well and quickly will receive much quickly.

162. He who dies when he wishes dies justly.

163. Good words do not burn the mouth.

164. A good reputation shines even in the dark.

165. When your neighbour's house is on fire, carry water to your own.

166. Tell your friend the truth even though it might anger him, and he will love you.

167. A man who is satisfied is rich; a man who is always yearning for others' goods is poor.

168. When you marry off your daughter, give her a man and not money.

169. He of whom people speak well possesses great wealth.

170. A good woman, who serves her husband well, governs him.

171. Patience is a remedy for every suffering – therefore have patience in your tribulations.

172. If there is something that you must do one time and no more, do it with great deliberation.

173. Gain that is acquired with a bad reputation should be considered a loss.

174. Suffering and affliction of the spirit are worse than suffering of the body.

175. It is useful to have wisdom in times of trouble.

176. It is said that envious people are their own tormentors, for envy only hurts the one who has it in him and is envious of his neighbour's good fortune.

177. A wise man looks after his own interests and takes care not to harm the interests of others.

178. Be more wary of hypocritical men than of forthright ones, for they are more dangerous when they wish to harm their enemies.

179. To avoid greed is to acquire every treasure.

180. He who refuses to help his own country deserves to have great hardships in another's.

181. As long as you conduct your affairs well, you shall have many friends.

182. Don't let go of what you have for what you don't have.

183. A woman should be solicitous at home and modest outside the home and devout in church; she should love her husband above all the other men in the world.

184. He whom Fortune helps too much plays the fool.

185. You cannot lose your faith unless you have it. He who loses his faith cannot lose anything greater.

186. If a man serves you with actions, serve him with actions; if he serves you with words, serve him with beautiful, fine words; if he serves you with promises, make him promises as well.

187. He who praises you to your face – keep him close by.

188. "If you frequent taverns, you will leave your money there." Therefore do not frequent them, for as the saying goes, "Have your wits about you when you enter, and when you leave, either money or credit," says the innkeeper. So leave taverns alone, for too much evil comes of them.

    If you heed me,
    great good shall you derive.
    Believe me, for I have long
    Experience in many lands.
    In taverns you will find brawling and evil ways,
    Carousing, and scheming.
    Words fail me to tell
    how greatly carousing is to be avoided
    wherever it may be found.
    It starts with comely ways
    and ends up in an evil dance.
    It empties your purse
    And leaves your throat ruined.

189. An angry man is not prudent.

190. A man who loses his friends is worse than dead.

191. Perilous is the enemy who keeps his enmity concealed.

192. Flattering words have their own poison; therefore beware of them.

193. If you do what is in your heart, you will never tire of doing it.

194. Do not take to sea during the winter if you do not wish to incur great harm.

195. The face reveals what the tongue withholds.

196. It is very good to delay in dubious matters; therefore do not be precipitate. It is better to endeavour to withdraw an offer to stand surety than to do something that will bring you great harm.

197. He who conquers his anger conquers a great enemy.

198. Forgetting is a remedy for anger.

199. Where there is harmony, there is always victory.

200. There can be no legal quarrel without damage to one party and enmity to the other; therefore avoid legal disputes whenever you can.

201. A sick man who makes a physician his heir does evil to himself. Therefore do not leave anything upon your death to a physician who is caring for you, lest he be eager for you to die. But if he cures you, bestow gifts upon him, so that he will love you your whole life long.

202. A woman's tears are the root of wickedness.

203. A whore does not repent unless she finds herself pregnant.

204. Never tell your secrets to a woman, nor to a young man. Any secret they know, everyone will know.

205. Every man is deceived by himself.

206. A woman who marries many men displeases many men.

207. He errs who puts his faith in luck.

208. It is very perilous to desire something that many people want. Therefore do not be desirous of having too beautiful a wife, nor too fine a horse.

209. Both a good horse and a bad horse need the spur; both a good woman and a bad woman need a lord and master, and sometimes a good caning.

210. Miserable and wretched is he who is not envied by anyone.

211. Act according to your inner feelings.

212. Live every day as if it were your last.

213. A small spark can make a great fire; therefore take care to avoid mischief-makers and gossips.

214. Test your friend, and then serve him as he has served you.

215. He who praises himself sullies himself.

216. A wicked man who passes for good will soon be unmasked.

217. A trade in hand is an advantage in every land.

218. He who thinks of things he has lost torments himself.

219. People are not happy in a divided city.

220. The good can be learned from the bad.

221. Never cause distress to anyone from whom you may need a favour.

222. If you want to support your family and conduct your affairs well, don't seek the advice of your relatives or friends, be they great or rich, humble or poor. Only take counsel with those who have the reputation of being wise and fair and whom you see conduct their own affairs well, for they will also give you good advice for your own affairs.

223. If a friend of yours tells you his secrets, it is either a sign that he loves you well, or that he is foolish and crazy.

224. He who is a friend of God can overcome any whim of fate.

225. A man who becomes angry to his own detriment is mad.

226. He who is his own man will not belong to another.

227. A man cannot be a teacher who has not first been a pupil. Therefore do not disdain serving in a trade that you want to learn, for one learns by serving.

228. He who wants everything will lose everything. He who hunts too many foxes will lose one as soon as he catches another.

229. It is better to be a good pupil than a bad teacher; better to be a good squire than a bad knight.

230. No one is offended by a man who demands his rights.

231. Don't be so bitter that every man spits on you, nor so sweet that every man sucks you dry.

232. Be well mannered in everything you do, and you shall be praised for all you do.

233. Take care that no one should hate you for any evil you may do.

234. Spend according to how much you take in, and give as you can from what you have to worthy men.

235. Take care not to eat herbs with which you are unfamiliar, for not all herbs are free of poisons.

236. Don't eat all you have, nor say all you know.

237. Do not relinquish that which is rightfully yours.

238. Demand proper service if you do not wish it to be denied to you.

239. If you work in a warehouse or shop, you must be humble, fair, solicitous, steadfast, honest, and orderly, and do everything in your power to do a good job for your master. If you did not do so, you would have to make restitution. And be very careful not to enter into any transaction

in which you appropriate your master's money. Likewise, do not do anything to your own advantage with your master's money without his permission, for that would be robbery and embezzlement, and you would
have to make restitution for what you had gained.

240. If you can, endeavour to marry your daughter to a man who has a
profession or trade, for you can't go wrong.

241. If you wish to be a decent man, take care not to do lewd things; be
ashamed of doing such things.

242. Always endeavour, if you can, to remain in your own homeland;
and if by chance it should come about that you cannot stay there, choose
another place to dwell in, and establish relations with the citizens there,
and not with foreigners, because you will have to live and die there.
However, if you should have many sons and daughters, try to have them
marry someone from your homeland, for you might still return there.

243. It is possible to do everything in the world. Therefore if you do
not want to fail, take care to do everything in the proper way.

244. It is a wonderful thing to learn a profession, and to gain knowledge and skills at someone else's expense. Therefore when you see your
neighbour in adversity, protect yourself lest the same thing should happen to you.

245. Whenever you have any document drawn up, have a special book
and write in it the day that the document was drawn up and the notary
who executed it and the names of the witnesses, and the reason and with
whom you did it, so that if you or your children should need it, they can
find it. And in order to avoid lawsuits and the dangers of false men, a fair
copy should always be made, and keep the copy in a safe place.

246. When you buy property, be sure to have good, reliable guarantors, and make sure to obtain the necessary legal consent of women
or children or other close relatives of the family, so that you can't be
cheated after the death of the seller.

247. Avoid gambling and women of the world like fire, for almost all
troubles come from these two things. If you lose at gambling, you incur
damage, and if you win, the winnings aren't truly yours – indeed, you
should give them to charity if you cannot give them back to the man
from whom you won them. And if you frequent women of the world, you
lose your honour and your money; however, if you must of necessity frequent such women, do what you need to do quickly, then pay and leave.
Never make credit with such women, for then they will want double the
money. Take care not to fall in love with any such woman on account of
her caresses or her beautiful face, for women like that don't caress you,

they caress your money. Of the signs to see if a woman loves you, the greatest is if the woman gives you some of her own money or treasured possessions, for women are stingy by nature. So if a woman acts against her nature she does so for one of two reasons – either to get more things and more money from you, or for the love she bears you. Therefore avoid at all costs giving large gifts to women, for you would be foolish and would lose what you had given.

248. Health is a wonderful thing; therefore when you are healthy, protect yourself from all of those things that you see are bad for your body, so that you can save and possess such a great treasure as is health. But if you should become ill, immediately put all of your affairs in order, make your confession and take communion and make your will, if you didn't already make it while you were healthy. Do all of these things before you become too ill to do anything, for the danger is too great for the soul and the body for you to say when you are sick: "Tomorrow I will do such and such a thing." For there are many sick people who one day seem fine, and the next day have lost the power of speech and hearing and understanding. Therefore take care not to become such a one as these. Immediately put your affairs in order, and let the rest go as it will, and commend your soul to God.

249. Do not be stingy nor lazy in keeping yourself healthy; indeed, do whatever you can, also for your friends and relatives, to stay healthy. Likewise, if you have sick people in your home, never abandon them. Have them waited upon and assisted up to the moment of death, for God says: "Help yourself, and I shall help you," and when he sees that you help yourself with good doctors, good medicine, and good prayers and alms, He will hasten to help you. Therefore never give up hope when you are ill; always have hope that you will recover, and do everything you can to help yourself. Do the same for any sick people you may have in your home, and for sick relatives or friends that do not live with you.

250. If you are on the point of dying and are uncertain to whom you should give any money of dubious origin that you may have, give it in the name of God before you die. You can give it to poor friends or relatives; and if you leave the money to be given after your death, entrust it to the bishop. It is better if you give the money away to whomever you wish before you die; and if you don't have money, draw up a document leaving a piece of land to him or her to whom you wish it to go; and the value of the land should correspond in value to whatever you have acquired in a dubious manner. But be careful not to be deceived by your conscience – that is, do not give money to any relative of yours who does

not need it. Also take care to guarantee the money so that your relatives cannot take it away from the person to whom you want it to go. It is better to give money to widows or maidens who do not have a dowry than to give it to men. Also, it is better to give any dubious money you have to six poor men than to two, if you have it. It is a great act of charity to enable a young maiden to marry well, in a position that is appropriate to the status of her family.

251. If you are a merchant, and letters for you arrive along with other letters, always remember to read your own letters first before giving the other letters to the people to whom they are addressed. And if your letters should advise you to buy or sell some merchandise for your own advantage, call immediately for your agent, and do what the letters say, and then hand over the other letters that came with yours. But don't give them until you have concluded your transactions, because those other letters might say things that could ruin your own dealings, and the service that you would have done to your friend or neighbour or some stranger would turn into great evil. You are not obliged to help others if it is a disservice to your own affairs.

252. When your sons are small, place them in the trade in which you want them to become masters, for whatever they learn and practise as children, they will retain and love as adults. Likewise I tell you to send them to be raised and trained in a profession or trade in whatever country, town, or city where you wish them to be citizens or inhabitants. And do not say: "I will send him as a boy to France, and there he shall grow up and be raised, and learn the ways of merchants in France, so that when he is thirty years old or so, he can return to Florence." In this way, he will not be as good a merchant in Florence as he was in France, for he has been raised and has grown up and has made many friends there, and his heart will always be in France. And at every difficulty he has in Florence, he will say: "If I were in France, I wouldn't be going through this!" And the same goes for other countries.

253. Away from your homeland, you live well and die badly.

254. Stalling is the same as doing harm – "Wait a little and I'll take care of it" places a man out of the way of gain.

255. He who sleeps too much wastes time.

256. I am certain that I was born
and I am sure that I will die,
but I know not where nor when;
for the world is shrouded in darkness.

257. Riches ill gained are akin to poverty.

258. A fool and his folly may go on for some time, but not forever.

259. If you can remain in your own homeland, don't yearn to go abroad, for going about the world involves great expense and risk. Therefore avoid this as much as you can.

260. When you receive a letter to which you should respond, don't fail to do so. Respond point for point, and you will never err nor can you be reproached.

261. When you go abroad, if you are a gentleman you should always frequent gentle folk; and even if you are not, always try to consort with men who are of higher rank than you, and you shall be honoured and revered, and they will think that you are of higher rank than they are, and just as good and just as great. Always be well-mannered and courteous as much as you can, not so much in spending, but in speaking and in everything else you do.

262. Solomon says that he who renders service to others can never be praised sufficiently.

263. Do not be in a hurry to leave your home when you hear a commotion outside; rather, stay inside, and make a show of knowing nothing about it. In this way you shall avoid trouble and embarrassment and you shall stay safe.

264. Man has four more things than he believes: the first is time, the second is sin, the third [*text missing in the original manuscript*], and the fourth is fear. Man has six fewer things than he believes he has: sense, wealth, friends, life, health, and strength. There are six salutations you can make, and whichever one you make will be seemly and good, to wit: "May God give you sense," "May God give you strength," and so on.[3]

265. Strive as much as you can to remain among your own kind.

266. Cicero says that for certain he who is the legitimate son, and not a bastard, of the man whom he takes to be his father, loves and fears and honours and obeys his father, be he young or old or poor or rich or healthy or sick, and he always feels deep kinship for him. And there is good reason that it should be this way, for existence is the noblest thing there is; and if a son didn't have a father and a mother, he would not exist. Therefore you should love and honour your father and mother more than you do yourself.

267. Always be on good terms with your neighbours, for they are always asked about your affairs before you yourself are asked, and they can hurt

---

3 For the various forms of salutation of the time, see Francesco Torraca, *Fatti e scritti di Ugolino Buzzuola* (Rome: Stabilimento tipografico dell'Opinione, 1893).

or help you in obtaining public office, and when the time comes for you to marry off your daughters or for you or one of your sons to take a wife.

268. For anything that you wish to accomplish, you need to have three things: power, knowledge, and will. If you have these things, you will achieve what you desire.

269. A sin is greater if it is committed on a Sunday or other holy day or solemn feast day than if it is committed on a working day. Therefore whenever you wish to celebrate in honour of a particular saint, do not do so with games nor banquets nor other worldly things; do so by giving alms and praying and avoiding sin – these are the celebrations that are acceptable to God and to his holy saints.

270. If you have money that you want to invest in grain, buy small grains before you buy wheat, if you don't have much money; for you will make two *soldi* on every bushel of grain and only one on every bushel of wheat; and the grain will cost you a third of what the wheat would. Also, during times of shortage you'll find more buyers. And if you buy other goods, buy them when the prices are low and there is little demand for them, for in time you will derive profit from them, and you cannot lose in the process.

271. When you buy wine for your own use or for resale, always ask the man from whom you buy it how he treats the wine he keeps for himself and how much time it takes the wine to turn, and you do the same. Thus you will not be deceived, and the wine won't go bad on you.

272. Never make a wager for anything for which you are contending with another man, for "he who wagers loses his head."

273. [*text missing in the original manuscript*]

274. Never pass judgment until you have heard the other party's side.

275. If your city or lord should send you on a mission, make sure to do four things, and you shall be well received. The first is to speak briefly; the second is to speak openly and clearly, so that you are understood; the third is to use unusual, unique words when you speak, for people delight in this; the fourth is to say what you have to say in a modest, gentle manner.

276. Keep in mind that there are five chief joys in life, just as there are five chief sorrows that man can suffer in this life. The first joy is revenge; the corresponding sorrow is to be injured by an enemy. The second joy is to be released from prison; and the corresponding sorrow is to be imprisoned for wrongdoing. The third joy is to have a good wife, and to love her dearly; the corresponding sorrow is if she dies. The fourth joy is to be very rich; and the corresponding sorrow is to become poor. The fifth joy

is to become a gentleman; and the sorrow is not to be able to maintain a gentleman's style of living.

277. If you can, avoid taking a widow as your wife, for you shall never be able to satisfy her. For every time you deny her something that she requests, she shall say to you: "My first husband did not treat me thus." Of course, if you have had a first wife, you can certainly marry a widow, and if she says to you: "My first husband did such and such," you can say to her: "My first wife didn't torment me constantly, bless her soul!" And always take care that your second wife not be higher born than your first, so that she won't be able to say to you: "I am more worthy than she, for I come from a better family and have more honourable parentage." And if you can, chose a woman who is healthy.

278. Be very careful not to have relations with your wife during her time of the month, for children who are conceived during that time run the risk of being sickly or scrofulous. You see what a risk this is, so always avoid it. You can also do great harm to yourself.

279. Our Lord God gave man two ears and two eyes and two hands and one mouth, and he did all this for our moral teaching. Therefore you should listen and see and touch two times before you speak once, for the tongue can wound where the knife cannot. Take great care not to speak too much or frivolously, if you do not wish to err frequently.

280. Practise what you preach.

281. Almsgiving is very pleasing to God; therefore have charity and compassion, and give alms from what you earn with your sweat and toil – that is proper almsgiving. Giving money or food or lodging in God's name is not the only way to give alms; it is also a great charity to give assistance to widows and wards of the court and orphans and the helpless and strangers in their hour of need. Likewise it is a great act of charity to make peace, get men out of prison, and similar acts: these are the things that annul sins, as when you say your confession and make an act of contrition.

282. Take great care to read many books, and you shall learn many things. And once you have learned good things, retain them and put them into action to good effect.

283. You can never ask enough questions; therefore do not disdain to ask what you do not know. It is good sense to ask about things that one does not know. That is why it is said that one is remiss if he reads and does not understand.

284. Love your teacher, and do your utmost to fear and honour him.

285. Judge not, lest you be judged.

286. Keep in mind not to curse yourself, O you who read this book, and not to condemn yourself by the imprecations you make. For it is an abominable thing to curse strangers or to condemn them, as we said above, not to mention men or women condemning or cursing themselves. There are many examples of men who have sworn so much that they end up hanged, or drawn and quartered, or beheaded, or some similar death, and they end up dying the kind of death that they used to evoke in their curses. For very good reason, those who curse themselves [*text missing in the original manuscript*]. Therefore avoid doing this, and you shall do well.

287. Be very careful not to do anything for which everybody can say behind your back, "It serves him right!" For "it-serves-him-right" is a bad thing that every man should endeavour not be said of him, neither in jest nor in seriousness.

288. The saying goes, "A thing put off becomes a vice." Therefore never put off doing a good deed. Julius Caesar felt he had accomplished nothing, when he had left something unfinished.

289. "Habit becomes second nature," the saying goes. Therefore avoid bad habits, so that you don't become wicked. Likewise, make a habit of good behaviour, and you shall persevere in it. Always have good thoughts in your heart, and your outward behaviour will not be bad.

290. When you teach or train someone, impart sound lessons – that is, teach what you have to teach in a straightforward, open manner, so that you will be well understood.

291. Always keep in mind that when you want to do something, you should think and ponder to what end you can succeed in doing it. And if you see reasonably that it can turn out well, do it; but if for any reason it might turn out badly for you, do not do it, so that having begun it, you won't repent and say: "I wish I hadn't begun this thing, for it puts me at risk of damage or dishonour."

292. A man who puts all of his trust in his wealth puts himself in great peril.

293. If you have poor relatives, do not shun nor reject them, for if you do, you shall gain a reputation for cruelty. Therefore love and support them as much as you can, so that those to whom they speak will not become cruel toward you as you have been toward them.

294. When you give a banquet for women or men, always do it cheerfully and with a good mien. And always order the things necessary for the banquet well ahead of time, so that you will have everything that is needed without scolding or raising your voice to your servants, for it is

an unseemly thing to raise your voice in anger when you have guests to dine. Also, be very careful, while at table with your guests and friends, not to murmur into the ear of your servants or any other member of your household, for it is an unseemly thing, and gives rise to suspicion on the part of your guests. Any of them who has some shortcoming or shows bad manners, or who is eating or drinking too much, will immediately think that you are speaking about him. And other things might transpire that would bring great dishonour and blame to you. Therefore speak and give orders to your servants openly and with a pleasant countenance, so that what you say will be heard by everyone who is there.

295. [*text missing in the original manuscript*]

296. If you wish to save your soul, take care that good actions prevail in your behaviour. For if a man never did neither good nor evil, his soul would be condemned to Hell. It might seem wrong for a soul to go to Hell, having done no evil; but there is a good reason for it to go to Hell, for he who does no good commits a great evil, for he is ungrateful to God for the blessings that he gives him in this life. Therefore strive to do good works if you wish to save your soul.

297. When someone else has begun to speak before you, always remain silent until he has said what he began to say, and then say what you have to say, and you shall be the wiser for it. For "he who interrupts another wastes both his breath and his words."

298. He who can boast of having two or three good friends can say that he possesses a great treasure.

299. It is no wonder that a man who refuses to hear censure for his faults from good men or from the law should end badly; indeed, it is only by God's mercy and a great miracle that he lives. For he who flees reprehension flees virtue and reason, and he who lives without virtue and without reason is worse than dead, and places himself at great risk.

300. A young woman who is a virgin should follow the example of the Blessed Virgin Mary, who was the first, supreme virgin of virgins, and queen and mirror of all other virgins; and I say the same of all other women. She did not stray outside of the home, nor did she wander about here and there, hearing or seeing vain men or other vanities; rather, she remained shut up in a concealed, decent place. Our Lady lingered over her prayers, and spoke much with Our Lord God; she did not do as the vain eye does, which sees what it wishes to see and does not see what it wishes to ignore. All faithful Christian women should learn from the Virgin Mary, and follow her example. If they do, they will be acceptable to God and to their husbands and to the other people with whom they associate.

301. A man who does not punish his child does not love him. Therefore if you have children, always punish and admonish them temperately and appropriately, depending upon their transgressions. For I wish you to know that he who does not punish his child loves him not; indeed, he gives him reason to turn out badly.

302. A good woman should be greatly honoured, not only by her husband; everyone should honour her and support her in doing good works. Always do great honour to all women, for two reasons: first, because it is good manners, and second, because if you believe that your wife is good, you should likewise believe that all other women are as good as or better than your own wife.

303. A wise man always lives in fear, for he knows not today what may befall him tomorrow.

304. If you are a good mentor, you will chastise and admonish yourself, for he is mad who chastises and admonishes his son or neighbour for things for which he does not chastise himself. Therefore in mentoring and chastising your neighbour, you should hold yourself not to do the things that you forbid him to do.

305. Always strive and endeavour to earn; and do not say: "If I am here today, I won't be here tomorrow. And I do not wish to leave a great deal after I die, for I don't have children, and my relatives love me not, and if I left them an entire city, in a short time they would have spent and wasted and squandered it." For you know not how long you will live, nor can you take your fortune with you. And I have seen great kings and lords and great citizens and great merchants lose their standing and, before they die, live in poverty and misery. Leave great riches to your relatives. It will bring you honour and fame to have left them well off rather than poorly. And they will be obliged to pray to God for you; and even if they do not do it, you will participate in the good that you do for them, and will partake of the honour that they have in the world. But take care not to earn in a bad way, expecting that those who survive you will make restitution, for they never will. You will bear the sin, and your bad reputation will survive you in the world. And your relatives will enjoy the possessions and wealth that you have amassed, without being grateful to you, for they are right that you shouldn't leave it to them, but to those from whom you have stolen and pilfered.

306. Take great care not to be vile or cowardly in spirit; and never, in any of your dealings, give in to or let yourself be conquered by the sin of apathy. Rather, strive to make valour and strength of purpose conquer cowardice, for a coward is vile in spirit. A coward tries to make a big show

of doing and knowing what he does not do and does not know. Take care not to do this yourself; rather, strive to make your goodness and merit and intelligence surpass what they appear to be, so that you will appear in your affairs and those of your friends to be better than expected, and not worse. If you do this, you shall be appreciated, respected, and held in great esteem.

307. Take care not to offend anyone. But if you should chance to offend, take care not to appear to be happy about the offence you have given, or about an offence that your son or relative has given – rather, show yourself to be sorrowful and distressed about it, and denounce the harm you've done as much as you can. In this way, you shall relieve yourself of the ill will caused by the offence. For if you appeared to be happy about an offence committed by your relatives, the offended party could easily turn against you as well, and might hate you even more than those who had offended him, for appearing to be happy about it. Therefore never appear to rejoice about any offence, for nothing but harm can come to you as a result, both before God and the world. Peace is always far from those who rejoice in evil acts; therefore avoid such rejoicing as much as you can, for if you should happen to offend a neighbour or a stranger and then you rejoiced about it, and later you wished to be forgiven by the offended party, he would say to anyone who spoke to him about it: "Why should I forgive him? You say that he is sorry, and that he did not deliberately offend me, but he is going about boasting to people. Hang him, for I will never forgive him until I pay him back for what he has done to me." He will say this more on account of the arrogance that you have shown than because of the offence that you committed against him; therefore, for God's sake, avoid such arrogance and such gloating.

308. A man who reproaches another man thoughtlessly only reproaches himself. Therefore when you reproach someone, do it with great prudence and thoughtfulness and with great deliberation and humility, and take care about the time and place. Speak gently, and not with pride nor anger. This is not meant for small children, but for men and youths who are beyond the age of being reprimanded like children, who are punished by beating with a strap or a switch.

309. If you wish to conquer and subdue the sin of envy, which eats away at a man and only does him harm, think of those who are worse off than you in this world, who are many, and worse off in many ways – some because of poverty, some for various illnesses, some who lack family, some who lack judgment, and some who are lower in social status. You will find many who are worse off than you for one reason or another.

310. [*text missing in the original manuscript*] … to reproach yourself in your heart and to punish yourself, so that you don't fall again into the same failing, or a similar one, be it greater or lesser. Consider that it brings less shame to you if you rebuke and punish yourself, rather than waiting to be punished by someone else.

311. The sin of lust is very grave and perilous and displeasing to God. As much as virginity is pleasing and agreeable to him, so much more does the said sin of lust displease him. Therefore always take great care to avoid it, for it is very dangerous, and it is that sin, or one of those sins, with which the Enemy of God harms us most, and occupies our minds with it in many ways, both in the commission of the sin itself, and in looking, and in wishing. And likewise in many other ways, which can be combated by a variety of methods. The first is to avoid the places and ways of lust … [*text missing in the original manuscript*] and the sin of gluttony is a strong inducement to lust. This sin can also be conquered and driven away by doing penitence – therefore have these three things in you if you wish to counter the sin of lust. But avoidance is the best way to defend yourself from it.

312. It is a great victory for a man when he conquers the evil urges that come to him. Therefore always strive to be strong and valorous in combating the evil urges that come to you, and do not indulge in vices or sins that come into your heart. Always remember that you must die, and that will be the shield with which you will conquer every evil vice and urge.

313. Whenever you commit a transgression, and your friend or teacher or someone else castigates or advises you about it or someone who loves you reproaches you for it, do not disclaim or deny what you have done, for by denying it, you err doubly. By confessing your transgression, you are already half forgiven, for you recognize that you have erred, and another time you will reasonably be more careful than if you tried to cover yourself by lying or denying what you had done. Therefore never try to sustain a transgression that you have committed by denying it, for you would be held to be either very evil and wicked, or very simple and foolish. And whether you lied or denied what you had done to cover yourself, you would be much worse off than if you had confessed your transgression to the person admonishing you.

314. A man can wish for more than a thousand men, or many more, can attain. Therefore carefully avoid giving in to your desires. For if you try to fulfil them, you shall never succeed, and thus you shall waste your time and shall always be tormented, and on the last day you'll be less happy than on the first, and thus you shall die. Therefore, if you wish to

live and die happy, temper your desires so that you are content with the things that are sufficient for your position and ancestry.

315. Always keep in mind that when you see or hear something being done that is not seemly or honest, whatever that thing might be, you must not participate nor join in with those who are doing or saying it. Indeed, if they are such that you can reproach and rebuke them for it, do so, or have someone of higher standing than you do so. If those who are committing the evil deed are such that it would be better for you not to reproach them nor have them reproached by someone else, leave them and do not tarry where the evil action is being committed, so that if you should condemn that action on another occasion, no one can say to you: "You were present, and you said nothing."

316. Many times it comes about that flatterers praise those with whom they associate or do business. And they do this to please them or to get money or gifts or favours from them, or to otherwise deceive them. Therefore always remember, when someone sings your praises, to judge yourself with regard to the act for which you are being praised, and you will immediately understand whether or not you are being flattered in order to deceive you. And if you see that you are being wrongfully praised, realize that he who is praising you knows what he is saying, and why, and beware of him. But do not say: "This man takes me to be much more wise than I am," for that would be an even greater foolishness; rather, always consider that he knows your worth to the penny.

317. Do not take it ill when you are taught something, but do take it ill if you do not know how to teach someone else.

318. I do not like a house where the hen sings and the rooster is silent.

319. The greater a man's worth, the more grave are his transgressions.

320. It is a great wisdom when a man knows how to separate his desire from that thing from which he cannot derive benefit; therefore never be obstinate in going after things that you know you cannot obtain, which would be a waste of time and a great foolishness.

321. Usury is a very damaging thing – and just as it damages one's wealth and honour in the world, it also damages the soul and the body. Usury has the characteristic of not making itself known either to those who practise it – that is, those who lend money – nor to those who borrow, until she shows you her tail and wounds you with it. Then you realize what usury is and what it does to you. In the end, usury deprives you of your honour and good name in this world, and in the next world it deprives you of your soul. So you see how much you have gained by it! And if you borrow money against land or a house or pledge something else,

you will not realize the damage that you've done to yourself until the very end, at the moment of reckoning, when for the hundred florins you borrowed you are obliged to pay two hundred gold florins and all the other expenses, which can mount up to more than ten per cent. Then you realize the harm that borrowing has done to you, when you end up a poor beggar, thrown out of your house and lands, or taken and put in prison, where you will die of hunger and shame. Thus usury takes away your body in this world; and, dying in this way, your soul runs a great risk on account of the offence that you feel you have received, and on account of the sorrow, and because you die unwillingly. Therefore take care as much as you can neither to lend nor borrow money, be it a small or a large sum, for if you do, you shall be ruined in the way that I have described. If you should need money, sell something for ten per cent less than its value, rather than pawning it, for the paperwork and other expenses related to taking a loan amount to ten per cent and more. Therefore avoid borrowing, and don't get into the habit of borrowing even small sums, for you will never be able to refrain from borrowing small nor large sums.

322. Of necessity there are good men and bad, for the virtues of the good man are known by the vices of the bad. And the good man learns and improves by hearing about and seeing the vices of the bad man, so that he does not imitate them; indeed, knowing them and hearing of them, he avoids them. For if he did not know them, he could not avoid them. Therefore always be eager to know about good and evil, not in order to practise both, but rather to practise good and to avoid evil. Now, I am not saying that you should associate with any evil man in order to be able to say: "I shall learn his evil ways and wickedness, and then I shall avoid him and other evil, vice-ridden men." For "habit becomes second nature," as the saying goes, so if you are in the habit of consorting with an evil man, you could become evil as well. Therefore always avoid every evil habit. But when you see and hear about the evil doings of a bad man or a bad woman, keep them in mind, and avoid them as much as you can, and always avoid vice and practise virtue.

323. The sin of pride is very dangerous; all the other sins derive from it. Therefore take great care not to become proud on account of your wealth or your relatives or friends or power that you might have. Rather, remember that in this earthly life no one is more powerful or more wealthy or more wise [*text missing in the original manuscript*]. Remember the weakness of our nature, which can be compared to a light little wind that quickly goes away. Here is a good example I wish to give

you: compare our life to a very large cask of wine. If a man goes to the cask every day for a glass of wine, and replaces the wine he has taken with water, and continues to do so, the cask that was originally full of good wine ends up full of water. In the same way, we little by little lose our natural warmth, and over time we begin to fail, and we die on our own without any accident befalling us. And neither money nor relatives nor friends nor power nor good food nor other worldly things can help you. Thus, see how our pride is brought down by itself; and therefore you should not strive for those things that cannot give you security – you should hope only in our Lord Jesus Christ and in the Virgin Mary his blessed mother, and from them take courage and valour, not from relatives or money or any other worldly thing. They shall give you courage if you follow their commandments and virtues and disdain earthly sins and vices. And the more you humble yourself on earth, the more they shall exalt you in heaven. Therefore always keep in mind that you were created out of the most base thing in this world – dirt; and if you keep these things in mind, you shall never have pride, and even if you do, it won't last long.

324. There are five things that are most pleasing to and valued most by the souls who have passed from this life for the remission of their sins and their punishment: the first is to have masses said for the soul for whom you wish to pray; the second is alms given on behalf of that soul; the third thing is to fast for that soul; the fourth is to make journeys to holy places and sacred festivals on behalf of the said soul; the fifth is to pray and to have prayers said to holy and good persons on behalf of that soul. Therefore never cease to do and to have done the aforementioned things on behalf of your departed ones; likewise for abandoned souls, for it is a great mercy to pray and have prayers said for abandoned souls, as I told you before.

325. When you give alms, make a habit of giving them to prisoners and to sick people and to poor people who are ashamed of their condition – those are good alms that are acceptable to God, to assist people who cannot help themselves.

326. St Bernard said that he who does not wish to be better is not very good, for when a person begins not to want to become better and to grow in goodness, then he ceases to be good. Therefore always strive to do better today than yesterday, and better tomorrow than today, and never tire of doing good deeds. For as soon as you cease to do good deeds, you begin to do evil ones. Keep in mind that it is a bad thing to do neither good nor evil acts; therefore do good deeds and leave the bad.

327. I told you before that if you have several sons, place them in various trades, not all in a single trade. Take care to do this, for as the saying goes, "A trade in hand means gold in every land, and you shall never lose it." We find in Roman history that the emperor Octavian had his sons taught to swim and bear arms and joust and everything that has to do with the art of chivalry, and he had his daughters learn to sew and cut and weave and everything that is necessary to know for the art of making clothing. And when Octavian was asked why he did this, he said that even though he was ruler of the world, [*text missing in the original manuscript*]. So should you do, if such a great ruler wanted his children to learn a trade. No wealth is more stable and more secure for a man than having a trade. Therefore place your sons in whatever trade they show the most interest in, and they will turn out to be better masters.

328. Keep in mind, when you are reprimanded by your teacher or by your father or some other person who chastises and admonishes you for some bad thing that you have done or said, to be very attentive and respectful in listening to what is said to you, and listen well with the ears of your mind to the one who chastises you. And do not say: "This man who castigates me has nothing to do with me." Indeed, consider that he who castigates you is your friend, or was a friend of your father or of your relatives or of your ancestors. Therefore listen to him with good grace, for a man cannot have a worse vice than not wanting to be corrected. For he who does not wish to be corrected and admonished for his faults does not love justice, and he who does not love justice nor reason does not love God. Therefore listen respectfully to your teacher or relative or other person or friend who castigates you, and keep his chastisements well in mind, and you shall often keep from acting badly. And I want you to know that he who does not want to hear the chastisements for his failings and the bad things that he does and says will end up acting badly habitually, and it will become such a habit that he isn't aware of it, and he won't believe that he is acting badly; and thus he never ceases to act badly. Therefore I pray you, if you cannot bear to hear worldly chastisements – that is, from your teacher or relatives or friends or neighbours – then listen to the spiritual chastisements – that is, the teachings of the saints and the good preachers of the Church. For if you listen to preachings, they will perforce touch your soul, and it cannot be that you would not chastise yourself for doing or saying evil. For the word of God softens the heart of an evil man more than any other thing that he might hear and more than any other earthly chastisement.

329. It is very seemly for a woman to be modest, for several reasons; for a woman who has a sense of shame within her shall not be without chastity. And a modest woman is held by everyone to be wiser and more decent than a brazen woman. A modest woman shines with comely behaviour and beauty much more than a brazen woman. And likewise many other virtues arise within a modest woman. Similarly, it is seemly for a young man to be modest, and it is very seemly for an old man not to be arrogant, although reasonably there should be no place for shame in old men, because they should not do anything for which they should be ashamed. In fact, rather than shame, we might speak of immorality with regard to old men. And it is an exceedingly unseemly thing for an old man to be immoral, and likewise for a woman; and likewise immorality is unseemly in the young. Therefore avoid it in all ages of your life.

330. When you choose a woman as a wife for your son or your friend or for yourself, take great care that her grandmother and mother were decent and modest women, for many times a young woman will take after the behaviour of her mother and grandmother.

331. Again I remind you that if you have girls or young women in your home, you must discipline them and keep them under control. And even if, as often happens, they or some of them are eyed by young men, do not let yourself be moved to fury or anger against those young men; rather, chastise and admonish the girls … [*text missing in the original manuscript*] The duke of Athens, who was called Peisistratos, was a very great prince. He had a noble, beautiful daughter whom he had not yet married off; and a young Athenian man fervently loved this girl. One day while the girl was on her way to a festivity with her mother and numerous other women, the young man stopped along the way and embraced and kissed Peisistratos' daughter. He was apprehended for having done this, and the girl's mother wanted him to be put to death immediately. When Peisistratos heard about it, he had the young man put in prison, and the girl's mother said that she would have her revenge for that. After several days, Peisistratos called together many wise men to confer with them, and he asked them what he should do with the young man, and they all responded that he was worthy of a cruel death for having had the audacity to lay his hands upon such a maiden. Then the duke, the girl's father, sitting in judgment, had the young man brought before him. And everyone thought that he would sentence him to death. The duke turned to his wise men and to the other people gathered there, and said: "If we kill those who love us, what shall we do to our enemies, who hate us?" And he turned to the young man, and said to him: "Go. And do

not let such a thing happen again," and he freed him. Peisistratos was greatly praised for this by the wise men and all the others who were present there. Therefore, do not rush to vengeance, since Peisistratos was so merciful as to pardon the young man.

332. If it should happen that you are called to pass judgment against malefactors or in some civil case, or if you were asked to advise your city or a friend, beware of two things that are contrary to passing judgment and giving advice: one is haste, and the other is anger. Therefore if you have to pass judgment about anything, take time to carefully deliberate about it before you render your judgment; likewise, if you have to give advice to your city or to a friend, think and think again before you give advice, and do not be hasty nor precipitate in judging or advising, if you do not wish to fail. Likewise I say to you with regard to anger: be very careful not to enter into the tribunal to pass judgment if you are angry, for it would be difficult for you to give a fair judgment. And take great care not to judge out of enmity anyone who has offended you or one of your relatives. You can seek vengeance against your enemy otherwise than with your judgment, for if you punish his fault with anger, it shall become your own. And it will be said that you did not kill the thief for the theft committed, but rather that you condemned him on account of the vendetta you had against him. Therefore take great care not to let anger enter into your judgment, for "he who is angry is not prudent," as the saying goes. Likewise, anger takes away every good judgment and obscures the truth. Therefore remember not to give a judgment that you reached when you were angry. Cambyses, the king of Persia, had placed a judge in his court to mete out justice to all of his subjects. This judge condemned one of his own enemies not for a crime he had committed, but as a vendetta. When Cambyses came to hear of this, he had the judge flayed alive, and he placed the skin upon the judge's son, who was also a judge, and put him in his father's place. And he commanded the son to always wear his father's skin while he was passing judgment as a reminder of the sentence that his father had passed in anger. Let this suffice with regard to passing fair judgment. A judge should also be compassionate; where he can work with words only, he should not use torture. And if it should be necessary to use torture, it should be done with prudence, and not cruelly. You can torture a malefactor in such a way that the punishment is either reasonable and compassionate, or cruel. Therefore if you must torture a malefactor, use great prudence, so that anyone who sees or hears you cannot say that you are doing it gladly or taking pleasure in it.

333. When you are in someone else's home, always take care not to speak ill of him. And take care not to say anything in the street or near a thin wall that you don't want everyone to know. Likewise, when you enter a room, don't speak or say anything until you know for certain who is in the room, for someone might be hiding behind the curtain or in some other concealed place, and could hear your business. As the saying goes, "Speak no lies when you're in the street." Never say anything in a place where you don't know that you cannot be heard by some man or woman whom you cannot see. If you wish to speak of secret things, speak softly, and in a place where the walls are so thick that you know that what you say will not be heard beyond the nearest wall. Or go to tell your secrets in a public square, or in a meadow or sandy area or field, out in the open, where you can see that there is no one nearby who can hear you. Beware of hedges and trees, and structures or walls or corners or any other place where someone can hide – man or woman, large or small – if you don't want your secrets to be known.

334. Keep in mind that there is nothing of greater spirit or greater virtue than forgiving offences. Therefore, always forgive those who offend you ten times rather than taking revenge one time, for in forgiving you attain merit from God, praise from those who hear of it, and love from the one who has offended you. Likewise, I tell you that in taking revenge you attain the opposite: that is, sin toward God, censure from men (that is, from wise men), and more hatred from your enemy. For you can almost never take complete revenge, no matter what you do. If you do more, you offend your enemy and incur his hatred, and people will say that you have done evil and villainy; if you do less, people will say: "It would have been better not to put himself at risk, than to have done so to his shame." Therefore always be a forgiver, if you wish to be a winner.

335. The sin of ungratefulness is an execrable thing. Therefore I pray you to take care not to be ungrateful. Indeed, you should always remember anyone who does you a service and honours you; and if it should happen that he needs your help or service, do not hesitate or wait for him to beg for your help; rather, rouse yourself immediately to help him, and respond and fight for him. Do not wait for him to ask for your help, so that it cannot be said that you are ungrateful or thankless for the benefit you have received. We also read that a man who does a service cannot be recompensed by the one who receives it. Therefore don't wait to be asked for a favour by one who has done a favour for you on another occasion, because then your assistance would not be freely given. As the proverb says, "a favour requested is half bought." Also, take great care not to

be ungrateful toward your Creator for the benefits you receive from him, which if you counted them would be many. I shall tell you about some of them. These benefits are the children he gives you, and wealth and health and worldly honours, and other boons, which you should recognize as coming only from him, and thank him for them. You should do as the good labourer does, who pays a tithe from the fodder and fruit that he gathers in his work. Thus should you also do – that is, you should perform good acts that honour God: praise him and thank him for the beautiful family that he has given you. Don't think that you have comely children on account of your comely wife, for then you would be ungrateful to God. Likewise, thank God for the health that he gives you and the honours that are given you by your fellow citizens and neighbours. This is paying a tithe to God – that is, recognizing the gifts that he gives you.

336. Be very careful, when you help a friend, not to enter into an assembly or contract or evil plot against your city, for anyone who asks you to do such a thing is not your friend, even if he pretends to be; on the contrary, he is your great adversary, for whoever acts against your city acts against you. How can he say he is your friend when he acts against your city? Therefore be very careful … [*text missing in the original manuscript*] … If he were your friend as he says he is, he would not involve you in things that could cause you to lose your honour and your standing in the community – rather, he would protect you as he would himself. He is your friend who helps and counsels you in your time of adversity, and who takes your tribulations on himself, and who helps you to bear them and comforts you so that you can bear them in peace. We read that there was a man named Rusillo, who was asked by a friend of his to perform a dishonest service, which Rusillo refused to do. When Rusillo did not want to help him, the friend said, "Then what good is your friendship to me, Rusillo, if you won't do what I ask of you?" Rusillo replied to him, saying: "Indeed, what good is your friendship to me, if I should perform a dishonest act for you?" Therefore you see that it is better to break off such a friendship than to continue it.

337. It is extremely foolish and simple-minded for a man to trust someone by whom he has already been deceived on more than one occasion. The second time, beware of one who has deceived you the first. As the wise man says: "May God curse the man who makes a fool of you; if he makes a fool of you twice, may God curse both him and you; if he makes a fool of you three times, God should curse you alone." And that is right, because you will have brought the third act of deceit upon yourself. Therefore, if you can't do better, follow the example of the ass,

whose nature is that where he falls once he doesn't return a second time if he can help it; and if he does return there, he always keeps in mind the first fall, and goes slowly and carefully so that he won't fall again where he fell before.

338. There are three chief things that someone who works the land and cultivates vines and olive trees and fruit trees and other trees should have within himself. You who have been assigned by God to do such work, listen and attend to me and put into action what I shall tell you, if you do not wish to fail both God and your fellow man. The first thing you must do is to know and fear God; the second thing is that you must be fair and honest with your fellow men; the third thing is that you must not be afraid of hard work. Therefore know and fear God when you praise and thank him for the abundance of blessings that he bestows upon you, and when you give a tenth of the fruits that you take from the earth to your priest and to the poor, as should be done. If you do not give away a tenth of what you grow, you err against God, and Our Lord will send storms and droughts and floods and other calamities upon the goods of the earth and upon your animals. Therefore, in order to avoid such evils, make sure to acknowledge the poor of Our Lord. I also said that you must be fair and honest toward your fellow man; therefore, be fair toward your fellow man when you give what is due to the master whose land you work, and when you pay what is due to your city. I also told you that you must not be afraid of hard work and toil; therefore work hard, as you assiduously do the necessary tasks at the proper times so that the earth will give up its fruits for your master and for you. Dishonesty does not only mean pilfering grain or other goods that belong to your master; it means not working your master's land as it should be worked.

Therefore you must toil with great solicitude; for whatever you do not do that you could have done, you should make it up to your master. That is, you owe him what he has lost of his rightful income on account of your defect, because you have not worked his land well.

339. When you see yourself in great tribulation and struggles, do not lament your fate; rather, you should grieve and mourn yourself, for those tribulations of yours and your affairs are permitted by God on account of your sins, or the sins of your father or mother. Therefore redress those adversities by confessing and doing penitence for your sins, and by alms and masses and prayers for the souls of your departed ones, and the said adversities will come to an end. And praise God for what he does for you, and have patience; and God will help and counsel you in your struggles, if you always have firm faith in him.

340. "This is the last will of Giovanni Cavazza: May he who gives his all to others be killed with this bludgeon."[4] This Giovanni Cavazza was a rich man who had two daughters. When they became of marriageable age, he married them to two noble young men and gave each of them a great deal, and later he gave them more of his own wealth on several occasions. But when he became impoverished, his sons-in-law wanted nothing to do with him, and likewise his daughters. Therefore always be wise to never in your lifetime make your children or other people rich, so that they will be subject to you and not the opposite.

341. Take great care not to drink so much that you are deprived of reason and consciousness, for drunkenness is a sordid, dangerous thing. Drunkenness leads men defenceless to their death; it reveals their secrets; it makes men slaves to the most vile thing there is, degradation and trouble; it induces them to lustful acts; it incites anger and brawling among brothers and neighbours and friends and comrades. What evil thing is there that does not proceed from drunkenness? Baltasar, king of Babylon, being heated with wine, lost his country and was killed by Cyrus and King Darius. King Herod Antipas, enflamed by wine, had John the Baptist beheaded, even though he loved him. Lot, who had been very chaste, fell asleep in a drunken stupor after he fled to the mountains, and slept with his daughters as if they had been his wife. Therefore beware of wine, for it is a very dangerous thing to drink it unadulterated and to drink too much of it.

342. Greed is a great and terrible sin. It is the sin that most vituperates our souls; it is the sin that most people commit. [*text missing in the original manuscript*] every man and woman, but one more than another. Greed leads men to usury, to playing with dice and other forms of gambling, to robbery, to bartering in civic affairs. On account of greed, men betray their cities, their armies, and other men; on account of greed, murders are committed, and many quarrels and legal battles and disputes arise; on account of greed, much money is gained by evil means. On account of greed, many women have taken an evil path and brought disgrace upon themselves and their husbands and relatives. Wise is the woman who, tempted by greed, succeeds in resisting and combating it. Judas Iscariot betrayed Christ on account of greed – what more could I say to you about greed than that our Lord Jesus Christ was betrayed because of it? Therefore be temperate, and do not desire more than your status requires.

---

4 In the original manuscript, there is a tiny drawing of a club under the words "this bludgeon."

343. Wrath is a dangerous sin: therefore take great care not to let yourself give in to anger, for anger deprives both men and women of reason, so that they know not what they are doing or saying. A man or woman who is without reason is like an animal; therefore it can be said that the sin of wrath makes men and women become like wild beasts. Once a man has lost his reason, he becomes enraged, cursing God and his blessed saints. Anger also generates rage against oneself, leading to despair. It causes men to lay homicidal hands on their fellow men, and causes their tongues to utter evil things. Anger doesn't spare family relationships, or friendships old or new; it rushes to have blood, and never rests until it sees blood spilled on the ground. What evil thing is there that is not born of anger? Certainly, there is no evil thing that an angry man or woman wouldn't want to see done, and do with their own hands. What relative or friend is spared by anger? Surely, none; indeed, the closer the family member, the more dangerous is his wrath. An enraged man is like an animal, or worse, for a lion will spare another lion and a wolf will spare another wolf, but a man won't spare another man. Therefore take great care to avoid this sin, for it is far too dangerous for the soul and for the body. What animal kills itself? Surely, none. Yet a wrathful man is lethal toward himself.

344. It is very bad for a man or a woman to be gluttonous and greedy, for gluttony induces men to be thieves and cowards and villains, and induces women to be thieves and to misuse their bodies, for the sin of gluttony engenders lust. Also, when a man or woman is very satiated and full, he or she has no desire to do anything that requires any effort, and therefore becomes a sluggard. When a man becomes lazy, he earns less, and earning less he becomes a thief, for he is accustomed to eating and drinking well. And when he finds that he no longer has the means to buy the good wines and foods to which he is accustomed, he can't do without them, and so he begins to steal and rob. And he can end up being hanged. Thus it is fitting that gluttony be the cause of his death. He is hanged by a rope and suffers for the evil he has committed. Likewise, a woman who is gluttonous and greedy begins to use her body in evil ways so that she can have money to buy tasty food; thus she loses her honour and that of her family, and she goes about in a wanton manner, and five out of six times she dies a violent death. Gluttony and greed bring many other evils upon you – they empty your purse, they lead you to sell your patrimony and send you out into the world like a beggar, poorly dressed and shod. They harm your body, and destroy your soul. And you can never satisfy their desires, for the more you give them, the more they want.

Even if your body is satiated and full, a gluttonous appetite is never sated; its nature is that the more it gets the more it wants, and no good work ever came of trying to satiate the desires of gluttony. Therefore take great care not to follow the desires of the table, for if you buy a spring chicken today, tomorrow you'll want a capon, and in this way the appetite continually grows. So, by God, avoid gluttony; for it is a very bad thing for a man or a woman, but it is worse for young men than old, and likewise it is worse for young maidens than old women.

345. Take care not to fail to make your confession one or two times a year, for a confessor often helps a man to avoid sinning, and makes him a friend of God. And do not fail every morning to go to church and hear at least one mass, and see Our Lord. Commend yourself and all of your affairs to him, and likewise all of your relatives and friends, and all your fellow men, and all faithful Christians, living and dead. Take great care to pray to God for your fellow man; for you partake of all the graces that he bestows. Always keep steady, honest faith and hope in Our Lord Jesus Christ and in his Blessed Mother Mary, ever virgin.

346. Prudence before the fact and during the fact is a wonderful thing; after the fact, it's not worth much. Therefore always have foresight, and think about past times, and the present, and the times that reasonably might be ahead of you. Remember that wasted time can never be recouped or recovered; therefore make sure to be diligent and far-sighted in all of your affairs, and avoid negligence as if it were the Devil, or a physical threat to you, if you want your affairs to turn out well.

347. When you go to stay in someone's home, leave the women alone, and do not steal, and do not tell lies.

348. "He who has more, leaves more, and passes on with greater sorrow." When you die, you will leave behind what you can't take with you (that is, wealth and honours and worldly prestige), and you'll take with you what you cannot leave behind (that is, your sins). Therefore always avoid sinning as much as you can.

349. "He who talks too much errs often." Therefore "speak little and listen much," and you shall be considered the wiser. And do not be a jokester: leave the joking to the jesters, for joking is often the cause of great trouble and bad feelings.

350. Always be honest and pure; and read the Epistle of St Barnabas[5] often, and make sure that you put your reading into action.

---

5 The so-called Epistle of the Governing of the Family, which Paolo copied out in his manuscript.

351. "Courteous speech is worth much and costs little." Therefore never speak in a rude manner to anyone, for it costs less to remain quiet than to say rude things to one's neighbour or friend or to a stranger. It is better to remain silent.

352. Always endeavour to earn money and to acquire wealth in your own right, and to never be waiting for some relative or other person to leave you an inheritance, for five times out of six people are deceived in this way. Therefore toil and earn for yourself, while you can.

353. Never engage in any business that your city prohibits, for nothing but evil can come of it. For every time that you gain from such transactions, you'll lose many other times. Love the honour and wealth and prosperity of your city and your lord, and place your wealth and yourself at their disposal, and never support any other position than that of your city. By your city I mean where you live with your family and your belongings and your relatives.

354. Never believe those who speak evil or gossip when they tell you something in order to make you rush off madly; instead, think and think again about what has been said, and whether or not it might be true. Then sleep on it, and think about it again, and don't be in a hurry to believe nor to follow what is said by gossips.

355. Everything that you have to do, do it with advice from a good friend. Don't tell too many people about your affairs, and don't do anything without advice.

356. If you have money, do not fail to use it. Do not keep it just sitting in your house, for "it is better to act in vain than to do nothing in vain." If you do something with the money, and end up not making more from it, you will still have your trade. And you will gain a great deal if you don't lose your capital and you don't abandon your trade.

357. Love and desire peace as much as you can, for it is above all other good things, for you and your family and your city and your fellow man.

358. Whenever you give, keep three things in mind: first, who you are and what it is fitting for you to give. The second thing is that you should consider what you're giving, and make the gift in proportion to your own status. The third thing is to look at to whom you are giving the gift, and whether he is worthy of it. If you do these three things, you cannot err in the gifts that you give.

359. If you have children, love them all, male and female, small and large, as you love yourself. Don't appear to love one child more than another, or not to love one, for you will create rancour and envy among them, and they will never get along together. Likewise, love all of the

members of your household, each according to his proper position, and honour each one according to his just deserts.

360. Always return home early in the evening, for all evil deeds are done at night and in the early morning, before daybreak. Therefore take great care not to go out before daybreak, unless you are well accompanied.

361. An old man should toil little with his body and much with his mind, thinking about good things for his soul and body and for his family.

362. Take care not to put off until tomorrow what you can do right away, and especially good acts. Anything can be overcome by continual diligence. And we read that as water drips on a stone, it makes a hole. Therefore be diligent and careful, and persevere in whatever you have to do, and you shall achieve it.

363. Listen well to what I say, if you want to be without fear: do good works and speak little.

364. If you live an unbridled life, you shall lose all you have.

365. "An open coffer is an invitation to sin." Therefore take care of your belongings and keep them safe, so that you take away the occasion to lose them, and your friend won't lose his good name and you won't lose your belongings.

366. When you give, take care to give temperately of your wealth or your services. Also, take great care to whom you give, and consider, as I've said above,[6] if he be worthy of receiving what you are giving. Also think of your own position, and whether you are able to continue giving what you have begun to give; and if you see that you are not able to maintain the gift that you wish to begin, do not begin to give it. For once you have given several times to a friend, he will begin to expect to receive such gifts, and it will come to pass that as long as you give to him he shall be your friend, but if you stop giving the usual gift or something similar, he will suddenly withdraw his friendship. He won't think to say: "My friend doesn't give to me any more, because he has fallen on hard times"; rather, he will say, "My friend has become so grand, he doesn't even speak to me any more. But if he should need me, I will remember him as he has remembered me." And thus he will have forgotten all the good that you have done for him because you are not continuing to do what he has become accustomed to. Therefore be very careful, as I have said; if you do not wish to lose your friends, you should not begin in any way to give gifts or render services to a friend or neighbour or stranger

----

6 A mark in the margin of the manuscript refers to precept number 358 above.

if you cannot continue to do so without diminishing your wealth or your status. And if you don't do so, when you have become impoverished on account of giving too much, and you need help from the friends to whom you used to give gifts but no longer do, you shall realize the error of your ways!

367. Always strive more to be loved than feared by your neighbours; and likewise I tell you, if you oversee some land or people, strive more to be loved by those over whom you have power than to be feared by them. But if you aren't able to gain their love on account of some defect of theirs, make sure that they fear you for your righteousness, so that you will be feared and obeyed by all. And have in yourself justice for both great and small, and you shall be feared and revered.

368. If you should have one or more children, take great care to put them to nurse with a good wet-nurse, and take care that she be wise and well-mannered and honest, and that she not be a drinker nor a drunk-ard. For very often children take from and resemble the nature of the milk that they drink. Therefore make sure that your children's nurses are not haughty, nor have other bad vices. Also be very careful, if you don't keep the child and the wet-nurse in your own home, to give the child to a nurse who has an abundance of milk, so that she won't give the baby goat's milk or sheep's milk or milk from some other animal because she doesn't have enough herself. For a baby who nurses on animals' milk does not develop like a child who is nourished with human milk; rather, he always seems somewhat stupid and empty-headed and not with full understanding. Therefore if you send your children out of your home to be nursed, visit them often, so that you can see how they are doing. And if they seem uncomfortable, move them immediately to another wet-nurse. Don't leave them there at any cost.

369. Never hesitate to forgive your fellow man, and never forgive your-self for anything.

370. It is a surer thing to remain silent than to ask someone else to be silent. Therefore always be careful not to tell any of your secrets, if you don't want everyone to know them, to one or more of your friends, even if you tell them to keep secret what you can't or don't want to keep secret yourself. Think and consider that your friend will not be able to keep your affairs secret any better than you; therefore keep to yourself any-thing that you do not wish to be known beyond yourself. For the moment it goes beyond you, it won't be in your power to keep it secret; rather, you will have to beg others to keep it secret. Thus by telling your secrets you lose the noblest thing there is – your freedom, and you make yourself the

slave of those whom you beg not to reveal the secret that you have told to them. It's better to be one's own servant – that is, to keep one's own secrets – than to tell them to your neighbour, and become enslaved to him because you are afraid that he will tell other people what you have done or said and revealed to him.

371. Boethius says that a happy death – that is, a fortunate one – is a death that does not diminish the sweet years of one's life, the years of prosperity. And a death that comes in sad, difficult times can be considered not to be a misfortune. Therefore, if Fortune first places you in great dangers and struggles and tribulations and illnesses, and causes you to lose your worldly goods, and then leads you to death, do not bemoan such a death, but rather you should welcome it, for it is better to die one death than to die a thousand. For a man who has bad fortune in this world dies a hundred deaths every day.

372. You should not nurture vain desires; that is, you should not desire things that you cannot have, and you should not desire things that cannot help you. Likewise you should not be afraid out of baseless fears; that is, you should not be afraid of things that cannot harm you. Boethius also teaches that you should turn your back on all rejoicing; that is to say, you should not rejoice excessively, nor should you rejoice in things that you can lose. He also teaches that we should banish hope: here he means that we should not hope for worldly things that are given to us by Fortune, for today Fortune gives you worldly goods and tomorrow it can take them away. We should only hope in our Lord Jesus Christ and in the most blessed Virgin Mary and in their blessed saints, and not in worldly goods, for many people have found themselves deceived by those who hope in temporal goods. Boethius also teaches to banish fear. What we should fear are those things that can harm our soul and body – that is, sins – and therefore take great care to avoid sinning. Likewise, do not be fearful or cowardly in the things in which one needs to be confident and bold, that is, in defending what is right and in helping your fellow man, and wards of the court and widows and orphans and those who are powerless and strangers, and in defending your own reputation. He also teaches us not to give in to sadness, and not to consort with her in the street, that is, in the Valley of Sorrow. Therefore never give in to sadness as you conduct your own affairs, or those of your friends; rather, endeavour to do whatever you have to do with care and joy and diligence.

373. Always strive, in all of your dealings with other people, to deal with successful men who are fortunate in their own affairs, and with people who are wealthier and wiser and of higher standing than you.

I am talking about when you consort with other merchants or tradesmen. Likewise with other things: for whoever deals or consorts with good men, it rubs off on them, and whoever deals or consorts with evil and false men can do nothing other than lose along with them.

374. If it should happen that you become ill, and for fear that you might die you make your will and leave behind your wife and children, avoid like fire leaving your affairs solely in the hands of your wife, even though she be the mother of your children. For almost all women are vacuous and light of spirit, and are easily led astray. In many ways and for many reasons, it could happen that your wife would leave your children and deprive them of their patrimony, or mistreat them, or let someone else mistreat them and not say anything, either out of some advantage to her or to her children by another husband that she may have had before she married you, or her relatives, or for some advantage to a friend with whom she has fallen in love, or out of fear of someone who seeks to appropriate their patrimony. In one way or another, almost no woman can be faithful and steadfast and not be led astray. Therefore never entrust your affairs and those of your children to a lone woman without some man to rein her in; especially if you leave your children well off; for the belongings of a poor man are regarded neither with rancour nor with envy. Indeed, it is a greater risk to leave your patrimony without legal restrictions to a woman who has poor children from another husband, for a woman understandably loves the children from her first husband more than those whom she has had with a second husband or friend or whoever it may be.

375. Be very careful when a man whom you do not know, nor whence he comes, is very kind to you and does you great honour and flatters and praises you both to your face and behind your back; don't put your trust in him immediately. Don't say right away: "This is the best friend I've got." First you must test him, not once but a hundred times – that is to say, many times. You must test him in many ways and in many situations before you accept him as a true friend. And I tell you that you should always hold back a little; even if you trust this man, don't trust him totally, for there are many examples of men who have trusted totally and have been deceived, especially where money is involved. I'll give you this example: There is no horse so loyal or so good in the bridle that when ridden for a long time without reining it in will not become spoiled. The same occurs with men: the son is subject to and obedient and humble with his father as long as his father has control of the household and his possessions; but once the father has given his son the authority to control

his own possessions, he is no longer subject to his father and hates him
and cannot wait for him to die so that he won't have to bear the sight
of him any longer. And while he was a friend before, he becomes your
enemy because of the trust you have placed in him. So, since I forbid
you to trust totally in your own children, you must be even more wary of
people whom you don't know. "He who trusts not, will not be deceived,"
says the proverb. Now, I am not saying that you should be completely
distrustful, but rather that there should be a happy medium in all things.
If you always keep to this happy medium in every aspect of your life, you
shall be praised and considered wise. Refrain from both immoderation
and excessive moderation; but if you have to sin in one, exceed in moderation rather than in immoderation.

376. If you borrow money and use land or property that you own as
collateral, deal with someone who is of the same social standing as you,
or lower. Take great care not to deal with a man of high standing, for it
might happen that after you have borrowed money from a great man
with your land as collateral, and you wish to sell the said land in order
to pay him off so that you won't be devoured by the interest, the great
man will not permit you to sell your property. He will say to whoever it
is who wishes to buy it: "I want the property, for what he can get for it."
In this way, no one will want to buy from you for fear of displeasing the
great man. Therefore you will have the burden of the interest on your
back, and you will lose your property. And if you still want to sell, you'll
have to give it to the great man as a lien. If you think that he wants the
land, pretend that you don't want it, and say that he would be doing you
a favour by taking it off your hands. Therefore take care as much as you
can not to enter into such dealings with men of higher standing than
you. And if you cannot help but do so, sell outright and do not borrow
against your property, for there is nothing worse than borrowing, as I've
told you above.

377. "Be well mannered in everything you do, and you shall be praised
for all you do." Without good manners, none of your affairs will ever go
well.

378. Here continues the example of the last will and testament of
Giovanni Cavazza, written above where I made this mark.[7] Having
given all he had to his sons-in-law, and having ended up a poor man

----

7 In the original manuscript, three asterisks in the margin refer back to precept number
  340.

acknowledged neither by his sons-in-law nor by his own daughters, Giovanni decided that he wanted to live as he had before, like a gentleman, for as long as he lived. And he said to his sons-in-law and daughters: "I am now old, and may not live long, and therefore I wish to make my will." He saw to it that he had a sturdy chest with two locks, and inside it he placed a large iron bludgeon, and a paper on which was written what is indicated above where I drew the bludgeon in this book, that is: "This is the last will of Giovanni," etcetera. He carefully locked the chest with two keys, and gave one to the Franciscan friars and the other to the Dominican friars. And he said to them: "Do not give these keys to anyone as long as I am alive; after my death, give them to my sons-in-law, for I wish them to be my heirs, and after I am gone I wish them to have what I kept in case I might urgently need it." And he said to them: "These are the keys to a chest where I put what I have kept for myself." Then he went to a dear old friend of his, and said to him: "Lend me two thousand gold florins." And he lent them to him. Then Giovanni Cavazza invited his daughters and sons-in-law to dine, and after they had eaten he said to them: "Wait for me here in the dining room." And he shut himself up in his bedchamber, and began to count the money over and over. The sons-in-law and daughters were at the keyhole, and the saw the money, and heard Giovanni saying to himself: "Whoever treats me well, I will do the same for him; and if these sons-in-law and daughters of mine behave well with me, I will leave them all this money. And truly, even if I were starving to death, never in my life would I touch one of these coins, for I want them to go to my daughters." The husbands and the daughters heard what he was saying; and he remained in his room for a long time. Then he made a show of putting the money back in the chest, but he came out of the room with the money on him; his sons-in-law believed that the money was still in the chest. Giovanni rejoined them, and said: "Help me, and treat me well, and I will leave you rich men." And from that day on, they strove to outdo one another in honouring him, with clothing, food, and keeping him company. In the end he made his will, and he left a great deal of money to friars and priests and hospitals and to the poor for the love of God, and he made his sons-in-law his heirs, and they pledged to pay those bequests. And he ordered that as soon as he had been buried, the friars should give the keys to his sons-in-law, and he said to them: "You shall do me honour at my grave, and you shall be well able to do so, for I am leaving so much to you." They both said they would do so. Giovanni lived a long time with his sons-in-law and daughters with great honour, and at their expense; finally he died, and they buried him with great pomp. When they returned home, it seemed like a thousand years to them that they had to wait to go for the keys, and they went to get them. First they paid the bequests, as Giovanni had ordered; and when they had paid them, they got the keys, and went home and opened the chest, and inside they found the bludgeon and Giovanni's message. You can imagine how they felt! And it served them right, for they were ungrateful for the benefits that they had received earlier from Giovanni. Therefore, son, brother, friend, relative, neighbour, or whoever you may be who read this book, do not be ungrateful for the favours you receive, lest you harden the heart of the one who has helped you so that he does the opposite.

379. If at any time it should happen that you have a malady for which you cannot find any medicine or any physician who is familiar with it nor is capable of curing you of it, which often happens, remember, if the said malady is in a part of your body that you can keep exposed, keep it exposed during the day, and at night apply the medicine that is most beneficial. And show it to everyone. If you do so, in a short time you will find a man or woman who will recognize the malady and will give you medicine for it. If it is in a place that you cannot expose, tell every appropriate person about it and do not conceal it, if you wish to find a physician and a medicine that will cure you.[8]

380. I told you above that if you have sons, you should place them in a trade.[9] And if you have more than one or two sons, don't put them all, as I told you, in a single trade. Likewise, I tell you that you should endeavour as much as you can to place them in a trade that they can do both as young men and when they are old. For there are trades or crafts that a young man can do, but as he grows older he has to leave them because he can no longer endure the labour. Thus your son would find himself in great need and without a trade and unable to make a living, and he would become impoverished in his old age. Therefore place your son in a trade or craft that he can practise for his whole life, at least as long as he has his wits about him. So take care not to make him a sawyer, or a cart driver, or many other professions that I could mention, such as needle maker or armour maker. For someone who is not strong cannot saw wood or load a cart, and someone who is losing his sight cannot

---

8 Horace's affirmation that "Fools through a false sense of shame hide their open sores" (*Epistles*, Book I, Epistle XVI, 24) was proverbial in Paolo's day.

9 Two asterisks in the margin refer back to precept number 327.

make needles or chain mail for armour. As a man ages, it is natural that his strength and sight should begin to fail; and the same goes for other characteristics that a young man has much more than an old man. An old man must make little physical exertion and much spiritual exertion, thinking of good things, and doing them; and thinking about his soul and the affairs of his family, always admonishing and correcting his family members and providing them with the things that they need in the house and outside.

381. There is a proverb that says "An open coffer is an invitation to sin."[10] Therefore take care of your belongings and keep them safe, so that you take away the occasion to lose them, and your neighbour who finds them will not be tempted to sin. For he might take something if he found it in an open chest, thinking that no one would know.

382. If you want to live without trembling and fear, do good deeds and speak little about others' affairs.

383. Have restraint in all of your affairs, for "if you live without restraint, you will lose every good thing." Therefore have restraint and good manners in all of your affairs.

384. If you listen well to what I say and you put it into action, make sure to be very diligent and careful and provident in all of your own affairs and in those of others, if you should be involved in them. For a drop of water falling on a stone makes a hole in it. Likewise, everything can be achieved through unflagging diligence and care; therefore make sure that you are careful and diligent, and persevere in doing good, and you will obtain what you want in the right way, for you should not wish for nor desire anything that is not right.

385. Just as I told you to be careful and diligent, I also want to tell you what will happen to you if you are negligent and lazy in your affairs. If you are negligent in conducting your business, you can never be anything but poor. For even if your father left you a rich man, if you are negligent in taking care of and managing your affairs, things will go from bad to worse and you shall end up in poverty. And the larger the amount and the abundance of your wealth, so much more care and diligence are necessary, and so much less negligence. For example, if there were a king of a realm, and he was negligent in taking care of his affairs, little by little his realm would be taken away from him. If the king says: "I let

---

10 This is a somewhat expanded repetition of precept number 365.

my barons or household staff or stewards or servants take care of things," and the barons say: "When I see that the king doesn't bother himself about things, why should I kill myself to defend his realm?" And even worse, seeing that the others don't care and the lord doesn't bother, the one who previously was the most faithful to the king will withdraw. Likewise I say it will happen down the line: the stewards will do the same, and the household staff and servants. And you shall come to such a pass that not only will you not be able to keep stewards or servants, you won't have enough to live on yourself; indeed, you shall have to seek work as a servant to your neighbour, who helped you throw away your fortune. And even worse often occurs: you become the servant of your steward; and where you once refused to exert yourself for your own good, and did not take care of your own affairs, now you are obliged to toil and take care of the affairs of one who had been your servant or your steward. And if you don't do it, he will throw you out; he won't do as you did when you didn't care about what he was doing. And when he throws you out, you won't have anything to live on, and you'll come to a bad end. Therefore remember, my son, that you must be diligent, and not negligent nor lazy, either for yourself or when you are working for another. And do not say: "I shall take care of it tomorrow," when you have something to do; rather, do it right away, and be vigilant in your own affairs so that you won't have to be vigilant for another's. Take heed of what I have told you, if you wish to end up well.

386. There are four cardinal virtues: prudence, that is, intellect; justice, that is, doing what is right; fortitude, that is, being steadfast, and not cowardly nor proud; and temperance, which is being wise in both great and small things. A man or a woman who possesses these four virtues cannot help but be good and pleasing to God. Therefore, my son, be sure to strive to possess these four virtues, and you shall be pleasing to God and to the people of the world.

387. There are four rivers that flow from the Garden of Eden, all from a single source. The first is called Phison, and it flows through India and ends in the sea in the West. The second of these rivers is called Gihon, and flows for a little way over the earth until it ends in the sea … [*text missing in the original manuscript*] … dividing into seven parts and flowing through Egypt, and ending in the Great Sea. The third of the four rivers is the Tigris; and the fourth of the four rivers is called the Euphrates. These two rivers, the Tigris and the Euphrates, flow through Armenia and pass through many countries, until they reach the Persian Gulf, where they end, as is their nature.

388. I said earlier in this book that the soul should have two spiritual eyes, one kept open to Heaven, hoping for eternal life, and the other open to the fear of the sufferings of Hell. If you do this, you will never do an evil thing, out of fear of the torments of Hell. But what good will it do you not to do evil things out of fear of the sufferings of Hell and to merely hope passively for the glory of eternal life? Surely, if you ever hope to go to Heaven, it will do you no good not to do evil, if you don't do good deeds as well. Our souls should fear Hell and its torments; and, as I have said, always have an eye on those torments, and you shall never sin because of that fear. But the other eye should be kept on God, and not only out of hope, which would deceive our souls, but out of love and charity. We must serve God with good actions and good thoughts. With good works, the soul acquires merit; and by acquiring merit in this life, in the next life the soul shall bask in the glory for which it had hoped. With hope alone, and no good works, our souls would not attain that glory, and would be disappointed in the end.

Memoirs

Giovanni di Paolo Morelli

Because nothing in this book has been written before, I, Giovanni di Paolo di Bartolomeo di Morello di Girardo di Ruggeri (or rather Gualtieri, son of Calandro di Benamato d'Albertino de' Morelli) became desirous to write about our family and our early situation and what followed, to the best of my ability. I do this to pass the time, and also so that our family will know something of our forefathers, for today every man claims to be of ancient lineage. Therefore, I wish to show the truth about our lineage. And, as you see, I name each of our forefathers in order as you see here above, according to how I found their names written in certain books and very old documents.

I shall call this book *Memoirs of Giovanni di Paolo* etcetera.

In the name of God and of his glorious mother the Virgin Mary and of the blessed St John the Baptist and the blessed St Anthony and the glorious virgin St Catherine[1] and of all the most excellent and holy heavenly court (to whom with devotion we humbly pray that I, unworthy as I am, may be granted such grace that for the good reputation of my family I shall write what is chiefly of honour and glory to God the highest, infinite joy to the souls of our departed and of our present family members and those who by the grace of God are to come, with honour and praise of the virtuous, good, and holy life led by us and by

---

1 St Catherine of Alexandria, virgin and martyr, an extremely popular saint during the Middle Ages, is invoked several times by Morelli, who was particularly devoted to her.

those who by the grace of God shall descend from us), begun in the year of Our Lord 1393.[2]

Origins of the Morelli family: Beginnings

Our earliest ancestors came to live in the city of Florence 300 or more years ago, but did not leave any record of their beginnings – or rather, since they were not wealthy but rather needy, they did not preserve nor save any of their humble writings and many were lost or disappeared in the course of time. At present, wishing only to shed light on things that clearly happened – in the following chapters I, Giovanni, will set down a record of things that we know because of documents or because they have been told to me, written with the help of God in the fashion and form in which they are truly known to me, without adding or omitting anything.

Firstly, to give order and a foundation to what I have in mind to write, I shall outline all of the sections that I wish to write, one after the other, according to the clarity granted to me and with as much brevity as is possible to my intellect. In the first part, I shall mention the place where our family first came from. In the second part, I shall record not the first member of our family who came to live in Florence, nor shall I write about the time that this first Morelli was born, which is not clear. I shall only mention the first member of our family whom we know about through our books and writings, and the name of this ancestor and where he first lived and in what period, conjecturing without deceiving myself. In the third section, I shall write about the descendants of that first Morelli to come to Florence, their profession, and where they lived. In the fourth and last section, I shall record certain great events that occurred in our city that had a particular effect on our family, recounting only the things that happened in my own lifetime and before – that is, the things that I remember because I saw or heard about them, and not others. I shall interpose the aforementioned sections among the other materials as shall occur with time, in the hope that the outcome will be as written above, and ultimately I desire in part to teach our children and descendants by true examples and things that actually happened to us.

---

2 Like Pitti, Morelli began writing his memoirs at a particularly inauspicious time for his family, which was in danger of being marginalized from Florentine political life.

If they frequently ponder these things, they shall receive by the grace of God health and good fortune, and if not in everything, for what I write is not of such great value, at least in some part thanks to the help of God and their own intelligence.

I

["THE PLACE WHERE OUR FAMILY FIRST CAME FROM"]

How the Mugello is Situated with Beauty, Goodness, and Greatness of Men, Land, Fortifications, Etcetera

Our family had its foundation and beginning a long time ago, five hundred years or more. We were known for our wealth and properties in the beautiful Mugello region, in the parish of San Cresci in the town of San Martino a Valcava, to be precise. It would be ungrateful of me not to mention the many noble qualities of that region, which gave us our wordly beginnings with an honourable and decorous life, giving us the gift of part of itself in the form of the virtues of our ancestors. This is where our ancestors first chose to establish themselves. We came from those beginnings, and our family increased, as is stated above. Many noble and perfect qualities can be ascribed to this land of Mugello. But in order not to overtax my humble intellect in those things that clearly I would not be able to express, and also to avoid writing at too much length, I shall distinguish three things only. The first is the beauty of the Mugello, the second is its fertility, and the third is its size. And in order to make myself clear and to not complicate my description, I shall briefly distinguish each of these aspects in three short sections.

I shall begin by saying that the Mugello is the most beautiful place in the Tuscan countryside, and it is reputed thus by the greater part of the citizens of Florence. Although this testimonial is quite adequate, nevertheless for the greater glory of the Mugello I do not wish to limit myself to saying this, but shall go into greater detail at various points in these pages. To my mind, in order to fully demonstrate what I have said, one must go over three main points, which encompass everything. First, we must see and examine the people who own property and govern the place; second, what is owned, which we shall divide into two parts – that is, first we shall tell about the lands and then about the buildings, because each have distinct characteristics. I have now established how we shall proceed in the three following sections.

The beauty of the Mugello can be seen clearly and manifestly in its people, for there are a great number of men who are farmers and honourable people, proper and upright in their profession; their womenfolk are comely countrywomen, cheerful and pleasant, all very affectionate, always singing and dancing and rejoicing. Likewise there are many noble citizens, men and women of all ages, who make the countryside blossom with their hunting and birding and banqueting and courtly life all the year round.

Then look at the countryside itself, which is so charming and pleasant, with all the pleasures you could think to ask for. The Mugello is situated in the middle of a beautiful cultivated plain adorned with delightful fruit trees, all cared for and as beautiful as a garden. An enchanting little river[3] runs through it, and along its banks are nurseries that slope down from the lovely hills that surround the plain. All around, like a pretty garland, are slopes and hills for climbing; there are also high mountains that are no less enchanting.[4] There are wild parts and cultivated parts of the Mugello, and some are neither wild nor cultivated, but something in between, and very lovely. The lands near the dwelling places are well kept, adorned with fruit trees and beautiful vineyards, and numerous fresh-water pools or springs. The hills are wilder, with woods and forests with many chestnut trees that provide a great abundance of fine fat chestnuts. There is a great deal of game in these woods, such as wild boar, deer, bears, and other wild beasts. Near the dwelling places there are many lovely oak groves; some of the people who live there have arranged these groves as places of pleasure, clearing the ground so that one can walk barefoot beneath the trees with no fear of hurting one's feet. You also see big groves of broom trees, where there are large numbers of hares, pheasants, and other game. Closer to the dwelling places, you see large fields of fragrant herbs – thyme, veronica, strawflowers, and juniper, with charming fountains that flow everywhere. The area is full of partridges, quail, pheasant, and hares. It is a delightful place to hunt.

Third and last are the buildings, which are large, solid, and well situated, and made of noble materials. There are many spacious homes, surrounded by lush, charming places in which to walk and disport oneself.

---

3 The Sieve.

4 This joyous, not particularly realistic depiction of the Mugello as a *locus amoenus* is one of the strongest echoes of Boccaccio in Morelli's prose (compare the conclusion to Day VI of the *Decameron*).

To give this last part, which is no less lovely than the others, its due, I shall describe it in some detail. In the centre of the built area, where the heart, head, and government are located, there are six main fortresses built by the government of Florence to guard and protect the whole area. These castles are built on lovely sites, nobly arranged in the centre of the plain, about three miles apart. They are surrounded by wide, dark moats full of good water, and are bounded by high, thick, strong walls surmounted by sturdy towers with high corbels. Inside the castle walls are numerous houses arranged in charming neighbourhoods abounding in knowledgeable and experienced artisans of every kind, who know how to receive strangers honourably. In an area of about two or three miles surrounding these castles, on the plains and hills and slopes, there are many dwellings of citizens in charming, delightful locations, with lovely views of the fields and gardens and meadows. The houses are large, with halls and chambers worthy of great lords, and pools of clear, cool water. On the higher slopes, six or eight miles from the castles, are many large, noble fortresses owned by noble gentlemen, who attract the peasants by giving them official appointments, honouring them so that they are glad to stay in these fortresses with them for company and for pleasure. In the wilder places and where it is necessary, there are many fortresses kept and guarded by our government, which are marvellously strong and fine and suited to the needs of the peasants. One couldn't write fully about all the beauties of this place on six sheets; so I shall bring this description to a close, and settle for having only touched upon some of them.

In the second section, where we have promised to describe the goodness of the Mugello, I declare that reasonably, being perfect, this goodness should be manifested in the same ways as we saw the beauty of the Mugello manifested above. And wishing to show this clearly, it follows that goodness appears in most of the people of the region; this is manifestly clear.

Firstly, the people of the Mugello are devout and charitable, according to their station in life. This can be seen in the many places of devotion that have been built, and the great aid and alms given by the people to support these places. Among others, there is the monastery at Monte Asinaio,[5] where the cloistered monks are very devout; there are also the

---

5 Mount Senario, to the north of Florence, famous in Italian literature for the story of the young man and the "geese" (*Decameron* IV, introduction); it was the site of a colony of hermits, and later of a famous monastery.

Franciscan friars at Bosco ai Frati, near San Piero a Sieve, a place of great devotion. And there are many others.

You will also find many people who are faithful to the Florentine state and to the Guelph party; they have shown their faithfulness on many occasions and in their good deeds. Among other things, with the help of Florence and their own vigilance, they drove out the tyrannical Ubaldini,[6] who are Ghibellines, enemies of the Guelphs and of the Florentine state. Our allies in the Mugello received great damage to their people and property at the hands of the Ubaldini, and were involved in many skirmishes with them. These country dwellers were strong and faithful in their devotion to Florence, and never capitulated to the many promises and large gifts with which the Ubaldini attempted to bribe them. They have always been against the Ubaldini, and it is never necessary to alert them to defend the lands and castles, for they have always lovingly and zealously followed the triumphal banner of our city-state and likewise the Catholic banner of the venerable Guelph party. The people of the Mugello are likewise faithful to each citizen of Florence individually; they are loyal and upright in their professions; diligent in their work; well-mannered, pleasant, reverent, and full of courtesy; knowledgeable about all things, but especially those that delight gentle folk, such as hunting for game and birds, and fishing. They are always ready with the appropriate persons and things for whatever you request. Their womenfolk, like the men, are well-mannered, pleasant, honest, wise, and hard-working, with all the virtues desirable in country folk.

The great bounty of their abundant harvests can be seen in their lands. On the plain of the Mugello, you see the best and most bounteous farmlands in the Florentine countryside, where you will see two or three generous crops harvested each year. Anything you could wish for is raised there to perfection. The lands on the slopes are perfect; a great abundance of wheat and grain and fruit and olives is grown there, as well as a great quantity of wine grapes, wood, and chestnuts, and enough livestock to supply a third of Florence's demand. The Mugello also produces a large quantity of cheese and a great deal of lambswool cloth, chickens and other domesticated fowl, as well as game in great abundance.

---

6 The Ubaldini were a powerful family that dominated the Tuscan-Emilian Apennines; often allied with the Romagnoles and Ghibellines against Florence, they were repeatedly defeated by the Florentines from 1251 onward, and their castles were dismantled between 1358 and 1373.

And all of these things are supremely good – better than anything else in our countryside.

There only remains to be seen the goodness and utility of the buildings: and this can be seen first, as I've said, in the five castles that are on the plain. These are strongly fortified, with moats and walls and towers so that there is no need to fear attacks from anyone. Within, they are well equipped to harbour when necessary both people and the whole harvest along with livestock, and everything is safe and sound without any lack of water or any other necessity. You can see markets that are held at all of these castles every fifteen days, alternating among the castles in turn, and at these markets you see all of the Mugello – everyone is there to sell or buy produce. There is a great abundance of anything you could ask for. And in order to avoid any troubles that might arise for many reasons, at each of these castles there is a *podestà* who is a citizen of Florence, who has complete authority over everyone, and keeps the peace among those who are subject to him. These castles are held to be the best and the most pleasant and the most courtly of any other in the countryside in that region. The rest of the area – that is, in the hills and everywhere else – has, as I've said, many dwellings, which in addition to being attractive are solid and well situated and with good air, with many dovecotes and wells and everything that is useful and good. Likewise, there are fortifications sufficient for defence against any attack, and capable of sheltering everyone in the area, with all of their belongings. This is of the utmost advantage to all of the citizens there.

In order to fulfil what I promised, even though it might be superfluous, for I've said almost everything in the two sections above, we shall say a few brief things about the population and size of the Mugello. And in order to proceed in order, I say that the Mugello has a large number of inhabitants; and truly I believe that fifty years ago, ten thousand soldiers could have been recruited from the Mugello. But I believe that the number has diminished, as it has everywhere else, due to plagues and wars and other troubles on account of which a large number of people have been forced to leave in order not to be captured and languish in captivity. I believe that today you could recruit between six and eight thousand men there, and these are mostly men of some standing.

Next, you see the large size of the area: in length, it stretches from the town of San Godenzo to the border of Vernia, below Barberino, about twenty-five miles; in width, from the village of Uccellatoio to the ridge of the Ubaldini mountains. Many people say that the area extends well beyond, but even taking the lesser area, it is about eighteen miles. You will find few areas in the Florentine countryside that surpass the Mugello in size or in any other respect. You have already seen that it is rich in castles and fortresses and other buildings and houses. The Mugello has several large castles. And even if you said to me, "Decomano and Barberino are not castles," I would reply that it is true, because they don't have walls structured the way that castles should, but they are as large and as heavily populated as castles. They don't have the same type of walls, because they aren't necessary, for they are already strong in terms of their location; that is, they are in narrow, well-protected areas. Besides these, there are many fortresses that belong to the government of Florence, more than twelve, I believe: there is a great quantity of fortifications and dwellings, as I've said, because the place is strong and large. And of this there is no doubt.

I have lingered over the description of the Mugello in a longer discourse than I had planned in the beginning. And because what I write is not of much usefulness or worth preserving, I apologize, having been carried away by the love of our ancestors. After I started in order, wishing to recount each part as I had promised, it wasn't possible for me to sum everything up in a shorter text. I also think I should be excused because, according to what I've seen and heard, I have written the truth. For which reasons and motives I was not able to make my account shorter.

What follows is an account of the history of our ancestors, may God grant them eternal repose. And likewise we shall recount the history of all their descendants, invoking with devotion the help of almighty God.

II

["ON THE FIRST ANCESTOR KNOWN TO US THROUGH BOOKS
AND WRITINGS"]

I find, written in some notary papers that are frayed, torn, and almost destroyed by age, mention of one of our ancestors, named Ruggieri di Calandro di Benamato d'Albertino de' Morelli. This was written in the year of Our Lord 1170. And in order to be able to write something about that first known ancestor of ours, I say that it can be presumed that Ruggieri, before he reached his majority, as can be seen in his papers, must have been at least twenty years old. Thus he would have been born around the year of Our Lord 1150 or thereabouts. I shall record here the information, according to my judgment, of that time, and in the chapter below we shall write about Calandro, to the extent that it is possible.

Our Ancestor Calandro

As stated in part above, we find no written record of Calandro; therefore, as I wish to write something about him, it has been necessary to seek out the most reliable and reasonable accounts that mention him. Beyond these, wanting to be more clear, I questioned our male and female relatives. And they, who have heard accounts from our elders, say that this Calandro was born in Florence and lived in the area of San Simone and took a wife from a very old Florentine family and was continually working with others in the craft of dyer and got very far in life on account of his skill. And it seems (and this is patently clear from several written accounts, as we recounted above) that he and his legitimate wife had several children. Among the ones whom we find mentioned, he had a son named Ruggieri, also known as Gualtieri, who was his heir. And it seems that he left Ruggieri very well off both in terms of his business and even in the form of some cash. We shall write about Ruggieri in the following section. No record can be found of Calandro's death; but in order not to give too sparse an account of him, it seems to me that we can arrive at an approximation of when he was born and died. He was born in the 1120s, as stated above. And from this we can deduce that if he was born in Florence around that time, and took a wife in 1150, and if he left a flourishing business to one or more of his sons, since he was well established and experienced in the profession of dyer, we can presume that Ruggieri must have been at least twenty years old when Calandro died, which would have been in the 1170s or thereabouts.

I added this information not out of necessity, but rather because I deem it important to show when our family was first established in Florence. Taking this further, and in order to err on the side of less time rather than more, I posit that the father of this Calandro was the first one in the family to come to Florence. And as I've said, since I don't know for certain who was the first, whether it was he or someone else before him, I shall choose him in order to err less. And I say that if Calandro was born at this time, of which we can be almost certain, his father (assuming that he was the first in the family to come into the city), who we can certainly assume did not come to Florence as an old man, nor with a wife, must have been young and experienced in noble things, not in vulgar ones, and that he had noble ways. For already at that time, and much earlier, we find that our ancestors owned land. And, as happens to many, this man came to Florence at the instigation of citizens from old, noble families, who saw in him virtue and gentility. So, out of love and friendship for our family, or out of his own wish and incited by our family (it makes no difference to me, since both reasons are laudable), he came to live in Florence. And we can deduce that when he arrived in Florence he must have been about twenty years of age, which at that time was like being twelve years old today. We can assume that he lived in Florence for fifteen or twenty years before he was well enough established in his profession to set up a household and have real security and stability.

And because the Florentines saw that he was truly talented, practical, sensible and a good earner, and also having learned that his father and forefathers in the Mugello were wealthy, respected, and revered and that his home abounded in all kinds of good things, many of which came from his father and his relatives in the Mugello, many favourable offers of marriage were proffered to him. In addition to the reasons given above, the fact that he had noble friends and neighbours in the Mugello was also in his favour. On account of this and for many other reasons, he came to associate with good, honourable people, and could obtain a wife with a good dowry by the time he had reached the age of forty or so. I do not want you to be astonished about his age, for at that time it was the custom to marry much later than it is today. At that time, a man of forty was considered like a man of between twenty-six and thirty would be today. And at that time women got married at twenty-four or twenty-six years of age, and had four or six children in all and were healthy and strong and lived a long time.[7] For this reason, I reckon that within two years of marrying he had had a son, that is, Calandro, if he was the first born. If Calandro wasn't the first, he must have had him later; but, however it was, I calculate that he had him earlier, and I say that if Calandro was born in the 1120s, his father must have come to Florence, if he were the first (and either he or someone before him must have been), around the year 1100, having been born around 20 years earlier, which would make the year of his birth around 1080, or earlier. I do not know the exact date of his birth, but I would be grateful to learn it, because it would bring much more honour to us. But as I said at the beginning, I shall take care not to make mistakes, and if I should make a mistake, I'd rather make it against myself than against time, erring on the side of less rather than more. There is nothing more to say about this. And my ignorance is my excuse for the length of this text, because I don't know how to make myself understood in a briefer way.

---

7 In canto XV of *Paradiso*, Dante's great-great-grandfather Cacciaguida states that in his day (late eleventh century) girls did not marry too young. By the mid-fourteenth century, the average age for girls to marry was fifteen.

Gualtieri or Ruggieri

What follows is a record of Ruggieri, also known as Gualtieri di Calandro di Benamato d'Albertino de' Morelli, son of Calandro. Many good and virtuous actions of this man could be recounted, which are seen by manifest experience, and which have truly given a good, strong foundation to our ancestors who descended from him. But so as not to go on writing at too much length, I shall briefly recount several things about which I know the most. During his lifetime, Ruggieri lived in the house where his father lived, that is, in San Simone, which was near to the city walls of Florence.[8] He continued in the dye trade and got on very well, and made money most of the time. We can also presume that he did well because he took a wife, I know not from which family, but he got a good dowry with her, around five hundred *lire*[9] – this is a sign that she came from honourable people. He had several children from her; among others, there was one called Giraldo, of whose dealings we have records. Giraldo inherited Ruggieri's business after the latter's death. I believe, based on what I have learned, that Ruggieri departed this life and rendered his soul to God in the year of Christ 1220 or thereabouts; I believe this because I have found papers from that time written by his son Giraldo, and nothing by Ruggieri. I believe that Ruggieri was buried in the church of San Simone, because they lived nearby, so their family tomb was probably there. I shall say no more about Ruggieri's affairs, for I would have to be guessing. We shall continue our account of his son Giraldo in the following chapter.

III

["RUGGIERI'S DESCENDANTS, THEIR TRADE, AND WHERE THEY LIVED"]

Giraldo Morelli

Giraldo was born in the year of Our Lord 1199 or thereabouts; I cannot say exactly, because there is no record of it, but I find that in the year 1205 he was at school, which means he had to be five or six years old, or a little older. When Giraldo reached the age of twelve or so, he was called

---

8 Morelli is referring to the second circle of city walls of Florence, built in 1173; the area of San Simone was located between the first and second circle of walls.

9 Morelli refers to *lire* (perhaps of Pisan coinage) and not florins, which began to be minted only in 1252.

Calandro by almost everybody, I think out of respect for his grandfather. By the time he was a man, the only name he was known by was Calandro, although he always signed his name as Giraldo. He continued to live in San Simone and he, too, practised the dye trade. We find papers indicating that he lent money in addition to being in the dye trade, because he found that he had some money at his disposal and did not have another occupation. He took a wife in the year of Our Lord 1226, give or take a year or two; he got a good dowry and a respectable girl (she was a Barucci),[10] and they had several children. Among others there was a son whom they baptized with the name Morello, who became Giraldo's heir after he died. Giraldo lived a long time for those days, and he was buried in San Simone. I believe this not because I found it in writing, but because I find, as I shall say here below, that Morello returned to live in that neighbourhood. I find that Morello returned to the area of San Jacopo when Giraldo had already been dead for several years, which is why I believe that he was buried in the same church as his father – that is, San Simone. I do not record any particulars of his death, in order not to say anything inaccurate. Let us leave our account of Giraldo, and turn to his son Morello, here in the following section.

Morello Morelli

We find a great deal written about Morello di Giraldo, called Morello di Calandro, both in books on parchment, as was used in those days, and on cotton-fibre paper and other similar paper used by notaries. We find more written about Morello than about those who came before him, because he had achieved a certain level of wealth, both because of what he had inherited and also because he himself knew how to make money better than anybody in his family, for he had a knack for it. According to what we find written in Morello's own hand, he began to lend money after his father died. This did not last long, and he took up another occupation, that is the wool trade, especially dyes and dyer's woad.[11] In this trade, working with his relatives and friends, he honourably made great advances as a merchant. Morello left San Simone to live in the Dyers' Way, in order to facilitate his

---

10 The Barucci were an old Florentine family, Ghibellines, who lived in the area of Santa Maria Maggiore; they later switched their allegiance to the Guelph party (Giovanni Villani IV, 10 and V, 39); Dante's Cacciaguida mentions them as among the most illustrious of his day (*Paradiso* XVI, 104).

11 A blue dye extracted from the leaves of *Isatis tinctoria,* woad or goad was an extremely important commodity during the Middle Ages.

work. I don't know the exact time that this happened, but I do know from hearing our elders speak that the Dyers' Way was outside of the city walls of Florence at that time, but during Morello's lifetime the city proper was enlarged to its present size, so that the road came to be inside the city walls.[12] He took to wife a woman from the Iscermi, an old family of good standing, who lived across from the Baldovinetti family;[13] her name was Monna Lapa. He had several children; one whom we shall mention who remained after Morello's death and was his heir (his name was Bartolomeo) shall be remembered in the following section. Morello di Calandro died a weathly, well set-up man, with a good reputation and well liked by upstanding men. His body was interred in the church of Santa Croce, beneath the arches, in a new tomb that he had had built there. I do not know exactly when he died, but he lived a long time, more than eighty years, by which time his son Bartolomeo was almost an old man himself – I believe that Bartolomeo was one of the last children he had. We can deduce this from his own writings, not because he specifically said so, but from transactions that he recorded in his account books in his own hand. I also found that he was a consul of the Wool Guild in the year of Our Lord 1334.

I must of necessity record some things from the very distant past, which, as you shall see, had to do with Morello di Giraldo, called Calandro or some other cognomen, I know not which.[14] We shall record this as a lesson for those who shall come after us, by the grace of God. I shall not specify the exact time, because I do not know it, and I don't believe that it's necessary. And for the sake of brevity I shall leave out many other circumstances, as you shall see in the following section.

Cardinal Ottaviano Degli Ubaldini

At the time when the Ubaldini family were lords of the Mugello – that is, of the Tuscan Apennines – one of them was made a cardinal, and was called Cardinal Ottaviano.[15] He was a haughty, almost tyrannical man,

---

12 Morelli is alluding to the third circle of city walls, begun in 1284.

13 The Baldovinetti and Iscermi were two old noble Guelph families. "Iscermi" was more commonly written "Schelmi" or "Schermi."

14 Morelli is referring to the additional name, often a patronymic or place name, added to one's given name. In many cases, this name became the family name or "last name" as we understand it today.

15 The famous Ottaviano or Attaviano degli Ubaldini, who was bishop of Bologna from 1240 to 1244, cardinal from 1245 on, and died in 1273. In Dante's *Inferno*, Farinata degli Uberti shows Ottaviano to Dante among the heretics, along with Frederick II.

who enjoyed great wealth, and was not at all a model of ecclesiastical restraint. While he was with the Pope, who then had his curia at Avignon,[16] Cardinal Ottaviano got the idea, in his tyrannical aspirations, to build a fabulous fortress in the Mugello. He quickly began to carry out his idea, first consulting with the great master builders and with wise, experienced military men. With their advice, he had a castle designed with all of the noble appurtenances and fortifications that could be devised. Having determined what was the strongest and best situated place in the Mugello for such a fortress, he sent his representative and the master builders with the designs to his relations, instructing them to build the fortress on Montaccianico. They were all exceedingly pleased with the idea, and began immediately to build it. So with all the greatest master builders of Tuscany and with the help of everybody on the mountain, where there was a large number of people, the fortress was completed and furnished with every appurtenance for its defence. In addition to the fortress, the mountain itself was so well fortified that with no danger of any impediment, sufficient provisions of wheat, grain, wine, and other things were gathered every year on Montaccianico to provide amply for the men who were needed to guard it.

Finally, when Cardinal Ottaviano heard that his fortress was built and that it was surpassingly fine and strong, he had the audacity to invite the Pope[17] and all his court to see it, with these very words: "Holy Father, I have had a fortress built that is one of the most marvellous in the world. It has a lush, elegant garden, twenty-five miles long and eighteen miles wide, all enclosed by high, strong walls. May it please Your Holiness to come and see it." With these and other fawning words, he made the Pope and his brother cardinals and all the papal court long to see this place. Once they had promised to come, he ordered that on the plain of the Mugello, where there is a church called the Holy Cross, there be built several large, beautiful, spacious palaces; he did this so that the Pope and his court would have a fitting place to stay. When it was all ready, the Pope and all the cardinals and many other high-ranking prelates came from Avignon to see the castle and its garden, which took up almost the whole Mugello. Its walls were the surrounding hills, which are situated just as if they were real walls. When they had seen the castle

---

16 The pope actually was not residing at Avignon at this time.

17 Pope Gregory X, who passed through Florence and the Mugello in 1273 on his way from Rome to Lyon. The chronicler Giovanni Villani (VII, 42) has a long section on this episode.

and the garden, they all agreed that it was just as Cardinal Ubaldini had described it, and the court remained at Holy Cross for several days, with great pleasure, and then went on to Rome.

When Cardinal Ubaldini died (I don't know how long he lived after this, or if the same Pope was alive), the Pope consulted with his cardinals, and it was decreed that there could never be another cardinal from the Ubaldini family, on account of the man's capricious, exceedingly proud ways. And it has ever been so, by the grace of God.

The magnificent, sublime people and state of Florence have always been enemies and persecutors and destroyers of iniquitous tyrants, robbers, and destroyers of the people, and especially enemies of the Ghibellines.[18] When they saw and heard of the tyranny, theft, and outrages that the Ubaldini, tyrants of the Tuscan Apennine and of the Mugello, were committing, they determined to extinguish that thievery as they had put down many others in the area (they had already taken many of the Ubaldini's castles, but the Ubaldini still had many others, especially the one on Montaccianico, of which they were exceedingly proud). The Florentines decided to take the fortress at Montaccianico from the Ubaldini, and in the year of Our Lord 1300 or thereabouts, they laid siege to it.[19] The castle called La Scarperia acted almost as a stockade for the Florentines as they waged war against the Castle of Montaccianico. The siege lasted seventeen years before the Florentines finally captured the fortress, and then a treaty was made. In truth, force of arms was of little avail, for it was like waging war against one of the stars in the sky. But it pleased Our Lord God, help and defender of all good, that the Florentines should capture that fortress and many others with great honour and victory. Some of the fortresses were dismantled, as they were costly to guard and were thought to be superfluous and of no usefulness to the State.

---

18 The Guelphs and the Ghibellines were rival political factions in northern and central Italy from about the twelfth to the fifteenth century. These parties originated in Germany in the early twelfth century during a struggle for the throne of the Holy Roman Empire between two noble houses. In the thirteenth century, the Guelphs were the party that opposed the authority of the Holy Roman emperors in Italy and supported the papacy, while the Ghibellines supported the imperial authority. In the fourteenth century, after the emperors had ceased to be a major power in Italy, the contest degenerated into a struggle of local political factions, as described here by Morelli. In 1334 Pope Benedict XII forbade the further use of the Guelph and Ghibelline names, but they were occasionally used as late as the sixteenth century.

19 The siege of the fortress of Montaccianico took place in 1306, and lasted from April through September (not the seventeen years of Morelli's extravagant retelling). Villani (VIII, 86) gives a detailed account of it.

Later, on account of the wars we had with the Visconti of Milan (some of which you shall hear about here below), it was deemed best to dismantle all of the fortresses because of the expense of guarding them and the great dangers that would arise should one of them be lost to our enemies. So all of the fortresses in which the Ubaldini had lived in the Tuscan Apennine were dismantled, also in part so that the Ubaldini wouldn't think about trying to regain them for the income they could provide. But then it happened that in the third war that Florence had with the Duke of Milan,[20] we lost Bologna to him, and with the Duke's help some of the descendants of the Ubaldini came to the Apennine and almost won back their former land in the mountains and villages; and certain stockades that they had were a worry to Florence. This had come about because there were no fortresses left from which to put up a resistance; so the Florentines realized that it had been a mistake to dismantle them all. It is impossible to foretell future events without great foresight; one would practically have to be a soothsayer. Thus it is important to take counsel with old men, who are wise and experienced and have seen many things. One must not be precipitate the moment one gets an idea, but should ponder it for a long while and follow reason and counsel rather than one's own wishes or desires.

In those days, and well before, as it pleased God, who does not want to give complete glory to those who live in this miserable world, it happened that in Florence there were many divisions and discords among the citizens for many reasons, and especially because everyone wanted to have power, and they used all kinds of covert stratagems to achieve that end. At that time there were factions of Whites and Blacks, derived from the sects of the Donati and the Cerchi, or if you wish the Guelphs and Ghibellines. Many wrongs were done to a great many people, depending upon who was in power at any given time. And in the struggle for power, more harm was done with the sword than through political channels, as we do today. The populace was very divided; those who sided with the Cerchi were Whites, and those who sided with the Donati were Blacks. Many powerful old families sided with one faction or the other, and

---

20　Gian Galeazzo Visconti (1351–1402), the son of Galeazzo II Visconti and Bianca of Savoy, was the first Duke of Milan. His marriage to Isabelle of Valois brought him the title of Count of Vertus (a village in the region of Champagne); this is the title by which he was known during his early career. He became Duke of Milan in 1385 after overthrowing his uncle, Bernabò Visconti. After Isabelle's death in 1373, he married his first cousin Caterina Visconti, the daughter of Bernabò, with whom he had two sons, Gian Maria and Filippo Maria.

many families were divided within themselves, with some members siding with the Cerchi and others with the Donati. There were many clashes on account of these divisions, and many evils arose every day among the citizens of Florence, who fought house to house with crossbows. And for this reason many high, strong towers were built, many of which you can still see today within the first circle of city walls.

Now it happened that on account of certain clashes that occurred, and our ancestor Morello having spoken in defence of the Guelphs with certain Whites of the Cerchi faction, they came to blows. And the thing went so far that several Ghibellines were wounded. So, in order to avoid certain arrest, Morello had to leave Florence, and he went to stay at Arezzo. There was a law at that time that permitted Guelphs to bear arms within the city of Arezzo. Morello, realizing that he could easily request this right, entreated the venerable Captains of the Guelph party, notifying them of his situation and requesting the right to bear arms within the city of Arezzo as a true Guelph. The Colleges made a declaration to the effect that Morello was a true and legitimate Guelph and presented it to the rulers of Arezzo, who granted the request to Morello or to his father; I'm not sure which of them it was, but I know that this is what happened. And for this reason, because we always sided with the Blacks, we were called Morelli.[21]

Since this story calls to mind another, which was the continuation of it, I shall write it here below, although it happened much later. You shall see how in Florence the Captains of the Guelph party sought to increase their power; I shall record the later years below, as they happened in time. But it happened that during all this turmoil in Florence, Messer Lapo da Castiglionchio,[22] who was a most ardent Guelph, having come to know about the situation of our ancestor Morello (for he was a neighbour of ours), wanted to reward Morello's actions, which had been done for the benefit and glory of the Guelph party. Lapo met his neighbour Bernardo Morelli near the church of San Romeo, and asked him about the affair. He wanted to see the declaration that had been made in favour of Morello by the Captains of the Guelph party in former times, as

---

21 *Morello* means "black" or "blackish."

22 Lapo was a famous jurist and politician, a friend of Petrarch, and a professor of canon law in Florence. After the Ciompi Rebellion, he taught in Padua and Rome, where he died in 1381. He was one of the most tenacious and ardent leaders of the Guelph party.

I wrote above. After having seen it, Lapo told Bernardo that he wanted it to be renewed by the current Captains. Bernardo was content and agreed, because Lapo was advising him to do so. For truly, Messer Lapo was a most worthy man, a great citizen and well loved by the Guelphs. So he arranged this for us, and he was happy to do it. When the Captains and their adjutants had assembled, Messer Lapo got up and told them the story of our ancestor Morello, and how the Captains of the Guelph party had made a declaration on his behalf to the government of Arezzo, and he showed them the document. Then he asked them to renew it, thus reaffirming what had been done in the past by that same body. The resolution was immediately put to a vote, and it was proclaimed again with all due solemnities that our family were members of the Guelph party, for which our ancestor had done so much. And because we always sided with the Blacks, we called ourselves Morelli – indeed, Giraldo, out of respect for the Black party, to which he was greatly devoted, named his son Morello.

Bartolomeo Morelli

Continuing with the history of our forefathers, it behooves us to tell the story of Morello's son, Bartolomeo. Bartolomeo was a very wise, good man, an honourable citizen and a good merchant; he imitated his ancestors in all of the virtues, and surpassed them as a merchant, and in his wealth and connections. He continued in the dye trade, on a much larger scale than his forebears. And because of his efforts God made him prosper more and more, for he was a man of conscience, charitable and of good spirit. Bartolomeo spent a good deal of money on property, both inside and outside of Florence; he had houses in the Corso and in the Via Vinegia area; certain houses that he rented out; and he also bought a considerable amount of property in his native land, that is the Mugello, whenever sellers presented themselves. I believe that he bought two estates on the other side of the Eme stream, at Galluzzo, which today belong to Giano di Giovanni Morelli. He took to wife the daughter of Geri di Ruggieri Cigliamochi. He lived where the loggia of our Seignory is today, and there his family had their houses; they were an old Guelph family and greatly honoured in our city. Bartolomeo and his wife, who was called Monna Dea, had seven children, four sons and three daughters. We shall write of his sons below. I do not know exactly how long he lived, but I believe he lived to be about sixty; he died of a fever, and passed from this life well disposed in his soul in the year of Christ 1347, on the 3rd of April. His body reposes in the church of Santa Croce, in a tomb located in the aisle where the men sit, as you enter the church from the direction of the Guidalotti Chapel.

Morello had another son, who was illegitimate; his name was Cietta. He was, during his life, a bold, daring man, ready to quarrel and fight more than anything else. He lived a short time; I know nothing further about him.

Giovanni and Dino and Calandro

Bartolomeo's first son was named Giovanni, of whom we shall now write. He was born in the year of Our Lord 1308. He was a worthy man who followed in his family's business – that is, the dye trade. He was already quite grown when his father died, and had a good grasp of the business; the family had obligations to certain of Bartolomeo's colleagues, so Giovanni was obliged to continue working with them. Giovanni was 36 years old when Bartolomeo died, and was in charge of the warehouse; he took over the business at his father's death. He went on like this for a while, but not too long, for he soon acquired other associates. Finally, he went into business with his brother Dino di Bartolomeo Morelli, as we find written in their books. Giovanni took to wife the daughter of Rosso Bagnesi; her name was Monna Lisa.[23] He was wise, as we have said, and he showed this also in the match he made, for he allied himself with a family from his own neighbourhood and *gonfalone* who were Guelphs of long standing. The Bagnesi were and continue to be prominent and well liked. Giovanni and Monna Lisa lived together for a long time and had several children, of whom we shall speak in due course. He left this earth and went to Heaven on the 8th day of July in the year of Our Lord 1363, dying of the plague. He was survived by four sons and a daughter, to whom he left an estate worth fifteen thousand florins or more. He was buried in the church of Santa Croce, where his father had been buried.

Bartolomeo's second son was called Calandro, after his great-grandfather. He was 11 months younger than Giovanni. Calandro was an evil man, less moral than any of his forefathers. He did not want to devote much time to business; but he did become a wool merchant and went into business with his brothers Giovanni and Paolo. The association did

---

23 The Bagnesi were a noble old family, among the leading Guelph families, from the area of San Piero Scheraggio (Villani V, 39 and VI, 33).

not last long, because his brothers became aware of the fact that Calandro had swindled them to the tune of no less than a thousand florins. He then went into money-lending, and if he had lived longer he would have become a very rich man. He took to wife Monna Cilia, the daughter of Ristoro di Piero, from whom he got a dowry of five hundred gold florins. He had three children with her – two sons and a daughter, of whom we shall tell below. He gave up his soul to God on the 19th of June 1363, dying of the plague; he was buried with his family in the church of Santa Croce. He left an estate of about four thousand florins. His wife survived him, and later married Messer Antonio Machiavelli; she is still alive today, in the year of Our Lord 1402.

Bartolomeo's third son was named Dino; he was born in 1323. He was wise and upstanding, practical and knowledgeable in business. He was a partner of Giovanni Morelli in the dye warehouse, where they did very well and made a great deal of money. If they had lived longer, they would have become very wealthy. Dino never married or had children. He departed this life, as it pleased God, on the 7th of July 1363, dying of the plague, for, as you can see, there was large-scale loss of life in Florence at that time, and it touched our forefathers, for of the four brothers only one survived, the youngest. Dino left an estate of six thousand florins. Paolo[24] inherited half of the estate, and Giovanni's heirs inherited the other half; they also inherited half of Calandro's estate. May God forgive him and the others. Dino was buried honourably in the church of Santa Croce alongside his ancestors. May God truly have forgiven them all.

Paolo di Bartolomeo Morelli

Bartolomeo's fourth and last son was named Paolo Morelli. Although he was the youngest, it seems fitting to me, for no other reason than for his virtues, to honour him by remembering some of his open-hearted, serviceable, wise, good acts, which were so many and such that my mind is incapable of comprehending them. But failing to record his great, lofty deeds would not be honouring them, but rather would diminish his honour, even though I could never write about him on the level he deserves.

Paolo Morelli was born in the year of Our Lord 1335, or thereabouts; I believe that some daughters were born to Bartolomeo between Dino and Paolo. According to what I heard our mother say, Paolo never knew

---

24 That is, the father of the writer of this diary.

Bartolomeo, his father; it seems this happened because Paolo was sent out to a wet nurse in the Mugello and kept there until he was quite grown. Paolo told our mother that this nurse of his was the strangest, most beastly woman that ever lived, and that she had beaten him so much that just remembering it made him so angry that if she had been within his reach at that moment he would have killed her. These memories of his, and the fact that he said "I never saw my father," tell me that he remained living in the country for a long time. And I believe that since Bartolomeo already had older sons who were on their way to becoming men, as you have heard before, he didn't trouble himself much about this youngest one. Perhaps since the boy's mother was already dead, and Bartolomeo was an old man by then, he didn't want the trouble of raising him; and to save money, or for whatever reason, it happened the way I've said. As I understand it, when Paolo moved back to Florence from the Mugello, his father was already dead; Paolo must have been ten or twelve years old by that time. Just think, having always, or most of the time, lived in the country, what he must have been like – little better than a peasant! But Nature, which is gentle in itself, always attracts virtue, and those who develop late because of neglect soon recover their breeding. The reasons for this are clear, and shown by effects. That is just what happened to this boy, who had been abandoned, and with the help of God I will tell about some of these things so that his descendants may remember them.

The boy returned to Florence; he was as pure and simple as he was courteous and intelligent. He found himself with no father, in the hands of his older brothers, who had taken their father's entire estate for their own, and didn't bother much about their younger brother, whom they left on his own, doing little to help him along. But as simple and unpolished as he was, on account of having had such a poor upbringing in the country, Paolo decided by himself to go to school and learn to read and write. Because he was so inexperienced, and was ashamed of being older than the other students, the schoolmaster beat him; so he left the school and did not return. For this reason, Paolo changed schools on his own many times. According to his wife, Madonna Telda, with some schools he made an agreement that they shouldn't beat him. If they kept the agreement, he would stay; if not, he left. In this way he learned to read and write and do sums; he had a very good memory, and was driven solely by his own virtuous will, desirous to learn and to make up for lost time. When with the help of God he had reached the age of eighteen years or more, he desired his brothers to give him his own share of the business; before that, he had worked with them on salary for a few years in their warehouse. Since his three older brothers had already taken over almost the whole of their father's estate for themselves, there was no one to look out for Paolo except himself. And although he tried to stand up for himself, his brothers paid him little heed, and he got nothing from them, either because he didn't know his rights or because he was still inexperienced and timorous. In the end, they assigned what they pleased to him from his father's estate: some land in the Mugello, a portion of some houses they had in Florence, and about five hundred florins in cash. He remained a partner of Giovanni and Dino at the warehouse. Paolo stayed there with them for several years on a salary, as we find in his books. He was never able to get any of the money assigned to him without a struggle, and with no benefit or profit to himself. His salary was all promised to him, but only a part of it was actually paid. He later went into business on his own, except for a certain period of time when he and Dino went back into business together, each putting up half of the money. Giovanni was the one who made the most money; Paolo made out the worst of all.

But he tried to better himself as much as he could. When he reached his majority, he complained to his relatives and friends and made many deals with Giovanni and the others, and managed to accomplish many things. But he always got the short end of the stick, because Giovanni was a grown man, cunning and experienced in the ways of the world, as were the other brothers. Giovanni was the eldest; the business was in his hands, and he could make people believe what he wished – they gave him more credence. Because he was the eldest, he had a wife; the relatives helped him, and he had many advantages. Paolo, who by his own talents showed himself to be diligent about his business, wasn't listened to or supported except in part, and more out of conscience than out of willingness or love, for he wasn't held in as high esteem as Giovanni and the other brothers.

Fortune and his own industry and hard work favoured Paolo; for he never wasted a moment of time, and was always careful to earn the love of God his Creator by his almsgiving and good works, and by winning the friendship of good men as well as respectable and powerful ones. He frequented such men, showing his great friendship by being of service to them in anything he could, asking their advice about his affairs, and showing his faith and hope in them. He honoured them by inviting them to dine, and in many other ways. He acted as godfather to their children and did similar and even greater things, as occur every day when one frequents people with whom one wishes to ingratiate onself. In this manner, and in other prudent, far-seeing ways, he was able to win such friends that at the time of his greatest need, as I shall tell, they – and not his relations – helped and supported him so that ultimately he was not wronged, chiefly through the aid and will of God, without whom nothing can be accomplished. If we wished to be faithful Christians and friends of God, we would acknowledge his power and supreme justice every day; but we are blinded by our sins and would rather judge and believe that good or bad fortune befalls us either by chance or on account of our greater or lesser intelligence, rather than by the will of God. But this is not true, for everything proceeds from God, according to our just deserts. Therefore I say that wise men have an advantage, for they know God and act well and help themselves better. For God helps those who help themselves, and who accomplish things through their own toil. This can be seen clearly and manifestly in Paolo, as you shall hear.

You have already heard about the behaviour of Paolo's elder brothers toward him, and how all three of them died and how they had arranged their affairs. Along with several others, Paolo was named conservator of his brothers' heirs, and inherited half of two of the brothers' estates, as I have already recounted. Paolo, who was still really a boy, had to take care of everything. With God's help, I hope to tell you how difficult and risky it was, so that you will be able to picture it all. Paolo's brothers died at the height of the epidemic of 1363; after contracting the plague, they went to God in the space of twenty days. As you have already heard, two of them were involved in the dye trade, in which they had invested around fifteen thousand florins. The third brother, Giovanni, who was the first to die, had a young wife, who survived him. Giovanni was involved in usury, and little else; and not only in Florence, but throughout the whole surrounding countryside, mostly with labourers and poor people, as well as with great, powerful men both inside and outside of Florence.

At the time of the plague, Paolo – young, inexperienced, and alone, with only the help and advice of his friends, shaken by the death of his relations and fearful for his own life – found himself embroiled in thousands of florins' worth of debits and credits; many of his brothers' creditors and agents had died, and he had to search not only in Florence and the surrounding countryside, but also in Arezzo, Borgo San Lorenzo, Siena, Pisa, and other places, in order to locate merchandise, sell it, and keep everything going, which he did with great diligence and much toil. Just think how you would feel if you found yourself in such times and with such a job to carry out! And yet Paolo took care of everything, from the biggest task to the smallest, well and assiduously.

At the same time, he had to repay five hundred florins to Calandro's wife; to inventory his brothers' belongings and homes; and to take care of the funeral arrangements, bequests, and all the other things that have to be done at such times. He had to contend with female relatives, with grown children about the disposition of their fathers' estates, with conservators and with other relatives. And, as you shall hear, all the relatives were standing by ready to steal whatever they could and to vex Paolo and interrupt what he was trying to accomplish. He had to cash out their capital, and the money that Calandro had lent in places all over Florence and the countryside. He had to negotiate with the bishop and with the most powerful men in Florence; he called in all debts, no matter who owed them. At the papal court, he achieved his goal, even though he had many people against him. And he did all this not through the power of money, but through his own reason and diligence. Besides this, he dealt in the wool trade with Tommaso di Guccio and others. He dabbled in the Public Fund and negotiated several thousand florins in personal loans and letters of credit; he traded in French fabrics and many other things. Around this time he took to wife the daughter of Matteo di More Quaratesi,[25] Madonna Telda, a beautiful girl thirteen years of age or younger. You will find the date and the amount of the dowry written in his papers. He pledged his troth to her on the 13th of December 1663, the feast of St Lucy, and married her on January 17th, 1364. The marriage certificate was drafted by Messer Francesco di Messer Gianni d'Antica. Paolo paid the marriage tax on the 21st of February, 1634, as indicated in his Book A, folio 109.

Just when he had taken care of all his brothers' affairs, through no one's toil but his own, and thought he might rest a little, Giovanni's widow, with her brother, Niccolò Bagnesi, acting in collusion with the other conservators, went after Paolo in an attempt to wrest from him the money and the guardianship of Giovanni's children; they made many false allegations against Paolo, as he carefully noted in his papers. He himself recorded the final decision of the court about all of this. To further their cause, unbeknowst to Paolo and with the advice of Madonna Lisa and the others, they married Giovanni's son Bernardo to the daughter of Gucciozzo de' Ricci in order to have more support against Paolo; for Gucciozzo was a powerful citizen, feared by many and possessed of

---

25 A prominent family in the Black Guelph faction, already wealthy by the early 1300s (Compagni III, 7).

every worldly good.[26] With all their own power and that of their relatives and friends, they took Paolo to law several times, using every dishonest trick they could. In the end, they were shamed, with the help of God and of justice, as well as Paolo's friends and his own constancy and virtue, as he recorded in his own papers. Thus it is unnecessary for me to go into any further detail about this.

Around this time, Paolo's family began to grow; he and his wife had five children, first two girls and then three boys, about whom I shall write in due course. Paolo conducted himself well and wisely in all of his affairs, applying himself to noble, virtuous things. If it had pleased God to give him even ten more years of life, he would have become rich to the tune of more than fifty thousand florins, and would have had a large family, for he had at least one child every year. He would have taken part in affairs of state for every good reason and cause. His name had already been put forward for the election of 1366 by Dino di Geri Cigliamochi, who was one of the Priors at that time (he was Paolo's uncle). His name was chosen as one of the Priors after his death; I think he was the first of our ancestors to be named a Prior.

It pleased Our Lord that Paolo should render his soul up to God just when he was about to flourish in all of his affairs, on the 14th of June, 1374. He had been married about ten and a half years earlier, for he had married his wife on January 18, 1363.[27] He left an estate of twenty thousand florins. His soul was well and devoutly disposed, as can be seen in his last will and testament. Paolo was a man of good character, very loving and charitable. He never refused anything that was asked of him, neither from a poor man nor a rich one, and was especially generous with money. He was a good relative to those who didn't attempt to undermine him. He died of the plague, and his body was interred with great honour in the church of Santa Croce, beside those of his father and brothers. He was survived by two daughters and two sons, three of whom were still nursing at the time of his death. I shall write about them in the proper place and time.

Lapa, Lisabetta, and Ermellina Di Bartolomeo

As we said before, Bartolomeo was survived by three daughters. The eldest was called Lapa; she was a nun and had taken her vows in the church

---

26 The Ricci were a powerful family belonging to the White Guelph faction (Villani VIII, 71); Gucciozzo was the head of a rich, prosperous company.
27 Morelli gives this date as the 17th on the preceding page.

of San Piero Maggiore in Florence. The second daughter was called Lisabetta, and she was weak and sickly; she took vows as a tertiary of the Franciscan order, but did not enter a convent. The third and last daughter was named Ermellina; she married Pagno di Gheri and had many children, as we find in our family's records. I do not know the dates when Bartolomeo's daughters were born and died, for I found no records about this. And since I do not deem it necessary, I omit these details – it suffices to record their names and what they did with their lives.

Bernardo di Giovanni Morelli

It is now time for us to recount the life of Giovanni di Bartolomeo Morelli's first-born son, who was born around 1356. He was called Bernardo. As a young man, he was very taken with society and was rather extravagant, for he spent money on foolish, pretentious things, and not very honourable ones. It's no wonder that he did so, because as a lad he was governed by his mother and her guardians,[28] who conspired together to rob and ruin him and his brothers, having cut out the man who should have acted in place of his father – that is, Paolo Morelli. And in fact Bernardo squandered a large part of the fortune that his father had left to him and his brothers, all in courtly extravagancies. When he was quite a young man, his mother and her guardians, not consulting Paolo but rather going against his wishes, chose as a wife for Bernardo the daughter of Gucciozzo de' Ricci, a wealthy, wise merchant with many connections and high status. Once Bernardo was married, he got out from under the control of the guardians, and, realizing that he had squandered much of his father's money, he began to act in a more judicious manner. And whereas before, when he had depended upon his brothers to maintain him, he had squandered money, once he was away from them and realized that money was lacking and having left behind the impetuousness of youth, he became the most sensible man in the world and the best administrator. He was a very pleasant man – jolly, outgoing in his speech and very diligent in his affairs. He often spoke with a double meaning – he was mischievous, affectionate, friendly, and a wonderful storyteller. He never had any children with his wife Simona;

---

28 Morelli uses the word *manovaldo*, from the Latin *mundualdus*, a male guardian or tutor. See Thomas Kuehn, "Understanding Gender Inequality in Renaissance Florence: Personhood and Gifts of Maternal Inheritance by Woman," *Journal of Women's History* 8 (1996).

he had many illegitimate children, some from a well-born woman, and some from a beautiful slave girl of his, whom he later married off to a man in the Mugello.[29] I don't want to mention names, because it is not seemly, and they are good people in their way.

Bernardo was a candidate for Prior in 1381, and served as a Prior in 1387. Messer Luigi Guicciardini was Standard-bearer of Justice at the time. Bernardo conducted himself very wisely, and succeeded in putting the affairs of our city into good order, and he assisted every reasonable request by citizens of Florence. When he left office, he was liked and respected by all Florentines. Later he was a standard-bearer of one of the militia companies, and one of the Twelve Good Men. And he carried out all of the other offices for which he was selected, both in Florence and elsewhere, in an honourable manner. Some misfortunes befell him, which I shall recount in part in due course.

Bernardo mostly did not involve himself in the business conducted by our ancestors and in other activities that involved commerce and gain. And he did this for no other reason than that he found himself wealthy and fatherless, influenced more by those who sought to teach him how to spend money rather than how to earn it. He departed this life on the 2nd of August in the year of Our Lord 1400; his body rests in the sepulchre of our ancestors in the church of Santa Croce. He died of the plague, which killed him in only a few days. He left behind five children – three boys and two girls. The oldest boy is named Dino, the second Cetta, and the third Benedetto. I believe that his entire estate was worth two thousand florins. May God in his mercy have received his soul into his glory.

Bartolomeo and Gualberto di Giovanni

Giovanni's second son was named Bartolomeo. He was quite a large man, with a physique like Bernardo's; they were about the same size. Bernardo was sturdy and quite stout, with reddish hair and freckles; Bartolomeo was fat and fresh, with clear olive skin. He took to wife the daughter of Ser Nicolò di Ser Ventura Monaci. Nicolò was at that time the notary

---

29 Slavery, usually of people coming from Asia, was still common during the fourteenth century, as is also shown in literary texts. Boccaccio mentions slavery several times in the *Decameron* (e.g., II, 6; V, 7), and Sacchetti had a female "Tartar" slave.

of the record office,[30] very well set up in all his affairs. He lived near San Romeo. Bartolomeo's wife was called Monna Lena; she was a wise woman, very eloquent and sagacious, and knew how to achieve whatever she set her mind to, with her own hands. She read and wrote clearly. Bartolomeo had three children with Monna Lena – two boys and a girl; the eldest was named Gualberto, the second was Giovanni, and the girl was called Lisa. We shall write of them later, if necessary, depending upon what direction we take. Bartolomeo passed from this life in the town of Forlì, in 1383; he died of the plague, in just a few days. He was buried at the monastery of the Franciscan friars in Forlì; later his body was taken to Florence and interred in the church of Santa Croce with our other ancestors, honourably as was done with the others. His wife survived him, and lived as a widow with her children until the plague of 1400. She died during that pestilence, leaving her children as her heirs. I believe that 4000 gold florins were left to them, including what belonged to their mother.

Now it behooves us to write about Giovanni's third son, who was named Gualberto. He was taller than average for the time, slender but not skinny, with a beautiful complexion. He was well educated; I believe he also studied law. According to what we understand, Gualberto turned out to be a very accomplished man, and he demonstrated this well throughout his life. Among other things, he did this: during the plague of 1374, when all of Giovanni's remaining family and all of Paolo's family had fled to Bologna and were living together in the same house and sharing expenses (which was greatly to the advantage of Giovanni's family), there were continually more than 20 people in the house, including men, women, children, wet nurses and servants, strangers and friends. The expenses and everything needed for the household were entrusted to Gualberto, who had to account for the money that was given to him. And he, an inexperienced young man and unfamiliar with the city of Bologna, where he had only been for a short period of time, nevertheless took care of all the extended family's needs with great solicitude, in

---

30 The *notaio delle Riformagioni* was one of the highest officials in the chancery of the Florentine republic; he registered all new laws and decisions of the assemblies. Ser Ventura Monaci, chancellor of the republic from 1340 to 1348, was a poet and a friend of Boccaccio. His son Nicolò played a leading role in the Florentine chancery for many years. He was a friend of Coluccio Salutati and other prominent humanists, and wrote a book of memoirs.

an orderly way and without excesses, carefully keeping track of what he was spending. Now, if this might seem praise for a small matter, let me tell you that anyone who knew that unbearable, unruly family and the disharmony and the people coming and going all the time, they would judge that what I have said about Gualberto (taking into account his tender age and the demands of his family) shows that he was without exception a man of great strength, thoughtfulness, and consideration.

And Fortune showed this clearly, for when Gualberto was on the brink of death, after having carried out deeds worthy of an experienced older man and not a young lad, realizing that he was sick with the plague and thinking about his death and the salvation of his soul, he asked for all the holy sacraments, which he received with great devotion, devoutly commending his soul to God, with holy, good, and pious prayers. Then with good and gentle words he asked the forgiveness of everyone in the household, old or young, commending his soul to all of them. And finally, in the presence of all of them, he confessed that he had taken about ten or twelve *lire* from the household money and used them for his own affairs, and he asked that the money be replaced. In the end, when he passed from this life, to the very last moment with the priest there reading, he said all of the prayers of extreme unction loud and clear, to that everyone could hear. And he repeatedly urged the priest to read faster, for he felt that he was about to die. By the grace of God, when Gualberto and the priest had finished saying the prayers, at the last words, "Deo gratias amen," he closed his eyes and gave up his soul to God. This was in Bologna. His body was honourably buried in Bologna in the church of the Franciscan friars, in a sepulchre that had been newly built, between the choir and the church wall, almost at the end of the choir – that is, close to the main chapel. I believe that there is a plaque with our family's coat of arms on the wall. Because he had been so honourably buried, Gualberto's brothers decided to leave him there; thus his body was not brought back to Florence. There are many more virtues and good acts of this young man that could be recounted, but I shall stop here in order to write about the other members of the family and the other things that we still have to tell, as I promised in the beginning.

Giano di Giovanni and Monna Andriuola

The last son Giovanni had, of whom we shall now write and who by the grace of God is still alive, is called Giano. He is of average height, and has a fine head of hair. But all of the brothers in this family got white hair early, at the age of twenty or even before; I believe this is on account of their large heads. Giano is quite fat, and has gotten even fatter since he passed the age of thirty-five; for he was always fat, but not this much nor this seriously. He took to wife the daughter of Jacopo d'Alamanno Nettori, who is called Monna Nanna, and had many children with her. As of today, in the year 1403, they have had about sixteen or eighteen children, six of whom are still alive – four sons and two daughters.

The first son who is still alive is named Bartolomeo, the second is Paolo, the third Nicolaio, and the fourth is Antonio. It is not necessary to write about the girls, for they are very young; when the time comes for them to marry, if they reach that stage, then we shall write of them, if it shall please God. The same goes for those children who are still to come, for it looks to me as if Giano is more likely than ever to keep fathering children.

Giano was selected as one of the Twelve Good Men in the vote of 15 September 1399, as was his brother Bernardo. He was elected standard-bearer of one of the military companies on 8 September 1401.

He has yet to be elected a member of the Seignory; we shall write of it when he does.[31] Giano is not involved in any trading, but lives off of his private fortune, like his brothers. He is quite well off, and would live like a rich man if loans hadn't ruined him.

Giovanni di Bartolomeo was survived by a daughter named Andriuola. Her brothers married her to Ciriaco di Guernieri Benci, who was a business associate of the Alberti family.[32] He was a good merchant and had made many successful petitions. He died in 1398 or a few years earlier; I don't know the exact date. Andriuola brought him a dowry of eight hundred florins. He was survived by many children, who all died in the plague of 1400, except one of the sons, Simone, whom they called Mone. Andriuola now lives as a widow with her mother and her brother Giano.

Up to this point we have written about all of our ancestors and their consorts who have passed from this life, and also about our living relatives, except for the ones who are the descendants of Bartolomeo Morelli's last son – that is, Paolo. It is reasonable to keep him for last, since

---

31 Giano was elected Prior (a member of the Seignory) in 1404, 1412, and 1416. He held many other important offices, and in fact came to be known as "Giano the Great." He was born around 1359 and died after 1416.

32 The Alberti were one of the wealthiest Florentine merchant families, and were also very powerful politically.

he is the youngest of all. And not diminishing the good accounting that is due to them, in the following sections we shall recount the birth and names and nicknames and the looks and situations of their descendants, and how they turned out and why, with details for each, as an example for those who come after them, and their good and bad fortunes; and if we see remedies that can be used against the misfortunes that have befallen our family (which can be clearly seen, especially by those who experienced them), we shall recount them all, God willing, in a brief way – that is, we shall recount the misfortunes that hurt us the most and did us the most damage. And even though they be written in a rough manner, nevertheless I think that you shall find good fruit in them. This book is not intended to be read for pleasure, nor to be shown to anyone else – it is intended for you alone, not for people outside our family, who might mock us about it. I write this so that you can see for yourselves part of your family's history. Likewise you shall see part of the worldly fortunes that have gone against us. And by these you shall be able to consider the remedies, learning from these experiences. But one makes decisions about what actions to take depending upon the time and the particular situation. I mean that some bad things that befell us might have turned out favourably for others, according to the situation or the people involved, or according to what God has determined for you. Nevertheless, what I am writing here will give you something to think about and ponder and seek advice about; and you won't err if you act wisely, and this will be useful and a good example to you, by the grace of God, which will help you to act well and wisely and confidently. Be wise and comport yourself well, and you shall obtain everything.

Bartolomea di Paolo Morelli

The first fruit of Paolo's marriage was a baby girl; she was born on Monday, June 23rd, at seven thirty, in the year of Our Lord 1365. She was baptized in the Baptistry of San Giovanni the following Saturday morning, the 28th of that month. The names given to her were Giovanna and Bartolomea; Lione Lioni, Tommaso di Bese Busini, and the innkeeper Francesco Brunellini acted as her godfathers. She was always called Mea.

Mea was of normal height, with beautiful blond hair, a very fine figure, and so amiable that she dripped with charm. Her hands were like ivory, and so shapely that they seemed to have been painted by Giotto; they were long and soft, with tapering fingers and long, shapely nails, pink and clear. Her beauty was matched by her talents, for she could do any kind of women's work with her own hands; she was extremely adept in everything she did. Her speech was refined and pleasing, her actions pure and temperate, her words effectual. She was a spirited, frank woman with the mettle of a man, and abounded in every virtue. She could read and write as well as any man; she sang and danced perfectly, and could have served men or women at table as adroitly as any young man used to serving at wedding banquets or similar occasions. She was expert at running a household, without a hint of avariciousness or stinginess. But she made the most of everything, admonishing and guiding her household with good teachings and her own good example, living a joyful, happy life. She wisely set about making all of the various members of her household happy, allaying every trouble, anger, or sadness that she might see in any of them. She handled everything wisely and with benevolence, and, as you shall see, she had to deal with her husband's family, which was large and unruly.

The conservators of his family and hers arranged for Mea to be married to Antonio d'Agnolo Barucci; she had a dowry of one thousand five hundred florins. Antonio lived with his father and mother, who were quite old, but prosperous, and with a wretched brother of his, who also took a wife at the same time. They also had two sisters, both grown and married, and two nephews, good youths, by one of the sisters. I have told all this so that I might return to what I said before: that Mea, wise and discerning as she was, was loved by everyone, although there was little harmony among the other members of the family. Her goodness was the more commendable, for where there was great discord and scandal, she alone was loved by all. She managed to bring peace and harmony to many unpleasant situations among them.

Mea was married in 1380, and Antonio and his brother Francesco put on a great, joyful celebration. At that time the Barucci family lived in great state and had a fortune of twenty thousand florins; they were wool merchants, much loved by everyone, wise, pleasant, and very respectable. Mea had four children with Antonio, but none of them lived longer than two years; the last, a baby boy, was born on the 8th of February, 1387, and was named Agnolo. Mea had been unwell for about a week when she gave birth to this baby in the eighth month of her pregnancy; she never recovered, but died of that same illness on Saturday the 15th of February, at the eighth hour. The baby died the next day, so Mea left no offspring. She was buried in the church of Santa Croce, under the transept, on the left side of Agnolo Barucci's tomb.

As you enter under the transept of the church, there is a door that leads to a sort of vault on the right side, along the wall. I want to describe this very clearly, for seeing where her bones are buried should make us all think of her goodness. I especially entreat everyone who is descended from Paolo Morelli to go and see the place where Mea lies, at least on All Souls Day, and to pray to God for the well-being of her soul. For the true light and fruit of her soul are prayer and almsgiving; may God grant that they help her blessed soul.

Sandra di Paolo Morelli

After Bartolomea, Paolo and his wife Monna Telda had another daughter. She was born on the twenty-seventh of December in the year of Our Lord 1369, on the eve of the feast of St John the Baptist, at nine in the evening. She was baptized the following Saturday, on the twenty-ninth of December, 1369. Her godfathers were Benozzo di Benozzo and Raffaello di [*text missing in the original manuscript*], both from the neighbourhood of San Jacopo tra le Fosse. For the love of God she was given the names Sandra and Giovanna, according to what Paolo wrote in his Book A, on page 19.[33]

Sandra was of average height, with pale olive skin; she was neither fat nor very thin. Her face and figure were very shapely. She was knowledgeable about what a good woman should know: she could embroider, and read and write. She was very eloquent – a great talker who knew how to say what she wanted to say, very openly.

Sandra was married to Jacopo di Zanobi Arnolfi; she brought a dowry of one thousand five hundred gold florins. There was a great celebration when she was married; it was the most beautiful wedding in Florence that year.[34] Her husband presented her with lavish gifts of beautiful silver jewellery and pearls. She lived with Jacopo until the twenty-ninth of July, in the year of Our Lord 1400, when he died of the plague. He left one son, named Simone; he had no other sons or daughters.

Jacopo, may God forgive him, was a wise young man and very capable in whatever he undertook, and especially in the business and affairs of our city. He held every honour of the city, inside and out. He had a big heart, and was very frank about his own misfortunes, and did a great

---

33 Paolo was the first member of the Morelli family to write a book of memoirs, as
     Giovanni di Paolo mentions several times.
34 Sandra married in 1384.

deal of damage to himself and to all of his friends and relatives. He did everything believing that he could satisfy everyone. This was not because he thought he had enough money to meet everyone's needs; but he was confident of his own industriousness and valued it as if it were great wealth. And in this way he deceived himself and others – and most of all he deceived us – that is, Morello and myself, Sandra's brothers. We incurred great damages for having helped Jacopo with a loan of more than a thousand florins, and over time we lost more than a thousand florins more, plus interest, as you shall see in the books that Giuliano di Tommaso kept for us.[35]

I wanted to touch upon some of our misfortunes here, because if I say something now about the origin of this affair, I think that it will be useful should I mention it again later. I should also mention the damage that Jacopo's wife, our sister Sandra, incurred to her dowry (and this continues to harm us in more ways than one, as you shall see), for it was necessary for Sandra and for us, Morello and Giovanni, to take a miserable little house in the neighbourhood of San Giovanni and two small pieces of property and certain furniture valued at about eight hundred florins or so, because we could do no better with what was left of her dowry. We have had to hang on for three years already, and we still don't know how we will be able to recover the equivalent of Sandra's dowry. And this is all chiefly Jacopo's fault, and also on account of Sandra's foolishness. For she, out of obedience to her husband, seeing him in need of help, obeyed him too well, mortgaging several properties without saying anything to us, her brothers, or to any other relative or friend. This was also Jacopo's fault, for, knowing how sweet and obedient his wife was, he did not warn her about this ahead of time, but rather, like a criminal, he suddenly came to her with a notary and witnesses, telling her "Say yes!" with a distressed look on his face. So she, ashamed to contradict her husband in front of other people, said what he told her to say, even though it seemed to her to be a mistake; but she did it out of fear and a sense of obedience. And the outcome is that she now finds herself a young widow with a twelve-year-old son, no dowry, living in our house for the foreseeable future, unless God should send us some other help.

I wanted to record this as an example for my readers – that is, that no one, man or woman, on account of fear or flattery or any other reason, should let go of what is theirs, for ninety-nine per cent of the time they

---

35 Giuliano di Tommaso was the steward who kept the Morelli family's accounts.

will end up ruined, even by their closest relatives or friends. For those are the people whom one tends to trust the most, and thus it is easy to be deceived or betrayed. And once you have lost your wealth, those who took it from you shall be your enemies. I do not wish to say anything further about this at present, for later it will be necessary to return to this theme. I simply want this to be an example to married women never to let any of their patrimony go without consulting their closest relatives, and if there is no great need, don't ever do it, if you do not have some other kind of security, which people don't usually understand, especially women. I wrote briefly here about Sandra's life up to today; if there are further things that occur, I shall write of them in due course.

Morello Di Paolo Morelli

Paolo Morelli had a son with Monna Telda; he was born on the twenty-seventh day of November in the year of Our Lord 1370, on the eve of the feast of St Peter of Alexandria (thus wrote Paolo in the book he marked A, on page 19); it was a Wednesday night, at half past eight, when the bells of Santa Croce were about to ring. Paolo had the baby baptized the following Saturday, that is the 30th of November, with four of his friends acting as godparents: Simone di Bonarota from the neighbourhood of San Jacopo tra le Fosse, and Monna Agata and Monna Giovanna, the sister and daughter of Ser Guccio da Rignano, who lived in the area of Santa Croce, across from Paolo, and Miniato, the grocer from Porta Rossa. They gave him the names Morello and Andrea – Morello after his grandfather, and Andrea because of the day he was baptized.

Morello was of average height, and was very fat when he was a boy, and as an adult he had beautiful hair and healthy limbs; he was good natured, and very abstemious. Rarely or never, except when he was in company, did he eat or drink more than two times a day. He was intelligent, and gave good advice, without any malice. He was good and sweet tempered. Up to this day he has not engaged in any trading or done anything to earn a penny, and we are in the year of Our Lord 1403; you shall learn the reasons later. He took to wife, as it pleased God, Catelana, the daughter of Stefano di Vanni Castellani; the marriage was arranged by Nofrio di Giovanni Arnolfi and Messer Vanni di Michele. She brought with her a dowry of eight hundred twenty-five florins. Morello married Catelana in the church of Santa Croce, on the morning of the feast of St Anthony in the year of Our Lord 1389, that is, the 18th of January. Up to today he has had eight or nine children of her, and she has had three miscarriages. The first time she miscarried was, I believe, about two years after he married her, and it was a baby girl; later she brought two baby girls to term.

The first girl was named Bartolomea; she was born with a swelling on the side of her head, which looked and felt like a bladder. They had her treated by the doctor Francesco dal Ponte, who lanced the growth in several places, and blood and pus shot out. In the end, Bartolomea did not survive; she died after a few days, and was laid to rest in the church of Santa Croce. Then another baby girl was born, whom they named Antonia, and she had the same kind of swelling. This time they didn't have her treated, but instead kept her head warm with a little cap lined with soft cloth, and in the end the swelling went down and she healed well. Antonia lived seven years or so, and then she died of the plague in July of 1400, in the Spini Palace. Her body was laid to rest in the church of Santa Trinita, in the Spini family chapel – that is, the last chapel on the left, going toward the main altar. This was of necessity, considering that there was widespread mortality in Florence and it was almost impossible to find anyone to take the bodies of the dead out of the houses. And besides, there was no member of our family in Florence at that time except for Monna Filippa,[36] who had to take care of things by relying on other people. The third baby girl got the plague at the beginning of the outbreak; her name was Filippa. She lived only a few months, dying before Antonia. She died at Quinto Fiorentino, where she had been placed with a wet nurse, and was buried in the church there.

We have no other daughters of Morello and Catelana to write about; they had five sons, and thank God they are all still alive. The first is named Paolo, the second Matteo, the third Tommaso, the fourth Bernardo, and the fifth is Francesco. I or someone else shall record their other names and the dates of their birth and the events of their lives as they unfold, God willing. Up to today they have been living with their parents; they are being raised and taught well, as is fitting for boys of their age. And as far as we can see, they are bright, intelligent boys, very well mannered and obedient, and they are diligent students, learning to read and write, and some grammar – they have a good attitude, and they learn well and happily. I am certain that it pleases God by his grace and generosity to give them life and virtue and good grace, and I hope to be able to write

---

36 That is, the baby's elderly great-grandmother, Madonna Filippa del Bianco, wife of
   Matteo Quaratesi and mother of Monna Telda, the wife of Paolo di Bartolomeo.

good things of them in the future, if, as we hope, they follow in the footsteps of their father and mother and their ancestors, whose example they have before them. And we have written and shall continue to write this account as an example for them and for all of our other offspring, by the grace of God.

Giovanni di Paolo Morelli

It pleased our Lord God to grant to our father Paolo Morelli a fourth child, a son, with his wife Madonna Telda. He was born on Thursday evening, the thirtieth of October, in the year of Our Lord 1371, at a third past the twenty-fourth hour. He was baptized the following Saturday, the first of November – that is, the feast of All Saints. His godfathers were Giovanni d'Andrea, Lorenzo di Tennia, and the dyer Raffaello, all from the neighbourhood of San Jacopo, bosom friends of Paolo Morelli. He was given the names Giovanni and Simone: Giovanni for his uncle, Paolo's brother, and Simone because he was born on the feast day of St Simon.

Giovanni di Paolo was of average height and complexion; he had beautiful hair and was a little rubicund in the face. He was not strong by nature, not a big eater, and of gentle blood. He was displeased by evil things, especially those that brought harm or shame to his city. He denounced such things whenever he had occasion to discourse about them; likewise, he would take steps to correct them if it were in his power to do so.[37] He wished to live an honourable life, never going against whoever was in power in word or deed. He frequented the upstanding, established men of Florence, Guelphs loyal to the city-state. He never thought or desired anything but honour, status, and greatness for Florence. Of the new breed of Florentines, artisans and small-scale traders, he demanded duty, peace, and harmony. He did not like everything about their behaviour, but he did mingle with them on some occasions; for it is good to keep in touch with the humbler folk. He always devotedly embraced the holy Catholic Guelph party – may God keep that party as his devoted Standard-bearer, for it has always defended the Holy Church. Up to this day it has not yet pleased God that Giovanni be able to show his good will toward Florence and toward her good citizens and

––––––––––––––––––––

37 In writing about himself, Giovanni di Paolo adopts a deliberately impersonal tone; but his moral and political attitudes come through clearly.

merchants in a concrete way, but presumably God has done this for the best.[38]

God and his Blessed Mother the Virgin Mary granted much grace and many gifts to the aforementioned Giovanni di Paolo Morelli, not on account of his own merits, for he is a sinner like all the other sinners in this world. Rather, he obtained these gifts through his devotion to the Holy Virgin St Catherine, the bride of Christ. On the fifteenth of December in the year of Our Lord 1395 Giovanni was betrothed to Caterina, the daughter of Alberto di Luigi degli Alberti; the contract was drawn up by Ser Michele di Ser Aldobrando, who lives in Porta Rossa. Giovanni got with her a dowry of a thousand gold florins. He led her to the altar on Thursday, the twenty-seventh of January at the hour of vespers, on horseback, accompanied by twelve young noblemen, at Olmo a San Gaggio; the marriage certificate was drawn up by Guido di Messer Tomaso, who lives in Borella. They had a lovely, happy celebration, as befitted such an occasion. Up to this day, July 1st 1403, Giovanni has had five children with Caterina, of whom we shall write in due course. For the moment, I shall record their names. The first-born was a son named Alberto Giovanni; the second, Antoniotto Jacopo; the third, Lionello Francesco; the fourth child was a girl, whom they named Telda Margherita; the fifth was another girl, whom they named Bartolomea Lisabetta. God bless all those who came before them, and to the living may He grant long life and health for their souls. Thanks be to God, Amen.

Paolo Morelli and his wife Monna Telda had a fifth and last son, whom it pleased God to call back to him shortly after he was baptized, according to what Paolo himself wrote and what I heard from Monna Telda's mother Monna Filippa, the widow of Matteo, and from Monna Buona, who was the child's godmother and assisted Monna Telda during the delivery. They confirmed that the baby lived long enough to be baptized, for the salvation of his soul; thus it pleased God to grant him that blessing. He was born on 12 February 1372, when Monna Telda had carried him for seven and a half months; he was baptized at home that same night, which was the night of the holy Sabbath; they called him Giovanni. He died that same night and was buried on the 13th at San Jacopo tra le Fosse.

---

38 Up to this time, Giovanni had not held any public office; the first office he held was Company Standard-bearer, in 1409.

Proem to the Following Section

As you have seen, I have written about all of our forefathers, not as fully as I would have wished, but I have recorded everything I found written or heard.

I have yet to write about the grandchildren of Giovanni and Paolo di Bartolomeo Morelli; but I think I shall omit this, to avoid confusion, and because I am not well informed about their births and their lives. I don't want to ask them when they were born, lest they think that I am trying to discover their ages. So we shall not go beyond what we've already written. I shall write about our own children and descendants as the years go by.

Now, to continue as promised before, I shall write about the time following the death of our father Paolo, and I shall recount, briefly according to what I know, certain important things that happened in our city and especially certain wars, by which you shall be able to understand the great damage to and almost destruction of our family's property. Likewise I shall write about our activities starting in the year of Our Lord 1374. I shall recount the great damage and persecution that we underwent, due to bad luck or malice on the part of those who wished us ill or our own foolishness, so that you who shall come after us can take heed, avoiding as much as possible those things that harmed us, and imitating the things that in part saved us, as I hope to make clear in these writings of mine. By my adding these writings to what was written by Tomaso di Guccio and his son Giuliano,[39] you shall be completely informed. And if you are good, God shall bestow his grace upon you. And although we have had unpleasant things happen to us up to now, you shall have better luck; for things don't always go on in the same way, but change continually. Therefore help yourselves by being friends of God, for he is the one who gives and takes away the good things in this world and in the next, which is infinite.

Our Misfortunes

You have read above about the death of Paolo, in 1374, and you have seen that he left four children, two girls and two boys; three of the children were still nursing when he died. This was our first misfortune – to have been left fatherless as very young children. And from this misfortune our

---

39 Probably scribes or stewards employed by the Morelli family.

second misfortune derived – for shortly after the death of our father, we lost our mother, who remarried, because she was very young. She married Simone di Rubellato Spini.[40] Our third misfortune was that we were left in the hands of guardians, and although they were good, loyal men, a guardian cannot be compared to a real father. For a thousand reasons, everything seems to go against orphans. Our fourth misfortune was that of the twenty thousand florins that had been left to us, after a few years only five thousand remained. The money went for our father's funeral expenses, the many bequests he had made, for our mother's dowry, and for many other things that are done with the money that is left to unfortunate young children. For example, 500 gold florins were spent for Bernardo Morelli and the whole family when they went to Bologna to flee the plague in Florence. As always happens to young children who are left fatherless, someone else spends the money and uses it all up, and the children pay the price. Our fifth misfortune was that whereas our father had made money, we lost more and more every day. Those who owed us money always had excuses: some cancelled their debts and some denied that they owed us and some threatened us and some refused to deal with our guardians either because of what others told them or out of fear or to help their friends or for whatever reason. All of this was greatly to our detriment. Our sixth misfortune was that the Florentine government increased our tax burden to six times what it had been when our father was alive, while our income had been reduced by half. The seventh misfortune followed, for while children normally receive teaching and direction and status and every good thing from their father, we were left without any guidance. And although we were taken in by Matteo da Quaratesi and his wife Monna Filippa,[41] who loved us like their own children, nevertheless that cannot compare with having a real father. And as time passed, Matteo soon failed us, and this was at the time of our greatest need. From these seven misfortunes that I have named here, many others resulted that could never be imagined nor recounted, for they are infinite in number. But not to leave the poor unfortunate child naked and abandoned, I shall follow with seven brief sections in which I shall attempt to redress those misfortunes and give advice about each

---

40 The Spini were an important Black Guelph family with strong ties to the papal court and the British royal family. The Morelli family lived in the Spini palace in Piazza Santa Trinita. Giovanni's children Antoniotto, Lionello, and Telda were born there between 1397 and 1401, and Bartolomea was born in an adjacent house in 1402.
41 The Morelli children's maternal grandparents.

one, as my humble intellect permits, wishing to grasp any glimmer of a remedy that is possible in this thorny, cruel life of ours.

First Misfortune: "Good Advice."

In order to avoid the first misfortune of a young child suffering the death of his father, this is the path to take: When you reach the age of twenty, and let's say that you are all on fire to be free and begin to enjoy your life, you must nevertheless keep your head, thinking of the good and perfect things that will follow. First of all, take your own measure – who you are, and what your condition and nature are; then assess your status – what it requires and what you can achieve in terms of honour and substance. And do not deceive yourself, but rather follow the advice and foundation of your conscience. And if your conscience tells you that you are in a position to do so, and that you reasonably deserve a good life because of your virtues and your wealth or standing, then you can decide to take a wife and have children. And if you take this decision – that is, to marry in order to have children – you should determine to protect them from the dangers described above. Say to yourself: "If I have children, I want to raise them myself, I want to see them grow up, I want to set them on the right path and guide them with my knowledge, I want to see which is good and which is bad, I want them to be able to assist me in my old age. I want to have the consolation and take the trouble to be able to protect them when necessary."

Once you have made this decision, carry it out between the ages of twenty and twenty-five, according to how God sets you up during this time. But take care not to put yourself at a disadvantage by being in too much of a hurry. By this I mean, if you think that by waiting until you are thirty years old you will be in a better position to marry and have children, then wait. And always take care, in this act and in any other that involves your honour, not to let your desires blind you. Rather, in all of your affairs make your decisions with wise and mature thinking, and heeding the advice of your relatives and good friends. But if there is not a good reason to wait, take a wife around the age that I have indicated.

Beware of this first of all: do not marry beneath you; rather, strive to raise your status by the woman you take to wife, but not to the point that she would be the husband, and you the wife. Take care to marry into a family of good citizens, who do not need money and who are merchants who do not act high and mighty. They should be an old family in your city, honoured by the government, members of the Guelph party, and have an unblemished reputation – no tarnish as traitors or thieves or murderers or descendants of bastards, or other blameworthy or shameful things. They should have a pure, untarnished reputation, and be known as good, loving relatives. They should not be greedy for money, and should entertain temperately, as wise men and good citizens do. Next, make sure that the woman you choose is well born, with a mother from a good family and with honourable relatives, an honest woman and of good reputation. And her mother's mother should also have been honest and pure, and they should all have the reputation of being good, loving women. Take care to choose a woman who is calm, and one who is not haughty or prideful. She should be reasonable and intelligent, as much as a woman can be. And if you cannot determine these things clearly, look at the root of the thing: that is, that she is a gentlewoman, the daughter of a good man. Choose a maiden who pleases you, healthy and whole and large, thinking of the children that she shall bear. She should not have been on the marriage market for too long, nor have been rejected by any suitors, for women become corrupt when they do not have that which Nature requires. Make sure that she is modest and not too impetuous, that she not be too vain, for example about clothes, and not too eager to go to all of the celebrations and wedding feasts and other vain things. For nowadays great immodesty is rampant, and terrible slurs are made about people. And there is no woman, no matter how good, who won't become corrupted if she frequents these kinds of situations. Don't seek to drown in money when negotiating the dowry, for a dowry never brought good to anyone; if you should have to give the dowry back, you'll be ruined. Be content with this: to have what you need according to your own situation and that of the woman you choose to marry.

Since youth is difficult to rein in, if you do what is advised above, and for the reason that it is recommended – that is, to have children early, so that you can raise them yourself – you should use your head in this matter. That is, be temperate in your relations with your wife, and do not let yourself become excessive. And if you wish to do this, you would be wise to not let her get too intimate with you. For example, if she realizes that you are too eager to have relations with her, and she resists you, you should get out of the bed, if that is where she is, and go outside and walk for a while to tire yourself out. By the same token, you should get up out of bed before you are overtaken by lust; do not spend too much time at home – go to the country, take some exercise, to get your mind off of sex. And restrain yourself whenever you can. If you do this, you shall have children soon, and they will be hale and hearty, big and strong, and you shall have sons, while keeping yourself young and fresh. You shall be healthy and happy, and shall do all sorts of good. If you act in the opposite manner, you shall destroy your health, sicken, ruin your stomach and kidneys; and if you get even the slightest fever, you will be at risk of dying. You shall also wear out your wife, and it will be difficult for her to have children, and they will all turn out to be girls, and they will be sickly and never get ahead in life. You shall be dull, ignominious, melancholy, and miserable. You shall find no pleasure in word nor deed, and everything shall seem to go against you; you'll never attain anything good. In order for my advice about this to come to good effect, you must act as recommended; if you act in the opposite way, you shall be making a terrible decision, as I've said above. And because not all cases can be recalled, for it is not possible, suffice it to say that you must use your natural intelligence and think of all of the things that could occur, and consider carefully what you do; and you shall almost never err. I see no other way to avoid this first misfortune.

Second Misfortune

As I wrote above about what happened to us, so I think that in similar cases it would happen to most people: that is, being left fatherless with a young mother, children can assume that they will lose their mother as well when she inevitably remarries, and on top of that, they shall have to provide her with a dowry. But if we want to think of some solution to this situation, we can say that the best thing to do would be to act as I described above, when I wrote about the father. Since the advice is the same, there is no need to repeat it, for if you do one you shall also do the other. But I want to add something here. Even if you act as I recommend in the previous section, and it happens that God decides to call you to him while your children are still small and your wife is left a young widow, think and consider whether your wife had been faithful to you and has borne you love as a woman should toward her husband, and whether she loves your children and is of a restrained nature that would befit a widow. Also consider whether she be loyal (this you shall know by her attitude toward money), or if she has brothers or close relatives who are in need of money. Above all, if you know her to be decent and modest, and if on top of that she is wise, of good intelligence and fit to run a household, and that she is not so attractive that even if she wanted to be good, she could not be left alone – when you have contemplated all of these things and find them all to be good and perfect in her, so that you do not doubt her much, or, if you know her to be lacking in these things, take all of this into consideration in arranging your affairs.

If you know your wife to be fully endowed with the virtues described above, then you can confidently and without doubts name her executor in your will – free to manage all of your affairs. This liberality on your part will encourage her to associate with good people, and even if she does not want to, it will shame her into doing so. But because it is impossible to find a woman of this ilk (or, if she is, it won't last, for soon she will be led astray by her desires, or by haughtiness, or by some disaster), I say that you should not trust her entirely. If it is your desire that your wife remain in charge of your children, leave her as free as you can, but not in everything. Leave it in your will that, acting together with two or three trusted relatives of yours, she can do everything, and that they can do nothing without her consent. And if she does not want to remain in charge of your children, then she should have a dowry and nothing else – and this is something that will make her want to stay with them.

If you know that your wife is a good woman and you are content for her to remain with your children, leave her whatever you can from your estate in addition to a dowry if she should remain with them. But the condition should be that if she does not remain with your children, she only gets a dowry. Make sure to leave her enough to live on in the event that your children should turn out bad. And leave it so that she can manage the children's affairs in agreement with your relatives and friends. This seems to me to be the best way to keep the children's mother in charge of them.

If you know your wife to be not a wise woman, not loving, vain, libidinous, and wasteful, and if her parents are in need of money or she has other flaws, it would be better for her to remarry rather than remain a widow. For if she remains a widow, there is a chance of greater damage to your estate and greater shame for your children than if she married, for if she doesn't conduct her own affairs well, she will never do it for her companion. Make her executrix of your estate along with your agents for honour and duty, but inculcate in her that she must be careful. Be strict with her; put limits on her spending; don't leave her more than a dowry, whether she stays with the children or not. For there is no mother so bad who is not better for her own children than another woman. I do not think that anything more can be done about this type of situation.

Third Misfortune: Guardians

I wrote above, as you have found, that the third misfortune is for a fatherless child to be left in charge of guardians. As is clear and you can easily see, in this situation the wishes of one person are exchanged for those of many, and the love and charity of a father toward his child, which are infinite, are exchanged for that of outsiders, be they relatives or friends. I say "outsiders" because when money or any kind of personal advantage is involved, there is no relative nor friend who will not place his own interests before yours, putting his good conscience aside. So the result is that while the father believes that he is leaving his relatives or friends to protect and guide his children, in reality he is leaving his enemies, for that is what they become. For your relatives and friends stick by you as long as you have money and status from which they think they can benefit; once you die, they remember nothing. While they were benefiting or thought they would benefit from their relationship with you, they showed great affection for you; after your death, they become the adversaries of your children, taking for themselves that which the child is not free to give them. Once sheep have lost their shepherd, the wolves devour them, for they are ungoverned, and have no one to defend them. The same is true for children left fatherless: they are robbed, deceived, and betrayed by everyone, and above all by those closest to them. And they can never take revenge for this, because they are so impeded in every way that they cannot catch their breath, much less take revenge. And in every way, they are treated just as badly as they had been treated well when their father was alive.

The least negative solutions possible to this misfortune must be sought. I see few remedies (and truly they are scarce); nevertheless I shall present a few which, in my view, are good to some extent. If you as their father wish to provide for the well-being of your children, first and foremost strive to ensure that their mother will remain with them after your death. Then see to it that they have good company – that is, endeavour to find relatives who are loving, loyal, and devoted to God (but not religious fanatics, who are the most hypocritical) – they should be wealthy, or at least not needy. Don't worry if you don't choose your closest relatives; the important thing is that they be good people. But don't choose a friend over a relative, if they are both equally good. Furthermore, do not choose a large number – no more than six, who must be in a majority for decisions, and cannot act without the consent of the children's mother. Or, if the mother is not involved, appoint instead her father or one of her brothers, if they are men who can be trusted.

But don't put too much stock in this, for it is an indication to the woman that she should remarry, and really you want to discourage this in every way, as I have said. And if you are worried that your widow will remarry, and that your children will be poorly cared for by guardians, then it seems better to me to leave them as wards of the Florentine government. And if you have a scarcity of relatives, and you don't trust them, in that case, too, it would be better to put your children under the guardianship of the government, leaving every freedom to their mother; always do this if she is a good woman. Also, if you see that your affairs are too tied up in merchandise or in debts, or if you are owed money by strangers or people who are bad at paying their debts, in that case, too, it is better to leave your children in the hands of the government – for many reasons, the government is better than a relative or friend. And truly I believe that this is the most beneficial thing of all for a child who is left fatherless – as I've said above, first the mother, then good relatives who have plenty of money and no vices, then friends, and in the last resort, lacking all other possibilities, take the last option – that is, leave your children as wards of the government.

I also advise you, if you feel that you have a loyal relative or friend who has proven his worth to you (otherwise, don't put your trust in him), give him the power to act on behalf of your children, on the condition that he give an accounting every year to their guardians, who will have the responsibility of accepting what he does, or reining him in. Do this for their honour – it is sufficient for you to have made your desires known to them, and the faith that you have in the person you have chosen to act on behalf of your children. Freedom should not be taken away from someone like your agent, who is obliged to give an accounting. If you leave young daughters when you die, stipulate that they should not be married before they are fifteen years of age, and be careful about the dowry, which should depend on the family into which the girl marries: estimate the family's worth, and then lower it by one fourth. If you have a son who is already of age, leave the decision about the dowry to his discretion and that of your widow. If they deem it proper, they may give the girl to be married up to two hundred florins beyond the amount of her dowry.

Fourth Misfortune for Fatherless Children: Expenses

The fourth misfortune for a child left fatherless, as you found above, are the many expenses that occur after the death of a father – chiefly, the funeral expenses, which take a lot of money. Then there is the matter of a dowry, for whether or not the widow or the wife of the testator remarries, she wants a dowry allotted to her, and wants the net gains from it. Then there are the salaries for the agent or steward, moneys and goods that it is necessary to give to relatives or friends, for nobody will want to deal with any of the children's affairs if they are not rewarded in some way. Debts must be paid quickly, and it is a good idea to try to make up for the interest in some way. Those to whom the father owed money tend to make threats, or ask for excessive interest payments. So, as I clearly said above, a lot of money has to be doled out, for many reasons. Not to mention that, once the father has died, his earning power dies as well; and this is a misfortune that befalls everyone. But, taking into consideration all of these things, and attempting to at least partly meet the needs of his children in the event of his untimely death, a father should live every day as if it were his last – he should have solid business dealings, orderly and above board, and should not embroil himself with bad contracts, which are wealth that dies with the one who signs them; he should not become entangled with a lot of business dealings, contracts, or people.

If you decide to deal in wool or French fabrics, do everything yourself, and don't expect to get rich overnight. Use your own money; don't ever borrow money in an attempt to make money. Deal with people you can trust and who have a good reputation and credit, and whose affairs are out in the open. And if on some occasion you find that you have been swindled by someone, don't ever fall into his hands again. Don't believe it when someone offers you too much for your merchandise; don't be deceived by inflated prices. Always demand everything clearly in writing. Go slowly; play it safe.

If you go into the wool trade, do so with your own money; don't be eager to send out your merchandise if you don't have someone who is as interested in your affairs as you yourself are. If you can do without partners, do so; if not, choose your partner well – a good man, and with plenty of money. Don't choose someone above your station or from an uppity family. Don't go into any business or trade that you don't understand; do something that you know how to do, and stay away from things that you don't, for you will surely be duped. If you want to learn about anything, do so from the bottom up: spend time with men in warehouses and counting houses, and go out and familiarize yourself with merchants and merchandise; see with your own eyes the places where you intend to do business.

Test your friends, or those whom you consider to be your friends, a hundred times, before you trust them. Never trust anyone to the point that he could unmake you. Be wary about trusting people; don't be gullible. Whoever shows most by his words that he is loyal and wise, trust him the least. And trust in no way anyone who proffers himself to you. Enjoy listening to big talkers, braggarts, and showoffs, and give as good as you get, but don't believe anything they say that might bring harm to you, and don't trust them at all. Don't trust sanctimonious men, sycophants, or hypocrites who cover themselves with a priest's mantle; you're better off trusting a soldier. Don't have anything to do with a man who has changed businesses or partners or masters many times, nor with a man who gambles, goes whoring (especially with males), who dresses too extravagantly, dines too well, or is flighty; don't get involved with such men by entrusting your money or merchandise to them, or by putting your affairs in their hands.

If you trade outside of Florence, go in person often – at least once a year – to those places, to see what is going on and to settle your accounts. Observe how those who represent you live, and if they are spendthrifts; make sure they keep good credit, that they don't fling themselves into deals nor get in too deep. Make sure they are solid businessmen and don't go beyond their mandate. The moment they cross you in anything, get rid of them. Always conduct yourself wisely, don't get too involved, nor ever show off your wealth; keep it secret and always try to give the impression that you have half as much as you really do. If you maintain this style of life you will never be duped too much, nor will those who come after you. Be sure that what you do is written out extensively in your books; never spare your pen. In this way you shall make money without too much risk; you shall avoid disputes and swindles, and you won't need to fear having to make restitution, or that your children should be asked to do so. You shall live free, since you shall be firm and solid in your holdings, and with no worries.

In addition to this, you must take care not to leave your children with too many obligations. Since they will of necessity have to take from your estate to handle the necessary things when you die, you don't want to add too many things to what they have to pay, which is much more difficult to do than to say. Give alms when you are healthy; they will be more pleasing to God and will do less harm to your children. And if you do leave obligations, give them a specific time span; never, never leave any obligation in perpetuity; designate an end to what you want to be done. In leaving your estate, don't base yourself on your entire capital, especially if your children are quite young; reduce it by one fourth of your net worth. If you base yourself on this, you won't go wrong.

Designate only a few people – good ones – as guardians of your children. If you are a merchant and your trustees don't know anything about the trade, let them take your share out of the business. If you leave cash and your children have quite a bit of property, let them take what they need and put the rest in good, well-documented investments, as long as all the trustees are in agreement. Make it clear in your will that none of the trustees or their relatives can get their hands on what you leave to your children, and if they do, they must be held totally responsible. But if the trustees come to realize that their wards are ill equipped to manage their own money, and more likely to spend, gamble, and eat up their inheritance than to keep it, in this case, for the good of the wards, the trustees should spend the money to buy property near Florence, good land not too close to the river, in places where there are plenty of labourers; they should buy property that they can turn around and resell at any time. If you take this course, I truly believe that it will be the best for your young heirs.

Fifth Misfortune: Traps into Which Fatherless Children Can Fall

I wrote above about the fifth misfortune that can befall children after the loss of their father: that is, everyone becomes very aggressive with them, like birds of prey with tiny partridges, which they easily catch, plucking their feathers little by little, until they are naked. Thus is the poor orphan plucked bare by his relatives, friends, neighbours, and strangers – he is robbed, deceived, and betrayed by everyone with whom he comes into contact. Where before he had his father the good shepherd to protect him, now he is left alone among wolves and dogs. This situation has few remedies, if any, except for God and if some friend remains who is a man of God, which are few and far between. Young, inexperienced fatherless children may have many people around them who say that they are their friends, and then they end up being deceived by them. Therefore you should ensure your household as much as you can, in this way:

Do not trust any servant, male or female; do not trust, or trust as little as you can, any other woman or man who frequents your house, be they relatives or not. Arrange your affairs honestly and in a way of which others are not aware. First, make an inventory of what you have, and let everyone know. Don't leave anything in your house except for the household items that you need, and never wish for more than is necessary. Assign to the women the household goods that belong to them, and tell them to take care of them; they should be able to give you an account of them when you ask. Designate what belongs to your maidservant and tell her that she must be able to give you an account of it, and likewise with your manservant, if you have one. Lock up everything else. But make sure that there is always bread and wine available; have the key hanging in the dining room, in a place where everyone can see it. Lock up things like oil, salted meat, grain or flour or fodder; and if you can't lock them up, then keep only the amount that you need in the house, or a little more. Sell the rest and you shall see that you come out right at the end of the year, if you've diligently calculated what you need to consume at home. If you come out short, you'll say, "Somebody has cheated me." Find out who it is, and remedy the situation. If you discover that someone is stealing from you, send that person packing, or lock everything up.

Be on your guard with your workers in the country; go there often, examine your land field by field along with your worker, reproach him for work he has done badly, assess the harvest of grain, grapes, olives, fodder, fruit, and every other thing. Compare this year's harvest with those of past years, and see if your neighbour's land has yielded more than yours. Likewise, ask around to find out what your neighbour's reputation and status are. If he talks too much, is boastful, if he tells a lot of lies, if he praises himself for being loyal – don't trust him; keep your eye on him. Watch what goes on at his house and everywhere, see the harvest in his fields, watch his farmyard. Above all, continuously examine your own lands if you want your man to respond well to you, and make sure that you get what is due to you, down to the tiniest thistle. Don't ever gratify your peasants; if you do, they'll come to expect it. They wouldn't give a straw for you, even if you gave them half of all you own. Don't ever ask to see one of your peasants unless there is a need to do so; don't ask him to do you any service without paying him – otherwise, it will end up costing you three times as much. Don't be too friendly with your labourers; don't talk too much with them, don't let them talk too much to you, don't do them any harm unless they do harm to you. If any of your peasants fails to do his fair share of the work, punish him reasonably, and don't ever forgive him. Don't give them gifts, and don't expect gifts from them. And if they should give you gifts, don't give them anything better. Be fair with them, and help and advise them if they are wronged or hurt, and do not be too slow and deliberate in this. Help them in a timely manner, otherwise it's not worth the bother. Above all, don't believe anything they say unless you see it with your own eyes, and never trust them at any cost. If you act in this way, you shall not be greatly deceived by them and you shall be liked better than other masters; they will respect you to the degree that they are able, and you shall get of them whatever good is to be gotten.

In your business dealings with your fellow citizens and with relatives and friends, behave in this way if you don't want to lose them or be robbed or deceived by them. Act in a friendly way to all of your fellow citizens, love and cherish them all; and if you can, do courtesies for them. Try to spend as much time as you can with them; treat them to eat and drink occasionally, but take care whom you invite – stick with the good rather than the bad. Nevertheless, endeavour to be on good terms with everyone; never speak ill of anyone, never listen to evil things being said about anyone, and especially not about any of your neighbours. If you do hear someone speaking ill of one of your neighbours, either don't say anything, or contradict what is being said. If anyone asks you to do him a service that will not cost you anything, hasten to do it. Gladly be of service to anyone of any station in both words and deeds; take care not to offend anyone; base yourself on reason and give whatever you can properly and honestly give. In this way you shall offend no one. Endeavour to put anyone who departs from reason on the right path with kind words, if you can; and if you cannot, and you are in office and in a position to judge him, judge him justly.

If anyone asks you to lend him money or stand surety for him or enter into any kind of obligation that could bring harm to you, avoid it like fire, and don't go to any place that might be harmful to you, for you might incur two or even three damages: one, you could lose money; two, you could lose a relative or friend; three, he could become your enemy if you ask him for your money back two or more times. If it's only a small amount, I say you should do it for a friend, but assume that you'll never get the money back. Don't fret, and don't act upset – otherwise, you'll lose both your money and your friend. Just accept that you've helped him, and don't fall into the same situation again; and avoid similar situations with other friends, for more damage could come to you, so don't fall for this again. And if you make a big fuss, and he says "I shall repay your money in a month … I'll have it then," and on and on, then you will have closed the door completely. Listen with the ear of a merchant and don't let yourself be moved, neither by money nor by promises. Once you've said no two or three times, and he continues trying, endeavour to find out whether he can give you a good guarantee; and if he does and you see that you can help him, do so, but proceed very carefully. Never put yourself under any obligation without a guarantee, and take care that it be sufficient: don't worry about losing a little time, for you don't want to lose any of your capital.

You have to be very smart, for a man who needs to borrow money will use the most wily and subtle ways in the world. He'll start out by giving you his business tips and telling you about his gains and transactions and dealings, and then he'll say to you: "If I had two hundred florins, I would be able to double them. I would gladly give half of what I made to whoever helped me. If someone would only stand surety for me, I could borrow those florins at a low interest." And with these and other similar words he will try to get you to stand surety for him. And if you don't give in at his first attempt, he will press you further: "Sign the note for me; I shall have the merchandise put in your name, and shall keep it in your house. You can trust me, I assure you. I would rather be drawn and quartered … There are twenty men who would be glad to help me, but I don't want to give them this tip, nor this advantage. I want to give it to you, because I know you. I'm telling you the truth. Would to God that I had the power to do this, as I have the good intention!" He will go on babbling like this, and if you are not careful, he will entrap you and later he'll play you for a fool. This kind of trickery and many other ruses are used to entrap friends – some do it with gifts, some with offering dinners and other honours, some get you entangled before they tell you anything, along with two or three others who pretend to be going along with the affair, so that you would be ashamed to pull out of it. There are many ways to trick people out of money. Be wise, and never let yourself be entrapped. You can use any number of excuses: "My money is encumbered … I took an oath … I am in partnership with my brother, and cannot undertake any obligations without his agreement … I am beholden to my partner … Forgive me – I need to think about this … What need is there to take all these precautions with me? Weren't you telling me the truth? You make me doubt where I would not have suspected anything … I need to mull this over," and so on. Continue to stall for time, and get advice six times before you risk even a small amount. Above all – and keep this well in mind – never enter into any kind of financial obligation with a man who has gone bankrupt, no matter if he be your relative or friend. Never, even if he says he can double your money, never trust him, unless you have made up your mind to lose money in order to help him. Don't accept pledges nor anything of the sort, and never believe in big promises. Avoid this man's company (don't forget!); don't let yourself be deluded; hold firm and make it clear that he can't turn to you for help. Once he has calmed down, you can placate him with a little bit of grain, or with ten florins. And he'll consider that you've helped him ten times more than if you had fulfilled his original request, for he would have ended up with creditors after him; this way, he will get to keep whatever you've given him.

Therefore, be wise. I am telling you this because of more than three bad experiences that I have had myself, to my great detriment. Never trust anyone; do things above board, and try to stick with relatives or friends rather than getting entangled with strangers. Have all documents duly notarized. Have accounts written by a third person. There are many other things that could be said about this, but in sum keep in mind what I have said here, and you shall not be robbed.

Sixth Misfortune: Taxes and Duties

As I said above, the sixth misfortune that befalls a fatherless child are the taxes and duties imposed by the state. The same goes for honours: for in both cases, the fatherless son is ill treated. The chief reasons are because he is young and powerless, and doesn't recognize those who wish him ill. He takes nothing into consideration but childish amusements; he doesn't know how to talk about his family's business affairs, relying on the advice of others. In addition, he is not eligible for public office and does not frequent the places where business is conducted, so he is ignored. He needs to know what his assets are worth, but his affairs are managed and buffeted about by more than one person, so that knowledge is not all in one place. And what happens to him is similar to what happens to those who gamble: if he wins ten florins, he's told it's twenty, and he must spend them; if he loses, either he's not told at all, or he's told that he's lost less, and nobody makes up any of the money to him. This is what happens to the fatherless child; his evil guardians, since they have the use of his money, say: "He is rich; he has two hundred casks of wine – what does it matter if I take ten casks? He has several thousand florins in cash – what does it matter if I keep a thousand for myself?" A relative will say the same thing. And when the time comes for them to act on behalf of the fatherless child, the guardians and relatives will skim off a little for themselves, saying: "I toil to manage his affairs and many times neglect my own; so what does it matter if I help myself a little along the way?" A stranger will skim off money willingly in order to help anyone who can be of service to him, saying: "He is young and has no expenses; he can afford this. If he's going to lose the money anyway, it's better for it to go to the city; he'll get it back somehow!" Thus for many false reasons he is made a fool. The same goes for honours: the relatives want to further their own children's fortunes, neighbours the same, and others don't even think of helping the fatherless child; there is no one to speak on the fatherless child's behalf. Everyone is out for himself. If the fatherless child's guardian is going to pressure his friends for honours, he will do it on behalf of his own relatives; he will make very little effort on behalf of his ward, and won't press people too much for favours. The fatherless child, for his part, doesn't know how these things work; he doesn't know how men are, nor how to draw attention to himself. And even if he does manage to draw attention to himself, and it becomes known that he is seeking some honour or other, it's of little use to him, for he is told many lies. And thus in reality he gets but a fraction of what should be coming to him, and ends up paying much more than he should do.

Now, wishing to provide some solution to this situation as with the others – although there are very few real solutions – I say that in my opinion the following is what should be done. To my mind, there are two chief reasons why a fatherless child suffers misfortunes in this area: the first is that the value of his patrimony is usually falsely represented as being greater than it really is. The second is that he is powerless and therefore dominated by everyone, because he is unable to defend himself by word or deed, for he has no experience or knowledge. For the first situation, I say that the one who is harmed needs to find the remedy himself – for if he does not, no one else will do it for him. This is because men are more evil and vice-ridden these days than ever before, and they will only get worse in the future. If men were good, it wouldn't be necessary to protect oneself from evil, for evil would not be done. Therefore, having to defend himself, the fatherless child does not understand. Therefore you, his father, in order to help yourself and to help him after you are gone, should act in the following way.

First, if you do not deal in any kind of merchandise, make sure above all to sign legitimate contracts. In this way you will gain a good reputation and people won't say that you've gotten rich too quickly, and you won't make big loans and thus the evil reputation of usurer won't be associated with your children.

Secondly, if you do deal in some kind of merchandise, use only your own money; from this you will gain a good and honourable reputation, and you won't give the impression that you have more than you really do. For if you borrowed money from others, you would be ruined in the long run and you would gain a reputation for being richer than you really are, which can hurt more than help – if not you, then your children. Therefore do not become puffed up with pride, for it shall be the ruin of you. Likewise, if you conduct your business in the way that I recommend, your affairs will not become embroiled with many others', and everybody won't know your business. For if you did business with many people, you would make more money, and word would spread about that. And the benefit would not be greater, but the danger would be, in more ways than one. Avoid personal loans, which are not legitimate. They are very dangerous, and generally entrap those who are in need. If you make this kind of loan, you will immediately get a reputation for being very rich; and if you lend a thousand florins, word will get out that you lent twice as much, and you'll be inundated with requests for loans. And if you should die, your children will not be paid what is due to them, and if they do get something, it will be given with enmity. Therefore avoid making this kind of loan.

Next, do not boast of making large amounts of money, or of having great wealth. Do the opposite: if you make a thousand florins, say it was five hundred; if you deal in a thousand, say the same. And if you are seen to have a great deal of money in hand, say "It's somebody else's." Don't be ostentatious in your expenditures; if you're wealthy to the tune of ten thousand florins, live as if you had five thousand – in your words, the way that you and your family dress, the way you dine, how many servants you have, and how many horses. Do not reveal your true wealth in any fashion to anyone, neither relatives nor friends nor colleagues. Keep a secret hoard of olive oil and other good things in order not to show the world how much you've got. To make sure that these things are a secret, entrust them to a friend in the country, in a safe place. Do not appear to own too much real estate: buy whatever may be necessary for your style of life; don't buy properties that are too ostentatious – they should be useful, but not showy. Always complain to other people that you have taxes and duties to pay, that you have debts, that you have heavy expenses, the obligations of your father's estate, that you've incurred losses in trading, that you've had a poor harvest, that you need to buy grain and wine and firewood and everything else that you need. But take care not to exaggerate too much when you say these things, or you will be ridiculed. Always keep these kinds of lies close to the truth, so that you will be believed and won't get the reputation of being a liar. Avoid like fire telling lies except in this kind of thing – it's acceptable to tell lies of this sort, because you're not telling them to take something away from anyone, but in order to protect yourself.

Then, be courteous: endeavour to make one or more friends in your *gonfalone* and to do good things for them, and don't worry about spending some of your own money. If you are wealthy, you can use your money to acquire friendships, if you can't obtain them in any other way. Do your best to forge relationships with good citizens who are well loved, and powerful. And ingratiate yourself with anyone in your *gonfalone* who can help you get ahead. If you can get to him by means of family relationships, do so. And if you cannot, then seek out his company yourself, associate with his friends, make an effort to do him favours, offer yourself when you see he needs something. If you have the ability to give him gifts without too much damage to yourself, do so; invite him often to dine with you and other neighbours of yours; behave well with them, do not despise them, do not threaten them. If you are weighed down by fees and duties, complain about it honestly everywhere. Do not threaten anyone, but keep in mind anyone who has done you a disservice, and try to befriend him. If you can't befriend him with pleasant words and actions, then do him a disservice the way he has done to you. Make sure that he knows what you are doing and that he knows who you are and the reason for your actions, so that another man won't try to do the same thing and you won't be treated with disdain. People need to know that you are a man, not weak like a woman. Show your face where you need to, and your actions and your words. Don't ever act in a villainous way – act openly both when you win and when you lose. Do not inflict villainy on anyone unless it is necessary for your honour. Avoid disputes and unpleasantness as much as you can, for they are harmful to individuals and especially to the State.

Do not be eager for the products of your harvests, if you have a great deal, to be brought to your house. Have whatever you need brought to you, not all at one time, but a little at a time. For if you put on airs like this, your neighbours will resent you and will say that you have a thousand estates and that you have enough grain and wine and oil for six families. They will say, "He can certainly afford to lend money to the state and can well afford to make public loans, for enough food goes into that house to feed an entire town." And in this way you shall earn the reputation of being a very rich man, which can lead to being hit with a heavy imposition for public loans. Use just what you need, and don't make a big show, if you don't want people to talk about how rich you are. Avoid having a lot of work done to your house – that way, you won't have the bother or the expense of having workers around, you won't have dust and moths, and many other bothersome things. If the poor people see that you have grain to sell but are holding it back to drive the price up, they will slander and curse you and will rob or burn your house if they get the chance; all of the lower classes will hate you, which is a very dangerous thing. May God protect our city from ever being taken over by them.

In conclusion, remember this: conceal your goods and your earnings as much as possible, and make a show as much as you can of your expenses, debts, obligations, and bad luck, your losses and other misfortunes, especially when you get together with your neighbours and with the men from your *gonfalone.* This seems to me to be to a great extent what a father can do to protect himself, and it is also a good foundation for his children, should they happen to lose their father.

A son should learn from the mirror that we have placed before him, or should be taught by those whose ward he is. He should first and foremost endeavour to be a good student, to learn the science of grammar and how to do calculations, if he wants to live well. Further, he should be well mannered and respectful in dealing with his neighbours and especially with those who can do him some good – that is, with those of his own age who are the sons of his family's neighbours. He should strive to be liked by everyone, not to dress too lavishly, neither in silk nor in other rich fabrics; he should not have a manservant nor a horse, unless he needs a steward or a beast of burden in the country. He should not keep a teacher in his home, unless it is necessary because of his great wealth; if he is very wealthy, he should have a master in his home, so that people won't think that he doesn't have one out of avarice or lack of money. He should avoid bad habits and people of a lower station than he; he should not be desirous of luxurious things and should not talk about these things. He should eat all kinds of food. He should not play *zara*[42] or engage in any other game of chance. He should play children's games – with tokens, tops, horseshoes, tarot cards, *coderone*,[43] and the like. He should jump and run and throw the lance and other similar games that build physical prowess and are played by young people. He should occasionally consort with other young people at weddings, parties, and hunts, but he should not do this too often, for he would stray from the path of virtue. He should learn to play an instrument, sing and dance, fence, and in this he should become expert; he will become known by other young men of good standing, he shall be reputed to be virtuous, he shall be liked, he shall be well thought of in every good and honourable thing. He should be well spoken, courageous and open and good and bold.

---

42 A game played with three dice, popular during the Middle Ages. Dante mentions this
   game in *Purgatory* VI, 1–9.
43 Another game played with dice.

Banish vices from your life in every way; do not give in to them – fight them. Banish fear, timidity, laziness, greed, foolishness, sentimentality, and other similar things, which make you wretched and repulsive; all men will deride you and despise you and wish you ill. If these things come to you by nature, fight against them; do the opposite of what your wretched spirit tells you to do. In this way, you shall conquer your vices. For once you have experienced the virtuous life and consorted with upstanding, righteous people, you shall soon learn the virtues yourself. If your spirit is decent, you shall delight in the virtues, and you shall soon learn to despise the vices to which you formerly surrendered.

Strive above all to be courteous, and take care not to let greed come near you in any way. Be courteous and generous with youths and worthy men, but temperately and in a prudent way, so that you will not be considered uncouth. Follow the example of your peers: if they do you honour, do honour unto them. Invite them to dine occasionally in Florence, and also in the countryside. During the summer, have a cask of good Trebbiano wine, from la Torre or Bucine or San Giovanni[44] or from other places where they make good wine. Invite your neighbours, invite your young comrades and give them wine to drink, as should be done. Or for the feast of the Holy Cross or St Onuphrius, or whatever feast day is near, invite your fellow citizens and upstanding young men, and do them honour. You should have a cask of good, crisp, fragrant red wine, and on hot days you should invite your neighbours and other men and cheerfully offer wine and other good things to all of them. But if anyone behaves ungratefully or otherwise discourteously, scorn him. And let other people see this, so that they won't take you for a fool. Likewise, occasionally invite your neighbours and comrades to dine in a proper fashion, as is seemly and as you see others do.

Take pleasure in courting a pretty, gracious girl from a good family; go to see her at the appropriate time, when you leave your shop. Take a trusted comrade with you when you go to see her, and make friends with the honourable people who live in the vicinity. Be well-mannered and pleasant, and be courteous to the young men who are her neighbours. Perform good deeds that people will report back to her so that she will know that you are well bred and wise; make her love you for your virtues. Once a year have music played, but not with too much expense or ostentatiousness – get three or four honourable young men, and confer

---

44 All places in the Valdarno where wine was produced.

with them secretly, and have pipes and four trumpets play. Spend two florins, no more. And don't do this more than once a year, or you shall gain the reputation of a spendthrift.

This is how you shall become mature, known by your fellow citizens, build friendships with your peers, and gain the reputation of an honourable, well-mannered man. But above all be judicious in all things; if you can't do these things properly, don't do them. If you can do them without harming your business, do so, but be wise, for these are things that can lead young men astray, causing them to neglect their business, to gamble, and to mismanage their affairs. Beware of these dangers – and if you come to realize that these things are leading you into improper behaviour, leave off. Above all, avoid gambling and gluttony and evil habits.

If you should find yourself without relatives to help and advise you in times of adversity, endeavour to find someone who will act as your father. If you can, first look in your own *gonfalone*, and if you can find someone there, do it there rather than someplace else. If you can't find the right person in your own *gonfalone*, look in the immediate neighbourhood – don't go any further afield, unless you have the possibility of making a good connection in the neighbourhood where one of your relatives lives. But first look in your own *gonfalone*, then in the neighbourhood. And even though I have already written this several times, I want to remind you again: make sure to make a connection with a man who is a merchant, wealthy, from an old Florentine family, from the Guelph party, and with a position in the government. He should be well liked by many, affectionate and good in all his actions. Likewise, choose a wife as I have said above.

When you are about eighteen years old, try to see a little of the world as a merchant and visit other cities and learn about the ways and conditions of other places, if you can do so to your benefit and with honour. And if you enjoy it, spend three or four years doing this – you shall become more experienced and learn more about everything, and you shall know how to communicate with other men. Your reputation shall grow, and you shall gain more status.

Now, to conclude, these things that I have said above are useful for gaining experience and getting to know the world, to making oneself well liked and honoured and respected. And reasonably you should be able to defend yourself from adversity and from any wrong that should be done to you by doing these honourable things. But if you should find yourself in great financial adversity and these things aren't enough to help you, to the point that you are about to be ruined, don't pay all your debts. Lodge a petition with the city, and arrange your affairs so that what belongs to you cannot be confiscated. Make it be known that your money is pledged for dowries or for other obligations. But if you can't protect yourself in this way, give over; for confiscated goods are not quickly sold. If you have money in cash, arrange things so that it is not known that the money is yours. Or invest the money in wool, and then sell it in Venice or Genoa, or have it put in someone else's name. Get some good advice about this. Never use injurious language against the city nor against any man; but wait until an opportune moment, for example when a peace treaty has been signed, or when many debts are being pardoned, and make a petition to the Seignory to pay a third or two-fifths at the most. Entreat the Seignory to reduce your debt, letting them and their associates know what straits you are in – do everything in your power to get your debt reduced. Make a show to everyone that you are in financial straits and cannot pay. Above all, never borrow money at interest, especially for this reason. Rather, sell the most that you can, for if you borrow money it will be your undoing – you would have to pay interest, and in the end you would have to sell off things in any case. I think I have said enough about the sixth misfortune that can befall a fatherless son. And if you diligently follow these teachings, you should be able for the most part be able to face this kind of adversity.

Seventh Misfortune: Loss of a Father's Teachings

The seventh and last misfortune of a fatherless son is the loss of the good lessons that he would have received constantly from his father on every occasion. His father would have counselled him to avoid vices and would have taught him virtues. He does not benefit from the good advice that he would have had from his father in times of adversity, which occur all the time, showing him by reason and by example how to deal with the situation and the steps to take to remedy it. A father would teach you how to speak to citizens, officials, and rectors in the missions upon which he would send you. He would teach you the tenor of words, the necessary manners and courtesies, the preliminaries of various missions, depending upon whom you are meeting. And so on for the other types of tasks that occur every day – all this a father would teach you. He would say to you: "Do this, act in such and such a way." You would be with him and see how he acted and spoke and behaved, and you would learn a great deal. You would hear from him about certain cases that had occurred in your city, certain advice given by men of worth, certain good and useful solutions that were found, and also decisions that were harmful and brought shame. And as he spoke, wishing to instruct you, he would remind you of many things from the past that he had seen or heard or read in the books of the Romans or other poets or worthy men. Thus he would recount to you things that had happened to him personally or to his property, either because of his own mistakes or those of others, or in the affairs of the city or in business or other occasions that arise in the world; or he might recount to you things that had happened to his ancestors, and the solutions they found, or from which they derived status or advantage, or on account of which they were disadvantaged; who had been their friend in time of need and who did not help them, and the vendettas taken against those who hurt them and the services rendered to those who helped them. In this way, a son learns from the many examples recounted to him by his father, and keeps them well in mind. When a son lives with his father, he has so many advantages in so many ways and on so many occasions that they are too numerous to tell. But because we have already written a great deal about this, there remains little for us to say in this section.

But in order not to leave off so brusquely, we shall write here about some things that can be done to remedy the lack of a father in cases such as these; some we have already spoken of, and others we have not yet had occasion to write about. In my opinion the remedy that a son growing up without a father should take is this, among other things: He should assiduously, even when he is quite young, learn to read and write and to read as much as he can understand of the learned writers in Latin, as well as legal texts. Likewise, he should know how to write a well-composed letter in Latin. He should endeavour always to consort with young men of his own rank, both in school and out in the world – upstanding youths who study like him and who are well mannered and virtuous. He should be confident about talking, joking, and even scuffling with them, but not in a malicious way, so that he can learn how to play the games that young people play. And these pastimes, or other even more valuable ones such as studying music or fencing or other pleasant diversions, should be indulged in when he is not studying, for example at noontime, during the summer, in the evening after school is over, or on holidays. At all other times, he should study – he should take delight in studying, and be diligent; he should conquer himself, and strive to learn as much as he can.

Once you have completed your schooling, endeavour to study Virgil, Boethius, Seneca, or other authors for at least an hour every day, as if you were still in school. This will result in great benefit to your mind: by studying the teachings of these authors, you shall know how you should act in your present life, both for the health of your soul and for the usefulness and honour of your body. And although when you are young this might seem rather difficult and burdensome, when you come of age and your intellect begins to savour the reason for things and the sweetness of knowledge, you shall derive as much pleasure out of it, as much delight, as much consolation as you do out of anything in the world. You shall not prize so much wealth, children, status, or any great or honourable preeminence, once you have knowledge and can repute yourself a man and not a beast. Knowledge is what shall bring you to a lofty, honoured place; virtue and your own intellect shall lead you there, whether or not you wish it. You shall have all the great men at your disposal: you can be with Virgil in your study as long as you want; he won't tell you no, but will answer your questions and will advise and teach you at no cost whatsoever; he shall take away your melancholy thoughts, and give you pleasure and consolation. You can be with Boethius, with Dante and the other poets, with Cicero, who will teach you perfect diction; with Aristotle, who will teach you philosophy. You shall know the reason for things, and every little thing shall give you the greatest pleasure. You shall be with the blessed prophets in the Holy Scripture, you shall read and study the Bible, you shall learn of the great acts of those holy prophets, you shall be fully instructed in the faith and the advent of the Son of God, your soul shall have great consolation, you shall not suffer no matter what befalls you. You shall be open-hearted and know which remedies are good and healthy. You shall be so well instructed and knowledgeable that it would be superfluous to say more.

But because we are prone to vice and full of deceit and betrayal, I shall inform you of certain actions and precautions with which you shall humble the evil, leading them back in part to your own benevolence or to redress their evil actions, in this way: in your relationships, lean chiefly on those who are in power and belong to the Guelph party and have good credibility and no stains on their reputation. If you can't get to such people through your relatives, become their friend by speaking well of them, serving them wherever it is in your power, seeking them out, and offering to do things for them. Associate with such men, but try to get closer to one or two of them, who you see have power. Once you have made sure that they are not corrupt, seek their advice; show them your faith in and affection for them; invite them to dine in your home and do things for them that you believe will please them and make them condescend to be your friend, even if it costs you a little. In addition, try to stay close to whoever is in power in the Public Palace and the Seignory, and obey and follow their wishes and commands. Be careful not to speak ill of their undertakings, even if they are not good; hold your tongue, and don't speak except to commend them. Refuse to hear or do anything against them in any way, even if you should be insulted by them. If anyone should mention to you anything against whoever is in power, refuse to listen, and avoid him at all costs. Do not consort or have relationships with malcontents, and don't hold discourse with them except in the presence of others who participate in government. But if by some misfortune you should hear something ill of them, report it immediately and without a second thought to the Seignory or to the office charged with protecting our city. Thus should you endeavour to live upright and in the clear so that nothing shall stain your reputation in any way, and especially anything that might be against the Guelph party.

You should also endeavour to ingratiate yourself with all types of people, and this is the way: offend no one in word or need, neither by shaming them or impugning their honour or harming their property or person. Because there are deceitful people in Florence who will try every trick to corrupt you, and because you can't recognize all of them, always speak well of everyone and don't agree with those who speak ill of others; either hold your tongue, or speak well. Be pleasing in your discourse; say things that will gratify the company you are with; be courteous to every type of person; be hospitable to them, give them to eat and drink; by day and night consort with your neighbours in Florence and in the countryside; serve them however you can. If you realize that someone in your circle is bad, pretend not to know, but be wary of him and don't trust him a jot. Be brave and courageous in defending your honour and your rights; demand them openly, reasonably, and with confidence, with legitimate, reasonable facts. Don't be timid or hesitant, but put yourself forward frankly. In this way, you shall be honoured and respected and reputed to be a valorous man, and you shall be feared so that you shall receive no insult from anyone, and shall fully receive your just due.

Once you have won your friends and relatives (I mean, once you see that they love you and serve you and care about you), you must be sensible enough to keep their friendship, and even to strengthen it; and this is how to do it. Don't be ungrateful for favours received; offer your own property and yourself, serve others, frequent them, honour them. Rejoice with your friends during their good times, and in times of adversity commiserate with them and show them that you are pained for them; comfort and help them, offering to do whatever is necessary. If you see that you can be useful to them or honour them, do so; don't wait to be asked. But when you've done so, or rather before, tell them so, so that with your help the favour or honour will be attained, and they shall see that you neglected nothing. In this way and others like it, as occur every day, you can win friends and keep the ones you already have, or rather add to them.

But above all, if you wish to have friends and relationships, make sure that you don't need them. Strive always to have cash and to keep it carefully; that's the best friend or relative you can have. Endeavour to attain a little status; be open – you are intelligent enough to know how to comport yourself and to do what you have been taught. Keep in mind these verses taught by our authors for our training, as you shall find in Aesop, I believe: *Tempore felici multi nominantur amici; Dum Fortuna perit nullus amicus erit.*[45] In your studies, you shall find many more true teachings like this one. By God, don't ever give up studying, but keep it up until the end of your life; for you shall derive much pleasure, much benefit, and much good advice from it. And these teachings are such that, if you know how to appreciate them, everything else will seem to you futile and useless, and you shall derive good from them in proportion to how much you follow them.

You can also learn other things, to wit: if in your city, or in your district or neighbourhood, one or more factions should be formed, as happens every day, either to deal with city affairs, or because one citizen has a grudge because of something the city did to him or for some other reason, if you want to live in peace and be no man's enemy and be loved and reputed wise and be listened to in every dispute, this is what you must do: stay in the middle and remain friends with everyone and don't speak ill of anyone nor try to please one more than the other; don't be moved by anger. If you want to complain, do so with anyone but someone from the opposing party; thus you will protect yourself from those who go around repeating things to defame others. If you hear people speaking well of one of the parties, join in, and listen to them willingly; if you hear them speaking ill of anyone, hold your tongue, or reproach whoever is speaking, if you think he will tolerate it. Never repeat anything bad that is said about anyone; repeat good things, if you think this will please people.

---

45 A medieval distich based on one by Ovid: "Donec eris felix multos numerabis amicos; Tempora si fuerint nubila solus eris" (As long as your luck is good, you will have many friends; should your fortunes change, you will be alone") (*Tristia* I 9, 5–6).

Don't get involved if you aren't asked to, and then only say good things. If you see that you can go on in this way and make both parties happy, do so, and do so for the better; if you see that it's no use, either because of a grudge someone has against you or because you are reluctant to do what is asked of you, or because there is no faithful friend to support you, or because the two parties want to put their own friends forward, then hold back, if it is of no benefit to yourself. Then you can turn your coat. Observe which of the two parties is stronger, which is more reasonable, which has more credibility with the powers that be, which has more noble men and more Guelphs; associate yourself with that party, honour it, support it in word and deed. Be strong, and don't let yourself be dissuaded.

Keep to the straight path; don't be led astray by promises or anything else; if you did, you would be reputed disloyal, indecisive, and unstable. Nevertheless, you should always try to reason with everyone; if it is necessary to use different words, even unreasonable ones, to further your cause, do so, but let the outcome be reasonable. Don't be swayed unless you see that everyone is concurring in a case of great importance in favour of your party or your situation. You should concur, too, then, for otherwise you would be held to be suspicious and people would reject you.

You should also try to frequent one or two valorous, wise, older men, who are uncorrupted; study their manners, their words, their advice, how they run their families and their households. Learn from, and try to emulate them. Always keep them foremost in your mind, and when you do anything, imagine what they would do in your place. If you speak in public or in an official capacity, keep this kind of man in your mind's eye; take inspiration from his example and follow his style. If you do so, you will take on his ways and won't become discouraged and will be forthright and confident, for you shall always be encouraged by his example.

And just as you can take a living man as your model, likewise or a little less you can take as an example a valiant Roman or some other valorous man whom you have studied. But it is not possible to imitate men like these as you can men whom you see with your own eyes, and especially in the things with which we have to deal, which are more material than those of the great events of Rome. Except that, if you should reach the highest level of government, then I would I advise you to strive to resemble our Roman forefathers, for as we are descended from them in essence, we should show this in virtue as well as in substance.

It is not possible for me to give instructions for every occasion, for two reasons: first, because I'm not able to; second, because I am very ignorant. But I am not ashamed on account of this, first because I am writing for the benefit of my young sons and not for grown men, all of whom would know much more than I do; and secondly, because this book of mine is not intended for anyone outside of our family. And I am certain that for my own family, if for no other reason than love of one's own flesh and blood, I could not help but have spent this small amount of time well, which I have spent to pass the time and avoid idleness.

For the present, in this chapter I shall not say more, but in the following chapter I shall record fourteen mad things that men frequently do – young Florentines, and foreigners as well. And because I want you to avoid doing these things, I shall name them all. The reason why I am not writing them in this chapter is to give honour to the man who manifested them to me.

After I had written the preceding section, which was quite some time ago, I thought that I should go forward; and at the proper time I shall write to you about the worthy and devout friar Giovanni Dominici of the Dominican order and certain teachings of his, as I promised above.[46] For now, we shall continue to record many things that happened in our city that shall be useful to know about and may shed light on other things that have happened in the past. And they shall be a sort of teaching, for one should be wise and take the part of things that is useful, and leave the rest.

Of Plagues, and Ways to Guard against Them

In the year of Christ 1348 there was a great plague in the city of Florence, and many people perished. We hear of many terrible events from older people and find many writings. And among others, Messer Giovanni

---

46 Morelli was a friend and admirer of the Dominican friar Giovanni Dominici (1357–1419), who played a leading role in the religious life of the city of Florence between 1401 and 1406, when he went to Rome as part of a delegation to the new pope, Gregory XII. Gregory kept Dominici in Rome as one of his advisors, and made him a cardinal in 1408; he later played an active role in the Western Schism. He was known for his various ascetic works and his ponderous *Lucula noctis*, in which he inveighed against what he considered to be the humanists' excessive exaltation of ancient civilization. Contrary to his promise, Morelli never went on to list the "fourteen mad things" that Dominici had indicated to him.

Boccaccio wrote at great length about this plague in his book of one hundred tales, at the beginning of the book.

At first, people began to die of a certain swelling in the groin or armpits or in the neck just below the ears, accompanied by great pain and sudden fever. They would live between four and six days after the onset of the disease. Then the plague got worse, and people died in two days or less. And finally the infection spread to such a degree that it appeared as little boils that would erupt on any part of the body – and these boils were more dangerous and difficult to remedy than the swellings mentioned above. Later, at the height of the pestilence, people's skin was covered with livid red spots, and they spat up blood or it flowed from their nose or from below, which was the worst symptom, with no remedy. In short, people were dropping dead, both old and young, from one day to another; and in an hour you would see one of your friends laughing and joking, and in the next hour, you saw him die! Things came to such a pass that people were dying in the streets or collapsing on benches, without assistance or comfort from anyone. Bodies were abandoned until they were buried by neighbours, to avoid the stench. Many people went mad, wandering around in a delirium and throwing themselves on the ground; many threw themselves into wells, or jumped out of windows onto the ground or into the Arno River. People were killing themselves out of madness, or grief, or pain. Many died in their beds and were not discovered until their bodies were in an advanced state of decomposition. Many were buried while they were still alive. There was no one to help the dying, and no one to bury the dead. And if you needed someone to witness a last will and testament, you couldn't find anyone, or if you could, they wanted to be paid six or eight florins. You could see a cross being borne along with a body, and before it reached the church there would be three or four more behind it. Many bodies were left in front of the doors of churches during the night, and many were simply left in the streets. Many strange things were seen – sometimes when someone would approach a sick person and touch him or his clothing, suddenly he would drop dead. Among other things, Messer Giovanni Boccaccio says that he saw two pigs nuzzle and rip apart the clothing of a poor man who had died in the street; and the pigs dropped dead upon the tattered clothing that they had torn apart. You see what a great peril and risk this pestilence is: one cannot do too much to guard against it!

Now, as you have in part seen and been able to understand, the mortality was inestimable. It is said – and certainly it was so – that two-thirds of the population of our city died. At that time it was estimated that

120,000 people were living in Florence, and 80,000 of them died. Think what a disaster! It's no great wonder that this occurred, for there were many causes that inflamed the illness. In fact, it was a greater wonder, considering everything, that as many people survived as in fact did. And these were some of the reasons: this disease was not known in Florence, because it had not appeared there for a long time; the population of the city was larger than it had ever been; the year before, there had been a great famine in the city – I believe that there were not twenty people out of a hundred who had sufficient bread or grain, and those who did have some had very little. People lived on plants and weeds (you would not know them today), and they drank water, and the whole area was full of people who went around grazing on plants as if they were cattle. Think what their poor bodies must have been reduced to! Also, as we have said, there was no remedy or protection against the disease; and the plague was so great, and so harsh, that no one could help anyone else in any way, and for this reason people died with no remedy.

Now it has come to pass, because of that plague and the many other epidemics that followed it, that we have learned ways to protect against the disease, though it still does great harm. Yet I believe that many people do survive now because of the steps that are taken, for the physicians say that the rules they give for combating this disease are a protection against it. Not that someone who is well armed cannot die, if he is struck by a lance or an arrow or a bombard or a stone that kills him; thus a good man who has taken every precaution against the plague might be struck by a whiff or the stench of contagion or the breath of a sick man that is stronger than he, and it will kill him. But what of this? It is very clear that in a fight to the death, a well-armed man has a great advantage, and fewer armed men die than disarmed men. Therefore, I say, taking precautions is a good thing. One should consult good physicians and write down their advice and their prescriptions, and follow them diligently and take them very seriously.

I want you to heed this advice from me: you will hear about a plague a year or two before it reaches Florence, because it always strikes Romagna or Lombardy before it gets to our city, usually a year later. At least by the winter before, you will hear of some small outbreaks in the countryside or on the outskirts of the city, which is a clear sign that the plague is approaching Florence. By February, it will begin to be felt inside the city itself, and will continue to spread all the way up to July. Starting in mid-July, it will attack the more well-off people, and those who have lived a prudent life. Fewer people will die, but they will be of higher status.

This is because the contagion will have spread so much and people's resistance will have been worn down. And no matter how hard you fight, the disease will wear you out and little by little it will devour you, and in the end it will defeat you.

You should therefore take the following precautions: Begin in the winter to take the following measures for yourself and all your family: First, avoid humidity as much as you can, and never let yourself suffer cold. Have a fire every morning before you leave the house, and eat something that your stomach can tolerate: either a little bread and half a glass of good wine or malmsey,[47] or an appropriate pill, or a little theriac[48] if it's wet and rainy; do this two or three mornings in a row every two weeks. Take this before you get out of bed, and then sleep a little more. Then don't eat anything from that time until midday. If you feel like drinking something, it's all right to drink half a glass of malmsey, but don't drink any other heavier wines. If your stomach is weak or feels cold, every eight days take some preserves of ginger root and drink half a glass of malmsey, and then do not eat anything for five hours. Or you can take a clove and a little cinnamon or a spoonful of preserves or four portions of saffron or two or three cooked walnuts and two or three figs, with no bread – or any small thing that your doctor recommends. If you find that certain foods bother you, leave off eating them. And if you feel better on an empty stomach, don't upset it by eating. Do not leave the house too early; when there is fog and rain, stay inside by the fire. Have your midday meal at the proper hour; eat good things, and don't eat too much. Get up from the table still a little hungry. Beware of fruit and mushrooms – don't eat them, or only eat them rarely, and in small amounts. Take physical exercise, but don't exert yourself too much, so that you won't sweat and have to dry out your clothing. Avoid having sexual relations – in fact, stay away from women throughout that whole year. Do not eat or drink if you don't feel like it, and if you have something in your stomach, let it digest first, and then wait an hour before you eat or drink. In the evening, eat very little, and eat good things. Do not eat pork under any circumstances. If your stomach is strong, use vinegar and sour grapes, but not so much as to give you difficulty in digesting. Be judicious in caring for your body, and go out at least twice a day. If you are constipated or sluggish, take a laxative every eight to fifteen days. Don't oversleep;

---

47 A sweet fortified wine.
48 A mixture of honey and various drugs, thought to be a cure-all.

get up when the sun rises. In this way, you should pass the winter. And if you keep to this kind of regime, or an even better one, you will purge your stomach and your entire body, so that the contamination in the air will find nowhere to attach itself. In the spring, or rather in March, you will know where will be a good place to which you can flee. Wait until some of your fellow citizens leave Florence; don't be among the first to leave, but once four to six families have left, pick up and go where most people are going – preferably to a city where with your money you can find what is necessary to maintain your health. Don't be a fool by trying to save money. Don't hole up in the countryside or anyplace where there are no good doctors or medicines. You could end up spending twice as much and dying into the bargain, not to mention the sorrow and regret that will never give you peace. This is no time to be frugal – rather, it is a time to get money anywhere you can, and spend generously on the things that are necessary, with no economizing. For you will be spending money in order to survive, and to live with honour – not for entertainment or things of that nature. I urge you to flee the city as soon as you can in the spring – this is the safest thing to do. Make sure you have sufficient money. Do not gamble, for you could end up without a cent, and in times like this you'll find very few men who would be willing to lend you money for many reasons. Therefore, be wise: try to get together at least three hundred florins ahead of time, and don't touch a penny unless you need to, and don't tell anyone that you have this money, for they would ask you for a loan. Rent a comfortable house for your family – not a small one, but rather a house with rooms to spare. During the summer, partake of fresh things: good, light wines, fresh chickens and kids, horse tripe or trotters with vinegar and lettuce, or crayfish if you can get them. During the early part of the day, stay where it is cool. Don't sleep during the day if you can manage it, or if you do sleep, do so sitting up. Use an electuary,[49] which the physicians make with rhubarb; give it to your children, for it kills worms. Sometimes in the morning, you should eat an ounce of cassia fruit, with the peel. Give this also to your children. Always have this in the house, fresh, as well as sugar and rose water and syrup. If you are thirsty during the day, drink those things. And freshen your wrists, temples, and nose with good, strong vinegar. Don't frequent places where there are many people, and especially not enclosed places such as loggias or churches or similar places. Avoid as much as you can

---

49 A medicinal concoction made with sugar or honey.

anyone who comes from where the air is contaminated, or has sick people at home, or has had family members die of the plague; but try not to show that you are avoiding him, so that he won't realize it and become angry or uncomfortable. Avoid melancholy thoughts as much as you can, and frequent pleasant places where you can divert yourself with pleasure and gaiety, and not think about things that will cause you sadness or unpleasant thoughts. If a sad thought comes to you, flee from it, either by thinking of something else, or by going to some place where something that gives you pleasure is done. If you have the opportunity, you may gamble, but only gamble a little bit of money at a time. Endeavour not to lose a single florin; but if you do, let it go and don't give it another thought. If you have a horse, go riding for pleasure in the morning or evening, when it's cool. Be chaste as much as you can. Avoid every putrid thing and the air around it – do not tarry there. Delight in your family and lead a good, healthy life with them, living without worrying about saving money for the time, for it is already a great gain to be healthy and avoid death.

For now I will write no more about this matter, because in truth the doctors whom you trust and who know your constitution are the ones who can best advise you about taking precautions against the plague. Therefore, as I have said, you should get your advice from them, although the things written here above are useful and good to observe in times of pestilence.

IV

[AN ACCOUNT OF CERTAIN GREAT EVENTS THAT HAPPENED
IN OUR CITY AND TO US]

I promised above that I would give an account of the wars and other events that happened in our city from 1374 until the present day. I shall not write about earlier events, because in truth I am not well informed about such things, for one who has not experienced certain things is never in a position to speak about them. But it seemed useful to me to write something about the plague of 1348; thinking about how unsafe and perilous it was and how there are so many similar perils, I decided to recommend some precautions, as ineffectual as they might be, but nevertheless useful. Now I shall mention certain wars and other events that took place in Florence, but very briefly, because our purpose is not to recount the history of our city, but only our own affairs and those of our forefathers.

A Brief Account of the Disenfranchisement of the Ghibellines

It seems, according to what I have heard from worthy men, that in the Year of Our Lord 1357, because of the political divisions and ill-will of the citizens of Florence one against the other, the disenfranchisement of anyone suspected of Ghibelline tendencies began. That is, the Captains of the Guelph party, with twenty-four votes, were able to pass a law causing anyone who was a member of the Ghibelline party, no matter what office he held, to lose his position. And in truth, although this was the beginning of the ruin of our city, nevertheless at that time there were no charges made that were not justified, and only a few men lost their offices. And I never heard that at the time anyone was wronged.

The Epidemic of 1363

There was a deadly plague in Florence in the year 1363; many people died, but the total didn't reach a fourth of what it had been in 1348, when it was three times worse. In that epidemic, as I have recorded earlier, three of our father Paolo di Bartolomeo's brothers died: Giovanni, Dino, and Calandro. The days and times of their death are recorded above.

The War with the Pisans

During this same year the war with the Pisans began, and it was bitter and harmful for both us and for them.[50] If the Visconti hadn't helped the Pisans, the wars would have been quickly resolved. But the house of Visconti was always the enemy of the Florentines and of all Guelphs, and friends of the Pisans and all of the Ghibellines in Tuscany.[51] During this war, the white company of the English came to Tuscany; they were the noblest company of soldiers that had ever been seen at the time, and the richest. They wanted to be hired as mercenaries for the Florentines, and showed that they were more willing to fight for us than for the Pisans. The Florentines deliberated about hiring them; and the story goes that the city would have hired them if it hadn't been for Messer Nicolò degli

---

50 This war – one of many between Florence and Pisa – took place between 1362 and 1364, but it had really begun six years earlier.

51 The Visconti of Milan were natural, eternal enemies of the Florentines, for territorial reasons and on account of Florence's alliance with Genoa against Pisa.

Alberti, who was then Stardard-bearer of Justice and wouldn't allow them to be hired on account of the great expense, to which we were not then accustomed. Thus it came about that the Pisans hired the English with the help of Messer Bernabò Visconti, the Duke of Milan, who lent them a hundred thousand florins. With the English mercenaries, the Pisans had the better of the war at the beginning, and they sacked the Florentine countryside at will and wreaked great havoc, setting fires, stealing crops, robbing people, and taking prisoners and livestock. The captain of this company of soldiers was named Andrea Belmonte; he dressed in white and was an extremely handsome young man. He had sixteen thousand men. When our government saw that we had been both injured and shamed by the Pisans, our citizens attempted to recapture our honour by hiring part of that company of Englishmen. At the same time, we sent to Germany and hired a fine company of lords and gentlemen, which included Count Arrigo di Monforte and Count Menno, two exceedingly valiant men, and two other counts; in all, they had two thousand cavalry, at the request of Francesco da Carrara, Lord of Padua. In the end, the Pisans were bitterly defeated.

One day (the day that the race of St Victor is run),[52] after our captain, Galeotto Malatesta, had hurled every insult in the world at the city gates of Pisa, the chains were removed from the gates of the city, and many horsemen entered. The race was run, with betting going on and whores all around. Afterward, our troops went back and made camp about six miles from the city.

The weather was terribly hot that day; around the ninth hour, our soldiers, believing that they were safe, put down their arms and removed the saddles from their horses and took their ease and refreshment in the Arno River, bathing and splashing about. The Pisans got word of this, and their captain, with all their soldiers on foot and on horseback, and the whole population of Pisa, even women armed with ropes, emerged from the city to assault our men on the battlefield; they were certain that they would win, and take everyone prisoner. But it pleased God that the opposite should happen: before the Pisans were able to reach them, they raised a great cloud of dust in the air, which made the Florentine captain suspicious. He ordered all his men to take up their arms again, just before the Pisans attacked. Our men weren't totally armed yet, and because it was toward evening, they had the sun in their eyes and the Pisans at

---

52 28 July.

their backs; but, as God willed it, there was a group of Genoese crossbow archers at the barricades, some of the best in the world. You could see hundreds of arrows flying through the air; and they put up such a resistance that one of the companies of British and German mercenary soldiers in our employ were able to arm themselves. The first to emerge was Count Menno, who became angry when he reached the barricades and couldn't pass, and said: "What is this?" "These are the barricades," was the answer. He said: "Open the barricades for Count Menno!" and burst forth like a paladin against the Pisans and made the fiercest attack against them that was ever seen. Between him and a few others and the crossbow archers, they managed to hold off the Pisans until the entire Florentine army was armed again, and they overwhelmed the Pisans, who were exhausted from coming there in the great heat and dust. The Pisans who were on foot could barely stay standing up, and those on horseback had their weapons all hot and untempered, and their horses were so sweaty they couldn't go on. The skirmish lasted about three hours, and was bitter and cruel. While the fighting was going on, an eagle, one of the ones that the Pisans kept as symbols or mascots, flew out over the battlefield; when it was above our men, its wings seemed to give out. It fell, and was captured by our men. The Florentines were overjoyed at this omen, and the Pisans were appalled. In the end, the Pisans were routed by the Florentines, and more than fifteen hundred were killed or taken prisoner. Our citizens believed that if our captain had persevered, that day we would have conquered Pisa; but he did not choose to follow up that victory, and it was believed that he acted thus so that the Florentines would not become too powerful.

However it went, the victory was great. The Pisans who had been captured were bound with their own ropes and loaded onto fifty of their own carts; and in the first cart their eagle was hung, but not so that it would die, because its feet could reach the cart, and it was struggling violently. Their captain went in front, a prisoner, disgraced and humiliated. His name was Rinieri del Busso; he remained a prisoner for a long time in the Stinche.[53] At the gate at San Frediano, through which the captain entered, there was a little live lion cub,[54] and all the Pisan prisoners were

---

53 The famous Florentine prison at San Simeone. According to Villani (VIII, 75), the name came from that of a rebellious castle in the Val di Grieve, whose soldiers were the first prisoners.

54 The *marzocco*, symbol of Florence.

forced to kiss its arse. And the cub was taken all around Florence, so that everyone, great and small, could see.

And finally, realizing that their position was untenable, the Pisans surrendered to the Florentines. The Florentines, being merciful, not wishing to further persecute the Pisans, made an honourable truce with them. And among the other agreements was that the Florentines would be exempt from taxes and duties on any trading they did within the city of Pisa and its environs, and that the Pisans would give the Florentines 100 thousand florins over a period of ten years – that is, 10 thousand florins every year. And the Pisans sent the two large columns that are now on the Baptistry of San Giovanni in Florence. It is true that the Pisans deceived us, for whereas the columns had been clear and bright as a mirror, they dulled their lustre and covered them with scarlet when they sent them to Florence, so that they could not be seen. And from that time on, we Florentines were called "blind."[55] With this betrayal, the Pisans made up a little for their shame and humiliation at losing the war. We also obtained chains and other things, which are now hanging on the doors of the Baptistry of San Giovanni. Let this account suffice for now.

The War with Messer Bernabò

In the Year of Our Lord 1374 there was a great plague in the city of Florence. As I recorded above, Paolo gave up his soul to God in that year, and we all fled to Bologna. Between the time of the war with the Pisans and this year, our city had two wars. The first was with Messer Bernabò, who had taken San Miniato. His men had camped at Peretola, and after they had been there for several days, our captain, Messer Piero da Farnese, secretly rode out to San Miniato, where he had an agreement with a man named Luperello, who opened up his house, which was within the city walls there. During the night, the Florentines entered the house, and the following morning they retook San Miniato without any resistance on the part of the Pisans. This was on 9 January 1370. When the Pisans who were camped at Peretola heard the news, they left for San Miniato, but they were too late to help.

The next war was in 1372, with the Ubaldini – it was a big, unpleasant war, because the Visconti continuously helped the Ubaldini, but in the

---

55　Morelli seems to be mingling the story of the two blackened columns that the Pisans sent to the Florentines in 1117 to thank them for their help in defeating the Saracens with the story of the victory of Florence over Pisa in 1364.

end they lost, for the city of Florence ultimately triumphed. I shall not write any more about these two wars, because I am not well informed about them. Suffice it that I have spoken in part about their effects.

The War with the Church

In 1376, or thereabouts, at the time of Pope Gregory XI, the city of Florence was engaged in a bitter war with the Church, which oppressed it greatly – so much so, that in the beginning there was a risk that we might lose our freedom.[56] Realizing that we were in extreme straits, we bought off the soldier of fortune Sir John Hawkwood for a price of 130 thousand gold florins; he had previously been in the service of the Church. Cardinal Noellet felt that he had been betrayed by this deal. Noellet was the Pope's legate; at that time, he was cardinal at Bologna. The deal came about due to John Hawkwood's shrewdness, both because he wanted to serve us, but also because he wanted the money. I will not tell the whole story, for it would be too long. Our city sent Spinello della Camera[57] as an envoy to take the money to Hawkwood, who gave him 3000 florins; but Spinello, not wanting to accept the gift, gave the money back to the city treasury. He was a very loyal man, faithful to our city, and when he died, his portrait was painted in the government chamber. He was so poor that his relatives were not able to give him the kind of burial he deserved.

Soon after this, our city having been greatly oppressed by the Church as I have said, we wanted to avenge ourselves to some degree, which is why we hired Sir John Hawkwood to be our Captain. Eight citizens were named to the Eight on War, and their appointments lasted for the duration of the war. Among these were Giovanni Magalotti, Andrea di Messer Francesco Salviati, Guccio di Dino Gucci, Messer Tommaso di Marco degli Strozzi, Messer Alessandro de' Bardi, Giovanni Dini, Messer Matteo di Federico Soldi, and Giovanni di Mone the grain merchant. These were the most prominent, wise, worthy men that had ever been seen in Florence, as evidenced by their many good deeds and victories. And in short, Florence took away from the Church two-thirds of its territories, including Bologna, Faenza, Forlì, and the whole of the Romagna region; later, we took Perugia, Città di Castello, Assisi and all of its territory, the Marches, and the Duchy. This all took place over a period of about three years.

---

56 Morelli is referring to the so-called War of the Eight Saints (1375–8).
57 Spinello di Luca Alberti, known by the nickname "Spinello della Camera," was treasurer of the Florentine city-state.

A great amount of money was spent, but it was done gladly, because it brought to fruition the desires of our city. Finally, worn out and defeated, with no other way out, the leaders of the Holy Church asked for peace, showing themselves to be unworthy of victory because of their wickedness. And thus, more for the love of God than out of for pity for them, Florence gave them peace. May God give peace to us! It was the will of Our Lord God that the pastors of his own Church be punished; but because it was not up to us to punish them, for we are sinners as well, God later punished us as well.

The punishment of the Florentines began with the aforementioned Eight on War, who suffered great misfortunes – some died, some were forced out of the city, some lost their wealth. And even today their descendants continue to suffer the consequences – this was all the will of God. Florence spent 460,000 florins on this war.

How the Disenfranchisement Began

At the time of the Eight on War, toward the end of that period, many people were disenfranchised – about 200 families in the course of two years. And the citizens of Florence became so bold that they even disenfranchised members of the Colleges. Anyone who had hoped to become a member of the Seignory or to obtain some other office and was on bad terms with one of the Captains was immediately disenfranchised. Things came to such a pass that many members of the Guelph party and good, worthy citizens were being disenfranchised every day. During this time Giovanni Dini, who was one of the Eight on War, was disenfranchised. The people of Florence were very unhappy about this, but no one was willing to speak out, for fear of reprisals. In 1378, on the first day of May, Messer Salvestro dei Medici was made Standard-bearer of Justice, and he proposed a renewal of the orders of justice that excluded members of the nobility from serving in the government.[58] After having proposed this measure several times without success, Messer Salvestro stood proudly erect before the council and said that, since he saw that the people of Florence had been abandoned by their government, he

---

58 Salvestro, a member of the famous Medici family, commoners who had become rich merchants, was opposed by the leaders of the Guelph party and the upper classes, and supported by the guilds and the working classes. He would play a leading role in the tumultuous events of 1378, especially the Revolt of the Ciompi.

was going to resign from office and return to his home. When he began to leave by the stairs, he was asked to return; and finally the measure was passed. After this, the Seignory forced the Council of Eighty-one[59] to restore the men who had been unjustly disenfranchised, and 57 families were restored to their former standing. While this was going on, and because Messer Salvestro wished it to be so, certain proletarian leaders rose up and burned down the houses of 20 citizens who had played a leading role in disenfranchising their fellow citizens. Then things calmed down for a while, but the situation was quite unstable.

At the beginning of July, Messer Luigi Guicciardini took office as Standard-bearer of Justice. This seemed a bad sign to the Eight on War, who incited many citizens, especially the working classes, to stir things up. This plot was discovered, and Nicolò Cini was arrested; he accused the Eight on War of sedition, and was beheaded. At this point, the proletariat rose up. They held several assemblies, and finally they all went to the palace of Messer Stefano di Broye, canon of the cathedral. A large crowd gathered there, and some of the members of the Seignory came out onto the square, showing a certain amount of resistance. The crowd threatened to throw them to the ground and to drag the members of their families into the square and tear them limb from limb before their eyes. After these and other dire threats had been made, in the end the members of the Seignory left by a side exit and went home. Then a labourer named Michele di Lando rose up, and ruled Florence for three days, sending roving bands of men all around the city.[60] During this time, leaders of the guilds were made members of the Seignory; a third of the members were workers and minor artisans and members of the guilds. And the Standard-bearer of Justice, Michele di Lando, was a wool carder. All this time, the workers kept looting and burning houses. The entrances to houses were blocked, and at night lamps burned in every window. But not being content with this, after having many of their number made members of the government, the workers sent two ambassadors[61] to the Seignory and asked for three days to be able to loot and do whatever

---

59 The Eighty-one included the members of the Seignory and the Colleges, the Captains of the Guelph party, the Eight on Security, the Six on Commerce, and the twenty-one consuls of the guilds.

60 Michele di Lando was a member of the Florentine proletariat; he was a wool carder by profession. He was acclaimed Standard-bearer of Justice by the people on 21 July 1378, and held complete power until the new governors were instated on 25 July.

61 Marco di Ser Salvi Gai and Domenico di Tuccio, both members of "the Eight Saints."

they wanted and to burn the Chamber of the city as they had burned all of the documents of the Wool Guild. At that point, the Standard-bearer of Justice could take no more, and he struck them with a rapier and had them arrested and beheaded. Then he rode out on horseback carrying the standard and pursued the rebellious workers and drove them out.

Then the artisans took over the government, and ruled for forty-two months. The members of the Seignory were assigned in this way: a craftsman was always the Standard-bearer of Justice, and the members of the Seignory were half skilled and unskilled craftsmen; their leaders were Messer Giorgio degli Scali and Messer Tommaso di Marco degli Strozzi; Messer Benedetto degli Alberti also played a role.[62] They burned the houses of many leading citizens, and beheaded many, including Messer Donato Barbadoro, Messer Jacopo Sacchetti, Messer Gregorio di Pagnozzo de' Tornaquinci, and many other prominent citizens. They also drove out many important men, and in general kept the citizens of Florence in great fear and dread. They had many spies all over Florence, who robbed and spied day and night. You couldn't invite anyone to dine at your home or socialize in any way, or you would be held in abomination by the Eight. They did so many strange things that Messer Benedetto stopped playing along, and wanted nothing more to do with them; this drove them to commit even greater enormities. And among the last was when one of their informers, called Scatizza, had been arrested for robbery. Messer Giorgio wanted him to be released, and since the Captain did not want to release him, Giorgio had the walls of the prison scaled at night and removed Scatizza by force. Everyone thought this was very bad. Seeing how arrogant Giorgio and the others had become, four members of the Seignory, including Filippo di Ser Giovanni, decided to overthrow the government. They took away the keys and the seal and the standard from the Standard-bearer of Justice (who at that time was Antonio di Bese Busini, who was not to be trusted) and they asked the Captain of the People to arrest Messer Giorgio and to behead him in place of Scatizza. Messer Giorgio was told about this, but he refused to step down. He was arrested at the door of his home and taken before the Captain. When Antonio di Bese heard of this, he began to make a great fuss and said that he had been betrayed, but that he was going to sound the bell and bring out the standard, because he didn't want a hair of Messer Giorgio's head to be touched. Filippo di Ser Giovanni was sitting on the keys, and

---

62 All belonged to old families that were enemies of the Guelph party.

said: "Yes, if you can!" When Antonio saw that the game was up and that all of his carrying on was ridiculous, he unwillingly agreed to what the others wanted. Messer Giorgio was beheaded, and Messer Tommaso di Marco fled, and Messer Donato de' Rico's head was chopped off, and several other of their followers were beheaded. The government changed in the Year of Our Lord 1381. A vote was taken, and the first Standard-bearer of Justice was Messer Rinaldo Gianfigliazzi. Many of the votes that had been taken before were poorly timed. So Messer Benedetto degli Alberti, wanting to have a good, stable government for the Guelphs, as a wise, practical man established a new system of voting; and we still have and will always have that system. That is a sign that he did this out of love for good men and the Guelph party.

The government remained stable until 1387; then Messer Filippo Magalotti was chosen as Standard-bearer of Justice and Messer Benedetto was chosen Standard-bearer of one of the military companies. This election seemed suspicious, and Messer Benedetto and some of his associates were sent into exile. Then Bardo Mancini was chosen as Standard-bearer of Justice, and after his period of service he was given a vessel made of silver, gilded and enamelled and ornate, filled with new florins. This gift was brought to him at the New Market by a page mounted on horseback, with trumpets sounding. Messer Benedetto, as I have said, went into exile, and later he went to Mount Sinai, where the remains of St Catherine are buried. He died in Rhodes with all of his entourage, except for a single footman.

How the Count of Vertus Betrayed Messer Bernabò, Put Him in Prison, and Had Him Killed

At this time – that is, around 1388 or so – Gian Galeazzo Visconti, the Count of Vertus, traitorously invited Messer Bernabò to a banquet he was giving.[63] Bernabò started out for the banquet, all unsuspecting, and the Count started out with more than five hundred armed men on horseback. A man they called Medicina told Messer Bernabò: "Sire, take care, for the Count has more than five hundred horsemen with him and is

---

63 The first wife of Gian Galeazzo Visconti (1351–1402) was Isabelle of France, the daughter of John the Good; the county of Vertus was part of her dowry, from which Gian Galeazzo took the title of "Count of Vertus." Bernabò died in 1385, in the castle of Trezzo d'Adda.

coming to take you to prison." Bernabò laughed and said: "It cannot be true; it's just that the Count is a self-important man – that is why he comes here in this way." They met on the road; the Count came up to Bernabò and greeted him warmly. Then some men came up to where the Count and Bernabò were and said: "Sire, you are the prisoner of the Count of Vertus!" Disturbed, Bernabò said: "My son, why are you doing this to me? I have only your good at heart, and everything I have is yours. Don't do what no one in our family has ever done, and become a traitor!" The Count replied: "You need to go to prison, because you have tried to have me killed several times." And he took Bernabò to Pavia and put him in the castle there and had him well guarded until he could take control of everything; then he had him poisoned. Messer Bernabò was the Count's uncle as well as his father-in-law; the Count was truly an evil man to be capable of doing something like this. He dressed like a Franciscan monk, carried a rosary, and acted very benevolent toward his men, all with the aim of ingratiating himself with Messer Bernabò's people. But he also showed great friendship toward Bernabò's enemies, especially in Florence. Thus he was able easily to take over everything that had been his. Bernabò's sons tried to flee, but the Count had them captured and imprisoned.

There was great rejoicing in Florence, for Messer Bernabò was our enemy. But certain wise men said: "We are rejoicing about our own misfortune, for these men are one as bad as the other, and they are both our enemies." Then the Count maliciously plotted to get the lords of Padua and Verona to make war against one another, pretending to give his support to each of them.[64] Finally, when they were both worn down and battered, he attacked them, first capturing Verona and then Padua. Shortly afterward, he had a son, and sent word to Florence that he wanted him to be baptized; the Florentine government sent Messer Maso degli Albizzi,[65] and had the child baptized; he was named Giovanni Maria. Then the Count formed a league with Florence, Siena, and Perugia.

After building up an army and preparing himself well for battle, in 1390 the Count turned on us, and waged war against us continuously for two years. During that time, the thirteen thousand florins in capital

---

64 Francesco da Carrara was lord of Padua, and Antonio della Scala was lord of
    Verona. Verona fell to Visconti on 17 October 1387; after the armistice of 21 Novem-
    ber 1388, Padua was ruled by a Visconti lord, Jacopo del Verme, who took power on
    18 December.

65 Maso degli Albizzi was a strong personality who, with Niccolò da Uzzano and Gino
    Capponi, dominated Florentine politics for a quarter of a century.

that Morello and I had managed to save got eaten into, between money we had to pay out for forced loans, interest, and land and titles to public loans that we were forced to sell. Florence spent a great deal on this war, but the Count spent two million florins. We always fought our enemy in Lombardy, keeping camps in Siena and Pisa. We had the Duke of Bavaria come as a mercenary captain with more than five thousand cavalry, and paid him more than a hundred thousand florins. But then he betrayed us and left with the money. Then we called in the Count of Armagnac with more than ten thousand cavalry, and because of his mad folly he was routed by Filippo da Pisa and Antonio Balestracci and others the moment he arrived in the city of Alessandria in Piedmont;[66] and the Florentine state paid him 200 thousand florins or more. If one of these two mercenary captains had fought full force, the Duke would have been undone. Padua was won back in this war.[67]

Peace was made in 1392, thanks to the great master of Rhodes and the Genoese; the treaty was signed in Genoa. Wise men believe (and this has been amply borne out by experience) that if peace had not been made then and the war had continued even for a few more months, we would have totally undone Gian Galeazzo, the Count of Vertus, because he was worn out and had no money and all of his men were furious with him. They had been promised a great deal of money, but he couldn't pay them; so they would have been forced to leave him and we could have had them at a good price. After this war, in which he accomplished great things, Sir John Hawkwood died on 17 March 1394.[68]

How the Alberti Were Driven out of Florence, and the Bad Situation for Many

After peace had been made, the following year – that is, 1393 – there was turmoil in Florence. Messer Maso degli Albizzi was Standard-bearer of Justice and Messer Rinaldo Gianfigliazzi was a member of the Twelve. It is said that there was a plot going on – Messer Cipriano and Alberto

---

66 This famous battle took place on 25 July 1391; the Gascon mercenary soldiers led by Jean d'Armagnac in the service of Florence were routed by the tactics of Jacopo del Verme, as Ariosto wrote in *Orlando Furioso* XXXIII, 22.

67 That is, it was freed from the Visconti domination by Francesco da Carrara, on 21 June 1390 (the peace treaty was concluded in January 1392).

68 The great English soldier of fortune, whom the Italians called Giovanni Acuto, is the subject of the equestrian monument painted by Paolo Uccello for Florence Cathedral in 1436.

Grasso degli Alberti were arrested, and ran the risk of being executed. The Alberti had become very important, and several were sent into exile. The Ricci, the Medici, the Cavicciuli, and other families that had come up from the ranks were under suspicion. Many families of magnates enrolled in the guilds in order to have the rank of commoners, so that they could hold office. Nerozzo and Alberto were sent into exile to Flanders, and Messer Cipriano was sent to Rhodes for 20 years; and they had to pay fines, amounting to 3 thousand gold florins, I believe. Then it was ordered that six thousand men, citizens and Guelphs, should put on white over-garments called "togas" with the coat of arms of the people of Florence on the front and back, and in the quarter they should only wear the coat-of-arms of the Guelph party. A good number complied, but nothing came of it. Then six hundred men gathered in the square – 400 Genoese soldiers with crossbows who were paid 6 florins per month, and 200 men armed with large shields and lances. Then many of the members of all of the great families – the most prominent and powerful – enrolled in the guilds in order to become commoners. The Council of Eighty-one was given power for 5 years, thanks to Messer Viviano Viviani's efforts – they could raise money and draft soldiers. Then a vote was taken, called the Vote of '93. The names of whoever was at least thirty years old and who had been candidates in 1381, 1391, and 1393 were placed in three purses; the names of those who were younger than 30 years old and had been candidates in 1391 and 1393 were placed in two purses. The voting was very close, and mostly honest. The results were accepted by all the citizens, although certain members of the working class and some members of the Guelph party were cheated because they were under suspicion. We were among the ones who were seriously cheated, because of our ties to the Alberti family, which many of our evil neighbours knew about. But may God make it clear who is a Guelph and who is not.

The Birth of Paolo di Morello

A son was born to Morello di Paolo in the Year of Our Lord 1393, on the 22nd day of February at the 14th hour, on a Sunday. He was given the name Paolo Giuliano. He was baptized in the Baptistry of San Giovanni (his godmother was Monna Sandra, the wife of Jacopo Arnolfi and the nurse of Catelana, her mother) on the 24th of February of that same year, on the feast day of St Matthew the Apostle.

*How We Left the Neighbourhood of Santa Croce on Account of the
Terrible Pressure from Our Neighbours, etc.*

In the year of Our Lord 1394, Morello and Giovanni and I left the neighbourhood of Santa Croce and the district of the Black Lion, with all of our families, and went to a house in the district of the Cart that belonged to Stefano di Vanni Castellani. We had to get out of the district of the Black Lion on account of the public loans that were being forced upon us. At that time, Messer Donato Acciaiuoli was Standard-bearer of Justice, and he ordered that the forced loans should be managed in the following way: there should be votes on sixty men in three groups of twenty, and each group of twenty should lend money equivalent to all of their lands; then the highest and lowest numbers should be discarded, and the middle sum would be the amount of the loan. And each man should lend money according to the district in which he lived. We were advised by Jacopo Arnolfi to move to the district of the Cart; by doing this, we reduced the amount of gold florins that we had to lend to the government from eighty to twenty-eight. Piero di Jacopo Barconcelli was in the first group of twenty. Everyone met in the palace of the Guelph party, and we estimated that we owed less than twenty-eight florins. In the second group was Messer Michele di Vanni; that group met in Orsanmichele. The third group included Messer Antonio di Attaviano Gherardini as a magnate and Salvestro di Michele Nardi. Among the men in this group we were greatly favoured by Antonio di Attaviano, at the request of his brother-in-law, Jacopo Arnolfi. We remained in that palace for about twenty-two months, and during this time the amount of money that the *gonfaloni* had to give to the government was changed, and the tax was increased by two-thirds, so we ended up having to lend about thirty-six florins. Because this was obscenely onerous for us, we petitioned the Seignory and we were allowed to pay a third at first, and on another occasion half, and that is how we paid.

The Birth of Matteo di Morello

Morello had a second son on the vigil of the calends of May in the Year of Our Lord 1395, at the eighth hour of the night, on a Friday. He was given the names Matteo Filippo Jacopo, and was baptized on the 2nd day of May. His godparents were Monna Telda, the mother of Morello, and two other women.

Of the First Woman Whom Giovanni Morelli Took to Wife

On the fifteenth day of December 1395, I, Giovanni di Paolo Morelli, became betrothed to Caterina, the daughter of Alberto di Luigi degli Alberti; the middlemen were Messer Lotto Castellani and Agnolo Ricoveri. I got a dowry with her of a thousand florins (the document was drawn up by Ser Michele Aldobrandini, who lives in Porta Rossa). I married her on the 27th of January at our property near San Gaggio. I think that this marriage greatly diminished my honour and my prospects in the government; I would have done better if I had married into another family. I believe that God determines the day that the man and woman are born who are destined to marry. I say this because originally I had agreed to marry another woman, and in the hopes of being with her I lost out on the opportunity to make many advantageous connections that I could have made. The father of that woman betrayed me; he had promised me her hand in marriage, via an intermediary, and later he shook my hand in the church of Santa Croce, and I shook his. He did this because he believed that it would be to his advantage. I ended up suffering greatly because of this, because I loved the woman and had wanted to make her my wife from the time that she was very young. Later I came to realize that rather than a misfortune, this was a great boon from God and from St Catherine – who, on account of the great devotion I have for her, I begged to bring about what was most advantageous for me and for my family and for my soul. And I truly believe that she heard my prayer, as unworthy as I am. So I am content with what she granted me, and I hope that I will continue to derive the benefit that one can hope for in this world; I believe that it all turned out for the best. As far as my betrayal by a man whom I believed to be honourable goes, I have seen and continue to see that he and his family have been punished for it to the greatest degree; and it all is a result of his betrayal. I am sorry for it, and have beseeched God on several occasions to forgive him for that sin and others he has committed.

The Banishment of Messer Donato Acciaiuoli

That same year, 1395, on the 12th of January, the Seignory, the Colleges, and the Six on Commerce[69] and the Eight on Security[70] ordered that

---

69 The high commercial court in Florence.
70 A magistracy responsible for internal security.

Messer Donato Acciaiuoli should be sent into permanent exile in the town of Barletta, in Apulia. This was done because Messer Donato was working with several other citizens and had proposed that a petition be made to the Seignory to the effect that the members of the Guelph party who had been wronged during the unrest in 1393 because they were suspected of evil intentions or for some other unjust reason should be fully reinstated as citizens and their honour restored. And because those who held power believed that Messer Donato was doing this to bring them down (and indeed it was so), they sought a remedy to the situation; and being unable to dissuade him from his purpose, they defamed him before the Seignory and the Eight, saying that he wanted to overthrow the government and subvert the state and put himself in power. The members of the Seignory, wanting to prevent this, called in twelve citizens to see to the peace and tranquillity of the city and the preservation of the government; and Messer Donato was among these twelve. At last, they met together, but because Messer Donato was among them, no one dared to say anything. The Seignory continued to put pressure on them to do something, and I believe that it was Messer Francesco Rucellai who said: "We cannot do anything, because the one who started the problem is in our midst." So a pretext was found to get Messer Donato into another chamber; and finally, when the Eight on Security had learned everything about the affair, Agnolo, the son of Nicolò Ricoveri (who was Standard-bearer of Justice at the time) went before the Seignory and denounced Messer Donato, saying that he had said that if his petition were not granted he would find some way to get around it in order to obtain his aim. Because of this testimony, Messer Donato was condemned to exile.

Of the Death of Messer Piero Gambacorta

Around this time, or perhaps a little earlier, Messer Jacopo d'Appiano, Chancellor of the Republic of Pisa, gave the order that Messer Piero Gambacorta[71] and two of his sons were to be slain by sword, along with some other Pisans. Word of this got back to Florence, and the Seignory warned Messer Piero about it. Messer Piero believed that the Seignory had done this to undermine Messer Jacopo, who was an enemy of Florence. He committed the error of showing the letter from the Seignory to Messer Jacopo himself, who said it was not true. But he said that he

---

71 A Pisan sympathetic to Florence, who was the ruler of Pisa at this time.

wanted to avenge himself against Messer Giovanni Rosso, so he had sent
to Carfagnana for some soldiers. At last, when the soldiers arrived, he
had them kill Messer Giovanni Lanfranchi. Then, when there was an out-
cry, Messer Jacopo rode with a large group of armed men to the home of
Messer Piero. Messer Piero, whom they found at the door of his home,
cried out to Messer Jacopo: "O friend, what is this that you want to do?"
Messer Jacopo replied: "I want to save our homeland!" and he ordered
his men to slay Piero. And in the end Messer Jacopo became captain and
lord of Pisa and built a citadel there. And the rest of the members of the
Gambacorta family fled to Florence. Messer Jacopo was never able to
come to any kind of agreement with us; he offered us every possible kind
of deal, but we never trusted him, though he said that he wanted peace
between us and that we could trust him.

In the year 1395 a company of approximately a thousand lancers was
created, led by Lodovico Cantelli, Filippo da Pisa, and Messer Bartolomeo da Prato.[72] The company was formed when a few citizens petitioned
the government of Florence. It was said that the Gambacorta family were
the instigators; and in truth, they gave two thousand florins and were
in the area of Pisa for a certain period of time. Messer Jacopo was very
suspicious of the affair, and always kept an armed guard. This company
harassed him a great deal, but not as much as they could or should have.
For it was believed that if they had gone to Pisa sooner, they would have
overthrown the government led by Messer Jacopo. But it is true (and I
heard this from someone who had been one of the Priors at the time,
who saw it all) that Messer Bartolomeo da Prato informed Messer Jacopo
of everything that was going on. Money changed hands. And because the
traitorous Jacopo saw that he could not conceal his error, he denounced
Lodovico and said that he was the traitor. Lodovico was not allowed to
come and plead his case, as he wanted to do; and this was ordered by the
friends of Messer Bartolomeo.

The Second War with the Count of Vertus

After the armed Gambacorta faction went to Pisa, as I recounted above,
the Pisans complained to the Count of Vertus about this offence, and he
decided to take vengeance on us. He assembled his soldiers, including

---

72 Bartolomeo di Gherardaccio da Prato, called Boccanera, was one of the most famous
    military leaders of the time; he later became supreme commander of the Florentine
    armed forces.

twelve thousand cavalry, who were led by the great constable Count Alberico da Barbiano, along with Messer Jacopo dal Verme, Count Giovanni da Barbiano, Messer Ottobuono the Third, Facino Cane, Messer Antonio Balestracci, Messer Cione da Siena, Messer Jacopo dalla Croce, and several others.[73] There were in all sixteen or eighteen valiant captains, the lowest-ranked of whom had more than 150 lancers; they were all men of great fame and repute. They gathered together and went to Siena in the Year of Our Lord 1396, in the month of January, and stayed there more than two months. Then on March 20, they rode into our territory and fought for several days in the area of Rincine, where they destroyed all of the walls with bombards. The inhabitants put up a brave defence. Then they went to Val di Greve and fought on the land belonging to Gianpaolo da Panzano for several days. The son, or rather the nephew of the great constable died there. The fortress was a tower, and there were a hundred people within; there was little water, and they surrendered after a few days. The soldiers stole a great deal of what was inside the fortress. Then they burned Mercatale di Greve, and went from there to Beccamorto and to Santa Maria Impruneta, and camped for the night on the slopes of Pozzolatico, at the mouth of the Greve River. The great Constable realized that this was a bad place, and it seemed to him a thousand years before the dawn came and they could depart. The next day they proceeded to Galluzzo and Marignolla and Sofiano and then went down to Monticelli. They made camp at Lastra a Signa. Their runners went as far as San Gaggio. They did not destroy anything by fire at Colombaia and San Sepolcro; but certain men who had been banished by us destroyed the property of their enemies. Some of the Pisans who were in the company, and the members of the brigade of Count Giovanni da Barbiano, also did damage. Count Giovanni believed that he had been injured by our government in a war that had been waged in Romagna between Astorre Manfredi, the Lord of Faenza, Azzo d'Este of Ferrara, and himself. We had fought against Count Giovanni in that conflict, and had done him considerable harm.

When they got to Lastra a Signa, they were starting to run low on provisions, so they decided to fight, for they realized that there were many provisions there, and there was a good place to make camp nearby. They crossed the bridge, and this meant that the Ten on War had not planned

---

73 Among all of these soldiers of fortune, the most famous were the Lombard Jacopo dal Verme; the brothers Giovanni and Alberico da Barbiano (1344–1409); and Facino Cane (circa 1355–1412).

well; if they had had the bridge cut off, the enemy forces would not
have been able to cross there, for the waters of the Arno River were very
high. The Constable's forces attacked the fortress at Signa several times;
the inhabitants there defended themselves well. It happened that there
were several citizens of Florence inside the fortress, who gave orders, and
were obeyed; among others, Tomaso Rucellai was there. The Constable's
troops remained there for several days, and attempted to scale the walls
of the fortress. The ladders were knocked down and the banner of the
great Constable was captured and also the banner of Messer Brogliole,
who was among the company. Many men were killed or wounded. The
fortress received reinforcements, for one night Fabrizio da Perugia, one
of our soldiers, entered there with twenty-five cavalry. The enemy broke
camp; and because they were low on food, horseshoes, and other things,
they decided to return to Siena. As they were retreating, they passed
through San Casciano; and at Sant'Andrea in Percussina, they captured
two maidens of marriageable age, daughters of Ghiandone Machiavelli,
who had taken refuge in an old tower. One was taken by Count Giovanni
and the other by Conselice; it is said that he made her his wife. After
they had returned to Siena, they could never agree again to venture into
our territory, so they stayed there for a while, and rode into Colle and to
San Gimignano and many other places in the vicinity. Our government
hired Captain Bernardone for this war, and we took Biordo Michelotti da
Perugia away from the Duke of Milan. We had Paolo Orsini, Count Ugo,
Antonio degli Obizzi and many other *condottieri*, and about two thousand
lancers. When the Duke learned how little damage had been done to us,
and that he had not gained anything, he was very displeased and called
many of his men back to Lombardy.

So we sent large numbers of men to Lombardy, because we were in
league with Francesco Gonzaga, the Lord of Mantua. The war moved
to Mantua, where the Duke of Milan destroyed the bridge over the Po
River, which cost our government 20 thousand florins. He had the bridge
burned down by his military engineer Maestro Domenico da Firenze[74]
and passed the first and second barricades and captured several fortresses.
For several days he fought at Governolo, which resisted well. Francesco
Gonzaga knew that if he did not succeed in resisting, Mantua would be
lost; so he held firm. The fortification was greatly battered by the enemy's

---

74 Domenico da Firenze was one of the most famous military engineers of the time;
    he was in the service of Gian Galeazzo Sforza. He died during the siege of Reggio in
    1409, struck by a bombard.

bombards, but whatever got broken, they repaired it overnight. Feeling that he was in extreme straits, Gonzaga asked for help from his allies the Venetians, who arrived by sea; and they succeeded in defeating the Duke's galleons. And then Carlo Malatesta[75] broke up the Duke's camp, and it was said that a better equipped camp had never been seen. It was said that if Carlo had pursued them, he would have brought the Duke down. But he did not wish to do this; it was sufficient that he had freed his brother-in-law from the war with the Duke. It was estimated that the Duke spent 200 thousand florins on the large number of bombards used, plus large provisions of wine, grain, and fodder and weapons and lumber and tools and other things with which his army was amply supplied. Once this had happened, our ambassadors and those of the Duke, who were in Venice negotiating a peace agreement, began to get along better. Francesco Gonzaga made peace with the Duke and entered into an alliance with him, breaking with us. He did this because he felt that the war had happened on account of us and he would have liked us to assume all the responsibility and compensate him for all of his damages. But we neither should nor could have done that. For this reason, he broke off his friendship with us and allied himself with the Duke, who returned to him control of certain waters that he had taken away from him. Messer Filippo di Messer Alamanno, Messer Lodovico d'Arezzo, and Guido di Messer Tommaso went to Venice to negotiate the peace agreement on behalf of our government. A truce was reached on the 11th of May 1398.

At the beginning of this war, or a little before, Messer Maso degli Albizzi went as our ambassador to Paris, and made an alliance with the King of France. The agreement was that we would give the King a thousand lancers for his wars, and he would give us the royal standard for ours. The news of this misguided agreement reached us on the 20th of October 1396. The members of the Seignory (Messer Forese Salviati was then Standard-bearer of Justice) descended to the railing with the members of the Colleges and their followers, each with an olive branch, and a bell was rung to announce the alliance.

The Birth of My Son Alberto

During the aforementioned war, on Saturday the 10th of March, between 18 and 19 hours in the year of Our Lord 1396, my wife Caterina

---

75 Carlo Malatesta, the lord of Rimini, became governor of Milan at the death of Gian
    Galeazzo Visconti. He was a faithful *condottiere* of the Church's army.

gave birth to our son Alberto; he was born in the home of the Aliso family.[76] He was baptized on the thirteenth of the month in the Baptistry of San Giovanni in Florence. His godparents were Filipozzo di Nicolò Capponi, Marignano di Pepo Buondelmonte, Antonio di Vanni Ricoveri, and Giuliano di Tomaso di Guccio. He was given the names Alberto and Giovanni; later, when he made his confirmation, his sponsor was Antonia, his nurse. I had him registered in the Wool Guild on 19 December 1405.[77]

The Birth of Tomaso di Morello

The third son of Morello Morelli was born on the 22nd December 1397; he was baptized in San Giovanni and given the names Tomaso and Francesco on Sunday morning, the 24th of that month. His godparents were Monna Telda, Bobi del Guercio, and Antonia, my son Alberto's nurse.

How the Count of Vertus Became Duke of Milan

The Count of Vertus, who was called Giovanni di Messer Galeazzo Visconti, became Duke of Milan in the year of Our Lord 1395. On that occasion, our government sent three citizens – Messer Rinaldo di Giannozzo Gianfigliazzi, Messer Maso di Luca degli Albrizzi, and Messer Cristofano d'Anfrione degli Spini. The government provided each man with robes of silk and woven gold, and each was accompanied by four young men (each of whom received sixty florins for clothing) and numerous servants with trumpets and fifes. Their pack horses were covered with caparisons with the coats of arms of Florence and the Guelph party. The ambassadors and their retinue had more than sixty horses among them – it was the most lavish embassy of all that were sent for the occasion, and the most honoured by the Duke. Next in honour was the embassy sent by the Venetians. The festivities were as grand as they could be. The morning that they departed from Milan, our ambassadors presented the robes to the Duke's court, and they were the most lavish – twice as fine as any of the others.

---

76 Because of the difficulties he was in, up to the year 1404 Giovanni's children were born in other people's homes, as the Morelli family did not have a home of their own.

77 Alberto Morelli could be enrolled in the Wool Guild while he was still a child, because his father was already a member.

The Birth of Antoniotto di Giovanni

Giovanni's second son was born on the twenty-fourth day of December, between the eighth and ninth hour, in the palace of the Spini family. The baby was born prematurely, at seven months; and because he was very tiny and weak, they thought he might not live, so they had him baptized the same day in San Giovanni, giving him the names Antoniotto and Jacopo. His godparents were my mother, Monna Telda, and Morello's wife, Catelana. He received the sacrament of Confirmation on Holy Monday, the 9th of April 1403; his sponsor was Antonia, Alberto's nurse. On Sunday the 13th of July 1421, he passed from this life, at the 19th hour, in the inn at Empoli. His body was brought to Florence and buried in the family tomb.

How the Duke of Milan Became Lord of Pisa

After the death of Messer Jacopo d'Appiano, his son Messer Gherardo became captain of Pisa. And because Gherardo was a man of little worth and paltry reputation, he feared he would not be able to keep control of Pisa; so he tried to sell the city to the Duke of Milan. It is believed that he did this on the advice of his father, for Gherardo barely knew the Duke. Word of this got back to Florence, and an ambassador was sent secretly to Gherardo to try to dissuade him from this plan, offering him assistance from our government whenever he needed it, and asking him if he wanted to sell Pisa to us, offering him twice the price that he would get from the Duke. He replied that it was not true that he was trying to sell Pisa to the Duke, and that he wished to be a friend and brother to the Florentines, etcetera. And yet he continued to negotiate with the Duke, and, having reached an agreement with him, he went about surveying the land. Then, on the 19th of February 1399, he turned the city over to the Duke, or rather to his proxy.[78] Gherardo was supposed to receive two hundred thousand florins, plus the town of Piombino and the island of Elba, along with certain fortresses that belong to the county of Piombino. What he got was a hundred twenty thousand florins and a cap of the Duke's that was worth fifteen thousand florins or less; he was given this as pledge for the remaining eighty thousand florins. Later, Messer

---

78 Antonio Porro.

Gherardo demanded the money; the Duke laughed in his face and
threatened to harm him unless he remained content with what he had
got. So Messer Gherardo began to scorn him a little. The Duke placed
in the citadel at Pisa five hundred lancers and a large number of foot
soldiers, who were under the command of Messer Antonio Balestracci.
Then he dressed all of the Pisans, or most of them, in fine clothes; and
they all marched in a procession and solemnly celebrated the new government. Then he sent for all of the Pisans who had left the city, and returned their property to the ones who pledged obedience to him. Some
he kept in Lombardy, assigning them certain offices according to their
status. He also called some away from Pisa, offering them positions in
Lombardy as rectors or captains of citadels.

How Siena Went to the Duke

When the Sienese saw that the Duke had become the new lord of Pisa,
they were advised by his people to do the same, for their own well-being.
And so the men in Siena whom the Duke trusted most advanced the
proposal that they should freely give their city to him, showing by many
false arguments that this would be their salvation. It did not take them
long to convince everyone that this was the best course to take. Once
they had made the decision, they sent a large number of ambassadors
from every walk of life – gentlemen, men of the people, artisans – and
the Duke received them with honour. They explained that the people
and the government of Siena wished to give the city and county of
Siena freely to him, and they drew up the documents with a full mandate
to this effect. He accepted, and gave them all rose-coloured garments.
This happened on the 3rd of August 1399. They had solemn processions
and great festivities. It was not necessary to build a citadel, because the
Sienese had given themselves freely to the Duke so he did not need to
worry about them turning on him.

The Duke Becomes Lord of Perugia

The Perugians followed the example of the Sienese and decided to give
themselves to the Duke. In an attempt to prevent this, delegations were
sent several times both to Perugia and to the Pope, trying to bring them
to an agreement whereby they would go under the dominion of the Pope
rather than of the Duke. As middlemen and in order to move the thing
along, we lent thirteen thousand florins to the Perugians, who gave the

money to the Pope to make amends for certain damages; they promised to repay us within a certain period of time. These agreements did not last long, because the Perugians were very suspicious, especially about what would happen to their citizens in exile. So in the end they decided to give themselves to the Duke, because he had enticed them a great deal; he told them of the many perils that threatened them, and made them many offers. So they gave in to the advice of the Duke rather than that of the government of Florence, for they distrusted us. Once they had made the decision, things went as they had gone for the Sienese, and they handed over their territory to the Duke. He showered them with rose-coloured garments and other fabrics, according to their rank. He took over the government on the 21st of January 1399. He did not build another fortress at Perugia, because he considered them to be his old friends, brothers of the Sienese. He offered posts in Lombardy to the Perugians who had gone into exile, leading them to hope that he would allow them to return to Perugia, but he never did this.

How Many of Our Allies Rebelled

Around this time it came to pass that certain important men, friends of our government, came together and began to turn against Florence. These included Andreino degli Ubertini, Count Guido di Bagno, Bustaccio and Ciapettino degli Ubertini, Count Rupert da Poppi, Count Antonio da Palagio, and Count Antonio da Urbino. All of the Ghibellines were gravitating toward the Duke, for they believed that we Guelphs would be defeated by him. This was all after the second war, during the time of peace or rather the truce that was brokered between him and us. I believe that the truce lasted 10 years, with the agreement that whichever side violated it would have to pay 100 thousand florins. And I believe that later, when the treaty was in danger of being violated, peace was reached again in order not to have to pay the penalty. The Lord of Cortona also turned against us; but we were fortunate to capture one of his fortresses, and were able to pressure him to come to an agreement again with our government, so that he could get his fortress back. After that, he remained our firm ally.

Birth of Lionello di Giovanni

Saturday night, on the 12th day of June 1400, between the fifth and the sixth hour, Giovanni's third son was born, in the Spini palace. He was baptized the following Sunday morning, and given the name Lionello Francesco. He passed from this life on the 3rd of August of the same year; he was laid to rest in the church of the Holy Trinity, in the Spini family sepulchre. There was a plague in Florence that year; about twenty thousand or more people died. Morello was *podestà* of the city of Massa at this time; Alberto and two of his boys and his wife and I remained there with him there until the 7th of June. Then I went to Volterra and stayed for 40 days; Caterina joined me there. Then the plague began, and we returned to Settimello, where we stayed until the feast of All Saints; we remained healthy, thanks be to God. Two of Morello's children died, and one of mine. May God bless them!

Birth of Bernardo di Morello

The evening of the feast of All Saints, well into the night, in the year of our Lord 1400, Morello's fourth son was born at Settimello. When the epidemic died down, he was baptized in the parish church of San Donato, in Calenzano. His godparents were Andrea di Fico and some of the women who worked for Morello. He was given the name Bernardo, after the Bernardo di Giovanni Morelli who had died in that plague on the 2nd of August 1400. Bernardo di Giovanni was buried in the church of San Jacopo, where his wife, Monna Simona, had been buried earlier.

Of the Death of Count Rupert da Poppi

During this same epidemic, Count Rupert da Poppi died, and among others he named the government of Florence in his will. He did this because his men had advised him to do so. In truth, he again became loyal to the city of Florence at the end of his life simply because he knew he was dying – not on account of any true affection or loyalty that he might have had for our city. He treated Count Francesco like a son, having completely forgotten all of the injuries that his evil father had perpetrated, turning against our government for no good reason.

Of the Plot Hatched at Bologna in 1400

During the plague of 1400, most Florentines fled to Bologna, where a plot was hatched against many important citizens of Florence. The conspiracy was discovered on the 12th of November 1400. Sanminiato di Gucciozzo was arrested, and revealed the whole plot, giving evidence against his brother Ardingo, Antonio di Giovanni di Cambio de' Medici, Gherardo di Messere Benedetto, Bernardo di Jacopo, Altobianco di Messere Nicolaio, many members of the Alberti family, Stoldo di Simono Altoviti, Bernardo and Giovanni di Giovanni di Marco Strozzi, Checco Davizi, and many others. Sanminiato was beheaded, as was Checco Davizi. All of the others were banished as rebels. All of the Medici were put down. Later, Francesco and Giovanni de' Bicci[79] and the family of Messer Veri were reinstated. The Alberti family were banished, except for Altobianco. Later, when the others complained because he had been spared and they had not, on his last day in office (he was standard-bearer of his company), he was arrested at the Alberti villa, called il Paradiso, and was on the point of losing his life. He was accused of complicity in Gherardo's plot. This was not true, but it was used as an excuse to punish him. He was fined 3000 florins, and he would have been beheaded if he did not pay within a few days. Then he was banished as a rebel. All of the other members of the Alberti family over the age of 16 were sentenced to banishment within two hundred miles of Florence. And any male of the family who was born in Florence had to leave once he reached the age of sixteen, going within 200 miles of Florence. Altobianco was sentenced to exile within 300 miles of the city.

Of an Uprising in Florence by Certain Exiles Who Wanted to Overthrow the State

Before the aforementioned treaty was signed and after Messer Donato was expelled – that is, on the 4th of August 1397 – a plot was discovered. (I forgot to record this earlier, in the proper place; but in order that it should not be forgotten, I will mention it briefly here.) That day, after dinner, at almost eighteen hours, a group of eight men who had been banished emerged from the home of a certain shearer named Antonio di Pepo Caicciuli, where they had been staying for several days to hatch their plot. Their plan was to kill Messer Maso degli Albizzi, first of all; then they planned to raise a commotion and cry out "Power to the people and the guilds!" They planned to bring back to power those who had fallen in 1393 and overthrow those who had risen to power. Later, each one of them planned to kill certain particular enemies of theirs. As I said, there were eight of these exiled men; their names were Picchio di

---

79 Giovanni di Averardo, called Bicci, was the father of Cosimo de' Medici the Elder.

Simone di Messer Pepo Cavicciuli; Masino di Salvesto di Messere Rosso de' Ricci; Antonio di Jacopo di Monna Nicolosa de' Medici, known as the Little Bastard; Benedetto di Bartolomeo Spini, called the Blind Man; Baroncino Girolami, the brother of Azzo and Bernardo; Cristofano di Niccolò; Chiarello the junk dealer; and a certain Martino, the brother of Matteuzzo del Corso. They lay in wait for Messer Maso to leave his house, but he was not there, for he had gone to write some lines for a certain grocer. Not finding him, they went off and got drunk. Losing control of themselves, they went to the Old Market and raised a ruckus. They went among the grocers, and entered the shop of Piero da Firenze, intending to kill him. Not finding him, they killed his son, a good young man. Then they went down the street of the cloth finishers, shouting "Power to the people and to the guilds! Close your shops and follow us!" and many other things to bolster their cause. Then they came upon Fedele, the son of Messer Bartolomeo da Prato – he spoke harshly to them, telling them that they wanted to destroy Florence. They killed him there, at the entrance to the New Market. Then they turned toward the loggia of the Cavalcanti and headed toward the loggia of the Adimari,[80] and remained there for some time. While all of this was going on, men who had been disturbed by the uproar took up arms and headed toward the Palace. Several citizens reproached them; seeing that they were not being pursued, they took off. They were approaching the Via dei Servi, where they were told by Picchio Cavicciuli to turn back and wait at the cathedral, where they would receive help. They turned back, and entered the cathedral, closing the doors. A banished labourer who was with them said that he did not want to be locked up there or anyplace else, and that they were fools. He left the cathedral and went off; no one recognized him, and for this reason, he survived. The others remained inside the cathedral. The citizens and soldiers arrived, and the men surrendered. They were immediately all tied to a rope and taken to the Public Palace. Later, during the night, four were taken before the Captain of the People and four were taken to the Executor of the Orders of Justice. The following day, they were all beheaded on two tree stumps at the foot of the gate of the Rectors. Their bodies remained there a long time before they were taken away. Picchiello and Guglielmo di Campolo da Panzano were also beheaded; Salvestro and Tommaso di Messer Rosso de' Ricci, several members of the Medici family, and Leprone degli Alberti were banished.

---

80. Also called the Loggia Neghittosa or "Lazy Arcade."

Because he was a priest, Messer Alamanno was handed over to the Bishop; he was charged with participating in the conspiracy, and it was said that he had been seen carrying the insignia of the people, intending to join the uprising. His father, Messer Filippo Caviciulli, was in Venice trying to broker the peace treaty, as I wrote above. When Filippo heard what was going on in Florence and that his son had been arrested, he quickly returned and appeared before the Seignory. With cajoling entreaties, sobbing loudly, he begged them to have mercy on this son, moving to pity the members of the Seignory and the other citizens. They took into consideration the fact that he was old, and that he had been a good, loyal, and valiant gentleman, and so they returned his son to him with no impediment. Messer Alamanno left Florence and went to Rome, where he petitioned the Pope to give him the bishopric of Florence. After a long delay, the Pope gave our bishopric to someone else, and gave another bishopric to Alamanno. In think that this happened because Messer Alamanno's brother Salvestro had unwittingly revealed the conspiracy led by Sanminiato di Giucciozzo de' Ricci. But he was rewarded by the Florentine government in another way, so it all turned out well for him.

After all of the events described above, the Florentine state strengthened itself by getting rid of suspicious men, and building up the resources for protecting the state and its law-abiding citizens. Also, a larger salary and more soldiers were given to the rector charged with protecting Florence and its government. I wanted to record these events for several reasons, and chiefly so that all of our descendants can learn the lesson never to rise up against the government; they should be content to be ruled by the Seignory and to support it, especially if it is in the hands of good men from old Guelph families. For you see the harm and the shame that come from those who oppose the government.

How Giovanni Bentivoglio Became Lord of Bologna

When our citizens returned from Bologna after the plague had died down, they had changed to some degree; for the Bolognese had forged many friendships with leading Florentine citizens, and goods and gifts and flattery and such nonsense were involved. The Florentines could not see that this would be their undoing; for the supporters of the Duke of Milan wanted what he wanted, and the supporters of the Marquis of Ferrara wanted what he wanted, and the supporters of Astorgio, the Lord of Faenza, wanted what he wanted. Everyone was so stirred up, there was no peace. At a certain point, when the discord was at its height, a certain Giovanni Bentivoglio, a wise man of courageous spirit, quite daring, who was supported by a certain family called Beccherini, men of low degree, advised his fellow citizens that it was not possible for Bologna to continue in this way, and that a certain small number of citizens should bring order and peace to the land and the people; and he said other things to bolster his intentions. His supporters said that he should be the leader and that he should take certain leading citizens as his advisors, in order not to exclude them out of hand. And indeed he worked both inside and outside of Bologna so that no one objected, and he became Lord of Bologna on the 14th of March 1400. The Florentines had their doubts about Bentivoglio, because he was a friend of the Duke of Milan. He wavered for a long while between the Duke and us, and finally he allied himself to us, pledging friendship and brotherhood. And this lasted, as you shall hear, until he lost power.

The Birth of Telda di Giovanni

Saturday night, at 7:30 on the seventeenth day of September 1401, my wife Caterina gave birth to a daughter. I had her baptized on the 19th of the same month in the Baptistry of San Giovanni. I gave her the name Telda Margherita. Her godmothers were Catelana and Monna Gemma, who had been Caterina's midwife. She was born in the Spini palace. She passed from this life to a better one on the fifth day of October in the year of Our Lord 1401, at the seventh hour. I had her laid to rest with her brother in the church of Santa Trinita, in the Spini sepulchre. May God bless her.

The Election of Rupert of Bavaria to the Imperial Throne

In the year of Christ 1401, the lords of the Holy Roman Empire – that is, the electoral princes – were discouraged to see that the dignity of the realm was flagging because the one who ruled it was a worthless drunkard.[81] Fearing that they might lose the realm to the Germans, they decided to elect a new emperor; and they chose Rupert of Bavaria. He was to go to Lombardy to receive various honours, and thence to Rome,

---

81 Wenceslaus "the Idle," Duke of Luxembourg, King of the Romans (German king) from 1378 to 1400, when he was deposed.

to be crowned by the Pope. He also planned to travel to our city and to Padua, and wherever else it pleased him to go. The Lord of Padua learned of this, and because he had friends in the empire, he led us to believe that if we helped Rupert to pass through Italy, he would forge an alliance with us, which would be the undoing of the Duke of Milan, and would avenge both him and us. He so embellished this story that many Florentines believed we were home free – but not everyone did. The Lord of Padua's lies were endless. There was much conferring about this in Florence, and Aesop was the author invoked above all the rest.

It was decided to send a representative to Germany to test the waters. Andrea Salvini was the first one who went; he was familiar with the empire and knew those lords and especially Rupert of Bavaria. Once he arrived, nobody said or asked him anything except "How many hundreds of thousands of florins will we receive from the government of Florence?" Andrea would respond: "Do not waste your time demanding any amount of money, because it will show that this is all you are interested in, and the Florentines will be put off. Come to Italy with your forces, and if you succeed in defeating their enemy, you will be given florins by the bucketful without having to ask for them." But they continued to demand: "When will we get the money?" Finally, since Andrea would not tell them an amount, they said that they had letters from someone in Florence to the effect that they would be given six hundred thousand new florins. The letter was purportedly from a Florentine citizen who was in Bologna in the capacity of ambassador to Giovanni Bentivoglio; I never learned his name, but I heard the story from Andrea himself, who had seen the letter. When he returned, Andrea reproached the man for making this promise, but he denied having done it. He admitted that he had said certain things to someone, but he said that he didn't think that it would be written down, and similar pathetic excuses. To show that he was not basing his assertions on a fable, Andrea got the letter back.

Then Bonaccorso Pitti and Ser Piero da Sanminiato were sent to the Emperor in Germany. They were welcomed with great honour, and without having seen a single man on horseback, they promised a first instalment of four hundred thousand florins. Then they were joined by Andrea di Neri Vettori. This delegation wrote such miraculous things back to Florence about the Emperor's men that the Paladins of Charles the Great seemed mere lads in comparison. They were constantly writing such things, so back in Florence we were eager for the Emperor to take to the battlefield. It was at the beginning of the winter when the fighting began. The German lords thought that it would be better for them to wait to enter the conflict. We said that it would be better for them to come right away, because the snows had melted. What we didn't tell them was that in Lombardy the slush was neck deep, and that there was no fodder, nor even a hut to shelter a sheep, much less the Emperor. In short, because we wanted the Emperor to come to Italy, we told him that the moment his banners were seen in Lombardy in the mountains of Trent, all of the Duke of Milan's vassals would switch their allegiance, for they were only waiting for his arrival. Andrea di Neri, who wanted part of the money to be sent to the new Emperor at once, wrote to his son Neri that he had never seen such noble lords nor such wonderful people, and that the Emperor was supported by many lords, each of whom had many more armed forces than the Emperor himself. He said that they had forty thousand cavalry, not counting carriages – the most magnificent men who had ever been seen, with superb heads of hair. He wrote that he had seen such marvels, that "Neri, my son, if I were to die, I would die happy, knowing that I would never have seen such magnificent men." This letter was read all over Florence. Giovanni d'Averardo de' Bicci was sent to Venice with a first payment of a hundred and forty thousand florins.

The Emperor set out with perhaps four thousand cavalry and reached the border of Trent, near the city of Brescia. The Duke of Milan had twice as many men there, whose only desire was to engage in battle, for it would have made their fortune. And they were right: the Duke of Austria and several others of the Emperor's allies were easily turned back. The Emperor was left with perhaps a thousand cavalry, and did not dare to press forward. And yet he wanted to reach Venice, to get his money – for the agreement had been that he would be given two hundred thousand florins when he left Germany, and two hundred thousand when he got to Italy, or rather when he arrived in Tuscany. According to this agreement, we were exempted from having to pay tribute money, and Pisa was given to us as a fief – that is, Pisa would be given to us if the Emperor conquered it. The Lord of Padua came out to meet the Emperor, and escorted him as far as Venice. When he arrived in Venice, he found our ambassadors Messer Rinaldo Gianfigliazzi, Messer Maso degli Albizzi, Messer Filippo Corsini, and Messer Tommaso Sacchetti. He remained there for several days, waiting for us to make up our minds to pay him the rest of the money. Finally he started to get fed up, and made as if he were about to leave. We wanted to give him the rest of the money – and more, because we wanted to make him strong, and we wanted to be the ones responsible for him being crowned Emperor by the Pope. But we kept him waiting too long, and he returned to Germany, and we never heard from him again. But in order to make it appear that we had achieved something, Duke Ludwig of Bavaria, the Emperor's nephew, was brought to Florence along with the Archbishop of Speyer, who was rich, but not in money. They had a hundred cavalry, whom ten of our soldiers could have put to route, for they were not armed as we were and they were a miserable lot. In order to get them to go away, we had to give them four thousand florins for expenses; but that was all.

Third War with the Duke of Milan, with Many Great Events

As you have been able to understand from what I wrote above, the Duke of Milan had been well advised about the Emperor's forces, and he had spent a great deal of money to build up his own. He was well fortified with men, and with good and capable captains. If we spent 200 thousand florins, that incited him to spend even more. But what did he do? When he saw that the Emperor had turned back, and that he himself had a large army, he wanted the money that he had spent to bear better fruit than ours had. And seeing that Giovanni Bentivoglio was in league with us against him, and had not turned out to be his friend as he had believed, the Duke decided to send his forces against Bentivoglio in Bologna and destroy him, for he was a lord devoid of forces, with few men and provisions. Bentivoglio had driven Giovanni Gozzadini, a well-loved citizen with many followers, out of Bologna. The Duke of Milan ingratiated himself with Bentivoglio, and made him certain promises. Then he sent a force of about eight thousand cavalry and a great number of infantry to Bologna, led by Count Alberico da Barbiano. The Lord of Mantua, the Malatesta family, Messer Galeazzo of Mantua, Messer Jacopo dal Verme, and Facino Cane and many other noblemen, who were always allied with him, also fought on the Duke's side. They reached Bologna in the Spring of the Year of Our Lord 1402.[82]

The Florentine government sent five thousand cavalry led by Bernardone Brettone, reputed to be a most valiant man,[83] to assist the Lord of Bologna. And with him were Muzio Attendolo Sforza da Cotignola, Agnolo d'Andrea di Lavello da Puglia (called "il Tartaglia"), the Brigade of the Rose,[84] and several of our own brigades of good men, well armed. The Lord of Padua sent to Giovanni Bentivoglio two of his sons with

---

82 The Battle of Casalecchio took place on 26 June 1402 near the town of Casalecchio di Reno, near Bologna.

83 Bernardone da Serra was a famous *condottiere* from Gascony.

84 A company of French mercenary soldiers, the last in Italy to have its own name; they fought in Romagna, Tuscany, and southern Italy until 1410.

armed men on horseback and provisions. The Duke's men had pitched camp and were skirmishing every day with our men; according to what was said, our men usually came out ahead. Seeing this, Giovanni Bentivoglio took heart and wanted Bernardone to go into battle. Bernardone did not agree with this, because he did not believe that his forces were strong enough. Bentivoglio was a man inclined to take risks; he seemed to believe that he was invulnerable. He repeatedly urged Bernardone to go into battle, and Bernardone told him that he did not feel confident to do so; he preferred to wait, for he believed that the enemy could not last long, as they were not getting any provisions from the outside. Bentivoglio said that Bernardone was acting out of fear, and that he, Bentivoglio, was the Lord of Bologna, and would go out to meet the enemy himself, for he was determined to wage war against the Duke's forces. Seeing how determined Bentivoglio was, Bernardone said that he would do as he asked, but God help them! Two of our ambassadors, Niccolò da Uzzano and Bardo Bastari, who were constantly with Bentivoglio, seeing his determination, agreed that he should do battle with the Duke's forces. So he went with his men and pitched camp at a good place, well fortified, called Casalecchio.

After Bentivoglio had been at Casalecchio for a few days, the enemy realized that they could no longer remain in the field on account of many disadvantages. One evening the captain consulted with the valiant men and lords who were there with him, and told them that he believed that remaining camped there was not possible, and that they should deliberate as to what they should do. There was a great deal of conferring, and finally it was decided that they should break camp, but first they would attack Bentivoglio. There were three reasons for this: first, because they were much stronger; second, because our men, and especially Tartaglia, loved to skirmish; third, because it seemed shameful to them to have been in the battlefield for so long and not to have accomplished anything. Once this was decided, the next morning they positioned their troops and began to advance on the Bolognese in a tight, orderly formation, brandishing their weapons and making a great noise. There was little order in the Bolognese camp, because they were taken unawares. But Bernardone did the best that he could. The skirmish began; Tartaglia could not be held back; he entered the fray, and soon the Bolognese camp was half empty, for the enemy had managed to enter it. The Rose Brigade, which was the best and largest under Bernardone's command, took flight along with two hundred lancers who were looking out over the field from a high position to see where the greatest danger was.

Our troops were put to flight, the captain and the rest of the camp were captured, and no one was killed. The Rose Brigade returned to Bologna, bringing the news of what had happened. This defeat occurred on Tuesday the twenty-seventh of June 1402, at the 12th hour. The news reached Florence the same day. Bonifacio di Facino Cane was taken prisoner.

Then the Duke's troops began to approach the city of Bologna, which was in a state of tumult. The people rose up against Giovanni Bentivoglio. He armed himself, and he and his men managed to repel the people three times. But Niccolò da Uzzano, realizing that the people would win in the end, intervened, entreating Bentivoglio to give up; Niccolò said that he would try to reach some kind of agreement with the mob. Bentivoglio did not want to retreat, for in his heart he thought he could win; he said: "Niccolò, don't fear these people – I know them better than you. I shall punish them and banish them for the villains they are." Although Niccolò continued to entreat Bentivoglio not to take this action, for he believed that it would be better to come to an agreement, he said: "Do as you wish!" He believed that the city would be liberated and that Bentivoglio would be deposed. While all of this was going on, a man who had always been a friend to Bentivoglio, called Lando d'Ambrogino (he was a butcher), was keeping guard at one of the gates of the city, and seeing that there was no hope for Bentivoglio, he left his old friend and found a new one. Indeed, he opened the city gate to Giovanni Gozzadini, Bolognino Boccatorta, and their cohort. They gave aid to the rebellious populace and rushed Bentivoglio's palace. He tried to flee; he was found hiding behind a window, and was cut to pieces. So the people took control of Bologna. Then the Duke's troops sought to enter the city, but the people did not want to admit them. Giovanni Gozzadini told them not to worry, and, keeping a promise he had made, he let them in. They took over the city on behalf of the Duke of Milan and made Giovanni Gozzadini a knight; he had thought that he would become Lord of Bologna himself, but instead he was given some provisions and a castle, and told to keep quiet. The Duke immediately had a large citadel built at Bologna, and this was done within a month. It is said that it cost him, along with all the provisions he put there, 120 thousand florins.

When the news of all this reached Florence, it seemed to us that we were irremediably lost. For many people had fled Florence, and there were only enough provisions in the city for two months, and the harvested grain was all in the ricks on the threshing-floors. The city was in great turmoil because of the great hardships and tumult among the citizens, as you can imagine. The countryside was even more depleted and perilous than the city, and there wasn't a single peasant who wouldn't have gladly come to burn Florence to the ground. The city of Pistoia was in great tumult because of the discord between the Cancellieri and the Panciatichi.[85] Moreover, Messer Ricciardo Cancellieri had been banished, and Giovanni Castasanti had been beheaded on account of certain dealings he was accused of having with the Duke, though the accusations were false. The Duke went and captured Sambuca, which he held along with certain other castles in the mountains. He had devastated the whole countryside to such an extent that the rectors could barely keep Pistoia secure. Later, many of the Ubaldini faction emerged; we had thought that they had been wiped out. They took over power in Pistoia and whipped up the whole region of the Mugello; and many people in that area turned out to be supporters of theirs. Likewise, at Arezzo, Prato, and Volterra and throughout the region the Ghibellines were agitating, attempting to take over every town and fortress that was under Florentine rule. And, as you can understand, if the Duke of Milan had taken us over, as he was well able to do, leaving Bologna well provided for, he would have taken our entire harvest and would surely have captured our entire territory. I believe that all of our lands would have been his in a short period of time.

But it was God's will that this evil should not befall us. We were not taken over, and what could be done to remedy the situation happened quickly – chiefly, all of the crops were harvested in eight days, and most of the harvest was stored in Florence and the surrounding fortresses. The taxes on grain, fodder, and olive oil were lifted. Then, the Ten on War raised a force of two thousand wool carders and sent them to guard the fortresses; this was done more to get them out of Florence than for any other reason. Other citizens were sent out to help our allies. Many of our soldiers returned on foot or with their horses in such terrible condition that they were allowed to keep them. They were put back on the government payroll because they were so needy, and furnished with new horses to the degree that it was possible, except for the Brigade of the Rose. Those soldiers were not taken back, because they had behaved worse than the others. But they returned to Florence in as bad shape as the men who had been taken prisoner in Bologna. Our two ambassadors were taken to Lombardy; Bardo Bastari died of a wound on the hand that he had received from a Bolognese (because Bardo had been against

-----

85 The Cancellieri and the Panciatichi were the leading families in Pistoia, vying for
    power in the city.

the Bolognese when they rose up against the Lord of Bologna), and Niccolò bailed himself out with five thousand florins, which were paid by the Florentine government.

Once the Duke of Milan's brigades had taken Bologna, they began to quarrel among themselves and with the Duke on account of their payments and booty, and the Duke was constrained to delay their payments on account of all the money he had spent building the citadel. So they broke with him, and went off to Lombardy, and the Duke was unable to get them back. The Malatesta left him, as did Count Alberico and others, for they were disgusted that they could not get paid; also because the Duke took the town of Faenza against the wishes of Count Alberico, who was his enemy and wanted vengeance.

With affairs in this state, God and his mother, the Virgin Mary, and the blessed St John the Baptist did not let so much evil befall us, for the Duke of Milan caught the plague. One day, as he was dining at one of his estates, where he had fled to avoid the pestilence that was in Milan, he began to feel unwell. He immediately departed and went to a castle called Marignano, ten miles away from the town of Pavia. He rode the ten miles in haste, around the ninth hour, and the heat was great. When he arrived at Marignano, he drank more than half a flask of wine and water, for he was burning inside from the exertion of the journey. He took to his bed, and lived for about seven days. He departed from this life on the 3rd of September 1402. He left Giovanni Maria Visconti as Duke of Milan with a portion of his lands, and Messer Filippo Maria, Count of Pavia, with certain other cities and fortresses. To Messer Gabriele, his illegitimate son, he left Pisa and its county. The first person to send the news of the death of the Duke of Milan to Florence was the Lord of Lucca,[86] who wrote two short verses about it to Messer Rinaldo Gianfigliazzi, without signing his name. Then Ardingo di Gucciozzo, who had heard the news from Messer Jacopo della Croce, wrote from Genoa. A month went by, with some people believing that the Duke was dead, and others not; many bets were made, and there were people who made bets at five per cent that he was dead. And as it pleased God, he really was dead. We were happy that he had died, but we continued to make every effort to undo and exterminate his government. In October 1402, we entered into an alliance with the Church and with the Malatesta family, with certain agreements that

---

86 Paolo Guinigi, who had become lord of Lucca in 1400 with the help of Gian Galeazzo Visconti.

cost us a great deal of money and brought us little benefit; but we were trying to do anything we could to undo our enemy.

After we had entered into this alliance, the Pope named Baldassare Cossa[87] his legate, and sent him with the Malatesta to try to take Bologna. We hired Count Alberico and gave him fifty thousand florins over a period of two months without officially enlisting him, and he continued to work for the acquisition of Bologna. Facino Cane was in Bologna, where he had been acting as the Duke's lieutenant; he had four hundred lancers and two thousand infantry. Bread and provisions were in short supply. Messer Giovanni Gozzadini entered into a league with the cardinal, because he had already rebelled against the Duke. He gave access to certain fortresses that were under his command, and was very helpful to us in acquiring Bologna.

The Birth of My Bartolomea

At this time, or a little before, a daughter was born to me in the house of the Pantaleoni family. This was on the twenty-second of October, on a Sunday night, at the tenth hour. She was baptized in the Baptistry of San Giovanni on the twenty-fifth of the same month. She was given the names Bartolomea and Lisabetta; her godparents were Giuliano di Tommaso and Monna Piera d'Arezzo.

What Followed the Death of the Duke of Milan

A few days after the death of the Duke, all of his enemies – that is, all of the noblemen who formerly had been lords of the cities of Lombardy or powerful in their own lands and had been defeated by the Visconti (such as the Rossi in Parma, the Cavalcabò in Cremona, the Scotti in Piacenza, the Guelfi in Brescia, the Beccaria in Pavia, and so on throughout the land) – rose up, the greatest and most powerful, both Guelphs and Ghibellines. Some became allied with our government, such as Piero de' Rossi, and others took measures to gain power in their own territories. We were happy to befriend anyone who wanted to remove the Visconti from power.

Later, there was an uproar among those who were left in charge of the Duke's sons;[88] the chief reason was envy of Francesco Barbavara,

---

87 Cossa was the cardinal-deacon of St Eustachius; he later became the anti-pope John XXIII.

88 Giovanni Maria Visconti was fourteen years old and Filippo Maria was eleven years old when their father died.

who was a clerk of the chaplain of the Duchess of Milan; and because he was very sly and ingratiating, the Duchess favoured him greatly and promoted him, and he was so clever that the Duke had made him one of his councillors.[89] In the end, the Duke favoured him over everyone else and placed all of his trust in him. And at his death, the Duke left the Duchess and Barbavara as the chief executors in charge of his estate and his children. Since Barbavara was a man of low birth and had risen from such a lowly position to such great heights of power, the hatred of him was great. There was also rumour that he was the Duchess's lover. Finally, a certain Messer Antonio Porro, a great citizen from a leading Milanese family, and very wealthy (it is said that he had an income of 10 thousand florins from feudal duties), led an effort to drive Barbavara out of Milan. Barbavara was expelled from the city, and the Duchess and her children took refuge in one of their fortresses. The turmoil continued in Milan for three years, and many hundreds of people died on both sides, Guelph and Ghibelline. Power was wrested from the Visconti, and then from the people, and then from the Duchess, and then from Giovanni Maria Visconti. Francesco Barbavara fled and never returned.

Messer Antonio Porro was betrayed, and beheaded. Since he was the leading man in Milan, and acting as leader not of the government but as the lieutenant of Giovanni Maria, the Duchess, who had taken refuge in the city fortress, sent for him. She distrusted him, and he distrusted her. But she assured him that he would be safe, saying that she was in great need of talking to him, and for good reasons. He trusted her, thinking that she wouldn't dare to have him harmed. When he arrived at the fortress, even before he saw the Duchess, he encountered Count Guido di Bagno, who grabbed him by the neck and said: "Now you're here, traitor!" and threw him to the ground and had his head cut off before he could say "Lord, help me!" But the Duchess still did not regain power; a certain Antonio Visconti came to power, and later Francesco Visconti, and the Duchess was poisoned.[90] Then the city was divided in two: one half went to Giovanni Maria Visconti, and the other to Messer Francesco.

---

89 Francesco Barbavara had been one of Gian Galeazzo's chief financial advisors. He was made count of Valesia, where he took refuge during the period of his disgrace (from 1403 on); later, he reconciled with Filippo Maria Visconti and in 1412 returned to Milan, where he died in 1415.

90 Gian Maria Visconti, who suspected his mother Caterina of treason, presumably had her poisoned.

Today, Giovanni Maria has power over the whole city, but he has to fight and struggle to keep it.

There were upheavals in other cities as well. Piero Rosso took over Parma, which was later taken from him by Messer Ottobono Terzi; this was in March 1403. Messer Ugolino Cavalcabò became lord of Cremona. The Beccaria family took over the government of Pavia, but in the name of the lord of that city. Messer Francesco Scotti took Piacenza, and later Messer Ottobono rebelled, breaking an alliance that he had made with the Lord of Padua, with Pier Maria Rossi of Parma, with the Lord of Cremona, and with us. It is said that he did it because the Lord of Padua did not give him the money that he had promised him. It is also said that he was getting money from the Venetians; and that could very well be, for if Ottobono had prevailed, all of Lombardy would have revolted, and the Lord of Padua would have become extremely powerful. The Venetians did not want this to happen, so they intervened, bolstering the government of Milan, which was in ruins.

While things were going on in this way, our government, in order to keep the turmoil going, suddenly ordered the Cardinal Legate, who was in Bologna, to go to Lombardy with all of the men who were camped at Bologna, which were more than four thousand cavalry. We also sent Alberico, who was then officially in our employ, with six hundred lancers. They were received in Lombardy by all of those who had rebelled against the Duke's government and by Messer Francesco Visconti, who had signed a document repudiating the Ghibelline party and declaring his allegiance to the Guelphs. After our government had issued these orders, the cardinal and Carlo Malatesta kept stalling, because they did not want to go to Lombardy. They argued that they wanted Bologna, threatening to leave if an agreement was not reached giving them that city. Finally, under these threats, the Duke agreed that Bologna should be given to the Cardinal Legate, if he would promise not to go to Lombardy to attack his forces. On the advice of Carlo Malatesta, the Legate agreed to this. For Malatesta was worried that we might do worse things, or even destroy those who opposed us. He kept all of these deliberations to himself – that is, he avoided us, and never conferred with our ambassador about anything. Once the agreement was reached, the papers were drawn up without saying anything to Vanni Castellani, who was representing Florence, nor to Alberico, who was in our employ. He turned to the Marquis of Ferrara, who did not want to agree without the consent of the Florentine government. The agreement was reached under threat of retaliation against any ally who would not ratify it. The Pope was able to do this because he was the one who could make peace treaties and agreements in all of the league's affairs, and we and the others were obliged to honour all of those agreements. The papal legate, Messer Baldassare Cossa, entered Bologna on September 3, 1403. Back in Florence, we heard about this indiscriminate affair and felt that we had been deceived by the Cardinal Legate, but it seems that it was the fault of Carlo Malatesta, so then we felt that we had been injured by him. We never ratified the agreement, but sent an ambassador to lodge a complaint with the Pope, who made a show of being sorry about it, and said that we were free to ratify it or not. So we sought to do damage to the Visconti in some other way, and we would have done so, if the Venetians hadn't interfered, as I recounted above. That is, after the defeat at Bologna, we entered into an alliance with Messer Ottorino and the Lords of Padua and Ferrara, and Messer Francesco Visconti and other enemies of the Visconti clan. The alliance was disrupted by the Venetians, as I said above.

The Birth of Francesco di Morello

At this time, or rather a little earlier, the wife of Morello di Paolo Morelli, Catelana, gave birth to a son, on Easter Sunday the 15th of April 1403, about a quarter of an hour before the 22nd hour. He was baptized in the Baptistry of San Giovanni on the 16th, in the large baptismal font. He was given the names Francesco and Pasquino. Francesco was born in the home of the Pantaleoni family, in the Via Larga de' Legnaiuoli, in the parish of Santa Trinita in Florence.

Of the War That the Marquis of Ferrara and the Lord of Padua Made against the Heirs of the Duke of Milan, the Florentines, and Their Unfortunate Neighbours, in Several Chapters

Having seen that luck was against us in the affair in Lombardy and that things were falling apart, the government of Florence decided to leave it entirely in the hands of the Lords of Padua and Ferrara. They began to try to take over certain portions of the deceased Duke's dominion; the Lord of Padua went to Verona, which he attempted to acquire by his own efforts and with the help of Master Dominico the engineer. Messer Ugolotto Biancardi was the Duke's lieutenant in Verona; he had something like two hundred lancers.

But the government of Florence was not idle; we continued to struggle with our enemies the Perugians, the Sienese, and the Pisans, and

Count Bagno di Andreino and Andreino degli Ubaldini and Bustaccio and Ciappettino degli Ubertini and Count Antonio da Palagio. Finally, Jacopo di Alamanno Salviati, with the forces of the Florentine government, defeated the Counts of Bagno and captured more than forty fortresses from them. Likewise with Andreino, who had few fortresses left, and he would not have had those if Carlo Malatesta and the Pope's treasurer hadn't sent him reinforcements on several occasions. Once he had conquered Bagno di Romagna, Jacopo d'Alamanno returned to Florence on October 12, 1404. He rode to the public palace, and the members of the Seignory came down to the railing, and he was knighted by Messer Lotto Castellani, who was the Standard-bearer of Justice at the time. The Seignory gave him a gift of a helmet decorated with gold and a sword and spurs and the coat of arms of Florence on a shield and horse with livery (but he returned the horse). I think that the Captains of the Guelph party also sent him gifts. And on that morning he took to wife the daughter of Piero Faselli, who was a widow. All of these honours were given to him not so much on account of the territories he had acquired with our forces, but because he had acted loyally. For he never wanted a tithe or any portion of what he had acquired on our behalf, nor did he ever demand to be recompensed or rewarded in any way, as soldiers usually do. He never wanted to receive gifts or presents, and he could have gotten two thousand florins worth of household items and rich furnishings that he found in the homes of the counts he had defeated. But he never wanted any of it – he had everything turned over to the Florentine government. And because there are so few men like that, he was greatly honoured in order to give an example to others.

How Perugia Rebelled against the Duke's Heirs

The Perugians perceived that they were under threat from the men whom they had exiled, who had allied themselves with Florence, and on the other side they were being assailed by the Pope, who had sent his forces against them. They felt that they had been abandoned, with no hope of assistance and fearing what the men whom they had exiled might do, for they had already captured several fortresses; and they saw that the Church was prospering and had already taken Bologna, as I have recounted above. So they decided that the best thing to do was to surrender to the Pope. And in fact this idea pleased those who had been loyal to the Duke's heirs – including Andreino di Messer Biordo degli Ubertini, who still had control of a fortress. The Malatesta, at the Pope's urging, had promised to protect such fortresses. And they did so in order that Andreino would not go over to our side. On November 20, 1403, Andreino left Perugia, now in the hands of the Church.

How Pisa Went Over to the King of France

The Lord of Pisa, Messer Gabriele, also had to decide with whom he should ally himself. Because he was being greatly harassed by us and felt that he was in danger of losing his state, he sent ambassadors to Genoa to the lieutenant of the King of France,[91] Boucicault.[92] The Lord of Pisa pledged allegiance to the King, promising to send him a peregrine falcon and two racehorses every year. Boucicault did this to please the Genoese. And so the Lord of Pisa handed over the fortresses of the city and county of Pisa to Boucicault, becoming the King's viceroy in Pisa. Once this was done, Boucicault sent an ambassador to Pisa with a full mandate; this man officially took over all of Pisa's holdings and placed them under the guard of men whom Boucicault had chosen. He did all of this on his own.

How Siena Came Over to Our Side

The Sienese were also feeling very threatened by our government, which had formed an alliance with the noblemen who had been expelled from Siena because they would not submit to the Duke's lieutenant there. We had succeeded in putting them into an intolerable position; they had lost several fortresses and had no hope of assistance from anywhere. So they went hat in hand to beg for mercy from our government. Messer Cristofano Spini was Standard-bearer of Justice at the time, and decided to make peace with Siena; so their exiles were left out in the cold. In the agreements that we reached with the Sienese, we agreed to return five fortresses to them, and they only returned the fortified town of Marciano to us; they kept Lucignano, which we had been fighting to get back for a long time. This peace treaty was disliked by all of Florence's leading honourable citizens; it was only liked by malcontents, or people with big problems, or ignorant people. And even if I am one of the people with

---

91 Charles VI Valois.
92 Jean le Maigre, called Boucicault, was marshal of France from 1391, and governor of Genoa from 1401 to 1409.

problems, I disliked the treaty, for I love my city and the honour of the Seignory more than I love my own self-interest. For it was certain that in a short period of time we could have gotten back not only Lucignano but also other even better fortresses, if we had wanted to. Nevertheless, the peace treaty was entered into in an honourable fashion, for the Sienese came in person to sign the agreement in the Public Palace. Our government magnanimously wanted to show that it could be gracious to those who repented and humbled themselves. The treaty was signed on the 6th of April, 1404; seven days later it was publicly proclaimed, and great festivities and jousting took place.

The Capture of Verona by the Scala Contingent

On the 11th of April 1404, a Friday, we received the happy news of the capture of Verona, and how Messer Guglielmo della Scala,[93] with the help of Francesco da Carrara, the Lord of Padua, had taken the city by storm. Later, on the 2nd of May, we got the news that he had captured their fortresses, and there was celebrating among the Seignory and the citizens of Florence. The Marquis of Verona knighted Messer Michelino di Vanni; he also wanted to knight Vanni di Carlo, but Vanni was wise and said that he first wanted to be sure that he could keep the position before he accepted it. Once Verona had been taken over, Francesco da Carrara regretted that he had made Guglielmo della Scala, whom he had raised like a younger brother, lord of that city. He decided that he would rather give the lordship of Verona to one of his own sons, so he secretly had Guglielmo and his sons killed, and took back the lordship of Verona for himself.

How Boucicault Informed the Florentines That Pisa Had Gone Over to the King of France

On the 18th of April 1404, Boucicault sent a French ambassador to Florence. Speaking on the King's behalf, the ambassador informed the Seignory that Pisa had allied itself with France, and that from that time forward any offence against the Pisans would be considered an offence against the King, and he would wreak vengeance. This man was not well

---

93 Guglielmo della Scala was the natural son of Cangrande II della Scala (who ruled
　　Verona from 1351 to 1359).

received; and the reply he got was that we had always held the King and his predecessors in reverence, and we were devoted to him, and had never gone against any of his wishes, but had always tried to magnify and increase his dignity, like devoted children and servants of his holy crown. We said that we were not surprised about what had occurred in Pisa purportedly on behalf of the King, but we did not believe at all that this had been what the King wanted. For the man who had taken over Pisa was our enemy and had, like his father and the rest of his family, attempted to undermine our liberty.[94] And we said that it was legitimate for us to seek vengeance against the Lord of Pisa and the Pisans and that no one had the right to prevent us from doing so. But because he claimed to be speaking on behalf of the King, we said that we would try to learn the truth from the King himself and we were sure that we could reach an agreement with him, as we and our forefathers had always done, and so on. The ambassador departed, and reported our reply to Boucicault. Around this time a Florentine merchant ship unloaded at Genoa, and Boucicault had all of the merchandise confiscated, and froze all Florentine assets in that city. But he didn't stop at that – he had all of the Florentines in Genoa arrested, and then released them on bail with the stipulation that they would not leave the city. The members of our Seignory wrote to him that we were shocked at what he had done, and entreated him to return to us what was rightfully ours. The reason why Boucicault had done this was that we had decided to withdraw all of our business from Genoa and not do business with the Genoese, nor use their harbour. And we had already reached an agreement with the Lord of Piombino and were planning to use that port for our business, and this decision had been communicated in letters to merchants outside of Florence. The Genoese were unhappy about this, and complained; the Pisans told them to confiscate our merchandise if we would not agree to do as they wished. We sent Bonaccorso Pitti as ambassador to him, and he was kept in long negotiations.

We wrote to France and sent a delegation to the King there. The King apologized for what had occurred at Genoa, and commanded that our merchandise be returned to us. What Boucicault had done was at the behest of the Duke of Orléans;[95] the King never wanted to receive tribute

---

94 Morelli is referring to Gian Galeazzo Visconti, and the Visconti family in general.
95 During King Charles VI's illness, the duke of Orléans practically ruled France, together with the duke of Burgundy.

money from the Pisans nor go against Florence in any way. Then Messer
Rinaldo Gianfigliazzi, Messer Tommaso Sacchetti, and Messer Filippo
Corsini went as ambassadors to Genoa, to join Bonaccorso Pitti. They
stayed there week after week; finally, on account of letters that the King
wrote, and because we agreed to many of the things that he wanted,
Boucicault returned the merchandise, but unwillingly, because he already considered that it belonged to him. The merchandise was loaded
up and taken to Lucca, and then to Florence. Because of the pledges we
had made with the Pisans, there was no more conflict between us, and
the road between Florence and Pisa was supposed to be safe for both parties; but there was no Florentine who dared to do business there. We remained peaceful, and we worked with the King of France and the Duke
of Orléans and with Boucicault and with the Pisans to secretly further
our own interests, or at least to extricate ourselves from our obligations.

Of the Villainy of the Lord of Lucca

Around this time, Paolo Guinigi, the Lord of Lucca, sought to hoodwink
us. He saw that we were in need of a port and that we didn't want to do
business in Pisa or Genoa. He would have been happy to forbid us to use
his port,[96] but his greed for money got the better of him. Blinded by our
need for a port, we let him do whatever he wanted as long as he would
allow us to use his harbour. The only ambassador he ever sent to us was
Maestro Andrea Gori, a peasant who had been banned from Florence
who sang about the Paladins.[97] Guinigi did this to mock us, and many
times he made us pay dearly for tricks he played on us. We always had
to make a show of not seeing what he was doing; and he was more of an
enemy to us, for the things he did secretly, than the Duke of Milan ever
was. But to return to the affair of the port: Guinigi manipulated us to
such a degree that we ended up giving him thirty-six thousand florins
over a period of twelve months, in addition to the customs duties, taxes,
and transit fees that we were obliged to pay. And when he saw that we
were willing to do this, he pulled back, thinking that he could get even
more out of us. I believe that God was displeased that this worm should
fool with us in this way. So it happened that Messer Gherardo d'Appiano,

---

96 The port of Motrone.
97 Gregorio dell'Incisa, a sort of troubadour, was the informer and negotiator of Paolo
   Guinigi, lord of Lucca from 1400 to 1430.

the Lord of Piombino, sent word to us offering us the port of Piombino, freely and at no expense except for five hundred lancers, which he would keep at our service to protect our merchandise. So we made an agreement with him and left the traitorous Lord of Lucca, who was sick with rage when he heard that we had come to an agreement with Messer Gherardo. Paolo Guinigi is a great enemy of Florence, as he has shown himself to be many times, bringing disaster to our government. And if he ever did anything good, he did it out of sheer fear and in order to better position himself for his trickery and betrayals. Some people (and I am one of them) believe that he spends a great deal of money in Florence so that he won't lose our support. But, God be praised, he has played so many tricks that everyone knows that he is a traitor. And may God permit that he will once again become faithful to our righteous and holy city and Guelph party and the liberty of Italy, which God shall always maintain in disdain of the evil!

The Birth of My Son Jacopo

On Sunday the 20th of July 1404, shortly after the sixteenth hour tolled, my wife Caterina gave birth to a son. This was the first child born in my own home in the neighbourhood of Santa Croce – and may God grant him the grace to live and remain there with better grace than I have had. He was baptized in San Giovanni on the 21st of the same month, and was given the names Jacopo and Domenico. His godparents were Monna Telda, the wife of Aliso, and Monna Ermellina, who lives in Prato. May God grant him a long life, if he is to be the best he can be. He is named after Jacopo Arnolfi.[98]

How the Council of the Eighty-one Was Stripped of Power

As is written above (where I wrote about the events of the Year of Our Lord 1393), the Council of Eighty-one was given power; most people understood that this was to be for a period of five years; but it lasted much longer. And it would have lasted forever if it had not been terminated. At that time Paolo Carnesecchi was Standard-bearer of Justice, after Messer Cristofano. At the urging of many citizens, he decided to

---

98 Morelli's uncle Jacopo di Zanobi Arnolfi, who died in 1400. In the manuscript, in another hand, is written: "Jacopo died on the 21st of September 1456."

deprive the Council of Eighty-one of the power to raise money and even to change the tax on personal loans. In order to ratify this, forty-five votes were needed – that is, the members of the Seignory, the Colleges, and the magistracy of Eight on Security; and all the votes were obtained. So the Council of Eighty-one was disbanded on the 10th of June 1404. The populace of Florence were very glad, and the men who wanted war were sorely displeased. May God restore us!

The Voting for Mangione

After Paolo Carnesecchi, Lorenzo Machiavelli became Standard-bearer of Justice. One of Lorenzo's comrades was Antonio di Cipriano Mangioni, known as "Mangione." The members of the council were the same as those during Paolo's time, and Niccolò da Uzzano was Standard-bearer of one of the the military companies. These are the only names I remember – they were the chief ones behind what happened at this time. They decided to hold a vote whereby whoever received enough votes and was thirty years of age or more would be in the voting for 1393, and whoever was twenty years of age or more would be in the voting for 1398, if not before. Any man younger than twenty years of age was not qualified to be in the voting. Again, forty-five votes were needed to pass this measure; and they got them, for they convinced the Eight on War to vote as they wished. They also passed a law to the effect that no one who had not already been a member of the Seignory, or a Captain of the Guelph party, or a member of one of the councils from 1381 on, could become a member of a magistracy. This voting took place in July and August of 1404.

Giano di Giovanni Morelli was qualified to run for office; he was nominated by Jacopo di Piero Bonaventura, who was Standard-bearer of the district of the Black Lion. At that time, Morello and I were living in that district, and we were nominated for that round of voting by Jacopo di Piero. It is true that, because we were not registered for the quotas for loans to the government, we were not positioned as well as we might have been, but he did us the honour of putting our names forward. And because this vote was so important, Morello and I did everything possible, not omitting any effort as long as it was honest. Whether it helped or not, I do not know. What happened should be taken for the best and we shouldn't take offence; we must conquer our ingratitude with humility, with courtesy, and with kindness toward those who we think wish us ill: this is the way to maintain one's honour. Also at this time, there were votes for all of the offices outside of Florence itself. Morello and I stood only for the internal offices; Giano also stood for the more important positions.

Many men in the government and especially many leading families were opposed to the idea of holding these votes. This was because they distrusted many people who were not of the upper classes, who they believed were not friendly to them. But I believe that this suspicion was unfounded, because those who do not wish well to those in power do so for no other reason than the fact that they are not among those in power (in the event that those in power have not attained their position through evil deeds). I believe that those who have acted and continue to act righteously should not be shunned, nor dishonoured. And if you should do so, such a man would be right to hate you. Now, I believe (and this is borne out by the facts) that whoever counted the votes at that time was very generous to all the men from wealthy old Florentine families; and this can be seen in the elections that were held in certain districts. I record this here for no other reason than to inform you of the things that one has to do in order to acquire the honours that the government bestows upon its citizens – that is, to do good works, obey the laws, pay honour to government officials, to the leading citizens, and to men from old families and persons of rank. Make sure that such people know you, commend yourself to them and remind them of the good acts of your ancestors. Do not attempt to acquire honours in other ways, for it is too risky.

How the Venetians Took Padua

You have heard how the Lord of Padua captured Verona, which the Venetians took very badly, because they feared that he would become too powerful. If the Lord of Padua had left the governing of Verona to Messer Guglielmo dalla Scala, they would have been content. But when they saw that he wanted it for himself, they decided that if he wouldn't let go of the city, they would make him do so. The Venetians saw that the Lord of Padua was determined to keep Verona for himself, for that is what he told them. So they made an alliance with Francesco Gonzaga, the Lord of Mantua. They also came to an understanding with the Duke of Milan, because he was afraid of the Lord of Padua, who was his enemy, and he didn't see anyone else who was willing to unseat him. So the Duke of Milan agreed to give the Venetians five towns under his power that were on the border between Padua and Verona, including

Vicenza, which I believe is midway between Padua and Verona – that is, in a very vulnerable place for him. Once the Venetians had taken over these towns, they put together a large army under the leadership of Malatesta da Pesaro and headed for Verona. Later they got rid of Malatesta because they did not trust him, and made Paolo Savelli captain of that army. The Lord of Padua left his son Jacopo in Verona, but with a small force, for he had few men. But Jacopo put up a strong resistance when the Venetians attacked the town; lack of provisions caused him to lose the town in June of 1405. Messer Jacopo took refuge in the fortress there, and later surrendered. The Venetians gave him and 25 of his companions safe conduct; and he, believing that he would be safe, left Verona and started out for Padua. He was captured by the Venetians and taken to Venice and put in prison under a heavy guard. When he invoked the safe conduct, they said that they had granted it to him for inside the town of Verona, but not outside. At this time, there was great mortality within the town of Padua and the surrounding countryside because of the plague, and Paolo Savelli perished. His place was taken by Messer Galeazzo of Mantua. The Venetians had also captured Master Domenico the engineer, and put him in a secure prison. Later they released him, threatening to do great harm to the Lord of Padua, and he believed them. When the Marquis Niccolò III d'Este saw that things were going badly for the Lord of Padua and that no one was going to help him, he allied himself with the Venetians, and the Lord of Padua was left alone. We were all sorry about this in Florence, but no one ever attempted to help him. The Venetians were very suspicious of us, because he was after all our friend and we would have liked him to win; there was much talk of this in Florence. And because the Venetians did not trust us, they always kept an ambassador in Florence, with our consent.

The Lord of Padua had repeatedly attempted to mount defences of his state, but when he saw that there was no hope, he decided to come to an agreement with the Venetians, who offered to give him 60 thousand ducats and let him keep his equipment and put his people in a safe place. He agreed to this; but then he heard that we had taken the citadel of Pisa and withdrew his offer to the Venetians, in the hope that we would be able to help him. Later he learned that we had lost the citadel; he would have liked to resume his negotiations with the Venetians, but they were unwilling. Realizing that he was in dire straits, the Paduan people understood that he was going to give in to the Venetians, so they beat him to it and surrendered first. He took refuge in the citadel, and later came to an agreement with Messer Galeazzo, agreeing to go to

Venice to resume negotiations with the Venetians. And if he could not reach an agreement with the Venetians, he wanted Messer Galeazzo to promise him that he could keep the citadel. Messer Galeazzo made the promise, and the Lord of Padua left the citadel. As soon as he emerged, they captured him, accusing him of trying to flee; they took him and his other son (I think it was Messer Francesco the Third). When the city of Padua was taken over by the Venetians on November 22, 1405, the Lord of Padua was in Venice, appearing before the Doge, humbling himself and asking to be pardoned. He was reminded of every benefit that had ever been granted to him and his people by the Venetians, and of every evil deed that he and his people had ever done. Then Venetians sent him to San Nicolò del Lido under heavy guard. They then debated among themselves and took several votes as to whether or not he should be beheaded, or whether he and his sons should be imprisoned for life; or whether he should be poisoned. The final vote won. He and his sons were put in prison, and a few days later were poisoned; they were buried in the most disrespectful way, and not all in the same place.

The Venetians struggled for eighteen months to take over Verona and its countryside as well as Padua, and spent around seventy thousand ducats in the process. And they had such good fortune that they took over both cities and conquered those who ruled them. For if the Lord of Padua or one of his sons had survived, they would have reconquered their dominion, or if they had not reconquered it, they would have caused the Venetians great trouble and expense. But everything went against them – God was against them, sending a deadly plague; the siege caused a great shortage of bread, so that the price of wheat went up to three ducats per bushel; there wasn't a drop of wine nor of water, because there are few fountains in Padua, and the rivers ran dry; and the siege was so terrible that the gates of the city were blocked for more than four months and nobody ever came out or went in; and there was no money to buy bread. Thus everything went badly for the Lord of Padua even before he was defeated, and then he lost everything very quickly.

How the Government of Florence Purchased the Citadel of Pisa from Boucicault

At this time, as I have already recounted in part, the government of Florence was plotting how it might take over Pisa, or engage it in a war. And since whoever has money and is willing to spend it can always obtain almost everything he wants, we offered so much money to Boucicault and to the Lord of Pisa and to the Duke of Orléans that they, who had formerly been so bitter toward us, began to give in and become as sweet as honey. They were happy to hear the sound of florins clinking, and they began to let us know this. Now, since we Florentines are always in such a hurry that it seems a thousand years to us before we get what we want, the Seignory decided that that Messere Maso degli Albizzi should try to entice Messer Gabriello Maria Visconti. So they met along the border between our territory and his. The Pisans heard about this, got suspicious, and found out what was going on. A citizen of Pisa called Messer Rinieri Saccio (he was a Raspante,[99] that is, a member of the faction opposed to Messer Gabriello Maria) heard about this meeting (which accomplished nothing, nor was it necessary, for Boucicault was the one we should have been dealing with). Messer Rinieri went to the Lord of Pisa and said to him: "We have heard that you want to sell us to the Florentines; this amazes us, because you are loved by our people and you should not doubt it." He told Messer Gabriello Maria that if he did not want to remain Lord of Pisa, he should leave the Pisan people free; and if he needed money, they would give him as much as he wanted. Gabriello Maria became angry and said that this could never be, and that that kind of thinking and that kind of talk displeased him. He said that they should banish such ideas and not give any credence to that rumour, and that if he heard any further talk like this, he would show them his displeasure.

Messer Rinieri departed; a few days later, the suspicion having grown, he got together with members of the other faction, and said to them, "Brothers, I hear that Messer Gabriello Maria wants to sell us to the Florentines. Let us become brothers as we were in the past so that we can work together to avoid falling into the hands of our enemies and your own." These words were very pleasing to the Bergolini faction, because they saw that it would be advantageous to them. They came to an agreement, and went again to Messer Gabriello to complain about what they had heard, and told him that if he didn't do something to remedy the situation, they would. Messer Gabriello apologized, trying to reassure them. And because he saw how ill disposed they were, he did not do to them what he would have liked to do, for fear that the situation would worsen. But he reproached them for their suspicions and for the things they were saying, warning them not to repeat them.

---

99 There were two factions in Pisa at this time, the Raspanti and the Bergolini, whom
   Morelli discusses in the following pages.

The members of the two factions left Messer Gabriello, sore displeased. And a few days later, that is on the 27th of July 1405, they all took up arms, shouting "Long live the people of Pisa, long live freedom, death to the tyrant!" Messer Gabriello took refuge in the citadel with his mother; and then, seeing that he had lost the city, he departed for Sarzana. His mother, Madonna Agnesina, went to Genoa, and signed a document handing over the city, countryside, and district of Pisa to Boucicault; she also gave him the citadel of Pisa, which he filled with Genoese and French soldiers to guard it well. While all this was going on, our negotiations with Boucicault continued to go forward. Messer Gabriello had never wanted to hear anything about this, and if anyone spoke to him about our negotiations with Boucicault, he would say: "I want the Lords of Florence to be like fathers to us, and for every citizen of Florence to be our brother, and I want them to be as free to move about in Pisa as they ever were; and I want to assure them of this" (which he intended to do by ceding some fortresses to us). "But I want the Seignory of Pisa for myself, and I want to live and die as Lord of Pisa, and I will never have any other desire until I'm up to here" (and he would touch his hand between his mouth and his nose). Boucicault was asking for two hundred fifty thousand florins for the citadel and the town of Ripafratta. He wasn't willing to give anything else, except the city of Leghorn. We offered him a hundred thousand florins, and he said he would take two hundred. We sent Gino Capponi and Messer Benedetto di Messer Lando Fortini and Nicolò Barbadoro to negotiate the deal. Messer Gabriello gave his word, saying, "I am willing to sell Pisa to the Florentines, because I'm barely keeping my head above water." The deal was struck in this way: He would sell us Pisa and its territory at the terms most favourable to us, and he would give us the citadel and Ripafratta. We agreed to give him a third of the two thousand florins at that time, and the second third six months after we took over the citadel, and the final third when we took over the city of Pisa, or when we came to an agreement with the Pisans. He promised to give us the use of the port of Leghorn as if it were our own, but not the citadel. Documents were drawn up to this effect, with our advisors and theirs in agreement. On the 24th of August 1405, the Florentine Seignory sent soldiers to take command of the citadel of Pisa; they passed beside the walls of Lucca.

Prior to this, on the 20th of August, the magistracy of the Ten on War was appointed for a six-month term; the members were Messer Lorenzo d'Antonio di Nicolò Ridolfi and Nicolò da Uzzano; from Santa Croce, Messer Filippo Magalotti, Francesco de' Pulci to represent the nobility and Antonio di Vanni Mannucci to represent the artisans; from Santa

Maria Novella, Messer Rinaldo di Gianozzo Gianfigliazzi, Messer Cristofano d'Anfrione Spini; from San Giovanni, Bartolomeo Valori, Paolo Carnesecchi, and Lodovico di Guccio della Badessa to represent the artisans. Complete powers were granted to the Seignory, the Colleges, the Captains, and the magistracies. There were four representatives for èach *gonfalone* (who were voted on by the Seignory and the Colleges) with full powers for six months, except the power to sell Florence.

We took over the citadel of Pisa on the 30th of August of that year, in the morning, at the third hour. Nencio Raffacani entered the fortress with three hundred infantry and Gino Capponi was the official representative of the Florentine government. The news reached Florence on Monday the 31st of August, the feast day of St Julian, at the first hour of the night. There was great celebrating; the Seignory did not set off fireworks, but many citizens did. On the 4th of September, the Ten on War sent two castellans, Siepe Peruzzi and Alesso Baldovinetti, who had the task of guarding the citadel along with Raffacani. They each received a salary of eighty florins per month. Messer Alamanno degli Obizzi was the captain of the mercenaries, and many others, good foot soldiers. And Messer Andrea di Neri Vettori was posted outside the citadel with eight hundred cavalry and a large number of infantry, to guard against any possible attacks by the Pisans.

How the Citadel Was Lost

On the sixth day of September, the Pisans scaled the walls of the citadel and entered through a tiny door into a tower that was supposed to be guarded by an officer and eighteen mercenary soldiers. Once they had entered the tower, they climbed up, and meeting no resistance, took the towers. Then they descended using our own ladders, which were leaning against the walls; they captured every man there.

Siepe Peruzzi, out of great fear, cast the banners of Florence down into the moat, and opened the gates to the Pisans; for after they had all entered into the towers as I have described, they didn't dare to descend until they saw the door open and the people come in. Raffacani opened the outer emergency gates and fled headlong with all of our men. The mercenary soldiers assigned to defend the battlements had quickly arrived, and when they saw our men emerging from the citadel, they started to flee; but Raffacani and the others cried out: "We are your prisoners!" They did this in order not to fall into the hands of the Pisans; for during the time that they had been guarding the citadel, all they had done was insult the Pisans and show them their arse. On top of this, they had tried to rob the infantrymen who were inside, so that many of them left. The "precautions" that these captains had taken were to hunt for quail and send for flasks of wine and rob the infantrymen and insult the Pisans and their women. The citadel was lost on Sunday, September 6. Messer Andrea came to offer aid to the Florentines at the second hour of the night; everything had been lost except one tower, and this they could barely hold. But they wouldn't surrender until Messer Andrea said that he could do nothing to help them until daylight. Then they surrendered.

The news reached Florence on the 7th of September 1405, the vigil of the feast of Our Lady; and the news was as gloomy and unpleasant as you can imagine. All true Florentines were saddened by this loss and never forgot it, on account of Florence's honour. And it shall never be forgotten, unless the proper revenge is taken, and that revenge shall be the taking of Pisa. Then we shall believe that God has permitted this to happen for the greater honour of Florence, though we have had to toil and pay for our sins.

After we had bought Pisa from Boucicault and Messer Gabriello, and with the will and consent of the King of France and especially of the Duke of Orléans, for 200 thousand gold florins in three payments (that is, a third on the day the citadel was taken over, the 20th of August, the second third six months later, and the last third once we took over the city of Pisa, as I said above), the Seignory and the various magistracies were given powers for six months. These powers included the ability to levy taxes and duties, and to change them as they pleased, and many other things necessary for an undertaking of this kind. Many cavalry and foot soldiers were hired by the Ten on War, and the cost climbed to 50 thousand florins per month. They hired Count Bertoldo degli Orsini to lead these forces for four months. He left Florence with a good astrological augury on the 5th of October at the fifth hour of the night. Orsini served the city of Florence badly, caring only to fill his own purse by ignoble actions; he achieved very little during his brief tenure, and when the four months were up, he was let go. He was such a miserable, dishonest man, it seemed like a thousand years to us before he left. Nevertheless, during his tenure he attacked the town of Vicopisano. He went there on the 12th of November 1405 with four thousand cavalry and two thousand infantry and many cannons and catapults.

After we had lost the citadel, the Pisans called back those citizens who had been banished, members of the Gambacorta family and the relatives of Giovanni dell'Agnello. They swore brotherhood to each other and attended a solemn mass, pledging peace and unity. Weeping and making a great show of love and tenderness, they embraced one another and kissed on the mouth. This love lasted only a few days, for the two factions, the Raspanti and the Bergolini, soon began to suspect one another, seeking to get back into power. A certain Pisan citizen by the name of Piero Gaetani, who was just as important and powerful as those who were in charge, realizing this, decided to rebel; he left Pisa and captured the fortress at Pecciole. Then he came to an agreement with the Florentines. Money changed hands and he ceded the fortress to us, going against the Pisans and helping us to capture several other fortresses. He was rewarded very well for all of this. It then happened that Giovanni Gambacorta became Lord of Pisa under the guise of making us happy: that is, he led the Pisans to believe that we would leave off trying to take over their city once we learned that the government was in their hands. News of this reached us on the 26th of October and we sent an olive branch at the 2nd hour of the night. The outcome of this was that Giovanni Gambacorta avenged Messer Piero and killed many Raspanti and banished many others, and stole what they left behind. And he dealt with them in such a way that they can't even sneeze without leaning up against a wall – that is how weak they are. We Florentines didn't get anything from him that we didn't get from others, but it is easier to understand his animosity toward us.

Birth of Costanza

On the fifth day of October 1405, a Monday, between the eleventh and twelfth hour, Giovanni's wife Caterina gave birth to a baby girl. She was baptized on Thursday morning in the cathedral of Santa Reparata. She was given the names Costanza Reparata; her godparents were Monna Lorenza di Matteo da Quarata and Monna Gemma, Caterina's midwife. May God grant good fortune to the health of her soul.

Birth of Andrea di Morello

On the 30th day of November 1405, in the evening, Morello's wife Catelana gave birth to a baby boy, on the feast of St Andrew; he was given the names Andrea and Leonardo. On the 14th of December the midwife who had been with him at Pian di Ripoli found him dead; we thought that she had suffocated him. He was buried in San Jacopo. May God bless him and our other departed ones.

The News Sent by the Venetians

In December 1405, the Venetians sent a messenger to Florence to report to the Seignory how Venice had taken over Padua and captured the Lord of Padua and two of his adult sons. There was sadness in Florence at this news, but we didn't want this to be known, for we did not want our government to be seen as opposed to Venice in any way. Later the Venetians poisoned the Duke of Padua and his sons, or else they had them strangled, and they were buried dishonourably in different places, as if they had been penniless prisoners. This was held to be great cruelty.

Encampment at San Pietro in Grado

On the 12th of April 1406, we sent forces to San Pietro in Grado, which is located between the city of Pisa and the estuary of the Arno River. We sent two thousand cavalry and one thousand five hundred infantry, including 400 Genoese with crossbows and two thousand men to build fortifications. They were sent to build two bastions on the Arno and to block off the river at a point between them, in order to block the Pisans' passage to the harbour. This encampment was supplied from Leghorn and Genoa – that is, from the Italian Riviera. The men toiled for three months before the two bastions were completely built and furnished with provisions. Count Antonio da Monte Granelli was put in charge of one bastion with four hundred infantry, and Count Gioacchino da Monte d'Oglio was put in charge of the other, with a similar number of infantry; they were provisioned according to what they could get. While they were toiling to build the bastions, about six thousand bushels of wheat arrived by sea for the Pisans, who had purchased it in various places. Twenty-two vessels suddenly arrived, including galleys and ships, brigantines and single-masted vessels, but they were in a bad position. They couldn't enter the harbour because the river was already blocked off between the two bastions – and besides, we had six galleys on the sea, and soldiers on the ground as you have heard. The vessels lingered in the sea for about a month before starting a skirmish. Then they were captured by our forces, and surrendered the wheat, which we had stored at Leghorn, where it remained at our behest. On the 10th of July, our forces broke camp and went to Pisa, where they pitched three camps in different areas.

The Illness of My Eldest Son Alberto

During these dark, unpleasant times for me, on account of the heavy, complicated burdens I have always had to bear, on Monday morning the 19th of May, 1406, my eldest son Alberto was taken ill, with blood flowing out of his nose. He had had three nosebleeds the previous day and night, before we realized that he had a fever. On Monday morning while he was at school, the fever seized him, blood flowed out of his nose, and he lost control of his bowels. It pleased God for him to live sixteen days, in great pain and suffering, until Friday night, June 5th, at the third hour. His illness took this course: he continuously had a fever, which would get higher every evening; he grew worse day after day. After two days, during which he hadn't been able to keep anything in his stomach, he got a pain below his liver, above where the thigh joins the body. The pain was horrifying and excruciating, and for sixteen days he got no relief, nor did those who were caring for him; he cried out in pain continuously. His body was swollen, and he seemed to be in a paroxysm of pain. There is no heart so hard that wouldn't have felt pity for him, seeing him in so much pain. He beseeched God and the Virgin Mary many times, asking that the painting of Our Lady be brought to him; he embraced it with innumerable supplications, prayers, and vows; no one could be so hard-hearted as not to be moved to great pity at the sight of him. He adjured his father, his mother, his relatives, and whoever was present, with such humility and such moving words that it was indescribable. At last he died; all the help we tried to give him, all our prayers and supplications and vows were of no avail; God wanted his life to come to an end!

May it please God to have brought to an end the strife, toil, and tribulation that to my mind followed my son from the time he was a little child. Of his own volition, at the age of four he wanted to come into my shop; at six, he knew the Psalms; at eight, the rudiments of Latin grammar. He knew how to write, and sent letters in his own hand to his cousins or mother when they were in the country. At nine years of age, he read the Latin authors and learned to read business letters. He had a good memory, spoke well, and could retain what he had learned; he had a pleasing appearance, and was gentle and well-mannered. He liked to take risks and was a little wild. The death of this child was an incalculable loss to me and his mother; it saddened his relatives and neighbours, his teacher, his fellow students, the peasants at our home in the country, our servants, and anyone who had ever known or seen him. His body was laid to rest on Friday, June 5, at the 11th hour, in the church of Santa Croce, in our family sepulchre, in the passage where the men are buried; it was not out of order to bestow this honour upon him. May God give his soul repose in Heaven, and may it please him to give life to Alberto's father, mother, brothers, and sisters, if that should be best for their souls; if not, may God do his holy will.

I could never have imagined that God taking my son from me, passing from this life to the next, could have been and continues to be such a knife in my heart. Many months have passed since the time of Alberto's death, and neither his mother nor I can forget. We continuously have his image before us – all his ways, the things he said and did – reminding us of him day and night, at breakfast, at supper, in the house, outside, sleeping, waking, in the country, in Florence. In any way we think about him, it keeps a knife in our hearts. And truly, this is not happening because we are obsessed with him; it's just the opposite. From the day he left us, we have tried to keep him out of our thoughts as much as possible, except when we are praying. After he died, we left the house and stayed away a month before any of us returned; and then for the entire summer no one slept in his room; and for more than a year after he died, I, Giovanni, didn't enter his room, for no other reason than overwhelming grief. May God grant that this shall not be a reason for hastening the end of our lives!

Of the Capture of Vico Pisano

On the 17th of July 1406, at the third hour, we Florentines captured the town of Vico Pisano. We gained control of the place by besieging it and reaching an agreement with the townspeople, as there were very few provisions within the town, except for wine, of which there was enough for three years; they surrendered because they were at the end of their rope. The fortress was in almost total chaos, and about 150 people had died within, from bombards and stones that had been hurled with catapults and other machines of our city. The fortress is very strong, so it was not possible to take it by force.

The Capture of Pisa and the Treaties We Made

At about the time of the siege of Vico Pisano, we were continually plotting to take over Pisa and the surrounding fortified towns, but it all came to nothing. In truth, many of the towns simply did what Pisa wanted them to do; but certain small towns came to agreements with us. One of these, and one of the best, was Pecciole. This was in large part due to Piero Gaetani, a citizen of Pisa, who rebelled against the Pisans and sold us the towns of Pietra Cassa and Laiatico. He helped our city a great deal against the Pisans. He was given a benefice and made a Florentine citizen, and was given a house in Parione that had belonged to the Gianfigliazzi. Once we had gained control of Pisa, he was knighted by the Florentine government and given the coat of arms of the Florentine people and the Guelph party.

On Saturday the ninth of October 1406, the feast day of St Domninus, at the third hour, three members of the Ten on War entered Pisa with a troop of mounted soldiers. Three thousand foot soldiers had entered earlier, at the second hour, and had taken control of the city and its fortresses. The names of the members of the Ten on War were Gino di Neri Capponi, Bartolomeo di Tomaso Parigi, and Bernardo di Matteo Cavalcanti. There were three thousand cavalry. Messer Giovanni Gambacorta emerged from the city gates to meet them, and came back with them into the city square, where he surrendered the Seignory of Pisa and presented the staff of office to Bartolomeo Parigi, who was acting on behalf of the government of Florence. Then he asked if he had completely fulfilled what he had promised, and if there was anything left that he should do. He was told no, that he had fully satisfied all of his pledges. Then the hostages were handed over to him – that is, 20 young Florentines who were placed in the custody of Sforza and other allies of ours, who promised Messer Giovanni to keep them until he should be fully satisfied. And then he received 20 thousand gold florins. Once this was done, they went before the Elders and sat down with them. The Pisans made some kind of official declaration, as is customary, and Bartolomeo Parigi gave them a response. Then the Elders departed, and the members of the Ten on War remained in their place. And as the Elders were leaving, they uncovered their heads and stood up before the members of the Ten on War as a sign of submission. At that point a great deal of grain, bread, flour, and wine was brought into Pisa, and each person was given enough to last for several days. The following Tuesday – that is, the 12th of October – at the ninth hour, Messer Giovanni returned to Florence accompanied by his brothers and all of the Gambacorta faction and certain intimate friends of theirs. And it was decided by the magistracies that they should be given everything that had been promised to them – that is, fifty thousand florins – in addition to the town of Bagno and the surrounding countryside, the fortress at Rocca Silana, their estates and those of the men who had rebelled against them, and three houses in Florence. They and certain of their friends were declared to be citizens and exempt for life. And Lotto Gambacorta, Archbishop of Pisa, was to receive 1200 gold florins every year from the government of Florence until such time as he would become Bishop of Florence.

These were important agreements for them, considering that there weren't enough provisions in Pisa to live for a day. If we had attacked the city a month earlier, we would have conquered it. For there were two thousand men left, but only eight hundred were capable of fighting, and these men were so worn out by hunger that they couldn't hold a crossbow steady in their hands, much less shoot with it. But our soldiers had not wanted to make the attempt. Several hundred people died of starvation, and if the siege had continued for two more days, everyone would have died; this is certain. We didn't know, or didn't want to know, what was the most honourable and useful thing for us to do. But in the end we got control of Pisa by spending a great deal of money: *omnia pro meliori*! Our sins and those of our enemies caused both them and us to suffer, but God in his grace helped us more. To him we should give praise and prayers, and know that we owe this and every honour and accomplishment of our city to him, and we should not be ungrateful for so many benefits, for everything proceeds from his will.

Three of our citizens received benefices from the government: Gino Capponi was appointed captain of Pisa for eight months, Bartolomeo Parigi was made *podestà* of Pisa for six months, and Bernardo Cavalcanti was made captain of Campiglia for six months. There were fireworks in Florence and the countryside for three nights, and there were processions for three days. On the last day, the painting of Our Lady and all of the relics in Florence and the countryside were brought forth, and the Te Deum was sung, and mass was said in the cathedral of Santa Reparata. The members of the Seignory and the Captains sent many men to spread the news throughout Italy, and they were all welcomed and honoured and rewarded well. Representatives from all our districts and dependencies and all the friends of our government and our neighbours came with lavish, stately retinues to rejoice with us. Then twenty of the leading citizens of Pisa came as ambassadors. During all of these visits – and there were many – there was jousting with eighteen jousters. Then there were tournaments of armed men ordered by the Captains of the Guelph party for three days; every day there were two brigades of ten men per brigade, all wearing special uniforms. The first day, one brigade wore white and the other red, with a particular insignia; on the second day, one brigade wore green and the other blue, with a particular insignia; on the third day, one brigade worn green with a diagonal red stripe and the other wore white and blue with a particular insignia. There were many honours bestowed each day. On the third day, Messer Piero Gaetani was knighted on the parapet by Messer Vanni Castellani, who was Standard-bearer of Justice at that time. Messer Carlo was knighted, and Messer Michele was clad in spurs with the coats of arms of Florence and of the Guelph party. Also that morning, Francesco Casali, the Lord of Cortona, was knighted by Messer Vanni, and Messer Nicolò Guasconi was clad in spurs; the Florentine government gave him the coat of arms of the people, a horse worth 130 gold florins, and a velvet-clad servant with a helmet decorated with a lion made of pearls and an olive tree rendered in silver all decorated with pearls and a sword beautifully decorated with gold and enamel. The Lord of Cortona arranged for a joust in the square in front of the church of Santa Maria Novella – he donated a helmet decorated with gilded silver. All of these things happened in October. At the beginning of November, the Lord of Cortona departed, and the Captains of the Guelph party gave him their coat of arms, a horse with livery, and a robe. He swore loyalty to the Guelph party and promised never to go against that insignia, but to always to defend it wherever he might be.

Around this time, many men – 300 or more – came from Pisa, and it was deemed that they should appear every morning before the *podestà*, and so they did. These citizens of Pisa were comely and honourable, and showed themselves to be the most valiant of men – there were gentlemen of great breeding, merchants, and artisans of every kind among them. And if many of them were not happy, they showed it in only the most decent way. They dealt with us Florentines with proper and wise words. A commission of ten men was formed, who could do whatever they deemed proper in Pisa for a period of ten months – they could fortify it any way, levy taxes, and even send away and call back whichever citizens they chose. These ministers were called the Ten on Pisa, and they were authorized to spend a thousand florins per month; if more money were needed, the approval of the Seignory and the Colleges was necessary. The first group of ten men was appointed without taking a vote; later, votes were taken. Two votes were taken to select a captain and *podestà* to be sent to Pisa. In the voting for the captain, twenty men voted on behalf of each *gonfalone*, and for the *podestà*, thirty or so men voted for each *gonfalone*. Two votes were held to select three vicariates for the territory outside of Pisa; the number of men voting was 153, and a two-thirds majority was necessary to win the vote. Subsequently, twelve *podestà* and one captain were appointed for the territory outside of Pisa.

Three votes were held, with a hundred voting per *gonfalone*. Both men of high standing and artisans took part in these votes: one-quarter artisans and one-sixth grandees. Chamberlains and other officials were appointed to collect taxes. The Ten on Pisa ordered that the citadel from which we had been driven out should be rebuilt, and reinforced in another way. They also ordered that another citadel be built near the Spina bridge at the San Marco gate, with two emergency entrances – one by land and the other on the Arno River. They also ordered that a strong bridgehouse be built above each entrance. Captains, castellans, soldiers, crossbowmen, and infantry were sent to guard the fortresses. One of the first men selected as a *podestà* was Giano di Giovanni Morelli. But because the place where they wanted to send him was ill situated and had unhealthy air, he refused. A few days later, Morello di Paolo Morelli was sent as *podestà* to the Colline, where the fortress is called Crespina (it is 32 miles from Florence and twelve miles from Pisa). Giano decided to go, on account of being the first. He left Florence in December 1406. Many of the men selected to go refused on account of the pestilence, which had already struck some of the men who had been sent to Pisa and Lucca. It was said that at least six of the men who had been sent to the territory of Pisa died. May God grant life and health to those who have gone forth, and to those of us who remain.

The Captains of the Guelph party announced throughout Tuscany and Lombardy and in Venice and in many other places that a joust would be held on the 28th of November, and they had a palisade erected in the square in front of the church of Santa Croce, where each competitor in the joust would enter accompanied by three men on horseback and four on foot. Anyone who was not there by the 18th hour could not enter. The joust was very orderly and fine, and many jousters competed. Two prizes were awarded. The first was a helmet decorated with silver and pearls, which cost one hundred forty florins; this was given to Felice Brancacci. The second was a helmet with a beautiful crest, which cost sixty florins or so; this second prize was given to Maso Betti. The winners were deemed to be well and reasonably chosen; they were selected by Messer Maso degli Albizzi, Messer Vanni Castellani, Messer Jacopo Gianfigliazzi, and Federico de' Nerli, and this was the culmination of the festivities for our victory over Pisa. Many other jousts were held later, but not as part of those festivities. But that event raised people's spirits, disposing them to spend lavishly on magnificent celebrations.

And it happened that our spirits were so high, that of all the sumptuary laws that had been passed with all proper judgment, none was observed. The laws were broken by people of high rank, by people of the middle class, and by people of the lower classes. In addition to precious stones, velvets, crimson fabrics, silks and satins, silk fabrics worked with gold thread, all of our women were so copious in the use of all these things that I believe that many of them could have passed for queens. The festivities were magnificent, and our spirits rose every day.

Before we took over Pisa, because the expenditures were great and the demands for public loans were not fairly apportioned, and especially for those in the government, several attempts were made to fix this. But it all came to nothing, and in the meantime eight or ten more public loans were levied. Lip service was given, to the effect that no more loans should be levied unless the burden were apportioned more fairly, but nothing changed, because the ones who had the power to make a change did not do so, for it would not have been to their advantage. But finally, after many violent and prolonged arguments, it was decided to change the way that the forced loans were imposed. I believe that God intervened, and this was the method proposed: 30 men from the major guilds and ten from the lesser guilds would vote. From a two-thirds majority, 18 votes were counted – that is, 14 from the major guilds, and four from the minor. Nine names would be drawn from these, 2 of which had to be artisans. One after the other, they would be obliged to make a loan to the government on behalf of their whole district. The second name would not be drawn until the first person chosen had deposited the money at the abbey of Santa Maria degli Angeli.[100] This distribution was better apportioned than any previous one had ever been. Certainly, some mistakes were made, but the people who would be affected by them did not complain. Florence was in a tumult, and everyone was complaining. For all the need that there was, in the end no forced loans were levied, because agreement could not be reached. In this way, we passed some very bad times.

***

[ON THE ANNIVERSARY OF THE DEATH OF MORELLI'S SON ALBERTO]

The course of a blessed year had already passed, but during all that time I could never forget the loss of my beloved son; I was continually sad and

---

100 This is where forced loans were deposited, and where it was decided how the loans would be imposed district by district.

afflicted, thinking about him and his misfortune. And as often happens, the closer one gets to a good or a bad thing the more affected he is by it, thus the closer I got to the anniversary of the cruel day and hour when my sweet son was taken without the hope of my ever seeing him again – I, his father who only desired his health, the more I remembered all of the agony, the pain, the sweet and gentle words of my blessed son. Afflicted in all of my senses, I felt as though my body and soul were being pierced by a thousand spears.

Realizing that never in the world could I be happy about him, yet hoping to give some comfort to his soul or at least some remembrance of me, his father afflicted with tribulations, having many times commended the well-being of the soul of my son to the merciful Son of God and his benevolent mother the Virgin Mary, I disposed my soul and body and all my feelings to more fervour and love, forgetting my own soul and any benefit to myself, before the figure of the crucified Son of God, to which I had many times commended the health of my son's body when he was ill. On my bare knees and clad only in my shirt, with nothing on my head and a scourge around my neck, looking toward the crucifix I began to ponder over my own sins, by which I realized I had sorely offended the Son of God. I thought about how the harsh, bitter, dark passion of the crucified Christ, upon whose figure I was gazing, had saved man from eternal damnation. He did not suffer to look upon me with harshness, but, I believe, granting me the gift of his pity, he moved my heart and all my senses with the greatest tenderness, and my face was bathed in tears.

I remained thus for quite some time; and when the weakness of my mind had been relieved and I felt comforted, I began to pray to the crucified Son of God with pious psalms and orations. And after having said many psalms and lauds in a piously modulated voice in reverence to him, I set myself to pray with my eyes, my heart, and my mind, uttering the following words: "O most holy and sacred Father, Son, and Holy Spirit, in whose majesty, divinity, and unity Heaven and the whole universe shine and glimmer, grant to your humble servant and faithful Christian your infinite grace so that I may utter in praise and reverence words that are worthy to be spoken in your presence, making them favourable to the blessed soul of my son, which you have received in your grace, and let that soul be beatified in your sight."

After I had said these few words, I felt greatly comforted, and God's mercy gave me as much confidence as if an angelic voice had announced these very words to me: "Faithful Christian, your prayers are pleasing to me, as are the prayers of all those who have faith and hope in me. And, as you see, I chose to be crucified so that this sacrifice would redeem all souls in the sight of my Father."

As these words were resounding in my mind, I began to pray, saying: "My Lord, father, creator and saviour of all who have good and sincere faith in you and firm and secure hope in your mercy, and who follow you with a pure mind and a fervent heart, grant me your mercy so that my request might be granted. And my request is this: I beseech you, if at this hour and at this point the soul of my son Alberto, which one year ago departed from his unfortunate body, should not yet have arrived at eternal glory on account of his sins, may you grant a special gift, and command him to appear before your most holy majesty, so that he may be granted his final wish. And since on account of my own sins I am not worthy of such a gift, my Lord, I ask it in the name of your most holy incarnation." And at this point I recited the gospel of the Virgin Mary Annunciate.[101] "And I also beseech you, my Lord, to make me a participant by the mercy and infinite gift of your sweetest and most gracious birth," again saying the Gospel. "And I beseech you by the worthy words and actions of your most beloved servant Mary, for which she was rewarded with the resurrection of her brother Lazarus," again reciting the Gospel.[102] "And finally, my Lord, I beseech you by your most holy, glorious, and victorious, though difficult and bitter passion." And I read St John the Evangelist's account of Christ's passion.[103] "After the holy Resurrection, my Lord and true Saviour, grant me grace, not because I am worthy if not through your infinite mercy; but I beseech you by the excellent gift and supreme happiness that in the hour of your passion you gave to the Holy Fathers, who were eagerly awaiting you in the darkness." And as before, I read the Gospel. "By the consolation that the Virgin Mary received when you, her sweet glorified son, appeared to her, and by the merit of the supreme happiness of the holy Apostles when you appeared among them, my Lord, and said *pax vobis*, I beseech you to grant peace in eternity to the blessed soul of my son. And finally I beseech you, my Lord, by the grace of your most glorious ascension; and as if at that point Heaven were full of fragrance and splendour and supreme rejoicing and gladness of the holy angels and the others who have been blessed with eternal life, thus I beseech you, O sweet and gracious Son of God the Father and the Holy Spirit, who are full of grace and the living source of infinite mercy, that, as you created the world and came down on earth to

------

101 Probably Luke 1:26–38.
102 Probably Luke 7:36–50 and John 11.
103 John 13–19.

save man from darkness and misery by your passion, and as you created the heavens and all the universe to obey your grandeur, and as you created the holy Paradise for your and our glory *ab eterno*, and you adorned and glorified the nine choirs of angels and cleansed them of the vices of pride and envy by your supreme justice; thus by all the graces and gifts and holy works, I beseech you to take pity on me and hear my prayer, and to grant my wish by your mercy and forgiveness, for the health, light, joy, and gladness of the blessed soul of my sweet son. For I wish his soul to be content in the life eternal, as much as, if that were possible, I would desire to have him alive again in this world."

Having said this prayer and become silent, but continuing to gaze upon the figure of the Crucified Christ, fixing my eyes on his precious wounds, in my heart I said these words: "My Lord, forgive my ignorance, which has not helped but rather hindered my prayer, which did not have the proper reverence nor the proper words to offer to your Majesty. But you, O Lord, see and know all and know that such graces are possessed neither by myself nor by other sinners. Yet I would fain have such graces in order to praise you. But I hope that my poor words will find favour with you, who are so full of grace."

My heart and mind having quieted, my eyes turned to the right side of the Crucified Christ, where, at the foot of the cross I saw his pure, holy Mother. I gazed upon her, full of the greatest grief and sadness; and realizing that my sins were the cause of so much affliction, my tongue did not dare to utter a single word. Considering in my mind the sorrow of that pure Virgin, mother of the pure and precious Son, and thinking of the many trials that she had undergone since the day of his birth, up to this time when he appeared before her eyes dead and flagellated by dissolute sinners, abandoned by his apostles and finding herself alone with St John to witness the cruel punishment and torture of the precious flesh of her beloved Son, having no comfort and remaining alone, abandoned with her Son, I felt such sorrow and pain that I truly believed that my soul would leave my body. For a short time I remained as if stunned, but then remembering what my son had suffered, I began to feel sorely ashamed, and I almost got up and stopped praying. But it pleased God that I should recover, and I remained kneeling where I was; and gazing upon the Virgin full of so much sorrow, I began to weep, and my anguish was so great that for a long time I was unable to restrain my tears.

But inspired by God, for I was weeping for the fate of all sinners, I took heart and was comforted. Drying the many tears from my eyes and my face, and making the sign of the cross, I said the *Salve Regina*. And having said that prayer, thus I began to speak, in my uncouth way: "Sweetest Mother, fragrant tabernacle of the Son of God, let me partake of your sorrow and affliction, so that with full justice, by participating in your afflictions, I shall become worthy to receive the blessing of that happiness that dwells in the wood of the holy cross. And make me worthy of the grace that I have beseeched your Son to grant me, and commend me and the soul of my son to the living font of his mercy. I make bold to ask this gift and this grace of you, the Queen of Heaven, by the words of the prayer that I just recited in your reverence and praise – that prayer in which you are described as our advocate in the sight of the Creator. We faithful Christians who are inhabitants of the city of Florence believe ourselves to be favoured by you, as unworthy as we may be; you, O sweetest Mother, have shown this by the many favours that you have granted to our City. Being greatly encouraged by these things, I turn again to your benevolence and your clemency, O immaculate Queen, beloved of the angels, supreme joy of the saints who dwell in your realm, true consolation of the Son of God, that you, moved by pity, shall pray to the divine Majesty for the well-being of the soul of my son, whom I desire to appear before you and to receive the gift of your blessing, so that, consoled forever, he shall enjoy the triumphal chorus of your beatitude."

Having said this prayer with the devoted reverence granted to me by God, I stood, and took up with a sense of devotion the painting that my son had so sweetly kissed during his illness, and kissed it in the same places that he had done, when he was imploring God to restore his health. Then I knelt again in the usual place and recited the Apostles' Creed and the Gospel of St John.[104] As I recited the Gospel, my eyes were fixed on the figure of St John in the painting, depicted on the left side of the precious cross, with as much suffering and sadness as it is possible to portray in the human body. Before I could finish reciting the blessed Gospel, I was unable to hold back my tears, which were flowing down my face and body and making a pool on the floor. And participating to some degree in the intensity of the saint's sorrow, not as much as I should have, but as much as it was granted me to do, I turned my eyes and my heart toward the image of the blessed saint, and said:

"O devoted and most faithful saint, sweet and loving brother of the transfigured Son of the devoted Virgin Mary, at the foot of whose cross

---

104 Obviously, Morelli didn't recite the entire gospel of St John, but probably the first part (1:1–14), which starting in the fourteenth century was recited after the mass and later incorporated into the mass itself (1570).

you are so sorely afflicted and are tormented body and soul so that it pains my eyes to regard you, I regret my sins because my iniquities are placed on your shoulders. You, immaculate, pure, and spotless, suffer and are afflicted by the dark, cruel death of the Son of God, which he, the Immaculate Lamb, chose to suffer in order to liberate me and other sinners from eternal suffering. I, the cause of your sorrow, am pained by the realization that I am unable to atone for my sins. Thus, not being able to do anything else, I beseech you, venerable saint who bears the burden of my wrongdoings, to let your sorrow be continuously before my eyes as a mirror of my sins, so that your splendour shall continuously illuminate the darkness of my mind. And not despairing because of my sins, because I am comforted by the meaning of your beautiful name,[105] I dare, as my heart desires, to implore you to grant your grace – which, deriving from the supreme light of your holiness and charity, will enable me to be received before the divine Majesty. And I shall remain content for having received the desired mercy. I realize that it would be superfluous for me to say more to your saintliness, for in your excellence you can see my every desire. And I know that it would be more useful for me, an ignorant sinner, to read the gospels in which you recount the most holy works of Christ, rather than to continue speaking. In order to satisfy in part my ignorant desire, I shall follow his will, in which, illuminated by the Son of God and inspired by the secret things inspired by the celestial bosom, I shall ask for the special grace and the excellent gift of the eternal health of the young soul of my son, whose body I gave back to Mother Earth. And so intense is my desire for this gift of the health of his eternal soul, that I offer every good thing that I ever said or did – as poor as they may be – for the health of his soul, and I implore you, O gracious St John, to exalt his soul in the glory of the face of the supreme Majesty."

Having said these prayers, giving great praise to God and his blessed saints, greatly comforted, it seemed to me that my prayers must have been heard. As I held the picture in my arms, I kissed the image of the crucified Christ and his Mother and St John the Evangelist many times, and then said the Te Deum. And having made reverence to the holy images, I left to go and rest my body. And thus, happy and full of good hope and great comfort, I went to my bed, and after making the sign of the cross I prepared for sleep.

---

105 According to St Jerome, the name John means "Dominus gratia eius." In Hebrew, the meaning is "God is generous."

But as soon as I had I disposed myself to sleep, the invidious Enemy, who I am certain was afflicted by my prayer, having for my sins partly deprived me of my liberty, assailed me grievously, attacking and oppressing me, and putting a thousand thoughts into my mind. He wished to show that my prayer and striving had been in vain, and that the soul is nothing but a slight breath, which is an impassible thing that cannot see nor feel heat or cold nor any suffering or pleasure. And he said that the only good or bad thing in the world was that which can be acquired, and that this is why I was ignorant, for I had never realized this. He said that I had been greatly oppressed by fortune, and that everything had gone against me, and that there was no other recourse but to become desperate, in this way: if Fortune takes a hundred florins away from you, you should steal a hundred; if Fortune brings you illness, when you are healthy you should break every law, and fulfil your every desire, and hold everything in contempt. As all of these things were going through my mind, I tossed and turned a thousand times in bed. Wanting to flee these vain, evil thoughts, I could not escape them. So, commending myself repeatedly to God, I felt that I was returning to myself and lessening that fire. But this was nothing – for suddenly, as when a wick flares up, the bad thoughts returned to my mind. After tormenting me so much, it seemed clear to me that the Enemy was trying to lead me into sin and error, and I endeavoured to take heart and gain control of my thoughts.

As I had decided this, all of the darkness in my mind departed, and I remained thinking of the good fortune that I had enjoyed since the day I was born. But then I began to think that I had never had a moment of perfect happiness, and that if it had ever seemed so, it was not true; rather, everything that happened to me had given me more sorrow and torment. Continuing to fantasize in this way, I said to myself, "Show me how this is true!"

Then the Devil, as if he wished to recall to my mind many things in great detail and with efficacious arguments, began thus to represent to me: "Giovanni, you are completely abandoned by good fortune; you never were, nor will you ever be, entirely content in this world. You can see very well that this is true, but so that you shall be very clear about this, I shall begin at the beginning. You were born, and it was fated that you should be your father's last child to survive, which was no small misfortune.[106] Then, when you were three years old, you were left without a father, and when you were age four, you were abandoned by a cruel mother.

____

106 After the birth of Giovanni, Paolo Morelli had a fifth son, who died immediately.

During this time, you were deprived of a large part of your rightful inheritance, which had been acquired by your father through toil and industry. When you were five years old, you were given over to the care and toil of the world – that is, to school; for many years you had to study, be submissive to your teachers, be beaten and terrorized. In addition to this submission and torment, in your sixth year you were doubly afflicted by the harshness of the city of Florence, and from all sides and in all ways and by many people you were unjustly robbed of your property and sustenance. In your sixth year, you had a serious, long illness, which denied you the pleasures of childhood. In your eighth year, you had a teacher at home, and were subjected day and night to his discipline, which, though beneficial, was unpleasant for a child's freedom. In your ninth year, you were plagued by illness and had two bouts of smallpox; the second brought you to the brink of death. Your tenth and eleventh years passed under the supervision of the teacher, which it seems to me was much harsher than is usual nowadays. In your twelfth year, you were taken to Romagna, and then to Friuli, under the supervision of Simone Spini, to the great disadvantage of yourself and your brothers and sisters. In Friuli you were taken ill and seriously affected by fevers, and remained for some time ill and unhappy. Finally, when you recovered, and had survived the fatal epidemic that occurred that year, the man who was a second father to you, Matteo di More Quaratesi, was taken away from you. He had treated you and your brothers and sisters like his own children, and cared for you devotedly. At his death, you lost half of what was rightfully yours and all of what had been his, which he had left to you as if you were his own children. You were saddened by the loss of this inheritance of which you defenceless children had been deprived, not so much for its value, but rather for the delightful country house in which you had lived in happier times. And whereas you used to take pleasure in the countryside, now that your fortunes had changed, you began to dislike it. If you consider well, you were at an age that should be the most pleasurable, but you were already beset by worries about your affairs. Your spirit was oppressed by constantly hearing how badly things were going for you; you wanted to take some action to set things right, and your powerlessness caused you much torment. This continued for several years, and still does to this day, but with less affliction now that the years have taught you how to understand and deal with suffering. From the time you were fifteen to twenty years of age, you had not a moment's rest, and were continually beset by misfortunes. Your eldest sister, who was married, died, and you had to find a husband for your other sister; you had to make several loans of money to the State (the war with the Duke of Milan had begun); you were beset by your in-laws and neighbours, who begrudged you what you had. You contracted a horrible illness that lasted a year. You were disgusted with yourself, with those who cared for you, with everyone you knew.

"When you had recovered from this illness, you contracted an even worse one, but you didn't realize it: you fell head over heels in love with a woman who caused you great torment and deprived you of much good and honour, and you lost a great deal of time on account of her. Finally, she was promised to you in marriage as you desired, and just to make you suffer more, her family reneged on the agreement and she was given to another man. You were devastated by this, not realizing that you were fortunate that it had happened. In your twenty-first year, you had to struggle with forced loans and reparations; you had to sell your best property. You lived in this hell, having to change your residence several times, until your thirty-fifth year. And your bad luck still continues. You have lost your position in the State, you have lost out on account of your evil relations, you are without money, without allies, without State honours; you can see no way you'll ever have them, and you have no one to comfort and assist you. You are related by marriage to people who can hurt you rather than help you.[107] You rejected those who could have helped you and brought you honour. You haven't enjoyed a penny of the inheritance left you by your father; it has brought you sorrow, not pleasure. You have had sixteen serious illnesses in your life; you've never had a piece of good news in your life, and if you did, it only brought you sorrow.

"The best news you ever had was when your wife had your first child, and this was turned into the greatest sorrow and the greatest torment you ever had. Your first child was a son, so that his death would really break your heart. You saw him intelligent and healthy, so when you lost him you would suffer more; you loved him and yet you never gave him any of your wealth. You didn't treat him like a son, but like a stranger; you never gave him a moment's rest; you never looked on him kindly; you never kissed him once; you worked him to death in your shop, and thrashed him cruelly and often. And finally, when he was mortally ill, you didn't realize that he was on the brink of death and so you didn't let him make his peace with God (though as young as he was, God surely had already pardoned him), so that his soul and yours might be comforted.

---

107 I.e., the Alberti family.

You watched him die in excruciating pain and torment, and never saw him have a moment's respite for the sixteen days that his illness lasted. You have lost him, and you shall never see him again in this world; and the memory of his death will make you always live in fear and torment for your other children."

Pondering upon and remembering these things and many other sad, painful memories, I became desperate almost to the point of putting an end to all those adversities. But then I turned to the Crucifix and commended myself to Christ and meditated upon his sufferings, which were infinite; and I took comfort in realizing that my own sufferings were nothing compared to the bitter Passion of Christ. I realized that I wasn't alone, for almost everyone is afflicted in one way or another. Thus, having found relief for my soul, I fell asleep.

Having slept deeply and without disturbance for an hour, my sleep became lighter, I believe because of the inspiration of God and his devoted saints, John the Baptist, St Anthony and St Benedict and St Francis and St Catherine, for whom I have always borne a special devotion and in whom I have had firm hope. And I dreamed the following things: I had gone for rest and recreation to Settimello. But not being able to get the image of my son out of my mind, in spite of all my efforts, I left that place and went up the mountain to Monte Morello.[108] I wanted to distract my eyes and my thoughts, but it was all to the contrary; for the more I endeavoured to forget my son, the more fervently his image, his manner, his words, his adversities, his toils, my reproaches of him, my threats, the fact that I did not make him happy, my way of estranging myself from him, my having taken little or no consolation in him – all these things and even more cruel ones came into my mind, saddening me deeply. Moving swiftly up the mountain, unaware of the time or the path I was taking on account of my thoughts and all the images of my son, I lost all perception of reality. And I remembered the hour and the place of his conception, and what a consolation it was to me and his mother. I remembered when he moved inside his mother's womb and the way I would carefully place my hand on her belly, awaiting his birth with the greatest desire. And after he was born, being a boy and with all his limbs and well proportioned, what gladness, what rejoicing it seemed that I

---

108 Settimello and Monte Morello are to the northwest of Florence. The Morelli family had a house in this area. Ascending a mountain – in this case, a mountain that bore the family name – is an allusion to purification, as in Dante.

received, and then, as he began to grow, how much contentment, how much pleasure in his childish words, pleasing in the sight of all, loving toward me his father and toward his mother, intelligent and wonderful in his childhood. And then, as he grew up, he learned to read and write twice as well as was required, and he learned how to pray to God with all the proper prayers and lauds. And thus, remembering every act of virtue and goodness in which he shone, my body was no longer able to bear the bitterness, so I decided to sit down, since I was a good two miles away from home. And there, weeping, I thought about the bitterness of my son's illness and of all the days and hours and pain and suffering and piteous words and actions. And finally, having lost consciousness and the ability to see and speak, his pure soul abandoned that poor body of his, as I gave him my paternal benediction and commended his soul to the true Creator. Cruel death twisted all of his limbs. Lamenting that I would never see him again, I let him go.

Saddened by these dark thoughts, I remained looking toward Monte Morello. At that moment, my thoughts turned to God; and considering the life of the servants of God, I had half a mind to go that evening to stay with the hermits who live on the mountain.[109] Thinking about this soothed my mind, and I almost decided to go there that evening to receive great consolation. But then I realized how far away it was, and it was already past the time of vespers, and I was alone and it was dark. Wavering between yes and no, I was leaning toward following my better instincts.

I remained there for half an hour, gazing toward the mountain, when I saw a bird about the size of a parrot flying down toward me. Its feathers were of the purest white, and its neck, breast, and wings were gleaming and adorned with gold fringe. Its beak was all gold; its legs and feet were brilliant green. In the dream, first it alighted on an olive tree, where it sang a song that was so sweet and gentle that it seemed like something from Paradise, and it gave me the greatest joy and comfort. I was a stone's throw away from the bird and in an open place, barren and without trees. I got up and began to approach the bird, and found myself standing at the foot of a fruit tree. With my arms around the tree trunk, I stood looking up at the bird, waiting for it to approach me, or to sing another song. The bird flew out of the olive tree and headed down

---

109 During the fifteenth century there were still two hermitages on the slopes of Mount Morello: one dedicated to St Jerome and Mary Magdalen, and the other to the Virgin Mary and St Catherine.

the mountain, alighting among the branches of a juniper tree. Hopping from branch to branch, it pecked at three of the juniper berries, and then sang a song much longer than the first, but not as sweet or as pleasant. When it finished singing, I tried to get closer, and saw that it had alighted on a fig tree. I went forward, waiting to see and hear more. Suddenly I spied two hogs and a sow near a ditch. One of the hogs mounted the sow at the foot of the juniper tree. Then the bird flew out of the juniper tree and landed in a myrtle tree near to where I was standing. The bird looked at me and I looked at it for a while, and then it began to sing a song, about as long as the first song. As sweet and gentle as that first song had been, this song was so much more bitter and fearsome, to the point that I plugged my ears. When the bird had finished singing, or rather lamenting, it began to peck at its feet until they bled. Unable to bear seeing it suffer so, I turned my back; and when I turned around again, it had flown into a sorb tree. I left the place, because I wanted to flee the horror and bitterness of what I had seen, and I returned toward the place where the bird had been in the juniper tree. I drove away the hogs, and remained with my mind clouded with many thoughts.[110]

I thought to rest myself, so I sat down at the foot of the juniper tree, gazing up toward the peak of the mountain, and thinking that I would like to go up there that evening. I still had the things that I had seen in my mind. I kept looking up, but could not see the way to go. And yet, drawn not so much by my initial desire to spend the night with the hermits, but rather by the vision of the bird (which I thought I would be able to find at the top of the mountain, for I was certain that was where it had flown), with this idea I started out. The ascent was difficult. I kept my eyes and ears open in the hope of seeing or hearing the bird. Suddenly I heard a great commotion in the nearby woods; it was the hogs again, and I shuddered all over. Then the sow appeared, alone, very hot and fierce, and she was headed toward me. As I tried to get out of her way, I fell; the sow trod on me as she ran by. A feeling of great disgust came over me at the incredible stench. And verily at that moment I resolved in my heart never again to eat the flesh of that animal, on account of the great discomfort, abomination, and danger that I had just escaped.

---

110 The symbolism of the trees in this passage is as follows: the olive tree symbolizes the peace and joy brought by the birth of Morelli's son Alberto; the juniper represents the bitterness of Alberto's illness; the myrtle is an allusion to death; the fig represents the forbidden fruit cursed by Jesus; and the sorb tree, with its dark, bitter berries, can be seen as an allusion to the hardness of Giovanni's heart.

After I had gone about a half mile up the mountain, I looked around me; it was almost night, and a little ahead of me I could see two lights that looked like two stars, so shiny were they. I headed toward the shining, and the closer I got, the stronger the feeling of aroma and sweetness became. When I arrived at the source of the light, I fell on my knees and prayed to God to reveal to me what it was. Having prayed, and resolved to follow the righteous path of God, it seemed as if a veil had been lifted from my eyes. The light was so dazzling that I closed my eyes. I wanted to see, but could not keep my eyes open. So once again I asked God to make me worthy of seeing this holy light. And then, as if through a veil, I saw a pure white maiden. Her eyes shone like stars, and in her right hand she held a palm frond, and in the left a wheel, with which it seemed to me she had completely rent asunder the sow that I had seen before. The maiden was surrounded by many birds similar to the one I had seen, and they were all singing the sweetest songs.[111]

As I gazed upon this sweet vision, wishing to know what it meant, I said these words in my heart: "O most holy Queen of Heaven, since in your benevolence you have made me worthy to see the magnificent glory of your bright, clear purity, let me partake in this mystery, so that I may correct my sins, using part of your infinite virtue."

With these thoughts in my heart, I saw one the birds most joyfully fly up to the maiden, and flying around her with the sweetest singing, it seemed to me that it wanted her to take it in her hands. Suddenly the holy maiden held out her hand; and what had seemed to be a bird became a spirit and knelt at her feet, and she put her hand on its head. The spirit looked like a white angel, and seemed to shine with golden beams of light. Turning toward me, it seemed to greet me with great rejoicing. Reassured, and trying to see better, for the splendour impeded my sight, I seemed to discern the face of my sweet son, for the salvation of whose soul I had been striving. My heart was bursting with happiness, and I longed to embrace and kiss him. Crying out, "O my son! My Alberto!" I rushed forward to embrace him. But every time I approached, it seemed I got no closer to him.

He seemed to realize that I was struggling, and said: "Have patience; do not attempt the impossible." I was bewildered.

The spirit turned to the holy and most pure virgin, almost as if he were asking permission to speak to me, and spoke these words: "Father, take

---

111 The maiden here is the traditional depiction of St Catherine of Alexandria, to whom Morelli was particularly devoted. Here she symbolizes the victory of chastity over lust (represented by the sow).

comfort, for your prayers have reached Heaven and have been accepted by our Lord God. And as a sign of this, you see me here to console you. May peace be with you; have hope in divine providence, and our benevolent Lord will answer your just and righteous petitions."

When the spirit had finished speaking, I replied: "My son, I thank God for giving me the consolation of seeing you in a place of eternal health for your soul, here with this blessed and devout virgin and queen who beseeched God to answer my prayer. And I entreat them to give you permission to respond to me and to answer my questions and resolve my doubts. Son, tell me if I am the reason for you being taken from this world on account of my sins, and tell me if your brothers will be of some consolation to me in this world, and if I will have any more sons. And I ask you, hoping in the virtue of God and not going against his commandments as I did after you left me, if I can hope that he will grant me good fortune in my business affairs and honour to my city; and finally, if I shall leave this life a young or old man."

The spirit, smiling, turned as before to the holy saint, and then replied: "O Father, my own flesh and blood, you ask many things, and God who is humble and gracious will satisfy you in part. It was God's will, for the health of your soul and of your family, to call me to him; the way and the form of my death were bitter for everyone, and this was on account of our sin. He shall safeguard you and your family; you shall pray to God to protect the sons you have – hold them dear. You have had many benefits from God and you shall have more, if you acknowledge what he has done for you; if you do the opposite, the Lord is righteous. Remember that you have received more benefits from him than you deserve. You ask if you shall depart this world as a young man or an old one. I advise you to live to be old for your own good and that of your family, if it pleases God, before whose Majesty I shall always speak in favour of your needs and those of my mother."

After the spirit uttered these words, the entire vision disappeared; and I awoke, very shaken and in part happy.

The Death of Pope Innocent

Pope Innocent departed this life on November 6, 1406.[112] The cardinals met in conclave to elect a new shepherd for the Church. Florence sent Friar Giovanni Dominici as an ambassador to the College of Cardinals

---

112 Innocent VII, who was pope from 1404 to 1406.

to entreat them to elect someone who could unify the Church.[113] But before Friar Giovanni could deliver our message, the cardinals elected Pope Gregory XII,[114] with certain agreements and conditions to ensure the unity of the Holy Church. Ambassadors then went out from Florence to rejoice with His Holiness and to encourage and beseech him to re-unify the apostolic seat. The election was held to be a good one, because Gregory was a devout man, and it was believed that he was well disposed in principle to reunifying the Church; but after a short time, he came to an agreement with the anti-Pope[115] and they decided to meet at Savona. Gregory got as far as Siena, and Benedict was approaching Genoa. But then Gregory decided not to go to Savona after all, alleging that he would surely be deceived by the French. This was the first obstacle put up by Gregory's nephews, and, it is said, by Friar Dominici. Then, on the 20th of January 1407, Gregory departed from Siena and headed toward Lucca; he passed through our territory, was greatly honoured, and neither he nor his cardinals spent a penny while they were here. There was a great deal of snow at this time, heavier than any in memory. It lasted for a good month before Gregory could get as far as Florence. He and Benedict kept avoiding each other; when one would approach where the other was, that one would go away. Things went on like this for some time.

The News of the Capture of Rome by Ladislaus Reaches Florence

Around this time, King Ladislaus of Naples built up a force of around 14 thousand cavalry, with good captains, and 3 thousand foot soldiers; at sea he had six galleys and 4 ships, in good shape. He went to Rome, where he came to an agreement with Paolo Orsini.[116] Seeing that Orsini was defenceless, Ladislaus bribed him, and Orsini turned the city over to him; this was on the 22nd of April 1408. The news reached Florence on the 25th of April; it was taken as a very bad sign, and our citizens were greatly disturbed. They reproached themselves, saying that it would have been easy to defend Rome, but we had not done it. But, with the good

---

113 This was the worst moment of the so-called Western Schism or Papal Schism in the Catholic Church, which lasted from 1378 to 1417. Innocent VII and then Gregory XII were opposed by a series of anti-popes: Benedict XIII, Alexander V, and John XXIII.

114 Angelo Correr was elected on 30 November 1406.

115 Benedict XIII.

116 The papal commander in Rome at the time.

counsel of the wise men of Florence, on the 16th of April we entered into a ten-year agreement with the Sienese to defend the Papal States. This was done solely out of fear of Ladislaus – for it was feared that now that he had taken over Rome, he would set his sights on Florence. Ladislaus wore a garment with the words "Aut Caesar aut nihil"[117] – clearly, he wanted to become emperor.

On Saturday, May 5th, King Ladislaus sent us an olive branch. On Sunday evening, the Gloria was sounded and fireworks were set off in the usual places – but not by the citizens, or by very few. The King's messenger was given a horse covered with golden draperies, and he was adorned with the same – all of this was done with a heavy heart. On the 10th of May, the King sent his ambassadors to Florence – Messer Benedetto Acciaiuoli, Messer Francesco d'Ortona, and Messer Gentile da Sermona, accompanied by eighty cavalry. They were hosted in the Acciaiuoli home, and were greatly honoured by the city government and by the citizens as well – especially Messer Benedetto. They delivered a request from the King, to the effect that we should not work to reunify the Church, and they complained about our league with the Sienese. They pressed us very insistently for a response. We took counsel together, and our reply was that we could not enter into a league with Ladislaus for many reasons, including our obligation to the Sienese. We said that seeking the reunification of the Church was our duty, and that of every faithful Christian, and thus we wanted to continue striving for the good of Christianity and for the King's salvation, and so on. Once they had our response, they went to Lucca to try to dissuade the Pope from every good intention, and the cardinals as well. They remained there for several days, and then returned to Rome with words that were more threatening than benign.

The Cardinals Named by Pope Gregory

Gregory named 4 cardinals, among whom was Friar Giovanni Dominici. The other cardinals were greatly displeased by this, for when they had elected Gregory, he had promised not to appoint any cardinals. Gregory's nephews threatened the cardinals who complained, attacking some of them with arms in order to frighten them. So the cardinals departed in secret, and went to Pisa; only one of the older cardinals, the weakest, remained. This was on the 14th of May. A few days later, the cardinals affiliated with the anti-Pope departed as well; they went to Leghorn, and

---

117 "Either a Caesar or nothing."

then, when they had been assured that they would not be harmed, they went to Pisa and joined the other cardinals, ready to make a true union. They both began to protest to Gregory and to Benedict.

The League with the Cardinal of Bologna

In June 1408 we joined a league with the Cardinal of Bologna. During that month, and after we had reached an agreement with him, we sent ambassadors to King Ladislaus, I believe in order to respond to his embassy and to reach some kind of accord with him and induce him to favour our league. We did not want to go against our allies, nor against the Holy Church or the Franciscans. We wanted to learn what the King's intentions were, and to persuade him to favour us. He was threatening to send 5 thousand cavalry to Lucca for the Pope; he was not doing this to ensure the Pope's safety, but rather to do harm to us in that area, if he could. Our ambassadors returned without achieving anything, and on the first of July, King Ladislaus sent word to the effect that he wanted to have a relationship with us and would not ignore our advice. He said that he was surprised that we were jealous of him and that he wanted what was good for us as much as he did for himself. He said many other chicaneries, traitorous words, lies, and falsehoods, all with the intention of deceiving us. And he almost achieved his aim. On the 2nd of July, we got the news that he had taken Perugia – and this after he had promised our ambassadors that he would not intervene in Tuscany. And that is just one of the things he did!

Because we were afraid that Ladislaus might send forces to Lucca as he had been threatening to do, we endeavoured to keep Pope Gregory safe at Siena. For this reason, at Gregory's request we sent 12 hostages to Casteldurante to ensure his safety. He was escorted as far as Siena by our soldiers and citizens; that was on the 4th of July. He remained there for several days, and then left for Rimini with a small escort, and poorly equipped.

The Letters Sent by Pope Innocent's Cardinals to Hold a Council

Innocent's cardinals wrote to our Seignory that they wanted to find a place to hold a Council. They said that various places had been offered to them, but that they would be happy to hold the Council in our territory in any place we liked, as long as it was to their satisfaction. We held long consultations about this. A few people counselled that we should not do this without the consent of King Ladislaus – they believed him to be dangerous because he wanted to be free of kings and emperors, and we would be putting our territory in danger, and it would cause hardship and unrest in our city. Others – the great majority, one might say – said that we should do it, and that we should negotiate with the cardinals about where and how the Council should be held, and that the King and the Emperor and any great potentate should be denied access. They maintained that this would be good for God, bring honour to the world, be beneficial for our citizens, and would strengthen our state; they also said that it would be a recompense to the Church for our past offences against her. With these and other arguments, it was decided to let the Council be held in our territory. On August 14th, two cardinals came to Florence – the Cardinal of Aquileia and the Cardinal of Turi – those associated with the anti-Pope. They were received with great honour. They dismounted at the church of Santa Croce and had a great audience. In the end, they obtained Pisa as the place where the Council would be held, under certain pacts and conditions. They went off to Pisa, well contented, and proceeded to organize the Council. They sent ambassadors throughout all of the Christian world, announcing the Council and explaining the reasons that were moving them to hold it. So all of Christianity sent representatives to Pisa, except King Ladislaus and the Venetians and a small part of the Holy Roman Empire. In the end, the Venetians gave in and came as well. On the first of February, Gregory was removed as Pope. And then on the 6th, there was a smaller council in the bishopric, to which all of the clergy of Florence and its environs were convoked. At this council, too, they agreed that they would forswear allegiance to Gregory in good conscience. The citizens of Florence received this decision with approval.

Around this time, Count Alberico passed through Perugia, trying to get to Bologna, with 800 cavalry. The Malatesta denied him passage, and also the exiles from Perugia. Our government wanted to intervene in order to get Count Alberico to come to an agreement with the Cardinal, by which he would have given his fortresses back to him. But he behaved in such an unseemly manner that even the legendary King Darius couldn't have pleased him. And because he could see that the situation was worsening, even though the King was writing every third day to say that we shouldn't worry (whereas all the while he was endeavouring to alienate all of our allies and was making treaties everywhere near our territory), after many vicissitudes it was decided to send 600 lancers and 2,000 infantry to help the Cardinal. There were still many who did not believe that the King was intending to betray us, because they believed the lies that he was continually writing to us, pretending that he was occupied elsewhere. Some people said, "He will go to Lombardy," others said he would go to Bologna, and others thought he would go to Arezzo. So we continued not to act, not without fear but with little forethought. And we didn't believe that the King would attack, until the time when he was upon us.

The Arrival of King Ladislaus in Rome

On the 20th of March 1408, King Ladislaus left Naples and came to Rome with eight to ten thousand cavalry and 4 thousand infantry. At this time, a magistracy of Ten on War was elected, and Malatesta da Pesaro was hired for a period of 9 months to lead a force of up to a thousand infantry. After reaching Rome, Ladislaus remained there for a few days and then departed for Florence, accompanied by people who were then in Rome – Paolo Orsini, among others. When they were only a few miles outside of Rome, there came such a deluge that they were forced to return to Rome, and their retinue suffered great damage. After remaining in Rome for several days, Ladislaus set off toward Siena and San Quirico d'Orcia, where he pitched camp on the 13th of April, 1409. Eight galleys and four armed ships of King Ladislaus arrived at the port of Pisa, and at that time they captured our ship *Nottona*, which was laden with English wool and other merchandise valued at one hundred thousand florins. The capture of this ship was a great defeat and brought great dismay to all Florentines, poor and rich alike. What is more, the King captured the island of Elba, which was then governed by our ally, the Lord of Piombino;[118] this was on the 18th of April. At this time there was great pressure on the Sienese, for the King's forces were approaching their city gates. And the King was offering fat rewards to anyone who would come to an agreement with him. We were very afraid that the Sienese would not hold firm, because they are not truly our friends, and they are voluble. The King's army was threatening them, the time for the harvest was approaching, and the King was promising to give them good terms if they would only let him pass through their territory. Our ambassadors were continually urging the Sienese not to give in – they were more effective and more firm than we were, and much more frank.

---

118 Gherardo d'Appiano.

Their actions saved them and us from servitude, for the freedom of Florence was in their hands – this is the truth. The King's forces left the area of Siena and arrived in Arezzo on the 2nd of May, and they would almost have captured that town on account of the idiocy of our people who were there, and especially the captain of the guard, who was playing chess when he should have been defending the town. The King captured a fortress of the Albergotti, and was in negotiations with Cocchi, Messer Antonio, and Borghese Albergotti. Since I was *gonfaloniere* at the time, it fell to me to question them. Then he decamped from Arezzo, went to Cortona on the 9th of May, and attacked that town quite violently. On the first of June, he captured Valiano, which had been under our control, and on the 3rd he took over Cortona thanks to the idiocy of the Lord of that city, Francesco Casali, who did not know to whom he should turn, and after vacillating he found that he had been tricked by the King. On the 26th of June, the King broke camp and went to Perugia; from there he returned to Naples with a small retinue.

The League with King Louis of France

On the 29th of June, we entered into an alliance with King Louis of Anjou for a period of twenty months. During the first twelve months, he was supposed to provide a thousand lancers, or five hundred, or eight hundred, and was also supposed to send armed galleys. The following year, we were supposed to provide six hundred lancers for eight months. Many people were against this alliance; it was proclaimed on the 7th of July. Our government sent eight ambassadors dressed in white damask, each accompanied by ten men on horseback, all dressed in white. The election of Pope Alexander V pleased everyone.

My Term as Gonfaloniere

On August 29, 1409, I, Giovanni Morelli, was appointed to the office of *gonfaloniere*; it was the feast of St John the Baptist. On the fifth of September, our office recommended that the Florentine government hire Muzio Attendolo Sforza as a *condottiere*, with a force of 660 lancers, and the Count of Tagliacozzo with 150; we were also supposed to hire Gian Colonna with a force of 200 lancers, but out of avarice this was not done. And it was almost on account of this that we did not take Rome. Around this time, we sent a force to Rome, and the expedition stalled so long that for every florin we spent, we lost fifty. On the 26th, the towns of

Orvieto and Viterbo rebelled; and on the 29th, our troops made camp in the area of St Peter's in Rome; they remained there for several days, but were never able to cross the Tiber River.

Departure of Our Troops from Rome

On the 10th of October 1409 our troops left Rome, heading into the countryside. A few days later, King Louis arrived in Prato, and Cardinal Baldassare Cossa[119] arrived in Orvieto. The King remained only a few days in Prato. Our ambassadors went there to discuss with him how things should go on. They came to an agreement, and the King returned to France; Cardinal Cossa went to Pisa. Later, on the 2nd of January 1410, we got the news of the taking of Rome.[120] This had occurred on the night before the 30th of December. On the 7th of January, the victory was celebrated with a procession, a Mass, and fireworks. Around this time, a certain Gabriello Brunelleschi,[121] a member of the court at Naples, offered us a peace treaty several times on behalf of the King. But we did not know if this Gabriello truly had a mandate from the King, so for a while nothing happened. Finally we sent word to him, to find out once and for all if he was telling the truth. He had been proposing just the conditions that we Florentines wanted, but he did not persevere.

The Rout of King Louis at Sea, the Death of Pope Alexander, and the Election of Pope John XXIII

On the 8th of May 1410, King Louis arrived at the port of Genoa with two galleys and two half-galleys; on that same day, Pope Alexander died in Bologna. On the 17th, Pope John XXIII was elected; he was the former Cardinal of Sant'Angelo and Lord of Bologna, Baldassare Cossa.[122] On the 19th of May, five of King Louis's vessels were captured, with all of his equipment, men, horses, weapons, money, and a great deal of grain. This was sad news, and greatly dismayed the people of Florence. This happened on account of the Genoese, who, after having promised King

---

119 A few months later, Cossa would be elected to succeed Alexander V as pope.

120 By the anti-pope Alexander V and the Florentines, with the help of Paolo Orsini.

121 A Florentine who had risen to a high rank in the court of King Ladislaus in Naples. See Alison Lewin, *Negotiating Survival: Florence and the Great Schism, 1378–1417* (Madison, NJ: Fairleigh Dickinson University Press, 2003).

122 There were rumours that Cossa had had Alexander poisoned.

Louis that he had nothing to fear from them, then betrayed him. On the 6th of June, King Louis spent the night at Prato; then he left for Bologna to ask the Pope for help. On that same day, eight citizens dressed in crimson went to the Pope to rejoice with him about his election. They were accompanied by a retinue dressed in rose-coloured garments. In all, there were eighty on horseback. On the 25th of June, King Louis returned to Prato and stayed there for about a month, in the home of Giovanni da Prato,[123] waiting for the Pope and us Florentines to send him money. These were tumultuous times of war, heavy spending, and suspicion. This always happens to our city when we get involved with a Pope, emperor, dukes, kings, or any potentate. To make things worse, it began to rain in March of 1409, and the bad weather – with rain, wind, fog, and sleet – lasted a long time.

On the 18th of July, we received letters from Paolo Orsini, in which he said that Sforza was plotting with King Ladislaus. We were very suspicious of Paolo, because he had been acting strangely. But later we learned that it was not true; he was a loyal, upright man. The King left Prato and went to Siena, where he stayed for several days and was greatly honoured by the Sienese. Then in August he went to Montepulciano, and stayed there for quite some time. On the 10th of September, he left Montepulciano and went to Rome, with our brigades and 600 lancers that we, or rather Sforza, our captain, had to give him. They subsequently defeated King Ladislaus at Ceperano in October 1410.

My Election to the Magistracy of the Twelve Good Men

On the 15th of September 1410 I took office as a member of the Twelve Good Men. On the 19th of October, Gabriello Brunelleschi came to Florence with an offer of peace. We negotiated and reached an agreement, and he returned to Naples. During the time that Gabriello was travelling back to Naples, new elections were held for all of the magistracies. Niccolaio di Niccolò Fagni was among my supporters. There was a great deal of fighting to keep our members of the Seignory and to include the results of the previous elections in the selection of the members of the Colleges. But this did not happen, because those who had been in the previous election would never consent. There was a great deal of division

---

123 Possibly Giovanni Gherardi da Prato, the author of the *Paradiso degli Alberti,* a
fictional miscellany written around 1390.

in Florence on account of this – there was discord between fathers and sons, between brothers, between partners, between neighbours; and between all the Guelphs and whenever votes were taken. This was only because of the selfishness of those who had previously been elected and did not want others to join them. The debate went on among all the subsequent Priors. But as I said, there was discord in all of the magistracies – some were for and some against – and they were motivated by nothing but their own interests.

The Peace Treaty with King Ladislaus

On the 22nd of December, Gabriello Brunelleschi returned to Florence with two ambassadors representing King Ladislaus, and with a full mandate to reach a peace agreement with us. An agreement was reached, there was a general council, and all the chapters – 15 in all – were notified. They were advised to ratify the peace treaty, with all due haste; so the treaty was executed. On the 11th of January King Louis was in Prato; he was visited by our ambassadors, and on the 13th he went to Bologna to see the Pope. On the 14th of January, peace was declared between King Ladislaus and the government of Florence, to take effect on the calends of February; this was because the league between us and King Louis was still in effect. The proclamation was criticized by wise men, and for good reason. On the 19th of January 1411, the olive branch reached us from Cortona. On the first of February there was a procession and a Mass celebrated, and in the evening the peace treaty was celebrated with fireworks.

The Arrival in Florence of One Who Claimed to Be Jacopo da Carrara

On the 19th of March 1411, a man claiming to be Messer Jacopo di Messer Francesco da Carrara, who had been captured by the Venetians when they took over Verona, arrived in Florence. Everyone was convinced that the Venetians had killed Jacopo's father and two older sons, because the father had been seen dead. The sons were not seen, but they had been sentenced to death and had received the last sacraments, and three holes were seen that had been dug for their graves. The man who said he was Jacopo went to the home of his brother, Marsilio da Carrara, who said that the man was not Jacopo; Jacopo's friends and the people who were managing his money said the same thing. The entire populace of Florence resolutely maintained that the man was indeed

Jacopo, and with reason, for his manners and demeanour showed this to be so – he was kind, cheerful, and outgoing. And he never lost heart or became discouraged, no matter how harshly he was rejected by many people. After much arguing for and against him, finally he was robbed, beaten, stripped naked, and driven away with many threats by those who he had believed were his best friends. He fled like a man pursued, going to Siena. When he wrote to his friends about what had occurred, the government and all the people of Florence were very sorry about what had happened to him. The government granted his request, or rather what his friends requested on his behalf; and he returned to Florence. He again suffered many hard and heavy vicissitudes – more at the hands of his brothers and old friends than from strangers. Ultimately, either because it was believed to be true or because it was his destiny, he was accepted as Jacopo da Carrara, and thus was he honoured by the people of Florence. Then, after a certain period of time, it became clear to us that in fact he was not Jacopo da Carrara, and this is still held to be certain. So much for being so constant!

On the first of April 1411, King Louis was in Prato. He had returned from Bologna to go to Rome, and he arrived in Siena. Honoured by the Sienese, he stayed there for several days.

Sunday, the 13th of July 1421, at the 19th hour or thereabouts, my son Antoniotto passed from this life. He had been taken ill at Laiatico, or along the way. On the 20th of June, he had accompanied Mea there. The letters I received said that Antoniotto had the tertian fever, continuously, and he had two phlegmatic fevers and was wasting away. Because of God's will or my own negligence, I did not go to him at Laiatico, much to my sorrow. He died at Empoli, as he was trying to make his way back to Florence. I managed to get to Empoli and see him before he died; he recognized me and gave me his blessing. He lasted about 3 hours after I arrived, and then passed away with his mind intact, having taken the last sacraments. I had his body brought back to Florence, and he was buried honourably with his mother. May Christ take his soul and make me worthy to not witness the death of my other sons; may they be granted a long, happy life with sons and daughters, all good Christians. May it thus please God, the giver of every good thing and every grace. Amen.

Memoirs

Bonaccorso Pitti

Here I, Bonaccorso di Neri di Bonaccorso de' Pitti, shall record the births of the children that I had with my wife, Monna Francesca di Luca di Piero degli Albizzi. On the first of June 1395 was born a son whom we named Luca, after Monna Francesca's father. His godfathers were Niccolò di Messer Luigi Guicciardini and Matteo d'Antonio Tanaglia.

Camilla was born on the 24th of December 1398. Her godfathers were Banco da Varazano, Chimento di Stefano, and Cocco Donati.

Rinieri was born on [*text missing in the original manuscript*] September 1400, in the palace of the Bianchi in Bologna, where we had gone to flee the plague. His godfathers were Ser Antonio di Ser Bandino da Romena, Ugolino da Lino, Bartolo and Richino di Ser Ciechino, Barlolomeo di [*text missing*], and Giovannino the miller.

Ruberto was born on the 25th of April 1401, the feast day of St Mark; I was born on the same day in 1354. I named him Ruberto after Rupert of Bavaria,[1] who was elected King of the Romans and new emperor, and who ennobled me and my brothers and our descendants, as we shall record here below. I chose Rosso di Piero and Fantone di Naldo to be Ruberto's godfathers.

Curradina was born on the 29th of October 1403. Her godparents were Bartolo di Berto da Marcialla and Monna Paola del Maciante Guicciardini.

---

1 Rupert of Germany, of the house of Wittelsbach, son of Rupert II elector palatinate of the Rhine and Beatrix of Sicily. He was elector palatinate from 1398 and king of Germany from 1400 until his death in 1410.

Our second Curradina was born on the 21st of September in the year 1404. Her godfathers were Ser Stefano Martini and Guasparre di Bartolomeo, representing the City of Pescia.

Neri Cipriano was born on the 4th of November in the year 1405. His godfathers were Ruberto di Francesco de' Rossi, the physician, Maestro Domenico di [*text missing*], and Ser Lapo Pieri of Certaldo.

Maddalena was born on the 15th of August in the year 1407; her godparents were Lupo del Guidicie and Lapo di Bicchiello, representing the City of Montespertoli.

Francesco was born on the 20th of October in the year 1408 at the third hour of the night; his godparents were Monna Costanza di Boccaccio Velluti, Monna Mea del Minna, and our tenant, Giovanna.

Primavera was born on the 22nd of October in the year 1409. Her godparents were Piero del Ciucco, Monna Caterina di Niccolò Malegonelle, and Monna Bandecca, the sister of Ruberto de' Rossi.

Pietro Vettorio was born on the 28th of July in the year 1410. His godparents were Don Simone Mattei, the prior of San Felice in Piazza,[2] and Ser Giuliano dalla Cicogna, a priest at the church of San Lorenzo.

Camilla Gaia was born on the 16th of August in the year 1413 at the fourth hour of the night. Her godparents were Francesco di Rustico, called the Fat Man, and Monna Costanza di Marco di Filippo and Giovanna [*text missing*], for the love of God. We named her Gaia after a sister of our father's, who when she became a widow entered the Hospice of La Scala, bequeathing her dowry to it.

Luigi Gimignano was born on the 22nd of November at nine in the morning. His godfathers were Ser Giovanni di Becci and Ser Ambrogio di Francesco in the name of the entire City of San Gimignano, and they gave gifts of many confections and wax and six silver cups valued at 50 gold florins in all. The moon was in the 15th hour, and the position of the stars [*text missing*] and 12 days.

This is to record that I, Bonaccorso, was born on the 25th of April in the year 1354, and my father, Neri, died on the 25th of April in the year 1374. I had a son named Ruberto who was also born on the 25th of April, as recorded above.[3]

---

2 San Felice in Piazza was one of the oldest parishes in Florence, located near the Ponte Vecchio, where the Pitti family lived.

3 Bonaccorso wrote below this: "Ruberto's son," and further down the page, on the left, he wrote: "Salvestro Francesco." At the bottom of the page, written in another hand during the sixteenth or seventeenth century, is the following authentication: "In the hand of Buonacorso di Neri di Buonacorso di Maffeo di Cione di Buonsigniore, son of another Buonsigniore de' Pitti."

On the 24th of March at three in the morning in the year 1419, the moon was in the third day and position 1053; Fioretta, the wife of my son Luca, gave birth to a son who was named Buonsoccorso Lionardo.[4] His godfathers were Nero di Filippo del Nero, Talento di Filippo di Bono, Antonio Fantoni, Antonio d'Antonio del Caccia, Jacopo d'Agostino Coppino, Giovanni di [*text missing*], a commander in the Palace of the Seignory[5] called Lancrescino, and Ser Festino from Visso.

Dionora was born on the first of September in the year 1421. Her godfathers were Niccolò dello Strenato and Jacopo Guidotti and [*text missing*].

Piero Amerigo was born on the 15th of November in the year 1422 around half past seven in the evening. On the 16th, we gave him his two names, after two of the sons of Francesco di Neri. His godfathers were Ser Antonio Melegonelle, Jacopo di [*text missing*] Guidetti, and Alessandro di Jacopo di Niccolò di Nome.

Filippo was born on the [*text missing*] of January in the year 1423; he was born in Corno di Val di Pesa. We named him Filippo after the father of the mother of his mother. The godfathers were [*text missing*].

Spinetto was born on March 26th in the year 1425. He was born in Verrucola in the region of Lunigiana, during the time that Luca was the commissioner for our city in the lands of the Marchese Spinetta. The godfathers were the Marchese Antonio Alberigo, the Marchese Bernabò, and Bernardo Nardi and Don Giovanni from Vinca, Bardino di [*text missing*], and several others.

Agnola was born on the 13th of July in the year 1426. The godparents were Giovanni, called the Baker, and Monna Giovanna Francesca di Piero Sciancato.

Lisa Caterina was born on the 4th of April 1429. Her godfathers were Gherardo Baroncielli and Papi Galli.

My son Ruberto di Bonaccorso Pitti and his wife Giovanna di Salvestro Gondi had a son, Salvestro, on the 5th of June 1429. The godparents were Foresta di Giovanni and Don Giovanni from Vinca in the region of Lunigiana.

4　Elsewhere, he is referred to as Buonaccorso – the names Buonsoccorso and Buonaccorso were equivalent. Here begins the record of the descendants of Buonaccorso's first-born son Luca, from Buonsoccorso to Lisa.

5　The Seignory (seignory), the chief governing body of medieval and Renaissance Florence, consisted of nine members, the *Priori* (Priors) who were chosen from the guilds (six from the major guilds, and two from the minor guilds). The ninth Prior was the *Gonfaloniere di giustizia* (Standard-bearer of Justice).

In the Year of Our Lord MCCCCXII

I, Bonaccorso di Neri di Bonaccorso di Maffeo di Bonsignore de' Pitti, in the year indicated above,[6] began to write in this book in order to leave a record of what I have been able to discover and hear about our ancestors and our early and modern relatives and events that happened or will happen in my own time. I shall also record things about the life and times of some of our progenitors and especially the ones I have seen. And if I cannot find or write about the founding of our family, the reason is that the earliest writings about our family, which were handed down from person to person, ended up in the hands of a man named Ciore di Lapo di Ciore di Maffeo di Bonsignore, son of another Bonsignore. This Ciore had the evil habit of speaking ill of others and was full of envy. It happened that on account of his evil ways he was not accepted into public office in the city of Florence. When Ciore saw that we sons of Neri were all accepted into some of the more honourable civic offices, he was extremely envious, and said that we were the ones who were depriving him of social status, and so he very erroneously believed himself to have been injured by us. So, when he died, in his will he left everything to a daughter of his who today is in a convent outside of the Roman Gate.[7] After he died, we went to see his daughter while she was still living in his home, and told her that we wanted the books and papers and writings relating to the early days of our family that Ciore had in his possession. She replied that she knew nothing about them, but that on several occasions she had seen Ciore sell a large number of books. And shortly before his death, she had seen him burn many papers and writings. We understood very clearly that she was telling the truth, for we searched the entire house and didn't find any books or writings, neither old nor modern. Thus it clearly appeared that Ciore had evilly wished that no writings that he had in his possession relating to himself or his ancestors should remain. Because of this loss, I went about searching for books and writings

---

6 This was a decisive year for Bonaccorso and his family, because 1412 was when their bitter dispute with the Ricasoli family, and their struggles with foreign affairs, came to an end. This had been an extremely difficult period for the Pitti family, who feared that they might be radically eliminated from Florentine political life. See Gene A. Brucker, *The Civic World of Early Renaissance Florence* (Princeton: Princeton University Press, 1977), 360 ff.

7 A community of Augustinian nuns founded in 1340.

of my grandfather Bonaccorso. These books are in tatters, poorly written and poorly kept, and yet I was able to learn some things that I shall record here. I shall also record what I remember having heard Neri our father say about the origins of our family.

Chiefly I find that we Pitti, who were Guelphs, were driven out of Semifonte[8] by the Ghibellines, who controlled that place. Evidently our family split into three branches. The first branch settled in a place called Luiano.[9] Today there are large numbers of descendants of that branch of the family in honourable positions in the countryside there, and they have wealth and rich estates. Their name – that is, the name of the whole family – is Luiesi, and they appear to dominate that area; and judging by their coat of arms, it appears that we came from the same family, because our coats of arms are identical. And I have heard from elders of their family and ours that the two families always maintained friendly relations. The second branch of the family went straightaway to Florence; they were called Ammirati and there are still some of them there today, living in the country very near to the hill of Semifonte, which was destroyed by the Commune of Florence in the year 1202. This family was once greatly honoured in Florence, and their coat of arms is the same as ours – that is, a shield with white and black waves.

The third branch of the family – that is, our family, the Pitti – settled in Castelvecchio in the Val di Pesa,[10] where we purchased fine, rich property, and especially a place called The Towers, where there were two large noble houses, and each house had a tower with a dovecote. That property is still ours today, but there is only one tower, because during my lifetime the other tower was demolished for reasons of safety, for it looked as if it was about to fall down.

A few years later, our ancestors came to live in Florence, and their first homes were those that are owned today by the Machiavelli family in the neighbourhood of Santa Felicita.[11] These houses were sold to them by Ciore and Bonaccorso di Maffeo de' Pitti.

---

8 A fortified town in the Val d'Elsa, not far from the town of Certaldo, cited by Dante in *Paradise* XVI, 62 as the antomomastic country place from which people migrated to the city. Semifonte flourished during the second half of the twelfth century and was destroyed in 1202.

9 At Impruneta in the province of Florence, where there was an oratory under the patronage of the Pitti family.

10 The Pesa is a tributary of the Arno River, in the Chianti area. The Pitti family's properties were about twenty kilometres from Florence, southeast of San Casciano in the Val di Pesa.

11 In the quarter of Santo Spirito, where Boccaccio also lived. The Pitti family later had a chapel in the church of Santa Felicita.

I, Bonaccorso di Neri, will record here my travels through the world after my father's death. Our father died in 1374 on the 25th of April, may God rest his soul. After his death, we his children – there were eight of us, along with our mother – left for a place of ours in the Val di Pesa, called The Horn, because there was a plague in Florence. Our brother Giovanni died there, at the age of 27, and during those days our cousin Niccolò di Cione also died of the plague, in our house. When the plague abated in Florence, we returned there. We found that Monna Margherita, Niccolò's mother, had emptied the house where they were living and had taken all of their furniture and valuables to the home of a sister of hers, the mother of Niccolò and Guido del Grasso Mannelli. It did not seem to us that this was a good thing to do, considering that Niccolò's brother Cione and his son were still alive; the son was in Venice. My brothers and I decided that I should go to Venice and take with me Cione, who was 18 years old, so that he could see to his affairs. I went to Venice; and on the way back to Florence with Cione, it happened that on the feast day of St Andrew we departed from Pietramala.[12] When we were on this side of the valley, on account of the cold we dismounted. Cione was walking behind his horse and gave it a lash on the rump; the horse kicked him in the head so hard that Cione fell, unconscious. I had him placed on a litter that I was able to obtain there near the church, and had him taken to Firenzuola,[13] and I immediately wrote to my brothers in Florence about what had happened. They told his mother, and they immediately brought Maestro Francesco the physician to Firenzuola, where they found Cione in such a state that no one believed he would survive. He lived, thanks to the good care of the doctor, and he remained there for more than a month, after which he was taken to Florence, where he recovered completely. I wanted to mention this incident because apart from the suffering I endured in those mountains for fear that my cousin's son would die in my arms, with his head on the ground and me sitting there, I feared that his mother – out of maliciousness or madness or to create a scandal – would say to my brother Piero: "You sent Bonaccorso with my son in order to kill him, which you have done, and you poisoned my other son in your home in the Val di Pesa."

---

12 A town in the Apennines, between Bologna and the Futa Pass, which descends into Florence.
13 A town about forty kilometres northeast of Florence.

I was even more distressed and upset when I had Cione placed on the stretcher and removed a bag that he had on a strap around his neck in which he had several opened letters from his Manelli cousins. They wrote to him saying that when his mother had wanted to return to the house where she and his brother had been living, we threw her out and beat her. I didn't want to give those letters back to Cione when he had recovered; I told him that I wanted to show them to our relatives, so that they could see the lies that the Manelli family were telling. Cione came to ask for the letters back, saying: "If you don't give them to me, I shall complain about what you have done to me, for you know that you struck me on the head with a sword, and I kept quiet and will continue to keep quiet if you give the letters back to me." When I heard those words, I considered that his mother and the Manelli family were making him say that, either to frighten me into giving him back the letters, or to upset me so that I would do him some harm. I said to him: "You are not saying these false words to me of your own accord. I know who is making you say this, and for what reason. I will not give the letters back to you no matter what you say, nor shall I out of anger do to you what you deserve for your evil actions. Now go away and complain and say whatever you like, for I don't care; the truth will out." I went immediately to the home of Bonaccorso di Rucco de' Pitti and took the letters with me; all my brothers were there, as well as Bonaccorso's son Luigi and his nephew Lionardo di Gieppo Pitti and poor Ciore di Lapo Pitti. I told them what Cione had said to me, and I showed them the letters. After much discussion, they asked for the letters and told me not to take any action about this matter; I should leave it to them. About a month later, they sent for me, and Cione was in their presence. After many words said in excuse for Cione, Cione asked me to forgive him, swearing that he didn't remember how he had gotten the blow to his head, and that he had foolishly said to me what he had been instructed to say by those who wished to create a scandal. But, he said, God had made him see the truth, which he firmly believed was that his horse had kicked him, as I had said. I forgave him freely, and many years later he entreated me to forgive his mother; he also wanted me to forgive his Manelli cousins. I did not wish to do so at the time, but a good 30 years later, on a Good Friday at the church of Santo Spirito, in order to obtain grace from Our Lord, and with no other intermediary than God, I had them called into the chapter house and gave them peace, which they accepted, humbling themselves and so on.

In 1375, being young, inexperienced, and eager to see the world and seek my fortune, I joined up with Matteo dello Scielto Tinghi,[14] who was a merchant and also a great gambler. We went to Genoa, Pavia, back to Genoa, and on to Nice and then Avignon. While we were there during the Christmas holidays, we were seized by the Pope's marshal and thrown into prison. After we had been in prison for eight days, we were interrogated; they said we were spies for the Florentine government. They produced a letter to Matteo from his brother in Florence, saying that Bologna had rebelled against the Pope at the instigation of the Florentines and with their assistance. After many questions and answers, the court realized that we were innocent of the charge. Nonetheless, they demanded that we pay 3,000 florins in bail to prevent us from leaving Avignon without the permission of the Pope's marshal. Matteo found someone to put up the bail, and once we were out of prison he wisely decided that it was very dangerous for us to stay there on account of the war that our city was waging in the Papal States.[15] He decided that we should leave, with the intention of reimbursing the merchants who had stood our bail if they should be forced to pay. We left, returning to Florence as quickly as we could; and we hadn't been there long when letters came from Avignon with the news that the Pope had imprisoned all the Florentines there, and seized all their records and property. We heard the same from everywhere in Western Europe, where people were being arrested and their property seized on account of Pope Gregory's decree against all Florentines. But for all that, our city did not cease to wage war against the evil clerics of that time; but I never saw a good priest before or since.

The next year, Matteo decided to go to Prussia[16] and to take me with him. He sent me on ahead, telling me to wait for him in Padua or Venice, where he would join me within a month. I visited Padua, Vicenza, and Verona and then came back to Padua, whence I left for Venice.

---

14 Tinghi was one of the leaders of an anti-government group in 1381, but later carried out several missions for the Florentine Republic. He was a powerful ally of the Albizzi family.

15 The war between Florence and Pope Gregory XI (1370–8) was called the War of the Eight Saints after the "Otto di Guerra" (Eight on War), the magistracy that presided over Florence's military activities.

16 This name was generally used to denote the northern part of Germany, which in Bonaccorso's day was dominated by the Teutonic Order.

Matteo came, and bought a thousand ducats worth of saffron. From Venice we set sail for Senj in Slavonia and then made our way by land to Zagreb and Buda,[17] where Matteo sold the saffron at 1,000 ducats' profit. Because I had fallen seriously ill with a fever and two swollen glands in the groin, Matteo left me in Buda at the home of Michele Marucci,[18] and left Michele 12 ducats for my passage back to Florence, if I should survive. And he promised that whatever Michele spent on my illness he would repay upon his return. He went on his way, leaving me alone and very poorly cared for. My bed was a large sack of straw in a warming room;[19] no doctor ever came to visit me, and there were no women in the house – only a servant boy who cooked and served Michele and two merchants who were staying with him. I was on the brink of death. After lying in that room for six whole weeks, on the night of St Martin a party of Germans gathered to play the pipes and dance in a large room across from where I lay on the sack of straw with a towel instead of a sheet under me and a shaggy blanket and my greasy fur coat over me. They stuck their heads in to see who was there, and finding me, forced me into my fur coat and dragged me around and around the room, saying to me: "Either you'll get better or you'll die and then you won't have to suffer any longer." They dragged me around the room for the better part of an hour in spite of all my entreaties, and only let go of me when I collapsed from exhaustion. Then they put me back on my sack, threw their lined cloaks on top of me, and went back to their drinking and dancing. They kept it up all night while I sweated under that pile of clothes. In the morning when they came for their cloaks, they forced me to dress again and to have a drink with them, which I did willingly enough. They left, and I rested for perhaps an hour and then went out to the home of Bartolomeo di Guido Baldi of Florence, who was master of the royal mint at Buda. He was happy to see me, and kept me to dine with him; after we had dined, we started to gamble. With 55 Venetian *soldini*, which was all the money I had left, I won 4 florins from him. At that moment there arrived several Jews and some more Germans, who used to come often to gamble with Bartolomeo. They began to gamble and I with them, and at the end of the day I brought home 20 gold florins that I had won. The

---

17 Buda was then separate from Pest, with which it would later form Budapest.

18 A Florentine merchant and speculator who acted as Tinghi's agent.

19 A *stufa secca*, a room warmed by hot air coming from below or the sides (see *Decameron* II, 4).

next day I returned and won about 40 gold florins, and so on every day for 15 whole days, by which time I found I had won 1,200 florins or thereabouts with my 55 *soldini.* Michele Mariucci kept begging me to stop gambling, saying: "Buy some horses[20] and go back to Florence and I will go with you as far as Senj, for I'm leaving for there in a few days." In fact, I took his advice and bought six fine horses and hired a page and four servants. When we reached Senj, Michele sold me five of his own horses. I hired a boat from Marseilles and loaded the horses on it; but there was a storm and the winds were against us, so I barely reached Venice in 24 days. And while we were unloading the horses one of the best of them put its shoulder out. When we reached Padua, I gave one of the horses to Giorgio Bagnesi, who was living there with his wife, Madonna Caterina, a daughter of Niccolò Malegonelle and a cousin of mine. I left Padua for Florence and took the Modena road on account of the war that the Bolognese were waging;[21] in the mountains above Modena another good horse was ruined, and I left it at Pontremoli. I made it back to Florence with eight horses, six of which I sold, and lost all of the money gambling. Indeed, six months later, between losses and money spent on clothes and other expenses, I was left with no more than about a hundred florins and two horses.

While I was in these straits, I fell in love with a woman named Madonna Gemma, the widow of Jacopo, the son of Messer Rinieri Cavicciuli, and the daughter of Giovanni Tedaldini. She was staying in a convent outside the city gates at Pinti,[22] and I happened to be passing by one day and some of her relatives invited me in for refreshments; I accepted. Although there were many people present, I managed to speak to her privately, and said to her respectfully: "I am all yours; I commend myself to you." "If you are mine, would you obey me if I gave you a command?" she replied, laughing. Said I: "Try me." She replied, "Go to Rome for love of me."[23] I went home and two days later set out with a servant, without

---

20 The market for horses in Hungary was very favourable at this time. See my *Venezia e Ungheria nel Rinascimento* (Florence: Olschki, 1973).

21 A consequence of the War of the Eight Saints, because Bologna was part of the Papal States and was governed by a papal legate.

22 Borgo Pinti, now one of the main thoroughfares in the historic centre of Florence, was in Bonaccorso's time outside the city gates.

23 This was a ploy that ladies used to rid themselves of importunate lovers, reminiscent of certain episodes in the *Decameron* (see for example *Decameron* IX, 1; X, 5).

telling them at home where I was going. I went to Siena and thence
to Perugia, Todi, Spoleto, Terni, Narni, and Orte, where the Florentine
league was fighting the Romans.[24] I begged Messer Bindo Bondelmonti
to accompany me to Rome one night with some of his men; he smuggled
me into the house of a Roman who was a secret friend of his, where I
stayed for several days. This Roman, whose name was Cola Ciencio,[25]
got me a safe-conduct pass for eight days. When I had been there for
six days, Cola had me taken to an estate that belonged to the Orsini
family,[26] and thence to Orte, whence I returned to Florence by the way
I had come. Between going and staying and coming back from Rome, I
was gone for a month. When I returned, I sent a woman to tell Madonna
Gemma how I had obeyed her. She sent back word that she had never
supposed that I would be so foolish as to take such a risk for something
she had said in jest. This was in 1377.

["TURMOIL AMONG THE POPULACE," VOLUNTARY EXILE
AND CONSPIRACIES]

In 1378, after peace had been made with Pope Gregory,[27] turmoil broke
out among the Florentine populace.[28] The *popolo minuto*[29] burned and
sacked a number of houses and drove the Priors from the Public Palace
and with them Luigi Guicciardini, who was Standard-bearer of Justice at
the time. They then proceeded to seize power and to appoint a Standard-
bearer of their own choosing, a certain Michele di Lando, who, however,
a few days later made common cause with the artisans, the Ghibellines,
and men who had been barred from office, and drove the populace out
of power. As a militiaman under the Nicchio standard,[30] I was on duty
in the square when the artisans and their allies were returning after the
mob had been expelled from the Public Palace. When all the others had

---

24 Again, this was part of the War of the Eight Saints.
25 Perhaps a member of the noble Cenci family.
26 The Orsini were a prominent Roman family who were traditionally friendly to the
    Florentines and their merchants, and enemies of Pope Gregory XI.
27 This is one of Bonaccorso's rare mistakes; Gregory XI died in March of 1378, and
    peace was made with his successor, Urban VI, in July of that year.
28 Bonaccorso is referring to the so-called Ciompi Rebellion that took place in July of
    1378.
29 Craftsmen, shopkeepers, and labourers who were not permitted to organize into
    guilds.
30 One of the four subdivisions of the civil militia in the Santo Spirito quarter.

quieted down, a stonecutter, who was clearly in a murderous mood, kept shouting, "Death to them! Death to them!" I walked over and told him to hold his tongue, whereupon he lunged at my chest with the point of his sword. I quickly drew a spear on him and, running it through his leather tunic, killed him on the spot. Several witnesses who had seen him start the trouble declared that I had acted in self-defence and that he deserved what he got. No more was said about it at the time.

I went home; and seeing that many Guelph citizens, and some of the best, were being driven out and banished, I decided not to stay in Florence. I went to Pisa, where I was joined by Matteo Tinghi, who had been banished. After I had been there for several months, we heard that a number of Guelph citizens were planning to start an insurrection in Florence with the help of a band of men who had been exiled, who were to come from Siena under the leadership of Messer Luca di Totto da Panzano. When they heard this, Giovanni dello Scielto Tinghi and Bernardo di Lippo organized and headed a contingent from Pisa of some 200 exiles, banished men, and sympathizers. I joined this group and, according to plan, went with them one night to the gate of San Piero Gattolino.[31] Messer Luca's men were supposed to reach San Miniato al Monte late the same night so as to give the signal at dawn. This was to be a signal for the conspirators in Florence to arm themselves, take to the streets, and open the gate of San Giorgio to us.[32] Accordingly, our party sent to find out whether Messer Luca was at San Miniato. He was not, for the plot in the city had been discovered, and Messer Gregorio Tornaquinci had been arrested along with several others, from whom the city authorities learned of Messer Luca's plan to come in from Santa Maria Impruneta with his men.[33] The Defender[34] was promptly sent out with a number of foot soldiers and sixty cavalrymen who, coming upon Messer Luca's party, captured seven and routed the rest. Knowing nothing of this, and hearing that Messer Luca was not at the appointed place, our group thought we must have come a day too soon. Accordingly, we retreated

---

31 The modern-day Porta Romana.

32 The exiles were approaching Florence from the south, as indicated by the places named.

33 About a dozen kilometres from Florence, the town of Impruneta had been famous since the early fourteenth century for its miraculous Madonna, its artisans, and its fair.

34 *Il Difensore* was a police functionary brought from another city to keep order in Florence, also against political conspirators.

from Florence towards Pozzolatico,[35] split up into small groups, and
sought refuge in the houses of friends. I went with Giovanni Tinghi and
Bernardo di Lippo to Giovanni Corbizzi's house in Pozzolatico, where
we found shelter for ourselves, 6 horses, and 12 foot soldiers. Around
three in the afternoon, a number of fugitives from Florence arrived with
the news that Messer Gregorio had been arrested and that the whole city
was under martial law. We were still convinced that we had arrived a day
early, and hopeful that Messer Luca might still turn up the next night
with his men. As soon as evening came, I mounted my horse and set off
for Santa Maria Impruneta with two comrades, who were on foot, to see
if I could get any news of Messer Luca. At about one in the morning I
ran into the Defender, who had the seven men from Messer Luca's party
who had been captured. Believing that this was Messer Luca's contingent, I happily joined them, but we were immediately surrounded by
men pointing their lances at us and saying: "Who are you?" Realizing the
fix I was in, I boldly replied, "Friends." A mounted mace-bearer came
forward and asked me: "What's your name?" I said, "I'm Bonaccorso."
Then he told the foot soldiers: "Let him go, he's a friend." By this time
they were all around me, and the path was so narrow and rough that I
could see no way of turning back. I pressed forward until I came to where
the Defender was with the men on horseback; he stopped and asked
me: "Who are you?" "I am Bonaccorso Pitti," I boldly replied, "the mace-
bearer back there recognized me at once." "What are you doing at this
hour, armed like this?" he asked me; for I was wearing a cuirass and had
a lance in my hand, and my comrades had lances on their shoulders. "I
have a quarrel with someone; I left Florence when they closed the city
gates and I'm on my way to San Casciano. I took this road for fear of being ambushed; I was also glad to take it because I knew you were in Santa
Maria Impruneta." "I believe you," he said, "but just in case you might
be one of the men I'm searching for, I want you to come back to Florence with me." Said I: "I am very happy to do so," and turned my horse
around. Then he asked my name again; I told him, and he questioned
me again. I gave him the same answers, without kowtowing to him in the
least. Then he said, "It doesn't seem right to me to make you turn back,
yet I am afraid of being blamed if I let you go." I boldly replied, "Your
Honour, don't worry about inconveniencing me, for I am very happy

---

35 About seven kilometres from Florence, near the confluence of the Ema and Greve
   rivers.

to return with you." Then he said, "Go with God." I left him, riding on; when I was out of sight of his men, I turned another way, and returned to the comrades I had left behind and told them what had befallen me. We resolved to lie low until daybreak, when I led them by back roads to Sorbigliano by way of Mezzola, where Messer Zanobi kept us to dine. After I had led them in safety to the road to Siena, I left them and returned to Pisa. All the roads were being guarded and I was in constant danger of being captured. But I didn't start to get frightened until I had reached a safe place not far from Pisa. Then I was so overcome with fear and exhaustion – not having slept for three nights – that I stayed at Pontedera and rested for two days. When I got to Pisa I heard that Messer Gregorio and the seven prisoners had been beheaded, and that I had been tried in absentia with many others and had been sentenced to be beheaded.

In the year 1379 I went to Genoa with Matteo dello Scielto; and when we returned to Pisa, Messer Piero Gambacorta[36] had me and many other people who had been exiled sent away from that city. I went to Siena, and after staying there for several months I returned to Pisa with Giusto del Citerna, who had also been banished from Florence. After I had remained there for several months, it happened in the year 1380, on the [*text missing*] of April, that Matteo di Ricco Corbizzi from San Piero Maggiore in Florence was in Pisa on business, and because he was a confidant of those who were then in power in Florence, went about speaking untruths to individuals, groups, and in public places like loggias and piazzas, speaking ill of every citizen who had been banished or exiled from Florence. And continuing to do so with unbridled audacity, it happened that one day he spoke very rudely to me. I replied to him that if he continued to defame and to annoy citizens who had left Florence or had been driven out, one day he would end up with blood on his shirt. He became all puffed up with pride and spoke twice as abusively to me. I left him, and sent Giusto del Citerna to tell him that I would never again go near him, nor would I speak to him, so that he could never again speak abusively to me, and if he should come near me, I would go away, and that if he continued to say things that touched my honour, I would show my displeasure with my actions. Giusto went, and returned, reporting that Matteo had said, "Go, tell Bonaccorso that I don't care what he says, nor fear his threats, but I won't rest until he and all the other exiles from Florence can no longer remain in Pisa." A few days later, I had dined

---

36 Piero d'Andrea Gambacorta was lord of Pisa from 1369 until he was killed in 1392.

with Matteo dello Scielto, and as we went out about midnight, we came upon this Matteo di Ricco. Matteo dello Scielto huddled together with him, because they had some business together. I left them and ran into Niccolò di Betto Bardi,[37] and while I was waiting for Matteo dello Scielto to leave the other Matteo, suddenly he left him and huddled together with Caroccio Carocci. Speaking with Caroccio about their business affairs, he lingered near where I was, and said loudly, so that I would hear: "Caroccio, I'm returning to Florence tomorrow morning, and I shall take action against all those who have threatened me." I understood that he was referring to me and to my brothers, who were in Florence; I put my hand on his chest, and shoving him, said, "What have I do to with you?" Against my wishes, Niccolò struck him in the head with a stock-sword, and he fell at my feet. A tumult arose, and I, stunned, did not depart. Some armed guards arrived, and they would have arrested me, if it hadn't been for Vanni Bonconti,[38] who came between us, and said to me: "Go away." I went to the home of Messer Gualterotto Lanfranchi, and Niccolò came with me. I told Gualterotto what had happened; he consoled me, saying: "Do not fear, for I will take you to a safe, secure place." That night, the wounded man died. I stayed for three days at Messer Gualterotto's house, and one day at the house of a nephew of his, where he had put us, because Messer Piero Gambacorta had told him that he knew where we were and that he wanted to have us arrested. On the fifth day Caroccio came to dine with Messer Piero, who was very fond of him. Messer Piero complained to him about what had happened, saying: "If I don't bring to justice the people who did this, the rulers of Florence will believe that I allow their merchants to be killed while they are in Pisa." Caroccio responded to him, saying: "Messer Piero, you can be certain that what happened was not intentional, and that Matteo died as a result of falling. I was speaking with him about our affairs, and walking along, and Matteo stopped in front of Bonaccorso and left off our conversation and said certain things to him. Bonaccorso reacted, and Niccolò as well. I later heard that Bonaccorso had had words with him several days previous to that occasion, and that he had had a message sent to Matteo, and Matteo had sent him a reply. And I also heard that Matteo had spoken so ill about some of the citizens who had been banished from Florence that if he hadn't left Pisa soon or hadn't died when he did, others would

---

37 Father of the famous sculptor Donatello.
38 A member of a family of noble Pisans, devoted followers of St Catherine of Siena.

have done him great harm." At these words Messer Gualterotto arrived, for he had been invited to dine. Messer Piero replied, saying: "Caroccio, you have greatly reassured me, and I'm glad that I did not have those two arrested. I would be happy if they would leave, if they are here, which I think they are. And Messer Gualterotto knows very well whether they are here or not." He called for one of his servants, and said, "Go and see to it that the guards whom I had posted at the gates to apprehend those men are dismissed." Messer Gualterotto came to the place where he had told us to go, and said, "You are safe," and told us about his conversation with Messer Piero. That evening we returned to his home, and the next day we rode off with him to dine at Santa Maria in Castello.[39] Later he gave me a letter that he had written to Ducino d'Armo in Lucca, recommending me to him. The letter was of great benefit to me, for after we had been in Lucca for several days, a brother of the chiseller whom I had wounded in the piazza in self-defence went to Ducino, whom he considered his lord and master, and asked him to give him sufficient men to carry out a vendetta against me, saying: "He goes every day to amuse himself at such and such an inn outside the city gate." Since I had given Ducino Messer Gualterotto's letter and he had offered to help me, he told the man, whose name was Michele: "Come back tomorrow and I shall give you some men." He came to see me that evening and told me everything, saying: "Do not go outside of Lucca." I remained there three days and then left for Genoa. After I had been there for several days, I began to gamble, and with about 50 florins that I had, I won about 1,500 florins in the course of a month. This was in June of the year 1380.

It happened that Giovanni di Bindo della Vitella came to Genoa, sent by several of the leading men who had been exiled from Florence, and on their behalf he told us how Messer Carlo della Pace[40] would soon be in Verona, and that the aforementioned exiles were all planning to go to Verona to get whatever help they could from him. I felt obligated to go as well, on account of a letter that I had signed along with many of the aforementioned exiles in Siena. I quickly bought five good horses and

---

39 In the Serchio river valley, between Pisa and Lucca.

40 Charles III of Anjou-Durazzo (1345–1386), also known as Charles the Short, was king of Naples and titular king of Jerusalem from 1382 to 1386, and king of Hungary from 1385 to 1386 as Charles II. He was known in Italy as "della Pace" (of Peace) because of the peace treaty he brokered between the Venetians and the Genoese, who were allied with King Louis of Hungary. The Anjou family were long-time allies of the Florentine Guelphs, and therefore also of the Genoese.

a great deal of armour, and I lent Niccolò 200 new florins. He bought three horses and armed himself well, and we left for Verona, where many of our leading exiles had already arrived. We all presented ourselves to Messer Carlo. With a large army of Hungarians, Germans, and Italians, he left Verona for Romagna,[41] and we went with him. We were riding with Bernardo di Lippo and Giovanni di Guerieri de' Rossi, and arrived in the area of Castello Sampiero,[42] where we found lodging. After we had supper, the stables caught fire, and I lost 4 of the best horses I had. The villagers came from the castle to kill us, and they would have succeeded if it hadn't been for a man from Firenzuola who had come to warn us that they were planning to ambush us. We armed ourselves, and with great toil we set out around midnight, some of us on horseback and some on foot, heading toward the battlefield, which was about 4 miles away. We went to Forlì, where I bought three horses, and then to Rimini where I bought another. We arrived in Arezzo where, thanks to the efforts of our leading men, the Bostoli and the Albergotti surrendered the city to Messer Carlo.[43] During the entrance of Carlo's army into the city, Tomasino da Panzano, Messer Bartolomeo da Prato (who was not yet a knight), and Moscone de' Beccanugi killed Messer Giovanni di Mone, who was in Arezzo as an ambassador for the Florentines, urging the Aretines not to surrender the city to Messer Carlo. Messer Carlo was very disturbed by this killing, and had a message sent to those who had done it not to come into his sight.

We left Arezzo and headed toward Siena, near Stagia.[44] After we had been there for several days, unable to go on because of lack of money (for Messer Carlo's brigades of Hungarians and others would not permit anyone to go on if they did not have money). The Hungarians wanted to leave, abandoning Messer Carlo. So he reached an agreement with the men who were in power in Florence, by which he received 25,000 gold florins, after which he left, returning to Arezzo.[45] All of us who had been exiled from Florence were there; he had promised to ride with us

---

41 Charles had been sent by Pope Urban VI to take over the Kingdom of Naples.

42 A village about fifteen kilometres southeast of Bologna.

43 The Bostoli and Albergotti were powerful Guelph families in Arezzo. The jurist Lodovico Albergotti would become one of the most influential advisors of Charles III.

44 A castle on the border of the state of Siena, owned by the noble family Franzesi della Foresta; it was sold in 1361 to the Florentine Republic.

45 Charles's agreements with the Florentine Republic stipulated, among other things, that rebels and exiles could not take refuge in Arezzo or in Gubbio. This explains Bonaccorso's heartfelt protest below.

to the city walls of Florence, so we cordially complained to him. Our spokeman was Messer Lapo da Castiglionchio.[46] Messer Carlo replied to us with a downcast look, weeping, that he had acted out of necessity, and promised us that if he acquired the Realm of Naples, he would never rest until he had returned us to our home. A few days later, he left for Rome. Several of us exiles went with him, but most of us took our leave of him, because we didn't have the means to follow him. I was one of the ones who did not accompany him, because out of the 1,500 gold florins that I had brought from Genoa, between cash and horses and trappings, I was left with two horses and no money, for I had either spent it or lent it to many of my fellow exiles.

["TRAVELLING THE WORLD IN SEARCH OF FORTUNE"]

Bernardo di Lippo and I decided to go to France. We went to Rimini, where we borrowed 50 ducats from Giovanni di Masino dell'Antella, who was living there, and without tarrying we left immediately for Avignon and then Tarascon, where we visited Messer Stoldo Altoviti and Messer Tommaso Soderini, who had been exiled from Florence. We left them and went to Paris, where we stayed only a short time, for Bernardo di Cino[47] sent me to gamble with the Duke of Brabant,[48] who was in Brussels with many great noblemen who were amusing themselves with great jousts and tournaments, dancing, and gambling. A few days after arriving in Brussels, I had already lost 2,000 gold francs[49] that belonged to Bernardo di Cino, with whom I had gone into partnership on the understanding that he was to supply the money, and I would contribute my foolish bent for gambling. I lost the money by making bets of 300 florins or more on each throw of the dice, having deluded myself that playing for high stakes would bring me greater profits. On my last night, I lost 500 francs, which I had borrowed from the Duke; since all I had at my lodging was about 550 gold francs, I left off playing.

---

46 Grandson and namesake of the famous jurist and influential Guelph. Lapo (or Lepo) the elder was a leading humanist, as profiled by Lauro Martines, *The Social World of the Florentine Humanists, 1390–1460* (Princeton: Princeton University Press, 1963), 339.

47 Bernardo di Cino di Bartolino de' Benvenuti, who by a privilege granted by King Charles V of France in 1379 called himself and his family nobles.

48 Wenceslaus of Luxembourg.

49 The three types of coins mentioned here had different values, since they contained different amounts of gold: the Venetian ducat contained 3.559 grams of gold, the franc 3.885 grams, and the florin 3.536 grams.

The Duke and a group of gentlemen rose and went into another room, where many ladies and gentlemen were dancing. As I stood enjoying the spectacle, a beautiful 14-year-old girl, unmarried, the daughter of a great baron, came up to me and said, "Come and dance, Lombard;[50] don't fret over your losses, for God will surely help you." And she took me by the hand and led me onto the floor. When I had finished dancing with her, the Duke called me over and asked, "How much have you lost tonight?" I told him that I had lost all that was left of the 2,000 francs I had brought from Brussels. He said, "I believe you, though if I had lost such a sum I wouldn't be able to show a face as cheerful as yours. Go back and enjoy yourself now. It can do you nothing but good." The next morning, I brought the Duke a purse containing 500 gold francs and begged his leave to depart, explaining that I wanted to seek better fortune elsewhere. He said to me: "Stay if you like, and try to recoup your losses with these 500 francs. If you lose them, you can pay me back some other time, when you're more prosperous." I thanked him, but said that I did not want to play any more for a while and that I had urgent reasons for going to England. He told me to keep the 500 francs anyway, and that I could pay him back if I ever returned and won back the money I had lost. Then he summoned one of his chancellors and told him: "Make out a letter for Bonaccorso saying that he is personally attached to my service and so on." I left Brussels and went to England; after I was there for about a month, negotiating the terms of a ransom to be paid for Jean of Brittany[51] as I had been commissioned to do by the Duke of Lancaster, in whose hands the prisoner was being held, I returned to Paris and reported to Bernardo about everything I had done in Brussels and England.

In 1381, after I had returned to Paris, I was very short of money because of my losses in Brussels, for I was obliged to return a fourth of the 2,000 francs I had lost to Bernardo di Cino; I gave him the 500 francs that the Duke of Brabant had lent me. In February of that same year, I returned to Brussels with about 200 gold francs, which I had obtained from several people, and in Brussels I borrowed 300 francs from Bernardo da Verrazzano. While I was gambling with the Duke and some other

---

50 In France, Burgundy, and England, all inhabitants of the northern and central regions of Italy were called "Lombards" (see *Decameron* I, 1).

51 Jean of Brittany or Jean de Blois, delivered as a hostage for his father Charles de Blois, who had been captured by the English in 1345. Jean remained a prisoner for more than thirty years; he was freed in 1387.

gentlemen, letters arrived from Florence with news that the exiles had returned there. I stayed in Brussels until the end of Lent, by which time I had about 600 gold francs. On my way back through Paris, I bought several fine horses; I reached Florence in the month of May 1382.

The following September, I returned to Paris; in November, on St Catherine's day, I took part in a battle that the King of France was fighting in Flanders near Ypres against the Flemish, or rather against the men of Ghent, whose leader was Philippe van Artevelde. The Flemish had a force of 40,000 armed men; we, on the King's side, were 10,000 men. The battle was fought on foot, at sunrise. What seemed miraculous was that, although at first the mist was so thick it was almost like night, when the King, who had divided us into three divisions, ordered his standard-bearer to unfurl a banner that is called the *oriflamme*,[52] which is supposed to have been a gift of God to his ancestors, the mist melted away and the two sides were able to see each other by the light of the sun. The French commander-in-chief opened the battle by leading the first of the three French divisions against the Flemish, who were drawn up in a single formation. It was all over in two hours; the Flemish were defeated by that single French division. The order was to take no prisoners; in the end, the number of dead Flemish soldiers was 27,500. As soon as the battle was won, we moved on quickly to Courtrai, a town about the size of Prato, which was taken and sacked and burned to the ground to avenge the defeat that the French had suffered near there many years before at the hands of the Flemish when, as one may read in the chronicles of Filippo Villani,[53] a great number of French knights lost their lives. After this, the King set out for Paris at the head of his victorious army.

Before I write about the King's entrance into Paris, I shall record the reason why that battle was undertaken. In the year 1381, the people of Ghent rebelled against their lord, the Count of Flanders, who was the father of the Duchess of Burgundy. They attacked Bruges, took it, and expelled the said Count and robbed and killed all of his officials; they did likewise in many other good lands that they took in Flanders.

---

52 From the Latin *aurea flamma*. This was the standard of the king of France: a banner of smooth red fabric divided into three strips, edged in green silk and hung from a gilded lance.

53 It was not Filippo, but rather Giovanni Villani who described the Battle of Courtrai (also known as the Battle of the Golden Spurs), which the French lost to the Flemish in 1302. Kortrijk or Courtrai is located on the Lys River in the province of West Flanders in modern Belgium.

Their captain was the aforementioned Philippe van Artevelde. The number and power of the rebellious Flemish grew, and they secretly sent ambassadors to the people of Rouen and Paris, urging them also to rebel against their rulers, and offering them help and succour. For this reason, those two cities rebelled against the king of France, beginning with the lower classes in Paris. The tumult was started by a female street vendor, because a tax collector wanted to seize the fruits and vegetables that she sold. She began to shout, "Down with taxes!" This caused all of the populace to rise up, running toward the homes of the tax collectors, whom they robbed and murdered. Since the populace was unarmed, one of them led the rest to the residence of the magistrate Monsieur Bertrand du Guesclin, the former Constable of France, who had 3,000 leaden maces that he had prepared for a battle that he believed he would have to wage against the English. The mob took hatchets and broke down the doors of the tower where the maces (which in France are called *maillets*) were being kept, and took them, going all about the city robbing the homes of the King's officials, many of whom they killed. The members of the bourgeoisie feared that they, too, would be robbed by the people of the lower classes, who were known as the Maglietti (and who were just like the Ciompi who rebelled in Florence). So they armed themselves and proved to be so strong that the Maglietti agreed to obey them. The bourgeoisie took over, and continued the rebellion against the Royals. So the King and his court retreated to the forest of Vincennes, where they took council. In order to prevent the whole kingdom from rebelling, the King ordered that all the barons, knights, and squires of the realm should come to him with all of their forces and follow him wherever he chose to go. But even after he had made the request several times, and issued the strictest orders that he could, no more men came than those who, as I indicated above, were at the battle. And the following year, that is 1383, the saying truly came to pass that applies to many unfortunates who say: "Long live he who wins." For having won the aforesaid battle, the following year the King gave the order to attack the English who had come into Flanders, as I shall mention below. At this command, about 10,000 knights and more than 16,000 squires came, and the army was estimated to have 200,000 or more cavalry. It's also true that many Germans came as well, out of friendship to the King.

Let's go back to the King's return to Paris at the time of the rebellion. He arrived one evening at Saint Denis, and the next morning he set out with three ranks of soldiers for the battle. When the bourgeoisie of Paris heard about this, they decided to come out to meet the King and ask his forgiveness. As many as 500 of the leading members of the bourgeoisie came, and when they arrived before the King they threw themselves on the ground, begging his forgiveness. The King said, "Return to Paris, and when I am in the seat of justice, come and make your plea, and I will render a decision." When the King was about a half mile from Paris, all of the knights and squires and armed men dismounted and formed into three ranks, except the King and his royals, who were in the second rank and remained mounted on horseback. All the others entered on foot, with their helmets on their heads, suspecting an ambush. We went to the main palace, and when the King had dismounted he sent out the order that before sundown every citizen should bring all of his weapons, offensive and defensive, to a large, fine fortress and royal residence there in Paris, under pain of the gallows. This order was fully and quickly obeyed. He also commanded that all of the chains in the city should be removed and taken away, and it was done. I saw one of the King's squires ask him if he could have all of the chains as a gift. The King, who never said no to anything that was asked of him, said that he would like the squire to have them. At the time, it didn't seem that the gift was of great value, but later it was seen and known that the squire got about 10,000 gold francs for those chains. About 40 citizens and Maglietti were arrested – the ones who had led the rebellion against the Crown – and they were beheaded in the square of Les Halles. Once that sentence was carried out, the King pardoned all of the others who had offended him. But he sent for all of the wealthy members of the bourgeoisie and merchants and had a fine imposed on all of them, which they had to pay according to their possibilities; a tax of 10,000 francs was levied on many of them, and many others had to pay 2,000 francs or more. And their creditors were all of the lords and barons who had been with the King in the battle. And I saw that the Duke of Bourbon,[54] to whom the King had assigned and given money amounting to about 40,000 francs, accepted the gift. The next day, the Duke sent for all of the debtors who had been assigned to him, and he released them from that debt, saying that it was paid in full. All of the other lords made their debtors pay, and the total amounted to about 500,000 francs. Thus the year 1382[55] came to an end, and in January there was great celebrating, with jousts, dancing, and gambling.

---

54 Louis, the king's cousin.
55 Bonaccorso uses the Florentine calendar; thus it was really 1383.

During the month of February, Bernardo di Cino gave his nephew Cino 200 gold francs and pearls and jewels worth about 3,000 gold francs. He wanted Cino and me to go to Holland to sell or gamble the pearls and jewellery with Duke Albert of Bavaria. We went as far as The Hague in Holland, where we found the Duke, but he wanted neither to buy nor to gamble for the pearls and jewels. Between expenses and gambling, we spent the 200 gold francs, and we returned to Paris, where we returned the pearls and jewellery to Bernardo in April 1383.

During that year, the English passed into France, that is on the border of Picardy with Flanders. There were about 10,000 soldiers, between archers and men of arms. They had already taken much good land in Flanders, and when the King of France heard about this, he sent out a command to the lords, barons, knights, and squires of the Kingdom of France. And by the month of August he was on the battlefield with about 200,000 cavalry and 10,000 Knights of the Golden Spurs,[56] as I mentioned above. I wanted to be part of these great events, so I joined company with a man from Lucca and another from Siena, and at our own expense with 36 horses and well armed, we went with the army under the banner and conduct of the Duke of Burgundy, who had 20,000 cavalry in all. When the army arrived at a fine place called Berg,[57] where some of the English were already ensconced, as soon as the King arrived he had the earth cleared all around, in preparation for the battle the next day. That night about midnight, the English wanted to flee but the inhabitants of the town did not want them to, so a struggle began between them, with many deaths, and finally all of the English and the townspeople who were able to fled before daybreak. When daybreak arrived, we approached the town, and broke down the city gates. Unopposed, we entered, and found that most of the houses had been set on fire, and that many English and citizens of the town were dead. I saw a frightening, cruel thing: a woman, who judging from the way she was dressed was a decent person, had a child of two years in her arms, and one on her back of three years, and one by the hand about five years old. She was sitting near the door of a house that was engulfed in flames, and someone made her get up and move away from the house so that she and the children would not be injured. But as soon as they let go of her, she quickly ran with the three children and entered the house, from

------

56 The title of an order of knights.
57 Today called Mons, the capital of Hainaut province in southwestern Belgium.

which large flames were issuing. And finally we saw her and the children burned to death inside the house. In the end, the city was completely burned and destroyed.

All that day we were on the battlefield; the next day we advanced to find our enemies, who were moving ahead of us from place to place, fleeing. Around the hour of vespers, we arrived at a large town where the English had taken refuge. The town was called Obourg. We immediately attacked from several directions, hurling fiery rockets into the town. When the town began to burn, the English began to defend themselves valiantly, wounding a great number of our men with arrows. The battle went on until one in the morning; it was a Saturday. We retreated with great injuries and little honour. And in our retreat, I became separated from one of my companions and from several of our servants who had accompanied us in the battle, and I could not find them for the rest of the night. Since it was nearly impossible for me to search for them in the dark, I lay exhausted in a ditch until daybreak.

On the Sunday morning, the Duke of Brittany, who was there with 20,000 cavalry in the service of the King, with the King's permission reached an agreement with the English, and in effect they agreed to leave with whatever they could carry, promising to return to England. They departed the following day, leaving the country of Flanders. The King returned to Paris and dismissed the brigades of lords, who remained in Paris to celebrate.

That same year, 1383,[58] in the month of February I went to Brussels and then to Holland to visit Duke Albert.[59] When I returned to Paris, I found my brother Francesco, who had come there from Florence. I remained in Paris all that summer, and also the winter of 1384. In May of 1385 I returned to Florence, and then in October I went back to Paris, bringing with me Berto da la Fonte. Then in the year 1386, I returned to Florence in the month of May, and in September I went back to Paris, and found that the king of France had gone to Flanders with a large army and he had a fleet of ships at Sluys ready to pass over to England. Francesco and Berto and I went to join the King, and we went well armed and mounted and eager to join forces with him. When we arrived in Bruges, I found the man from Lucca who had been my companion in the great

---

58 That is, 1384.

59 Duke Albrecht or Albert I of Bavaria, who had been feudal ruler of the counties of Holland, Hainaut, and Zeeland in the Low Countries since 1358.

army of the Duke of Burgundy. We joined company with him and with another man from Lucca, and rented a fine ship. We went to Sluys, where the King was waiting with all of his forces to pass over into England. In the harbour at Sluys, I saw 1,200 vessels, 600 of which were large sailing ships. After we had been at Sluys with all of the King's armada for about 15 days, waiting for the sea and the wind to be favourable, the King called all of the captains and helmsmen to ask them what they would advise him to do. And because it was already the end of November, they did not believe that the passage to England could be made with such a large number of vessels, saying: "If we find ourselves in a rough sea and with the wind against us, the ships will inevitably collide with one another, and many men will perish." The King and the lords of his Council listened to the advice of the captains and helmsmen, and we all returned to France.

During the time that we were waiting at Sluys, I lent the Count of Savoy about 500 gold francs to gamble with, and later in Bruges I lent him 200 francs, and then at Arras I lent him 400 gold francs to pay his expenses, and so it went all the way back to Paris, to the extent that when we arrived there he owed me around 2,000 gold francs. And during that whole winter when he remained in Paris, I lent him 1,500 gold francs, so that by the time he left, I had lent him a total of 3,500 francs. I sent a man with the Count when he returned to Savoy, as he told me to do; he said that he would send the money he owed me back with him, and if he didn't send the money back by a certain time, I should go fetch it. At the end of the agreed-upon period I went to Savoy, and stayed there for more than a month, and finally the Count set another date for six months from that time. I returned to Paris and remained there all winter, and then at Lent I went to Holland to visit Duke Albert, and then I returned to Paris, and from there I went to Florence in May 1388, and in September I returned again to Paris, bringing with me Francesco Canigiani,[60] who had sold an estate of his for 400 gold florins, which he gave me as a deposit, and I promised to give him 100 florins per year and cover his expenses. I stayed in Paris that winter, and won around 2,000 gold florins by gambling. I bought a house for 600 gold florins, and at Lent I went to Holland and Zeeland[61] to visit Duke Albert, and I won about 1,500 gold francs from

---

60 The Canigiani were a prominent Florentine merchant family.

61 Zeeland was an area contested by the counts of Holland and Flanders until 1299,
    when the count of Holland gained control of it.

him and from other noblemen. I returned to Paris and then left with the King for Avignon and Toulouse.[62] After following with the King for several days, I encountered along the way Messer Antonio Porro,[63] who was following the King as an emissary of the Duke of Milan. While we were travelling together, I won 1,200 gold francs from Messer Antonio before we caught up with the King. Later we arrived in Toulouse, where the King celebrated Christmas. In the church of St Sernin,[64] I saw the head of St James, which is in an underground chapel in which they say there are the bodies of six of the Apostles; I saw the sepulchres, but not the bodies. It is said that when Charlemagne travelled around the world as emperor, he sent all of the bodies of saints that he could find to Toulouse. That is why people believe that what is said about those bodies is true. After celebrating Christmas, we returned to Paris, where I found Messer Filippo de' Corsini and Messer Cristofano degli Spini, who were there as ambassadors from Florence to the King; at Lyon on the Rhone, they presented themselves to the King and delivered their message to him. He responded that they should come to Paris for a reply. We went to Paris and I immediately departed from thence for Holland, where I again won a great deal of money gambling. I returned to Paris for a short time, and then left for England in the company of the Count of San Paolo, with many gentlemen who were going to a great celebration, with jousting. I did not gamble there, but I gave 2,500 gold francs to Mariotto Forantini and Giovanni di Guerrieri de' Rossi, and instructed them to invest the money in wool and send the proceeds to me in Florence. I returned to Paris and stayed there for the entire winter. I found that I had 10,000 gold francs in wool, my house and furnishings and horses and equipment and cash, not counting the great deal of money that was owed to me, nor the money that the Count of Savoy owed me, nor a great deal of money that was owed to me by several people; so much so, that this amounted to around 5,000 francs.

As I was in this situation, my brother Francesco and also Francesco Canigiani advised me to return to Florence and in fact insisted that I do so, leaving them to collect my debts and take care of my affairs. I made

---

62 In October 1389, Charles VI went to Avignon to visit Pope Clement VI, who crowned his cousin Louis II, duke of Anjou, king of Naples, Sicily, and Jerusalem.

63 Antonio Porro, count of Pollenzo, would later serve Gian Galeazzo Visconti in the takeover of the city of Pisa.

64 The great Benedictine abbey church of St Sernin or Saturnin (the first bishop of Toulouse), later a basilica.

up my mind to return. I left my house in Paris and all of the furnishings and jewels to sell and money in cash amounting to about 3,000 gold francs. I left Paris, taking with me that ungrateful boor, my steward, and along the way I visited the Count of Savoy, but I could get nothing from him but promises and postponements.

[BONACCORSO'S RETURN TO FLORENCE; MARRIAGE, MISSIONS
TO FRANCE]

I arrived in Florence and decided to take a wife. Since Guido di Messer Tommaso di Neri del Palagio was the most respected, influential man in the city, I resolved to put the matter in his hands and leave the choice of my bride up to him, provided that he selected the woman from among his own relations. I calculated that if I were to become connected to him by marriage and could win his good will, he would be obliged to help me obtain a truce with the Corbizzi family. Accordingly, I sent the marriage-broker, Bartolo della Contessa, to tell Guido of my intentions. Guido sent Bartolo back with the message that he would be happy to have me as a kinsman and was giving some thought to the matter. A few days later, he sent Bartolo a second time to say that if I liked I might have the daughter of Luca, son of Piero degli Albizzi, whose mother was a first cousin of his own. I sent back word that I would be very happy and honoured and so forth. I was betrothed to her at the end of July 1391, and married her on 12 November of the same year.

I was a member of the Eight Magistrates on Security;[65] one day, before I got married, I happened to be in the Public Palace with several comrades when lightning struck the palace tower and grounded not far from where I was sitting, so close that the fire touched my calves. When I tried to stand up, I collapsed on the ground, paralysed from the knees down; my legs felt as if they were on fire. They removed my hose, which stank of sulphur, for the lightning had missed me by a hair. All the flesh on my legs was covered with welts; the skin was bleeding, and the hair was singed. They rubbed my legs, which were as cold as those of a dead man; thinking I was dying, I asked for a priest. Half an hour later, I stretched my legs, put on another pair of hose, and walked home on my own two feet.

The wool I had bought in England arrived on two ships before my marriage. The insurance for the consignment that was unloaded in

---

65 This group was in charge of the police, especially for the security of the state and of the city. They also had a voice in military and fiscal affairs.

Genoa was nine per cent of the cost; on the ship that came to Pisa, I paid fourteen. When the wool was sold and the money collected, I found that I had made 1,000 gold florins on the venture in 16 months. I deposited this money with Luigi and Gherardo Canigiani, to whom I had already entrusted 4,000 gold florins, for which I accepted letters of exchange when I arrived in Florence. This money greatly improved the credit enjoyed by the Canigiani family.

Before getting married, I spent about 2,000 gold florins on building costs and furnishings, and over the years I have had so many restorations and improvements done on this place that I have spent more than 2,500 gold florins to date just on construction and tending to vineyards and orchards.

Before I married, having decided to deal generously with that ingrate, my steward, I gave him 300 gold florins, though I only owed him 200. I also entrusted to him another 700 florins, and yielded to his request to let him go to Paris and engage in any profitable business he might find. We had agreed that for three years we would each get half of whatever money he made, and if he lost the entire 1,000 gold florins, I would repay him the 300 that I had given him. He went to Paris, where my brother Francesco got him together with our kinsman Luigi di Bartolomeo Giovanni. Since Luigi had stayed in my house and had worked for me collecting debts (I had sent him several times to Savoy, where he succeeded twice in getting 1,000 francs from the Count), I gave him 300 gold francs upon my departure from Paris. Having arranged this ill-fated partnership, Francesco left them in Paris and returned to Florence in April. I found him a wife, and he got married in June. In September he returned to Paris, taking my brother Bartolomeo with him. That December I went to Milan, taking with me Antonio Canigiani, and then I went to Pavia and Genoa. I left on February 2nd and arrived in Florence on the 5th at three in the afternoon. In March Francesco returned to Florence, leaving Bartolomeo in Paris. He told me that Bartolomeo and my steward had lost everything, and that all that was left was our house and its furnishings, which were worth a total of 1,000 francs. Thus of the 3,000 I had left them between cash and the value of the house and its contents, they lost 2,000 francs.

In May I took horse and set out for Avignon and Paris. While I was stopping at an inn in Pavia, I happened to be leaning on the banister at the top of a flight of stairs when a servant, running down, startled a large horse that was tied to a lower part of the banister. The beast gave such a tug that it pulled down the railing to which it was tied, the one upon which I was leaning. I fell into the yard below, hit my head against a bin of oats, and passed out. I broke no bones, and didn't bleed, but I lay unconscious for more than two hours. When I came to, I opened my eyes and asked whether I had broken an arm or a leg. Then I felt a strong ache in my head, and on the side upon which I had fallen. I asked, "What happened? Who hit me?" For I could not, nor did I ever, remember falling. But I did remember the horse that had been frightened by the servant. The Duke of Milan sent all of his doctors to me. They drew a great deal of blood from several veins, kept me in the dark with the windows closed for nine days, gave me medicines, and applied ointments and poultices to my head. On the tenth day I got up and went to thank the Duke. I took leave of him and went to Avignon and thence to Paris, where I found Bartolomeo sick. Between expenses and gambling, he had contracted debts amounting to about 600 gold francs since Francesco's departure. I also saw the other two sorry partners in mismanagement, who told me, truly or falsely, that they had lost or spent everything. I kept my temper and restored order to my affairs. By the winter of 1393, I had repaid the 600 francs owed by Bartolomeo and had given the 300 francs to the steward, as I had promised. I also satisfied Luigi and had about 500 francs left.

I returned to Florence in May of 1394, and left Bartolomeo, my steward, and Luigi in my house, enjoining them not to gamble until I returned. After arriving in Florence, I departed in October and took my brother Luigi with me to Asti,[66] where I had a commission from the rulers of Florence to speak to the Sire of Coucy, who was there at the time.[67] Once I got his reply, I sent Luigi back to Florence with it; that was why I had brought him with me. The Sire kept me in Asti until the 22nd of November, waiting to give me a secret mission to the Duke of Orléans, the King's brother, of whom I was an equerry.[68] On that day, he gave me the commission and a letter of credentials; and because this affair was very important for the Duke's honour, eight days earlier an embassy had left Savona for Paris to see the Duke, but they were working against what

---

66 The city of Asti in Piedmont was an important mercantile centre during the fourteenth century (see *Decameron* II, 4).

67 "Sieur" was a generic term for a great lord (see *Decameron* VI, 10). The lord of Coucy in Picardy at the time was Enguerrand or Ingelram VII, the last Sieur de Coucy, who was known for being valorous and prudent. He was married to a daughter of Edward III of England.

68 *Escuyer d'escurie* (squire of the stable), an honorific title at the court of France.

was honourable for the Duke, and if they had arrived before I did, they would have obtained from the Duke what they were asking. That is why I left Asti on the 22nd of November, and I arrived in Paris on St Andrew's day,[69] having travelled about 450 miles. During the last two days of my journey, I rode from Chanceaux to Troyes in a single day, which is 24 leagues, and from Troyes to Paris in day, which is 34 leagues (a league being equal to about 2½ miles). I ruined many horses on the road, for which the Duke compensated me.

In April 1395, the Duke of Orléans, the Duke of Berry, the Duke of Burgundy, the Duke of Bourbon, and many other lords travelled to Avignon to negotiate with Pope Benedict.[70] I accompanied the Duke of Orléans. During the month before our departure, having received 600 gold francs from the Duke of Burgundy for three horses that I had sold him, which had cost me 260 gold florins in Florence, I found a wine merchant from Burgundy from whom I bought 110 casks (which the French call *cuves*) of wine with a capacity of one *cogno*[71] each. I paid a thousand francs, giving him 400 in cash and a note from the Duke of Burgundy for the other 600. I had the wine placed in two cellars. I couldn't get anyone to offer me more than 500 francs for it, so I left the wine in the cellars and told my steward not to take less than a thousand francs for it. I departed with the Duke of Orléans, and when we arrived in Burgundy at the end of April, one night all of the vineyards there froze over. So I wrote immediately to my steward, telling him not to sell any of the wine until I returned to Paris. And it turned out that when I got back to Paris I sold a hundred casks of wine for 14 francs cash per cask. I made 400 gold francs out of it, and kept 10 casks for my own consumption. In this way, in two of the most risky dealings that there are (that is, horses and wine), I came out very well.

To return to the journey to Avignon, I saw and heard the Dukes in a public meeting ask Pope Benedict to do what he had sworn and subscribed and sealed with his papal seal – that is, to unify the Holy Church. He had promised, before he met in consistory or conclave with the Sacred College of Cardinals, that if he were elected Pope, any time that the cardinals should ask him to abdicate the papacy in order to

---

69 29 November.

70 Benedict XIII, the Aragonese Pedro de Luna, elected in 1394 as the successor to the anti-pope Clement VII (the pope at Rome was Urban VI).

71 A unit of measurement equivalent to more than 455 litres.

unify the Church, he would do so; and each of the cardinals promised the same, before they entered into the conclave. Benedict responded that he wanted time to think it over, and that then he would give them a reply. He kept them in discussions and negotiations for three full months, using all kinds of strange tricks not to give them a precise reply. One such trick was that one night when all of the Dukes were in Villeneuve, the town opposite Avignon, he had one of the wooden bridges across the Rhône secretly burned, so that the Dukes would have a more difficult time coming every day to Avignon to petition him for his reply. But the Dukes did not cease to come to Avignon on account of the difficulty or peril of crossing the Rhone by boat. They continued to press the Pope for a reply, and finally he gave it, but not from his own mouth. Rather, he gave them a public reply by means of a decree to the effect that he held himself to be the true Pope and that he was absolved from what he had sworn to do before his election, and that he could do this, and that he was willing to seek the unification of the Church in any way that did not involve his abdication. So the dukes and lords returned to Paris.

Then in September 1395, the King made a pilgrimage to Mont St Michel in Normandy, about 150 miles from Paris; the Duke of Orléans went too, and I with him. When we arrived, we visited the abbey, which is built on a huge rock five miles out to sea; you can reach it by land at low tide. On his way back to Paris, the King accepted the hospitality of a Norman nobleman, the Seigneur d'Hambye. The Dukes of Berry, Bourbon, and Orléans, and many other great lords and gentlemen who were travelling with the king, stayed there for a day and a night. To make things more festive for them, there were many beautiful women and great baronesses. I mention the Lord of Hambye because it was believed that he spent more than 4,000 gold francs that day in the King's honour, and it was said that this was his entire income for the year. The King brought him back to Paris and showered him with gifts of jewels, horses, and cash to the value of about 10,000 francs, so he paid well and generously for the hospitality he had received. Certainly, that feast was a marvellous and grand thing to see.

The next day after supper I accompanied the Duke of Orléans to the home of one of the King's equerries, whose name was Siferval. A number of gentlemen who had dined there were gambling when we arrived. The Duke sat down to play, and had me place on the table around 400 francs that I had brought for the two of us. It happened that when it was my turn to throw the dice, I played against the Viscount of Monlev,[72] a big gambler and a great, rich nobleman who had an annual income of more than 30,000 francs. People began to talk because I won twelve times in a row, both when I threw the dice and when he did. He had been drinking wine and had grown heated by the game, and began to say to me: "Ah, you villainous Lombard traitor, are you going to go on winning all night, you barbarous bugger?" I replied, "My lord, please speak decently, out of consideration for His Grace the Duke." He laid another bet; I won. At this he flew into a rage again, saying more foul words, and ended up with: "And I'm not lying." "Well, prove it, my lord!" I promptly replied. Then he stretched out his hand, grabbed the cap off of my head, and made as if to strike me. I pulled back and said, "I'm not a man to let myself be struck when I'm armed," and put my hand upon the short rapier I wore at my side. He screamed, "I've never failed to carry out a threat, so now I'll have to kill you!" Then the Duke whispered to me to go and wait for him in his chamber, and leave things to him. I left; when I had gotten about a hundred yards from the house, I heard someone running up behind me. I turned around and saw, by the light of the torches of a group of courtiers who happened to be passing by at that moment, one of the bastard sons of the Viscount of Monlev with a naked dagger in his hand. I drew my rapier and said, "Bastard, sheathe your dagger and go back and tell your father you couldn't find me." He looked around, and seeing that none of his friends were coming, decided for his own good to do as I said; he sheathed his dagger and turned back. The courtiers who had been passing told many people what had occurred, and I was greatly commended, for the bastard son was only 18 years old and was such a weakling that I probably would have injured him if we had fought.

I went to the Duke's chamber, and shortly afterward he entered, greatly agitated, without saying anything to me. He said to one of his grooms: "Go to the Viscount's home and tell him that before I go to sleep I want to know whether he intends to do what I asked him." The groom went, and came back with the message that the Viscount hadn't changed his mind. Then the Duke told me: "Don't leave this house without me, for I will protect you in spite of him, and will do him little honour." The next morning we took horse and set out after the King, who had already departed. We caught up with him at an abbey where he had dismounted

---

72 Probably Robert de Béthune, viscount of Meaux.

to take some refreshment, and the Duke told him everything that had happened the night before, and asked permission to protect his dependants, of whom I was one. The King replied, "The Viscount spoke and acted wrongly, and Bonaccorso could not fail to answer him for the sake of his honour; but I don't want this affair to go any further." Then he summoned to him the Duke of Berry and the Duke of Bourbon and several other lords, and said to them with an angry look on his face: "Send for the Viscount and tell him that before he leaves this room I want him to do as my brother wishes about the dispute he had with Bonaccorso last night." The Viscount came, and the Duke of Berry spoke to him in the presence of the King and everyone else, and told him what the King had commanded. The Viscount turned to the Duke of Orléans and said, "Sire, I am very pained that you should have taken the side of a Lombard against me, your relation and humble servant. There was no need for you to speak to the King about this, for I do not wish to disobey your orders. If I refused your request last night, I did so thinking that you weren't serious about it; but now that I see you are serious, I am willing to overlook the way that Bonaccorso spoke to me in your presence last night." The Duke replied, "You started things by speaking to Bonaccorso in such a way in my presence that if he had remained silent I would have thought him unworthy." I was standing nearby and had heard everything that the King and everyone else had said; I came forward and made the appropriate reverence to the Duke of Berry, who said, "His Majesty the King has heard about the words you had last night with the Viscount, and is greatly displeased. Bonaccorso, you were certainly overly bold to give the lie to such a nobleman, who is related to ourselves and who has the right to challenge and fight with any lord or prince, be they ever so great, with the sole exception of the members of the royal house of France. But since His Majesty is disposed to clemency and does not want this matter to go any further, he desires the Viscount to pardon you and the two of you to be friends as before. Therefore, Bonaccorso, beg the Viscount's pardon." I turned to the Viscount and said, "Sire, forgive me if I have said or done anything to displease you." He replied, "Since it pleases the King and my Lord his brother, I would forgive you even if you had slashed my face. So I forgive you, and I also beg your pardon, and wish to be your good friend."

When we returned to Paris, I invited the Duke of Orléans and the Duke of Bourbon to dine at my house. They came, bringing with them the Sire of Coucy and the Viscount and many other barons and lords. They were so well served with viands and entremets that they spoke handsomely of them, praising me before the King and other lords. That supper cost me 200 francs. My guests only had one complaint about me, which was that I refused to gamble that night, though there was a fine gambling session and for high stakes; but I had invited Bernardo di Cione de' Nobili, who was the most courtly and lavish gambler ever seen.

[BONACCORSO'S RETURN TO FLORENCE, AND MISSIONS TO FRANCE AND GERMANY]

After spending the winter in Paris, I decided to return to Florence for good, and to give up gambling forever. I sold my house in Paris to Bernardo di Cino for a thousand francs; it had cost me 600. I gave the household furnishings, which were worth a good deal, to my steward. And when I was ready to depart, I went to take my leave of the King and Queen.[73] The Queen commanded me not to depart before speaking to her again, and told me that she would send for me when it was time. A few days later, she sent for me. Her brother Duke Lodovico[74] was with her, and after many nice speeches she commissioned me to endeavour to get the City of Florence to send its ambassadors to the King to ask him to join in league with them against the Duke of Milan.[75] She said that she was sure that the King would be willing to do so. She gave me letters of presentation to the rulers of Florence. I left Paris and arrived in Florence at the end of May 1396. Before I presented myself to the rulers of Florence, I informed several wise, capable men who served on the Florentine Councils about my mission, and then I appeared before the lords of Florence and delivered my message to them. Much consultation took place. And because Messer Maso degli Albizzi[76] had gone as ambassador to the King of France before my arrival in Florence, to ask the King to give us armed men and captains if there should be a need of them, they decided

---

73 Isabella of Bavaria-Ingolstadt (also known as Isabeau de Bavière), daughter of Stephen III of Bavaria-Ingolstadt and Taddea Visconti. She became queen consort of France when she married Charles VI.

74 Ludwig (Louis) VII of Bavaria-Ingolstadt.

75 Isabella was hostile to Gian Galeazzo Visconti, her uncle-cousin, because he had deposed and imprisoned – and, according to some accounts, assassinated – her maternal grandfather, Bernarbò Visconti, Gian Galeazzo's own uncle, who died of poisoning in 1385.

76 A leading figure in Florentine politics of the time. The Albizzi family opposed the rise of Cosimo de' Medici.

that I should return to Paris. They gave me the commission and full mandate to Messer Maso and to me to make an alliance with the King. I left Florence on the 20th of July 1396, with a salary of 4 florins per day.

Before leaving Florence I purchased from Miglione di Gionta two properties at Montughi, in the area of the abbey of Fiesole. I paid 700 gold florins, and also paid all the taxes. I hereby record that in 1391 I purchased a property from Luigi di Bonaccorso di Rucco de' Pitti for 700 gold florins, and paid all the taxes. The property is called Bossoli and is located below Sorbigliano in the Val di Pesa. That same year, I paid Andrea Belincini 400 gold florins for a house that my brother Francesco had mortgaged to Andrea's brother Niccolò, and another 300 gold florins to Lisabetta, the daughter of the late Cione di Bonaccorso de' Pitti.

I departed Florence on the 20th of July 1396, and travelled to Paris via Lombardy, in great danger because of my mission on behalf of the City of Florence. I took with me the notary Vanni Stefani, and it was very burdensome for me to take him to Paris, because he was not used to riding on horseback; nor had he ever been outside of Florence. When I arrived in Paris, I learned that Messer Maso degli Albizzi had obtained what he had asked of the King. And seeing that he had gotten the King to agree, we promptly set about putting things into action, and in the month of September we entered into a league with the King of France. Because of my involvement in this, the Duke of Orléans, who previously had liked me very well, began to become suspicious of me, because the Duke of Milan was his father-in-law.[77] Before we entered into the league with the King, the Duke of Orléans secretly sent to me an equerry of his, Bonifazio del Madruccio, to entreat me for love of him not to enter into a league against his father-in-law, and he openly threatened me. I did not comply, but with fervent zeal and love for my homeland I persevered. We left Paris and headed for Avignon, hoping to board a ship and sail to Porto Pisano. When we arrived in Avignon, it pleased God and on the advice of Cardinal Corsini of Florence,[78] we did not board the ship, but instead continued travelling by land. The ship we had been intending to

---

77 In 1389, Louis I of Valois (1372–1407) had married Valentina Visconti, the daughter of Gian Galeazzo.

78 Piero Corsini, who became a cardinal in 1370, had initially been a supporter of Pope Urban VI. He later switched his allegiance to the anti-pope at Avignon, Clement VII. Piero was an expert on the law, and wrote a treatise that argued that the papacy of Urban VI was invalid. On the Corsini family, see Martines, *The Social World of the Florentine Humanists*, 221 ff.

take was wrecked at sea, and all the men aboard were drowned, including several Florentine merchants, among them Giovanni di Ser Lando Fortini. We departed Avignon on the feast of St Martin,[79] and when we arrived at Asti we sent a courier to the Duke of Milan to ask him for safe-conduct. Word got out about this in the whole area, and before dawn on the third day we left Asti and headed toward Genoa, avoiding the Duke's lands. We arrived in Genoa and then in Portovenere, where because of a storm we remained for many days, and finally we reached Florence on Christmas Day. The trip from Avignon to Florence took us about 46 days.

Shortly after we arrived, Messer Vanni Castellani, the lawyer Messer Filippo Corsini,[80] and I were selected to be ambassadors to France. I was ordered to go first, and to depart immediately. I left Florence on the 15th of January, travelling through Friuli and Germany. I was on the road for 34 days, always in the snow, except when I was indoors. I remained for five days at the foot of a mountain called Arlberg.[81] I finally got through thanks to men with shovels and oxen, who broke through the snow and made a passage for me. I arrived in Konstanz and then Basel and then Langres and then Paris. I found that the King was seriously ill, and that the news had reached Paris about the defeat of the French in Turkey.[82] For these two reasons, I was able to do very little before the arrival of Messer Vanni and Messer Filippo Corsini. They came, and my brother Luigi came with Messer Filippo. We remained for about 4 months, during which time there were continually funerals for noblemen and others who had died in Turkey, and the King was ill, in seclusion like a madman. His health began to improve once he began to take counsel with his advisors. We quickly appeared before him and his advisors, and Messer Filippo presented our message. He spoke so eloquently that all of the King's advisors, and many others besides, wished to have a copy of what he said. And we gave it in writing, for the King requested it thus. The gist of it was that we requested His Majesty to join with us in a league against the Duke of Milan. He responded that he would give us his answer on another occasion. We asked several times for a response.

---

79 11 November.

80 The brother of Cardinal Piero Corsini, Filippo was also an authority on the law.

81 A massif between Vorarlberg and Tyrol in what is now Austria.

82 The famous and bloody Battle of Nicopolis in September 1396, where a French army led by the duke of Nevers (known as John the Fearless) was massacred by the Ottoman troops of Sultan Bajazet. Charles VI's mental state, already unbalanced since 1392, worsened increasingly after this defeat.

The responses were ineffectual, saying that the King would do his duty; and thus he kept us waiting for more than two months. I got an idea, which Messer Filippo and Messer Vanni liked: I knew that the King did not understand a word of Latin, nor did any of the dukes, except the Duke of Orléans, who was on the side of the Duke of Milan. Because every time Messer Filippo had spoken he had done so in Latin, and had made our request well and clearly, and nothing had come of it, I believed that the King's chancellor and the other prelates, who did understand Latin well, were not translating accurately for the King what Messer Filippo had said. So we decided that the next time we appeared before the King and his council, I would be the speaker, and would speak in French. Thus it transpired that I spoke briefly, saying that the rulers and City of Florence, his devoted servants, entreated the King to keep his promise to enter into a league with us. When I got to the part about him keeping his promise, I saw the King's expression change; he looked upset. Our audience with the King came to an end. We later heard that as soon as we had left the council chamber, the King asked, "What promise am I being asked to keep? Bring me the document." The documents were brought, and when the King saw what he had promised, he strongly reproached the chancellor and the others who had heard and understood Messer Filippo and who had not given him the right meaning of the part that I had made clear speaking in French – that is, his promise to join with us in a league against the Duke of Milan. The King had us called back in, and first the chancellor apologized for the King not having given us a reply sooner, fulfilling our request, and explaining with forthright words the reason for the King's illness on account of his kinsmen who had died in Turkey. He said that the King was now ready to fulfil his duty to us. When the chancellor had finished speaking, the King spoke, saying: "I confirm what my chancellor has said. I do not wish you, or others, to believe that I will fail to keep my promise." Then he addressed me, saying: "And you, Bonaccorso, who have so strongly reminded me of my promise, do not do it again, for it was never nor never shall be necessary to remind me of a promise of mine; as long as I know that I am obliged to keep it, I will never fail to do so. I do not believe that I was ever asked to keep a promise by anyone except just now, by you." I stood up, for I had been sitting, and then knelt down, saying: "Sacred Majesty, if I have said anything to displease you, I humbly beg your forgiveness. I spoke out of necessity, seeing that you did not understand what Messer Filippo had requested of you several times." The Duke of Burgundy responded, saying: "Your Grace, the Florentines are so devoted to Your Majesty that they have made bold to speak to you as if they were your own subjects." The King replied that he was content, and smiling, he said, "But Bonaccorso must make amends to me!"

We left the King's presence, and a few days later the King and his council selected Bernard, Count of Armagnac,[83] to lead a thousand lancers and 5 thousand cavalry, paid by the King for six months, and go to Lombardy in the service of our league. The Count accepted. We went to visit him, congratulating him and entreating him to waste no time in setting out. He replied that it was his intention to set out with 10,000 cavalry and to pitch camp as close as possible to where the Duke of Milan was, and we encouraged him in this. A few days later, Messer Vanni set out for Florence, and Messer Filippo and I remained in Paris to hasten the Count's departure. Because the Duke of Orléans was delaying the Count's departure as long as he could, it took more than a month for the money to come for the Count to pay his soldiers. When he finally received the money, he sent for us, saying: "I want to return to Armagnac to assemble 10,000 cavalry of good men who are used to facing the enemy and not to frequenting the taverns and pastry shops of Paris. I shall have them in Avignon by mid-April; I cannot get such a large force together before then. I need your league to assist me with 10,000 florins per month for the period of six months that I shall be in our enemy's territory. If you agree to this, I shall go to Asti with the whole force, and once I am there, I should find 25,000 florins ready and waiting for me. In the event that you do not wish to do this, I shall not go in person, but shall send a capable captain with the force that the King ordered me to pay. Please let me have an answer, whether yes or no, at Avignon by the end of April." We decided that I should go. I took the road to Burgundy, and from Germany I went down to Friuli, and when I arrived in Treviso I learned that our ambassadors from Florence were in Venice with the lord of Padua and with the other ambassadors of the league.[84] I took two carriage horses, and sent all of my horses and household servants, except one man, to Padua. I went off to Venice, and after I reported to our ambassadors, they immediately conferred with all their associates and told them what I had recounted to them. They all agreed to contribute to the sum of 10,000 florins for the troops to be led by the Count of Armagnac.

---

83 Bernard VII, count of Armagnac was also count of Charolais and constable of France. He died in the insurrection that delivered Paris to the Burgundians in 1418.

84 That is, the ambassadors from Bologna, Ferrara, Mantua, and Rimini.

Our ambassadors charged me to go to Florence and report everything; they also sent a letter with me. I left Venice on the 22nd of March at nine in the evening and landed at Mestre, and at two in the morning I entered Padua, and the morning of the 23rd I took two good horses belonging to the lord of Padua and without having eaten or drunk anything I arrived in Ferrara at eight in the evening, and there I changed horses for two horses belonging to Niccolò d'Este and travelled to San Giorgio, about 10 miles outside of Bologna, where I slept. The next morning I arrived in Bologna before sunrise; I hired two nags and travelled to Scarperia,[85] where I slept, and arrived in Florence about nine in the morning on the 25th of March. Thus in two days and a third I travelled from Padua to Florence, having previously ridden from Paris to Padua in 16 days.

I reported everything to the Seignory and to the Ten Magistrates of War,[86] who quickly decided to send Berto Castellani to Avignon to tell the Count of Armagnac to go to Asti, where he would find the 25,000 florins ready, and that everything that he had requested would be done. A few days after Berto departed, about the 8th of April, I received a letter from the Count of Armagnac, informing me that he needed the 25,000 florins in Avignon. I showed the letter to the Ten Magistrates of War, who lost their patience and decided to break with him, sending word to our ambassadors in Venice that they should conclude the league with the Venetians, by which we obliged ourselves to make war or peace with the Duke of Milan how and when they saw fit, which was of little honour to our city. Shortly afterward a truce was declared, followed by the false, evil peace with the Duke of Milan, which didn't last long.[87]

The Count of Armagnac had arrived in Avignon with 10,000 cavalry and was expecting 100,000 francs (equivalent to 90,000 gold écus) from Paris; the money had already arrived in Point-Saint-Esprit.[88] Back in

---

85 A town about twenty-five kilometres northeast of Florence.

86 The members of the *Dieci di Balìa* (Ten Magistrates of War) were appointed magistrates who served for six-month terms only during times of war or potential conflict. See Gene Brucker, ed., *Two Memoirs of Renaissance Florence: The Diaries of Buonaccorso Pitti and Gregorio Dati,* trans. Julia Martines (New York: Harper and Row, 1967), 60, note 27.

87 A general truce of ten years was proclaimed on 11 May 1398 with the Venetians, with no Florentine delegate. Gian Galeazzo Visconti took advantage of the situation, taking over Pisa in February of 1399, Siena in August of that same year, and Perugia in January 1400.

88 A town on the Rhône River, site of a historic crossing.

Paris, the Duke of Orléans, who had delayed the sending of the money as long as he could, alleged in the King's Council that he knew for certain that our league would quickly make peace with the Duke of Milan. He received letters from Pavia that had been sent by the Duke of Milan seven days earlier, stating that he had reached a truce and that soon peace would be declared. The Duke of Orléans showed the letter to the King and to the Council, and they immediately sent word that the person who was taking the 90,000 écus to the Count of Armagnac should not pay them; the message reached him at Pont-Saint-Esprit. So the Count of Armagnac returned home, unhappy with us and with the rulers of France, after he had incurred great damages and expenses. The King of France was also unhappy with us, because we had made a truce without consulting him. And we were unhappy with the King for all of the delays, on account of which we incurred great danger and expense and damage, with little honour.

On the 15th of September 1398, I entered the College of the Twelve Good Men.[89] And then on the 30th of October we held a vote for the *podestà* of Pistoia. I protested as much as I could, both verbally and with the vote I cast, that we should not do this, for it seemed to me that it was doing an injustice to the people of Pistoia, because this would break the promise we had made to them, assuring them of their freedom. On the 2nd of December, we began a general vote and on the 11th of that month it was completed, and the secretaries were the farrier Lorenzo d'Agnolo, Nastagio Bucielli, Francesco di Neri Ardinghelli, and Andrea di Messer Ugo dalla Stufa.

On the first of July 1399, I became a member of the Priors. My colleagues were Giovanni di Messer Donato Barbadoro, Stefano Rafacani, Deo Bentacordi, Michele Altoviti, Antonio di Durante, Simone Biffoli, and Attaviano di Ser Tino dalla Casa. The Standard-bearer of Justice was Giovanni di Giovanni Aldobrandini.

During the time that I was a member of the Priors, the news arrived that King Ladislaus[90] had taken the city of Naples, and reconquered the whole Kingdom of Naples, and that King Louis[91] had gone back to

---

89 Along with the *Sedici Gonfalonieri* (Sixteen Standard-bearers of the militia companies), the *Dodici Buonomini* was one of the two major "colleges" that advised the Florentine Seignory on matters of policy.

90 Ladislas or Ladislaus the Magnanimous, king of Naples and titular king of Jerusalem and Sicily.

91 Louis II of Anjou, who had seized Naples from Ladislaus in 1390.

France. Everyone in Florence was moved to celebrate, but I argued that open celebrating should not take place for more than 15 days, because the term of our league with the king of France was not yet finished. But I did recommend that we send a messenger to console the King and to secretly give him up to 10,000 florins, which he must have been more happy with than the 6,000 florins that I calculated the celebration would cost. Finally, the celebration took place, with great jousts and tournaments and fireworks for three nights with the bells of the Palace ringing.

At this time there occurred a new phenomenon, which spread throughout Italy – people great and small all dressed in white linen who went about in large groups, with their heads and faces covered, shouting and singing and asking God for mercy and peace.[92] With all these people acting in this way, there were people who said, "Let us go to the Stinche[93] and release the prisoners." By the grace of God, this didn't happen and the city did not erupt in armed rioting, but the danger of this was very real. It ended well, because peace was brokered among many people. Our family made peace with Antonio and Gieri di Giovanni Corbizi, the nephews of Matteo di Ricco whom I had killed in Pisa, and with Matteo di Paolo Corbizi. Ser Antonio di Ser Chello drew up the documents.

On the 22nd of September in that same year, I entered upon my duties as captain of Pistoia.[94] During my term of office, among other things, it happened that I captured a public thief, and the Florentine Seignory sent a mounted guard to me, with a message that I should hand the thief over to him, so that he could be taken back to the *podestà* of Florence. I did not do it, but wrote back to them, imploring them to respect the rights that had been guaranteed to Pistoia. They wrote back to me that if in response to their second letter I did not hand the thief over to them, they would do something to me that would be a perpetual example to anyone who did not obey them. I continued to make resistance, and wrote to my brothers that they should inform our relatives and friends, and if they saw fit to go and beseech the members of the Seignory to let me mete out justice in Pistoia and observe the oaths that I had sworn to

---

92 Bonaccorso is referring to the famous religious cult of penitents known as the "Bianchi" because of their white clothing. The movement started in the Piedmontese town of Chieri in 1398.

93 A famous Florentine prison.

94 The captaincy of Pistoia, a city about thirty-two kilometres northwest of Florence, was an office in the Florentine dominion that involved administrative, judicial, and law enforcement functions. See Brucker, *Two Memoirs of Renaissance Florence*, notes to 62–3.

the people of Pistoia when I took office. My brothers went with many of our relatives and friends to entreat the members of the Seignory and their Colleges. When they emerged from the audience with the Seignory, Giovanni di Tignosino Bellandi, who was provost, made a motion to take a vote to have me banished for 20 years. There were 23 black beans[95] in favour, which were two short of the necessary number. My brothers were called back in and told about the vote. The members of the Seignory told them that if I did not turn the thief over to them in three days, it was their intention to repeat the vote as many times as was necessary for the motion to pass. My brothers informed me of this, saying that all of our relatives and friends were advising that I should not put up any more resistance. I met with the Priors of Pistoia and many of their citizens, told them everything that had transpired, and had the letters that I had received read to them; then I told them that they should decide what they wanted me to do. I said that I was determined and steadfast, and ready to suffer banishment and any other punishment in order to respect their rights, and that without their consent, those rights would not be violated by me. They retired to consult together, and then they replied to me, with tears and with sighs, saying that I had done so much for them, they would always be obliged to me; but that seeing that the Seignory was determined to take away their rights,[96] and the risk that I would run if I continued to resist, which could bring even greater harm to them, they agreed that, for fear of worse, I should send the thief to Florence; and that is what I did.

In the year 1400, I departed for Savoy to try to collect the accursed money that I had lent to the Count. When I arrived in Padua and told the lord of that city where I wished to go, he said to me: "You cannot cross into Savoy without making a petition to the Duke of Milan; I know this for certain because of the order he has issued, and he has been promised by the lords of the territories through which you would have to cross, and by others, that they will obey his order." I therefore resolved to turn back, and was glad to do so, because I had very unwillingly – indeed, with great displeasure – left my brothers and our families at Sorbigliano where they had taken refuge from the plague in Florence. When I got

---

95 Black and white beans were used in balloting, black indicating a vote in favour of a
    proposition, and white a vote against.
96 This policy on the part of the Florentines would lead to the complete end of Pistoia's
    autonomy in 1401.

to Bologna, I wrote to my brothers that they should join me there with all of our families, and I sent them horses and muleteers. They came to Bologna, and after about eight days I rented the palace and garden of the Bianchi family, about two miles outside of the city, and all of us brothers stayed there with our families, except Piero and his family, who remained in Montughi.[97] By the grace of God we all survived, except a son of mine who was born and died there. Between us and our families and other relatives, who had come there with us at our expense, there were always about 25 people staying in the house. We remained there around four months, and when we returned to Florence, we found that we had spent 480 new florins.[98] During that year, when many Florentines had fled to Bologna on account of the plague, the political exiles incited many young men to join them in a plot against out government; the ringleader was Salvestro di Messer Rosso de' Ricci. The plot was discovered, because it was revealed by Salvestro di Messer Filippo Cavicciuli. Samminiato d'Ugocciozzo de' Ricci and a member of the Davizi family were arrested and beheaded. Many men were banished, and many were pardoned, and calm returned to the city.

["AMBASSADOR TO THE NEW EMPEROR" AND CHAMPION AGAINST
THE VISCONTI]

That same year, I was elected ambassador and sent to the newly elected Emperor in Germany, that is, Rupert of Bavaria, Count Palatine.[99] My mission was, firstly, to congratulate him on his election; secondly, to entreat him to come to Rome for his coronation; thirdly, to persuade him to win back the regions of the empire that were then under the tyranny of the Duke of Milan; fourthly, to tell him that if he agreed to do so in that year, 1401, our city would give him 100,000 gold florins; fifthly, to ask him to reconfirm the privileges that had been granted to us by the empire, and to extend our vicariate to Arezzo, Montepulciano, and all of the other imperial lands that were then in our possession. I left Florence,

---

97 A hilly area in Florence.

98 Florins that had been minted since 1422.

99 Florence theoretically recognized that it belonged to the Holy Roman Empire, while at the same time jealously protecting its complete *de facto* independence of it. The city-state of Florence was willing to pay a substantial amount of money in order to maintain its independence, and its dominion over the lands it had occupied, albeit under the guise of a vicariate.

taking with me the notary Ser Pero di Ser Pero da Samminiato to draw up the necessary documents. I departed on the 15th of March. We travelled by way of Padua, where, as I had been instructed to do, I informed the local lord of my mission. The lord of Padua sent with us an ambassador of his own, named Dorde. We went by way of Friuli and then to Germany via Salzburg and Munich and Ingolstadt and then Hamburg,[100] where we found the newly elected Emperor. After I had presented the obeisance and compliments of our city, I said that whenever it should please His Majesty, I would expound my embassy to him, either privately or publicly, whichever he preferred. He received us readily, saying that he would inform us when he was ready to hear our message. At his expense, he had us lodged in a very fine house, where we were honourably waited on by his own servants. On the second day, he sent for us, and asked me to deliver my message in the presence of about eight members of his council. I delivered it, and though I said that we would be willing to make him a payment, I did not name the amount. He responded that he would appoint delegates to negotiate with us, which he did. During the negotiations, they asked us what amount our city would be willing to pay. I replied that they should ask for what they thought was appropriate, and they answered that the Emperor would need our city to help him with 500,000 florins, if he were to come to Italy that year. I said that I wished to respond to that point in the Emperor's presence. We went before him, and I said, "Your majesty, your delegates have asked me for an astoundingly large sum; and it seems to us that this is a polite way of refusing to come to Italy, for you must be well aware that it would be impossible for our city to pay such a sum." He said that I was right – he did not want to go to Italy that year, because he didn't have the money; for the 300,000 florins he had gotten before he was elected had all been spent for the two sessions of the imperial diet[101] that he had held after his election. He said that if we could wait another year, he would have more money, and would not have to ask us for so much; but if we still wished him to come that year, we would have to bear most of the expense. After much entreating to convince him to come, I finally told him the sum that I had been authorized to offer. He replied that, if I could not offer more, I should write to Florence, telling them everything he had said to me, to the effect that he had no money. That is what I wrote, in duplicate letters carried by my own couriers. I received a reply, instructing me to try to

---

100 Hamburg was at that time the capital of the Palatinate.
101 The highest representative assembly of the empire.

convince him to come to Italy that year, and giving the reasons: that it was a propitious moment for him and that if he delayed, the situation could change. I was authorized to offer him up to 200,000 gold florins, and also to give him the hope that once he was in Italy we would make every effort to help him. We went before His Majesty on several occasions on several days after that, and after much talk on his part as well as ours, before we concluded, I continued to increase the amount of money we were offering, until, having reached the limit of the second amount I had been authorized to offer, I told him that I could go no higher. He replied that he would send for his electors and barons to come to him at Nuremberg, about two days' journey away, and that he would consult with them and then give us an answer. While we were still waiting for a reply from Florence, it happened that we dined with the Emperor in one of his gardens, and I, having noticed that he took no precautions against poison, said to him, "Your Highness, it seems that you are not aware of the perfidy of the Duke of Milan; for if you were, you would take greater care for your safety than you do. For you may be certain that when he hears that you are resolved to cross into Italy, he will do his utmost to have you killed either by poison or by stabbing." His countenance changed entirely, and he crossed himself, saying: "Could he be so perfidious as to attempt to have me killed, when I have not declared war on him, nor he on me? I find this difficult to believe; nevertheless, I will follow your advice and take greater care." And this he did. And among other things, on account of the suspicion that I had aroused in him, whenever he saw someone whom he did not know, he immediately wanted to know what that person was up to. On one occasion, when he and we, who were continually with him, went to a fine estate of his near Hamburg to hunt, and were going out one morning to hear mass, the Emperor noticed a man dressed as a courier; he had him summoned and questioned him. The man said that he was on his way to Venice, and that he had come to that place solely to see the Emperor and to be able to give news of him at Venice. The Emperor ordered one of his knights to take the man to his chamber and to keep him there until he returned from mass. When he returned, the courier confessed to him that he had come from Pavia carrying a letter to the Emperor's physician from Master Piero da Tosignano, the physician of the Duke of Milan,[102] and that

---

102 Piero da Tosignano was a lecturer in medicine at Bologna, famous for his observations on the plague and for a very popular book of prescriptions, both of which were later published (the former in Venice in 1472, and the latter in Perugia in 1482).

he had carried such letters on other occasions. The Emperor read the letter, and sent for his physician, whose name was Master Herman, who had been a pupil of Master Piero da Tosignano. In short, the physician confessed that he was to have poisoned the Emperor with a clyster, for which he was to receive 15,000 ducats, 5,000 to be paid in Mainz and 10,000 in Venice. We left the estate to return to Hamburg, and the physician and the courier were brought along under heavy guard. During the ride back, the Emperor called for me and said, "You saved my life through your warning," and he told me what he had found out. We later went to Nuremberg; the archbishops of Cologne and Mainz, who were electors, came there, along with many other barons, whom the Emperor told immediately about the plot he had discovered. He sent for the authorities of that city and told them what he had discovered, saying that since he was involved, he did not want to judge the case himself, but asked them to take custody of the physician and to question him and to judge him according to what seemed right to them. They brought the physician to their palace, and after questioning him for several days and having determined that it was true that he had intended to poison the Emperor, they decreed that he should be dragged on the ground to the place of justice and that his legs and arms and back should be broken, and he should be tied to a cart wheel and raised on a pole and left there until he died; and thus it was done. After this, the Emperor held council for several days. Finally, because everyone who should have taken part in the deliberations as to whether he should go to Rome for his coronation was not there, they determined that they should go to Mainz to meet with everyone who needed to participate in the deliberations; and this they did. At Mainz, after holding many discussions and negotiations, we reached an agreement with the Emperor that if he would come to Lombardy with all of his forces for the whole month of September, 50,000 ducats would be given to his representative in Venice, and then 150,000 ducats in three instalments. We accompanied him when he left Mainz for Heidelberg, more than 10 German miles away,[103] whither he had summoned certain great merchants who had promised to lend him 50,000 ducats at Augsburg, where his forces were to assemble; we had to promise to repay them that amount at Venice once he had crossed into Lombardy. But when the merchants arrived, they said that they could not keep their

---

103 In German-speaking areas at the time, a mile had slightly different measurements: 7.042 kilometres in Bavaria, 7.5 in Saxony, 7.419 in Hanover and Brunswick.

promise, because the other merchants, from whom they had hoped to obtain the cash from them on credit, were absolutely refusing to give the money to them, because they had heard what they wanted it for. Finally, after many entreaties mixed with threats, when the Emperor realized that he could not obtain from the merchants what they had promised him, he sent for us and told us everything. And almost weeping, he said to us: "I shall be dishonoured because of these merchants, for on account of the promise that they made me at Mainz, I ordered my lords and barons and soldiers to join me in Augsburg for the whole month of August and then to cross into Lombardy. And now you hear how they have failed me. Therefore I entreat you, Bonaccorso, make haste to go and recount what has happened to my devoted sons in the Florentine Seignory, and entreat them to salvage my honour and their own interests if they want me to be in Lombardy at the appointed time. Tell them that in order for me to depart from Augsburg, I need them to advance me at least 25,000 gold ducats of the promised amount." I strongly resisted going to Florence, asserting that it would be safer and quicker to send duplicate letters. But the Emperor would not be persuaded by any argument that I should not go, so I decided to depart, fearing that if I did not, he would not come to Italy that year. I left Heidelberg on the 18th of July and arrived in Padua in 12 days, which is a journey of more than 500 miles. The lord of Padua was astonished that I had been able to arrive in such a short time; he wouldn't have believed it if it hadn't been for a letter that I brought him from the Emperor. I had had a fever for 4 days when I left Padua, and when I arrived in Rovigo I had to stay in bed for a day because my fever was so high I could not ride. On the second day, I got on a boat which took me by way of various canals to the Po River and from there to Francolino, where I again took horse and rode to Messer Egano's home at Poggio,[104] where I spent the night. It took me two and a half days to ride from Poggio to Florence, and I still had a fever. Once I had reported to the Seignory, their Colleges, and a special council, I returned home, and in a few days I recovered from my fever. When I was hale and hearty again, the Seignory and the Ten Magistrates of War resolved that I should go to Augsburg with Andrea di Neri Vettori, who was

---

104 Perhaps Poggio Renatico in the area of Ferrara, a town on the border between the territory of the Este family and the feud of the Lambertini family. The name Egano was common there: Egano di Gidantonio was made Count of Poggio Renatico during the fifteenth century.

later made a knight, and tell the Emperor that as soon as he had drawn up a document with the clauses and terms that we had agreed upon with him, he could send to Venice for the 50,000 ducats, which would be there in the hands of their delegate, Giovanni di Bicci de' Medici.[105] We departed from Florence on the 15th of August with the aforementioned Giovanni de' Medici, who came with us as far as Venice, where we left him. We continued our journey, and riding for many hours each day we arrived in Augsburg, where the Emperor had assembled about 15,000 fine cavalry. We delivered our message, to which the Emperor quickly replied in great distress, seeing that we had brought no money with us: "Now I am obliged to leave behind the flower of our army, around 5,000 experienced fighting men, who have no money of their own." He held council for a whole day, debating whether to go forward or turn back. Finally, he decided to leave the 5,000 cavalry behind because of the lack of money, and to go with the rest of his forces in slow stages to Trent, where he would wait for me to return with the 50,000 ducats. He gave me the documents and agreements with his seals, asking me to return to Venice with one of his knights and his bursar. This I did; when we arrived in Venice I immediately collected the 50,000 ducats and we departed with them for Trent, where we found the Emperor greatly distressed because of the time he had lost waiting for us (about 22 days). He would have been in Lombardy much sooner, and he would have brought all his men with him, if the 25,000 ducats had been sent to him at Augsburg as he had requested. His fears were later realized – that is, because of the Emperor's delay in entering Italy, the Duke of Milan had the opportunity to make preparations and strengthen his forces against his coming. And this he did, with the result that he inflicted great losses and brought shame both on His Majesty and on our city, as I shall relate later on.

When the Emperor received the 50,000 ducats, he immediately distributed them to his men, and begged and urged me to return to Venice for the second payment, which he wanted to receive at Verona. I resisted leaving him, saying that it was not necessary for me to go, and that if I went I would be in great danger of death or imprisonment. I said that I would be happier to die bearing arms in his service than to die as an envoy on the way to pick up money, because a more glorious memory

---

105 Giovanni di Bicci, the founder of the Medici bank, was the father of Cosimo de' Medici, considered the founder of the Medici dynasty.

would survive me, and more honour would accrue to my family. But in the end he insisted that I go, saying: "You will serve me much better by going than you would by commanding a hundred lances in my service." And he added: "Ask of me whatever you want that is in my power, and it shall be yours." I replied, "Sire, if it is your pleasure that I should go, I am happy to do so; but if I am killed or captured, what sign will remain for my family to show that I died in your service?" Then he said, "I wish to give you an emblem from my coat of arms – the golden lion[106] – to include with your own coat of arms. I ennoble you and your brothers and your descendants." And thus he commanded his chancellor to record this in his register, saying: "Go with good cheer, Bonaccorso, for God will accompany you in consideration of the deeds and actions that I hope to accomplish as a result. And if God grants that I castigate the great tyrant of Milan, this emblem that I give to you will be the pledge of great honour and profit that in time you shall receive from me." It turned out that the Emperor left Trent before I was ready to depart for Venice. I rode with him a little way outside the city, and left with him Andrea Vettori and Ser Piero da San Miniato, to whom I entrusted two of my horses and most of my armour, except for the breastplate, which I wanted to keep on me at all times.

I departed, taking the road through Germany to Venzone in Friuli. On my way, I composed one of my humble sonnets, which I transcribe here:

> In this year 1401,
> In the city of Trent King Rupert
> Decreed that my escutcheon should be covered
> With his own coat of arms, a golden lion rampant.
> He ordered and decreed in that moment
> That in his registry be openly written
> Our five names,[107] so that each
> Would have the lion on our wavy shield.[108]
> He gave us this privilege, and made us worthy
> Of nobility, with our descendants.
> We have the right to bear his emblem on our coat of arms,
> With other signs of noble eminence

---

106 The Palatine emblem is a golden lion rampant, with a red crown, claws, and tongue.
107 That is, the names of Bonaccorso and his four brothers.
108 The Pitti coat of arms has a background with white and black waves.

Recognized throughout all Realms
And we can receive feuds
from powerful Kings.
So, my esteemed brothers and sons,
Act and speak well,
As befits our noble estate.

The evening of my arrival in Venzone, I was visited by a man from Siena with whom I was on familiar terms, for I had gone to the spice shop that he kept there several times when passing through that town. He told me that he had learned of a plot to capture me on the road when I set out on the following day. This plot had been put together by a secret agent of the Duke of Milan, a man called Fra Giovanni Decani, who had promised the lord of Prampergh[109] 4,000 gold ducats if he would hand me over to him. This Prampergh had promised to do so, under the guise of a reprisal against the Florentines. I asked the Sienese man if I could trust the innkeeper where I was staying. He said that I surely could. So at about four in the morning I mounted my horse, and took with me the innkeeper and one of his servants so that I would not get lost, for I kept off the main road to Portogruaro. Without stopping to eat or drink, I reached Portogruaro, which is a journey of about 40 miles. There I boarded a ship and set out for Venice. I sent my horses to Padua. Later, after the death of the Duke of Milan, I encountered that same Fra Giovanni in Bologna, and he confessed to me that the story of the plot to capture me was true.

About three days after my arrival in Venice, the news came that the Emperor had been defeated outside of Brescia and that he had returned to Trent. There, he was prevailed upon and encouraged by our city and by the Venetians and by the lord of Padua to set out for Padua by way of Venzone. When he reached Padua, a new delegation arrived from Florence, consisting of Messer Filippo de' Corsini, Messer Rinaldo Gianfigliazzi, Messer Maso degli Albizzi, and Messer Tommaso dei Sacchetti. These gentlemen and Andrea de' Vettori and I had many negotiations and discussions with the Emperor and with the lord of Padua. But since we could not reach an agreement, the Emperor decided that we should all go to Venice and ask the Venetian government to help us reach

---

109 Perhaps Prampero, a noble Friulan family.

consensus. This was around the Calends of December, 1401. We went to Venice, and after much negotiation and councils held in the presence of the Doge, we still could not reach an agreement. So the Emperor set sail for Portogruaro in galleys that the Venetians lent him. As soon as he had departed, the Doge sent for us, lamenting the departure of the Emperor for our sake and on behalf of all of Italy, saying: "If you let him go back to Germany, there is no doubt that the Duke of Milan will make himself lord of all of Italy," and so on. The Doge entreated and begged that one or two of us should follow the Emperor, saying that if we would undertake to give the Emperor the amount of money that he had requested, he himself would send a delegation to entreat him to return to Venice. We agreed to do this, and returned to our lodgings. Since it turned out that no one else was willing to undertake the danger of following the Emperor, I went on behalf of everyone, to entreat him to return and say that we would give him what he had asked for. I caught up with him the following day, at a port about 50 miles from Venice, and delivered my message. He withdrew to consult with his advisors, and because I had told him that the Doge was also sending a delegation, he remained in council waiting from sunrise until midday. The Doge's emissaries arrived around the hour of the terce and went before the Emperor's council. After they had been there a short while, I was called, and the Emperor told me that he was willing to return to Venice on the condition that I would pledge my word and that of my comrades that we would give him the 60,000 ducats that he had requested to get his troops in order, and I promised him that we would. I accompanied him back to Venice, and the promise that I had made to him was kept. Then we went to Padua, where I left him in negotiations with the other ambassadors, and I returned to Florence to make my report about what had happened from the time the promise made in Germany had been broken. Later the other ambassadors returned, and the Emperor's nephew, Duke Ludwig of Bavaria, came to seek new agreements about aid for the journey to Rome and the continuance of the war in Lombardy against the Duke of Milan.

After much consultation and negotiation, we didn't succeed in getting any additional money in order to keep the Emperor in Italy. This decision would have cost us our freedom if death had not overtaken the Duke of Milan shortly after he had captured Bologna; he captured that city in late June of that year, and he died in September.[110] If he had lived to conquer

---

110 Gian Galeazzo Visconti captured Bologna on 28 June and died on 3 September, as
    recounted by Morelli in his lively narrative in this anthology. See page 203 above.

us, he surely would have become lord of all of Italy in a short time. And he was poised to beat us, for he was already lord of Pisa, Siena, Perugia, Chiusi, and Bologna and all of their fortified places, and the lord of Lucca obeyed him, and likewise the Malatesta family and the lord of Urbino. All of northern Italy was subjugated to him, except Venice. Thus his death saved us and increased our power up to today, as can be seen, more out of luck or the grace of God than on account of the virtue or wisdom of our rulers. For it seems to me that we have grown so arrogant and careless that if an emperor or other great lord were to take against us in our present state, we would surely lose, with our leaders divided as they seem to me to be; with their special interests and secret feuds, those who govern our City have abandoned her well-being and honour. In my opinion, because of the faults of our rulers, two sorts of citizens have managed to get into the government – upstarts and the very young – and these people have become so cocky on account of the disunity that they see in their superiors that I am sure that not too long from now, our state shall undergo a great change. May God grant that the elders of our government find harmony and work together for the common good rather than impeding the course of justice as they continuously do now, for their own personal interests. I do not wish to write any more about this matter at present.

[BONACCORSO'S PUBLIC OFFICES AND AMBASSADORSHIPS]

On 28 June 1402, I took office as captain of Barga.[111] That same day, I heard the news that the army that we had sent under Bernardone da Serra to relieve Bologna had been defeated at Casalecchio.[112] After the Bolognese were routed, the lord of Bologna, Giovanni Bentivoglio, died, and Count Alberigo da Barbiano entered Bologna with his army in the name of the Duke of Milan. Two of our ambassadors, Bardo Rittafé and Niccolò da Uzzano, were there. Bardo was killed and Niccolò was captured; he was ransomed after several months in captivity.

When Niccolò returned to Florence, he told me that he had been severely tortured and that finally they forced him to say what they wanted, and he wrote a false confession in his own hand for fear of being tortured more. Later he was taken to Marignano[113] and appeared before

---

111 An Apennine town in the province of Lucca.

112 Gian Galeazzo Visconti defeated the Bolognese and their allies at the Battle of Casalecchio di Reno, near Bologna.

113 A town sixteen kilometres southeast of Milan, today called Melegnano.

the Duke of Milan and many of his counsellors, and his false confession was read aloud. The confession recounted how Niccolò had carried out the commission that had been given to me when I went as an ambassador to Germany to try to persuade the new Emperor to come to Italy. There were many true things in the confession, and one falsehood, which was that I had been told to spend whatever it took and tell whatever lies were necessary to deceive the Emperor into thinking that the Duke of Milan was intending to poison him; this was purportedly to incite the Emperor. The confession also stated that the death of the Emperor's physician had been my doing. Niccolò told me: "When the confession had been read, I confirmed it in the presence of the Duke and his counsellors, and I was taken back to prison. So, Bonaccorso, take care not to fall into the hands of the Duke of Milan. And I beg you to forgive me." I concluded from this that the Duke was seeking to falsely clear himself, especially with the lords of France. So I wrote a letter to the Duke of Orléans, informing him about all of this and concluding that it was not true that I had in any way caused the death of the Emperor's physician Master Herman, as the Duke of Milan's people had alleged on the basis of a false confession that had been obtained through torture. I entreated him to advise me if he thought I should appear before the King and the other lords in order to assert the truth and maintain my honour; if he did, I would hasten to go to them in order to clarify what was true and to assert my innocence.

After I had assumed the post of captain of Barga, I received letters from the Ten Magistrates of War ordering me to blockade the roads from Pisa to Milan. I accordingly ordered the confiscation of 11 mules that were carrying 22 bales of English wool to Bologna; the wool had been bought in Pisa by Francesco Bonconti in the name of Lippo di Muccie-rello of Bologna. The mules were stopped on the Alberguccio road coming from Montecuccolo, which was under the protection of the Duke of Milan. No sooner had the confiscated goods been brought to Barga than the Lord of Lucca[114] sent a complaint to Florence, saying that the wool was the property of Lucchese merchants and demanding that it be returned, in an almost threatening tone. Fearing that he might become a sworn enemy of our city, the rulers of Florence wrote to instruct me to hand over the wool to a commissary of the lord of Lucca, and that I could leave the mules to the men who had confiscated them, because they

---

114 Paolo Guinigi, who ruled Lucca from 1400 to 1430. Morelli also writes about this
   incident.

belonged to men who were subject to the Duke of Milan. I did not obey; instead, I quickly wrote a reply to the rulers of Florence, enclosing letters that had been found on one of the muleteers, which confirmed what I said above, and entreating them not to deal unfairly with the men who had been following reasonable orders when they had confiscated the wool. My letter had little effect, for the lords of Florence, doubting what I had said, and also under pressure from Bartolomeo Corbinelli, a member of the Ten Magistrates of War who was and continues to be a particular friend of the Lord of Lucca, sent me letters by one of their guards ordering me to hand the wool over to the guard and clearly threatening me, if I did not do so, not to expect any more letters from them, and that I would be punished as an example to others. Having read the letters, I handed the wool over to their man, and I distributed the mules among the men who had confiscated them. The guard turned the wool over to a commissary of the lord of Lucca. Before I left the office of captain of Barga, that same lord of Lucca closed the roads from his town to Florence, whereupon the Ten Magistrates of War wrote to me that I should blockade the roads as before. I dispatched one of my notaries to them to say that I wasn't eager to expose the men and soldiers of Barga to hardship and danger only to have them wronged again at the request of the lord of Lucca. But I said that if they wanted to stop his hostile actions against our city, I would be happy to rouse all of the Garafagnana Valley against him and to wrest a number of villages from him, which I already had reason to believe they would like to do. If our city did not want it to be known that they were behind this, I told them to leave it to me, and that if they secretly gave me enough money to pay 50 cavalrymen and 200 foot soldiers and archers, I would get Barga and Sommocolonia[115] to rise up against him, and would offer refuge to anyone who deserted from the other side. To further dissociate Florence from this action, I was willing to let them banish me and imprison my wife and children. They considered my proposal, and replied that it was not the right moment for such action but that when it was the right time, they would remember me. Later, shortly before I left office, Maestro Andrea dall'Ancisa, who was in Lucca, secretly informed me via a trusted agent of his that the lord of Lucca, having been informed about my plan by one of the members of the Ten Magistrates of War, had ordered that certain soldiers of the Duke of Milan should capture me as I left Barga, and had seen to it that I

---

115 A hilltop village overlooking the town of Barga.

would be prevented from taking any road but the main road from Barga to Lucca. Having been thus forewarned, on the day that I left office, I did not depart from Barga. I remained there four days; and then at three in the morning on the 6th of January, I set off in the following manner. I sent my squire ahead of me on horseback dressed in my clothes and accompanied by my servants. I went on foot, with a shield on my arm and carrying a small club, accompanied by 20 stalwart foot soldiers and 14 archers from Barga. That night before daybreak I came to the bridge at Moriano, where I mounted and rode to San Gennaro and thence to Pescia. That night we encountered guards at the bridge at Calavorno, but seeing our strength and realizing that some of us had already stealthily got onto the bridge, for their own good they let us pass. At Chifenti, we again found guards, who had taken the bridge so that we could not pass; so we proceeded to the bridge at Moriano, which was unguarded, and were able to pass over.

During my term as captain of Barga, I was informed that a certain Cristofano di Barzuglino was secretly meeting with some men who had been banished from Barga, especially with a brother of his and with another man named Nerone. I had Cristofano arrested. When I first took office at Barga, and shortly after Bologna had fallen to the Duke of Milan, I had ordered that all the sheaves of harvested wheat be stored inside houses for safekeeping; so, many houses were full of wheat sheaves. I discovered that Nerone had put Cristofano up to setting fire to many of the houses of their enemies, counting on help from all of the exiles from Barga and many of the lord of Lucca's[116] foot soldiers. As soon as they saw the fire, they were supposed to start chopping down one of the city gates with the help of some of their own men, who were meant to have entered through a sewer to set fire to the houses. As soon as I arrested Cristofano, his father, Barzuglino, fled; his son had told him about Nerone's plan, and Barzuglino had reproached him for agreeing to take part in such a plot, but out of love for his son he had not revealed it to me. I had Cristofano beheaded, and banished his father and confiscated his possessions.

On the first of May 1403, I began a term as one of the standard-bearers of the militia companies. My colleagues were Giovanni di Lodovico di Banco, Fantone di Naldo Fantoni, Neri di Ser Fresco, the goldsmith Chello di [*text missing*], Fruosino di Francesco Spinelli, Lapo di Giovanni Niccolini, Niccolò di Marco Benvenuti, Nofri di Giovanni Siminetti,

---

116 Paolo Guinigi; see note 114.

Antonio di Jacopo del Vigna, Marco di Goro degli Strozzi, Lionardo di Tommaso da Careggi, Vieri di Vieri Guadagni, Bartolomeo di Jacopone Gherardini, Lorenzo di Tommaso Baronci, and the master mason Andrea Ciofi.

That year, a priest from Pisa informed the Ten Magistrates of War that there was a gate in the city walls of Pisa[117] that was unguarded; the gate had been bricked in many years before so that the outer surfaces were flush with the walls, and the interior was hollow. The magistrates consulted a master engineer, who, after he heard what they had to say, went in disguise to see the walled-in gate himself. Because of the holes that had been left in the exterior of the wall by the scaffolding that had been erected when the gate was walled in, he could see that indeed the wall was hollow on the inside. He returned to the Ten Magistrates of War and told them how he could insert gunpowder through the holes into the hollow space in the wall and then set fire to it, and that the force of the explosion would surely cause the brick walls to collapse both on the inside and the outside. The magistrates chose two of their own, Messer Rinaldo Gianfigliazzi and Messer Filippo de' Magalotti, with four citizens to accompany them – Messer Maso degli Albizzi, Bartolomeo di Bardo Altoviti, Betti di Giovanni Rustichi, and myself. We set out for San Miniato and then to Santa Gioconda with all of our cavalrymen and infantry, and with a large number of peasants from the district as foot soldiers. We left Messer Rinaldo at Santa Gonda, for he was unwell, and the rest of us continued on and found lodgings at the abbey of San Savino and in other houses in that area. The next day we remained there without budging, because we heard that the Pisans had reinforced the bricked-in gate by digging trenches on the exterior of the walls and posting a good number of men to guard it. We resolved to go to Leghorn and attack it with all of our resources and strength, but when we got there, we found that the city was being protected by a great number of skilled archers. We gave battle and lost a number of our men to arrows and artillery. We departed and returned to Florence, with little honour. I had gone with 14 cavalrymen, but only received pay for 4, which came to 2 gold florins per day.

On the 20th of February of that same year, I became Vicar of Valdinievole.[118] On the 26th of April 1404, the Seignory sent me as ambassador

---

117 At this time, Pisa was an ally of Florence's chief enemy, Gian Galeazzo Visconti, the duke of Milan.

118 A valley in the southwestern part of the province of Pistoia.

to Boucicault, the governor of Genoa,[119] to protest the large quantities of wool and other merchandise belonging to Florentine merchants that he had confiscated. He claimed that he was holding the merchandise as a guarantee lest we make war on Messer Gabriello Maria, the lord of Pisa, who was under the protection of the king of France.[120] Boucicault said that he had issued a warning before confiscating the merchandise, and when he did not receive an acceptable reply, he seized it. After he confiscated the goods, which were worth about 200,000 gold florins, he declared that we would have to accept this loss, because our people had waged war on Pisa before he had received Messer Gabriello on the recommendation of the King and had informed us about it. The rulers of Florence had sent me to make it clear that our forces had not made any offensive moves against Pisa since Boucicault had informed us of the pact with the King of France, and to entreat him to release our merchandise and our merchants. I was instructed to promise him that no further acts of war would be made against Messer Gabriello without informing him beforehand, and to beg him to let us continue to wage the war that we had begun before Messer Gabriello had sought the King's protection. I went and delivered my message, and Boucicault replied that he would not return the confiscated merchandise until we made peace or at least a secure truce with the lord of Pisa. I wrote to Florence, and the Seignory chose Messer Filippo Corsini, Messer Rinaldo Gianfigliazzi, Messer Tommaso Sacchetti, and Bartolomeo Corbinelli to go to Genoa, and gave them and me the task of reassuring Boucicault that we would not take any further aggressive actions against the lord of Pisa. The four emissaries arrived in Genoa and we appeared before Boucicault. He kept us in prolonged discussions, believing that we had been instructed to make an alliance with him. He had asked us to join an alliance with him on a previous occasion, and had entered into negotiations with Agnolo di Filippo di Ser Giovanni,[121] who had gone to him as an ambassador from Florence. The negotiations between Agnolo and Boucicault had reached the stage of drafting the clauses of an agreement, but it was not concluded, because Agnolo did not have the authorization of the Seignory. He said that he would go back to Florence to get that authorization, and return to Genoa, but he never returned; so Boucicault believed that he had

---

119 Jean II le Maingre, known as Marshal Boucicault, was the French governor of Genoa from 1399 to 1409.

120 Gabriello Maria was the illegitimate son of Gian Galeazzo Visconti.

121 Agnolo Pandolfini, author of a *Treatise on Governing the Family*.

been duped. He confided this to me alone, appealing to my affection for and loyalty to the King, and entreating me to tell him if we had a mandate to make an alliance with him. I swore to him that as far as I knew we did not have such a mandate, but that I would ask my colleagues who were superior in rank to me whether or not they had been instructed to make an alliance with him. I told my colleagues what Boucicault had said and what I had replied to him. They ordered me to return to him and say that they had no mandate to enter into an alliance with him. I returned, and gave him the reply. Then he said, "In that case, there was no need for them to come, for I could have reached an understanding more easily and more quickly with you alone." I went back to the others, and we decided that Bartolomeo and I should return to Florence to give a report. We went to Florence and made our report, and the Seignory, the Colleges, and the Ten Magistrates of War decided to write to the three ambassadors that they should agree to the truce that Boucicault wanted, for at least three years. In this way they were able to get back the confiscated merchandise with much more trouble than was necessary, according to what Boucicault said, and I believed him for many good reasons.

On the first of November 1404, I began a term as Prior together with Donato di Michele Velluti,[122] Luigi Mannini, Salvatore di Bondi del Caccia, Paolo di Cino de' Nobili, who was the Standard-bearer of Justice, the needle-maker Simone di [*text missing*], Lapo Martini, Jacopo di Francesco Guasconi, and Giraldo di Lorenzo Giraldi.

On the first of January 1405, I became a Consul of the Wool Guild, along with Piero d'Agnolo Capponi, Messer Forese Salviati, Paolo di Piero degli Albizzi, Antonio di Piero di Fronte, Bartolo di Nofri Bischeri, Antonio di Lionardo degli Strozzi, and Sandro di Francesco Baroncelli. Then on the 16th of January, I began to serve as one of the Eight Magistrates on Security, along with Messer Vanni Castellani, Bertoldo di Messer Filippo Corsini, Guglielmo di Bardo Altoviti, Jacopo di Messer Rinaldo Gianfigliazzi, Agnolo di Giovanni da Pino, the wine merchant Andrea di Berto, and Jacopo di Giglio Schiattesi.

On 15 September 1405, I began to serve as one of the Twelve Good Men,[123] along with Niccolò di Niccolò di Gherardino Giani, Brunetto di Prese da Varazzano, Jacopo Orlandi, Bernardo di Pierozzo Peri, Giovanni

---

122 The grandson of the Donato Velluti whose chronicle is included in this anthology.

123 Two elected councils, known as the *Collegi* (Colleges) were consulted regularly by the Florentine Seignory: the *Dodici Buonomini* (Twelve Good Men) and the *Sedici Gonfalonieri* (Sixteen Standard-bearers).

di Ser Bernardo Carchelli, Marco di Goro degli Strozzi, Giovanni d'Andrea Binerbetti, Corso Canacci, Agnolo di Filippo di Ser Giovanni, Piero di Giovanni d'Andrea dal Palagio, and Antonio di Giovanni Compagni.

On the 5th of January 1406, my brother Bartolomeo and I brought our wives to Bagni di Petriolo.[124] Lisa, Bartolomeo's wife, had been ill for a long time, and the doctors, not being able to diagnose her illness, had advised her to take the baths. She was cured, and after we returned to Florence she became pregnant and later gave birth to a son; all of the nine children she had had until then were girls. So it seemed to us that those baths were quite beneficial; thus I note it here.

On the 17th of June 1406, I went as *podestà* to Montespertoli.[125] During my term of office there, the Seignory and the Colleges selected me to go to Rome as an ambassador to King Ladislaus and the Pope. I refused, and because of the reasons I gave, I was exempted.

On the 16th of January 1407, I went on an embassy to the Pope[126] in Marseilles, and thence to the King and other lords in France, to try to obtain the release of two of Florence's ambassadors, Messer Bartolomeo Popoleschi and Bernardo Guadagni, whom the Dukes of Orléans and Burgundy had taken hostage in reprisal for our having taken the city of Pisa, which they claimed belonged to them. When I arrived in Paris, I found Messer Alberto di Pepo degli Albizzi, who was living there; he had been assigned to work with me on this mission. In short, the Duke of Orléans,[127] who was holding the two Florentines prisoner at Blois, three days' ride from Paris, agreed to let the prisoners come to Paris in exchange for our word and theirs that they would not leave Paris without his permission. They came to Paris, and while their release was being negotiated, in an act of foul treachery the Duke of Burgundy had the Duke of Orléans assassinated at three in the morning on November 23, 1407.[128] Before the murder occurred, while Messer Alberto and I were at Senlis[129] waiting upon the Duke of Orléans in hope of prevailing on

---

124 The fourteenth-century poet Folgore da San Gimignano had sung the praises of Bagni di Petrioli in the province of Siena, which was famous for its thermal waters.

125 A town about twenty kilometres south of Florence.

126 The Avignon anti-pope, Benedict XIII.

127 Due to the illness of Charles VI, the duke of Orléans, who as we have seen was very close to Bonaccorso, shared the ruling of France with his great rival, the duke of Burgundy.

128 A year later, the duke of Burgundy would be assassinated in the bloody struggle between the Orléans and Burgundy factions for control of France.

129 A fortified town in the region of Picardy.

him to free the prisoners, the Duke sent for me late one night. He was in a chamber gambling with some noblemen; when I came in, he told me that he desired me to play with them. I replied that I had given up gambling more than eight years before, and that I hoped he would not be displeased if I didn't play, especially since I was on an official mission. But I said that once he freed the prisoners, if he still wanted me to play, I would obey him. He replied that my being on a mission was not a good excuse, as that should make me all the more eager to please him by playing. I replied that I would play to please him, but that I had only brought enough money from Florence to cover my expenses. At this he said, "Go on, sit down and play with my money," and put a large amount of gold *écus* in front of me. I began to play, and the game went in such a way that in the end I lost 500 gold *écus* that night. Early the next morning, I rode to Paris to see if I could borrow enough money to repay the Duke and recoup my losses. When I got to Paris the first person I asked was the ungrateful steward, who told me he couldn't lend me the 200 florins I asked of him. Then I asked Bartolo di Bernardo di Cino for a hundred florins, which he lent me. I asked Luigi di Bartolomeo Giovanni for a hundred, and he lent them to me. I asked Michele de' Pazzi for 300, but he said that he had already lent them. I asked Baldo di Guido Baldi for 400, and he, too, said they were lent out. I asked Calcidonio degli Alberti for 500, and he said he didn't have cash but that he would give me a bill of exchange payable in some other place. I decided not to ask any more of my friends, but accepted a bill of exchange from Calcidonio for 500 gold florins, payable in Montpellier.[130] With that sum, and the money lent me by Bartolo and Luigi, I went to see the Duke and handed him a purse with the 500 gold *écus* I owed him. He was delighted, and commended me and so on. After dinner, the gambling began, and I won back around 200 gold *écus*. The next day, the Duke and all his retinue went to Paris. We had many more gambling sessions up to the time of the Duke's death, and I ended up about 2,000 gold *écus* to the good. After the Duke of Orléans's death, Messer Bartolomeo Popoleschi and Bernardo Guadagni were freed by the Duchess and her sons and given leave to go, and they returned to Florence. I stayed on in Paris until

---

130 Brucker observes how Bonaccorso turned to this Florentine banker working in Paris on other occasions, entering into transactions described by Raymond de Roover in *The Rise and Decline of the Medici Bank: 1397–1494* (Cambridge, MA: Harvard University Press, 1963), 109. This type of transaction involved an advance of funds in one place and its repayment in another, usually in another currency.

September; then I returned to Florence on October 12, 1408 to find myself a Consul of the Wool Guild.

On the 15th of December 1408, I began to serve among the officials in charge of the wine tax; my colleagues were Balcaro Serragli, Master Cristofano di Giorgio, Michele Acciaiuoli, and Nofri di Palla degli Strozzi.

On July 6, 1409, I took office as the Captain of the Guard of Pisa,[131] and the following day Pope Alexander, who had been elected at the Council of Pisa, which had been held at that time, was crowned.[132] Shortly afterward, King Louis came to Pisa as an ally of the City of Florence. I had promoted this alliance – that is, on my way back to Florence from France I had visited the King, who was then in Provence, and spoke with him about Florentine affairs and how there was discord between the Florentines and King Ladislaus of Naples. The result was that the King commissioned me to write to him when I saw that it was the right time for him to enter into an alliance with our city; unless he received a letter from me, he would not send his ambassadors. When I arrived back in Florence, I reported on this to the Seignory and the Ten Magistrates of War; shortly afterward, the Ten instructed me to write to the King that he should send his ambassadors. They came, and after much negotiating, the alliance was concluded. Later, the Pope also joined the alliance.[133]

While I was captain of Pisa, a damnable venture was brought to my attention: Messer Mariano Casassi,[134] director of the hostel at Altopascio,

---

131 After Florence conquered Pisa in 1406, the Florentines named the captain of the guard and the *podestà* of that city; soon afterward, the powers of the *podestà* were taken over by the office of the captain.

132 Pietro Filargo di Candia, the archbishop of Milan, had been elected pope under the name Alexander V at the Council of Pisa. Florence recognized Alexander as the legitimate pope, but most of the rest of Europe did not. Thus at this time there were three claimants to the papacy – Alexander; the Avignon pope, Benedict XIII; and the Roman pope, Gregory XII.

133 The alliance between France, the papacy, and Florence was reached in Florence on 12 June 1409. Later, Pope Alexander V, who had been elected at Pisa on 26 June, confirmed the agreements that had already been entered into by the papal legate Cardinal Baldassare Cossa. Cossa would later be elected Pisan pope (in 1410), taking the name John XXIII. At the Council of Constance in 1415, John XXIII and Benedict XIII were deposed; Gregory XII voluntarily resigned. Odo Colonna was elected pope on 11 November 1417, taking the name Martin V, and was regarded as the legitimate pontiff by the Church as a whole, thus ending the Western Schism of 1378–1417.

134 A Pisan nobleman; named Prior in 1408.

was ruining and impoverishing that benefice.[135] I found the allegation to be true – he had sold off many of the hostel's assets, and deserved to be deprived of the benefice. I therefore submitted a petition to Pope Alexander, entreating him to take the benefice away from Messer Casassi and to grant it to my nephew, Cione di Francesco. I did this on the advice of the cardinal legate of Bologna, Messer Baldassare Cossa, who later, by God's grace or disgrace, became Pope. He encouraged me to submit the petition, and said that he would do everything in his power to ensure that I would obtain what I had asked for. But after I had sent the petition, and entreated the cardinal to speak to the Pope about it, he replied, "I cannot keep the promise that I made to you about this affair, because a certain citizen, whose wishes I am loath to thwart, has spoken against the idea to me. But neither will I take his part against you. So get someone else to intercede for you, and you will surely succeed."

I complained to him, saying that I would have never undertaken this affair if it hadn't been for his advice and encouragement and the promise he had made me. But I said that since I had made the petition that I would follow through, hoping that justice would be done. Then he confided to me, swearing me to secrecy, that it was Niccolò da Uzzano[136] who was against me, and he advised me to endeavour to win Niccolò over. I spoke to Niccolò in the presence of Messer Bartolomeo Popoleschi, telling him what I had heard. He replied that he was so deeply obligated to Messer Mariano that he could not refuse to speak up for him, but that he had not known that I had petitioned the Pope about the benefice. He said that henceforward he would refrain from speaking in favour of either one of us. He promised this to me in the presence of Messer Bartolomeo. And the way he kept his promise was by immediately inciting all of his friends and supporters, and especially Bartolomeo di Niccolò Valori and Gino di Neri Capponi, to openly rise up against me. But I did not withdraw from my undertaking, because it did not seem to me that I could do so with honour. Also, I hoped that Mariano would rightfully be deprived of the benefice, so I persisted, at great expense.

---

135 The hostel at Altopascio in the province of Lucca was a stopping-off place for pilgrims travelling on the Via Francigena from France to Rome. The order of the Hospitallers of St James was founded there in the eleventh century.

136 Niccolò da Uzzano was a powerful citizen of the Florentine Republic, and a friend and ally of Cardinal Baldassare Cossa, later Pope John XXIII. There is a famous bust of Niccolò in the Bargello museum in Florence, attributed to Donatello.

As soon as my term of office ended, I went to see the Pope at Bologna; I remained there for two full months, and achieved nothing except to spend money. I returned to Florence. Pope Alexander died.[137] Pope John was elected.[138] I went to visit him and stayed about a month, at the end of which Pope John had Luigi da Prato tell me that he wished me to reconcile with Niccolò da Uzzano, and that if I did he would make sure that I was satisfied. He told the same thing to Bartolomeo Popoleschi, who was there with Niccolò on a mission. I replied that I was ready to do as the Pope wished. Messer Bartolomeo spoke to Niccolò, who replied that he was willing to meet with me and my brothers in Florence, and to be our friend. I returned to Florence; and when Niccolò and Bartolomeo returned from Bologna, they met with me and my brothers in the church of San Piero Scheraggio,[139] and after much talk, Niccolò promised to do nothing more against us. And the way he kept his promise was to get Mariano Casassi to receive a son of Giovanni di Lodovico di Banco as a monk at Altopascio, and to make the hostel over to him with all its assets under the jurisdiction of the City of Florence, while he himself retired to Lucca.

On the 24th of July 1410, I left for Rome as a representative of our city with Messer Jacopo Salviati[140] and King Louis of France,[141] in the struggle with King Ladislaus. On the way we went through Montepulciano, where we stayed for 24 days trying to engage Sforza da Cotignola[142] to fight for us at our expense. We finally got him to agree, but with great difficulty, as he had already made an agreement with King Ladislaus. Once we had won Sforza over, we gave him 25,000 new florins, and departed for Rome. After we had been in Rome for about a month, Messer Jacopo returned to Florence to report on several important matters, and I remained with King Louis. The King was stuck in Rome, unable to wage war, for he had been failed by the three most important captains – that

---

137 On 3 May 1410.

138 John XXIII was elected Pisan pope on 17 May 1410.

139 A small church near the Palazzo Vecchio in Florence, which had often been used for meetings since Dante's time.

140 For more on this mission that Bonaccorso undertook with Jacopo Salviati, see Brucker, *The Civic World of Early Renaissance Florence*, 263ff.

141 Louis II of Anjou, king of Sicily and Jerusalem, who was contending with Ladislaus for the kingdom of Naples.

142 Muzio Attendolo Sforza (1369–1424), a *condottiere* who was born in the town of Cotignola in the province of Ravenna. He was the father of Francesco Sforza, who ruled Milan for sixteen years.

is, Paolo Orsini, Sforza da Cotignola, and Braccio dal Montone[143] – and because the Pope had failed to send the money to pay Paolo Orsini, as he had promised. So on the last day of December, King Louis left Rome for Florence. On the way, we received letters informing us that a peace treaty had been reached between our city and King Ladislaus. Good King Louis was greatly vexed at this news, saying: "They could at least have waited until our alliance had expired at the end of January!"[144] When we arrived at Prato, the King departed for Bologna, and I continued on to Florence.

After I had been in Florence for eight days, I went to Bologna at my own expense to see about the Altopascio dispute. Finally, after having been there about 20 days, and after several audiences with the Pope, whom I entreated to treat my case favourably, he told me that he could not see his way to honourably grant what I had requested, on account of certain promises that he had made to several people, which he did not want to break. But he said that he was ready to give me satisfaction in any other way, even to the point of giving me a nice bishopric. I responded, complaining bitterly, that there was nothing else that I wished to ask for; and, greatly dissatisfied, I left his presence. I complained to King Louis about the matter, took my leave of him, and returned to Florence. Later, in the month of March, the Pope and King Louis both left for Rome. I went to Prato to visit the King,[145] who wouldn't let me leave him until we had arrived at Siena; along the way, he warmly entreated me to go with him to Rome, offering me money and horses and a steady salary. I decided not to go, for I was concerned that the Seignory might order me to return to Florence, and I did not want it to appear that I was going in any way as a representative of our city. I took leave of the King and returned to Florence, where I remained until the 25th of April 1411. Then, on account of the plague that was beginning to break out,[146] I left with my

---

143 Andrea Fortebracci, known as Braccio da Montone (1368–1424), another famous soldier of fortune, fought for Pope John XXIII against Ladislaus. In 1416, he became lord of Perugia.

144 The peace treaty was signed on 18 January 1410. The Florentines obtained the city of Cortona and the fortified towns of Pierle and Mercatale, for 60,000 florins. One of the articles of the treaty stipulated that it would not go into effect until 1 February.

145 As on other occasions, while in Prato King Louis stayed at the home of the famous merchant Francesco Datini.

146 Contemporary chroniclers reported that about four hundred Florentine families sought refuge in Pisa during the plague of 1411.

entire family for Pisa, taking with me my first cousins Nerozzo and Doffo di Luigi and Giovanozzo di Francesco. I also took two servants and a wet nurse for a 15-month-old baby.

In Pisa I rented a fully furnished house from Bindo and Jacopo and Filippo degli Astai[147] for 48 gold florins. Toward the end of June, one of my servants died of the pestilence; and a fortnight later, my 12-year-old daughter also died of the plague. So I left that house and went to stay on the outskirts of Pisa in a place belonging to Tommaso Grassolini, to whom I gave 20 florins for rent; I remained there until the 24th of November, when we returned to Florence. I reckoned that I had spent 1,300 florins in seven months. The place where we stayed outside Pisa is called Ghezzano.[148]

On the 26th of November, I arrived in Florence, and discovered that I had been named as an official of fortifications along with Giovanni di Bicci de' Medici, Jacopo di Zilio Schiattesi, Niccolaio Fagni, Masino di Piero dell'Antella, Jacopo di Francesco di Tura, Soletto del Pera Baldovinetti, and Niccolò di Bardo Rittafé; I also learned that I had been named a consul of the Wool Guild along with Schiatta Ridolfi and Alberto di Zanobi.

On the first of December 1411, I took office as Captain of the Guelph party along with Messer Maso degli Albizzi, Messer Bartolomeo Popoleschi, Ser Paolo di Messer Arrigo, Uguiccione Giandonati, Tribaldo de' Rossi, Lorenzo del Toso, Corsetto di Jacopo Arrighetti, and Davizino Ammirati.

Also in December of that year, I was named to the board of the Cathedral of Santa Maria del Fiore along with Paolo Biliotti, Niccolò del Buono Busini, Giovanni Minerbetti, Lorenzo Baronci, and Giraldo Giraldi.

On the 18th of August, 1412, I was appointed to the Ten Magistrates of Pisa along with Cristofano della Malvagia, Antonio da Rabatta, Bernardo Vecchietti, Luca di Messer Maso degli Albizzi, Michele di Salvestro, Tommaso di Giacomino di Goggio, Cristofano Carnesecchi, Amedeo Peruzzi, and Marco di Goro degli Strozzi.

On the 20th of August of the same year, I was chosen to participate in a secret vote of the Wool Guild, along with Messer Maso degli Albizzi, Nofri Bischeri, and Tommaso Rucellai.

––––––––––

147 The Astai were a leading Pisan family; the members named here were city Priors.
148 A village northeast of Pisa, in the Valdarno.

[QUARREL BETWEEN THE PITTI AND RICASOLI FAMILIES, AND THE
PITTI'S "BAD YEAR"]

May you, our sons and descendants, and whoever else may happen to
read or hear what I write here, see and learn from what happens when
one attempts to stand firm against those who are more powerful, no
matter how rightfully. It happened that in 1404, when my brother Luigi
was *podestà* of Bucine and Valdambra,[149] the Abbot of San Piero a Ruoti
di Valdambra[150] submitted a number of proper and reasonable requests
to Luigi, which he kindly satisfied. The abbot became extremely fond of
Luigi, and clearly showed it. Three years later, when the abbot was very
old and often harassed by powerful people, he came to seek refuge in
our home in Florence, where he had already stayed several times, and
we received him as our spiritual father. He told us that he had decided
to give up the abbacy that he had held for 34 years, because his age and
infirmity no longer permitted him to govern the abbey. He asked us to
act on his behalf in renouncing the benefice, and to try to obtain it for
one of our own sons. We responded that we did not think this was a good
course of action, encouraging him to remain as abbot and promising
him our support in all matters. But in the end, after much discussion,
we agreed to act on his behalf, although it was our intention to keep
him in his post and to defend and help him. He returned to the abbey,
where shortly afterward Alberto Ricasoli[151] and his people contrived to
implicate the abbot in a sham conspiracy, and they came to Florence to
declare to the Ten Magistrates of War that he had plotted to hand over
Valdambra to the Ubertini family, who were in rebellion against Florence. The Ten Magistrates of War ordered that the abbot be arrested;
but the abbot's suspicions had already been aroused by a man posing as a
servant who had called at the abbey and said that he had come on behalf
of Andreino degli Uberti to speak to him, and was awaiting a reply. The
false servant had timed his visit for when the abbot would not be there.
After the man departed, the abbot returned and was told what the man
had said. The abbot immediately took horse and came to our home.

---

149 Both towns in the eastern part of the province of Arezzo.
150 A very old Camaldolese monastery built by the powerful Ubertini family.
151 The abbey was in the middle of one of the territories of the Ricasoli family, who
     would not have been happy about a family like the Pitti, traditionally from a different
     political clique, gaining a foothold there.

After he had told us the whole story, Luigi brought him before the Ten Magistrates of War, who questioned him in great detail, and having established the falsity of the informer, they let him return to his abbey. I knew how powerful and determined the Ricasoli were, and realized clearly that they would not rest until they got the abbey into their own hands, either by force or by treachery, unless we quickly submitted the abbot's resignation and our own petition for the benefice. The rest of my family disagreed, fearing that we would be criticized, especially because, since we had agreed to act for him, the abbot had taken heart, seeing that we had extended ourselves and endeavoured to help him on several occasions. Both Luigi and I spoke to the abbot about the dangers of the situation, and he replied that he would agree to whatever we decided, but he entreated us to have a care for his honour. Francesco and Luigi took his words about his honour to mean that he did not want us to renounce the abbacy on his behalf; but Bartolomeo and I thought that we should do it in the interests of the abbot's own safety.

Having seen that we had come out openly in the abbot's defence, the Ricasoli realized that they could not achieve their evil ends by deceiving the City of Florence. So they had four members of their family – Pandolfo, Bindaccio, Galeotto, and Carlo – who were in Rome lodge an accusation against the abbot, saying all manner of false things about him. They made a petition to Pope John, whom they served as equerries and chamberlains. The abbot was summoned to appear, but because he was old and unable to travel to Rome, and also because he feared that if he went he might come to physical harm, he decided to send a representative. We sent Ser Giuliano della Cicogna, a priest at the church of San Lorenzo who was a friend of mine. Then Luigi and I spoke to Albertaccio,[152] gently entreating him not to pursue the case against the abbot for our sake, and explaining our relationship with him and how we hoped to obtain the abbey for one of our sons. He replied that he had not known about our arrangement with the abbot, and that if he had known, he would not have acted against him, even though he was an enemy of their family. But he said that he could not now withdraw without the agreement of his relatives in Rome, to whom he intended to write. Because we had heard that Ridolfo di Bonifazio Peruzzi, a relative of Albertaccio's, was in league with him to request the abbacy for his brother Arnoldo,

---

152 Alberto Ricasoli. "Albertaccio" is a somewhat denigrating way to say "Alberto," implying that he was big or ugly.

we went to speak to Ridolfo, told him all about our relationship with the abbot, and entreated him to withdraw from the affair for our sake. He replied that he had not meddled in the affair, and would not do so. We went to Messer Rinaldo Gianfigliazzi, the father-in-law of Albertaccio, and told him the whole story, entreating him to persuade Albertaccio to leave off. He promised to do everything in his power. A few days later, we went to the Public Palace and appealed to the Seignory and the Colleges to write a letter to the Pope, requesting that His Holiness instruct the bishop of Florence or Arezzo or Fiesole, or any other prelate, to investigate the charges against the abbot, and that based on their findings, His Holiness would pass judgment. After we had made our petition, Betto Busini, a member of one of the Colleges, at the urging of the Peruzzi and having been informed by them, said to the members of the Seignory: "Hear the other side." The members of the Seignory told us to go away and come back another time, because they wanted both parties to be present. We returned the following day. When the Colleges had assembled, in came Messer Michele di Messer Vanni Castellani, Papino di Messer Rinaldo Gianfigliazzi, Piero di Giovanni di Piero Baroncelli, and Bindaccio, the brother of Ridolfo Peruzzi. They all spoke before the Colleges, entreating them not to consent to write the letter that I had requested. I was called to speak for the other side.I entered and Binduccio Peruzzi entered behind me, and I again requested that the letter be sent to the Pope. Binduccio spoke against it, vilifying the abbot, and saying that his family wanted to request that benefice for one of his brothers. We withdrew, and the outcome was that the Seignory did not agree to write the letter – our request was not granted because of the power of the Ricasoli faction.

The abbot's representative, Ser Giuliano della Cicogna, appeared in Rome before Cardinal Orsini,[153] whom the Pope had appointed to oversee the case. When Cardinal Orsini made it known that he did not want to accept a representative in place of the abbot himself, Ser Giuliano gave the cardinal a letter that I had written to him. At Pisa I had attempted to enlist the cardinal as our patron, and gave him a goblet of gilded silver that cost me 32 new florins. When Ser Giuliano had presented the letter to Cardinal Orsini, he repeated: "Sire, I beseech you on behalf of the abbot for the sake of Bonaccorso, who is the devoted servant of both Your Eminence and of the Holy Father." Hearing this

---

153 Giovanni Orsini, one of the leading figures at the Council of Pisa, who had been instrumental in the election of Pope John XXIII.

recommendation, Pandolfo Ricasoli, who was present, said, "Sire, he has just named a thoroughgoing enemy of the Holy Church and of His Holiness the Pope. Bonaccorso's brother Luigi, when he was a member of the Priors, was the driving force behind the City of Florence making peace with King Ladislaus, in defiance of the Holy Church and of His Holiness the Pope." After that, the Ricasoli, who were constantly in company with the Pope, repeatedly brought up the story about Luigi being instrumental in Florence making peace with King Ladislaus, which was true. And the Pope was so displeased by this that he turned against all of us brothers, and we suffered continuously both in secret and openly at his hands and at the hands of his Florentine followers, and especially Messer Rinaldo Gianfigliazzi, Gino Capponi, Bartolomeo Valori, Niccolò da Uzzano, and all of their co-conspirators and followers. In the end this unjust Pope, iniquitously and against all sense of justice, deprived the abbot of his benefice and condemned him to perpetual imprisonment. And he granted the abbey to Arnoldo dei Peruzzi. When Binduccio and his brother had obtained the papal licence, they petitioned the Florentine Seignory to grant them possession of the abbey. A commission of three doctors of canonical law was formed to judge the matter.

While this litigation was going on, I asked the Seignory for a soldier to guard the abbot, and I had the abbot come to Florence to defend his cause. After the abbot, along with one of his monks, his representative Ser Giuliano, and Giuliano's brother Francesco had been staying in my house for about a month, I saw very clearly that he would lose his case on account of the papal bulls excommunicating him and anyone who might help or favour him, and also because of the power of those who were producing false witnesses against him and us. One day I was bemoaning our situation to Ser Giuliano; I told him that I saw no way to succeed against the power of the Gianfigliazzi, the Castellani, the Peruzzi, and the other relatives and friends of the Ricasoli and their followers and co-conspirators. At these words of mine, Ser Giuliano said, "I can see a way. The abbot could submit a petition to our Seignory, denouncing Albertaccio Ricasoli. If he does this, Albertaccio, for fear of being declared a magnate, will be forced to come to some sort of compromise with the abbot, so that some sort of agreement should come out of it."[154]

---

154 Brucker points out that for certain crimes against Florentine citizens that were not
    prosecutable in court, a person could be denounced to the Seignory. If by a two-thirds
    vote of the Priors and the Colleges the denounced person was declared to be a *grande*
    or magnate, he would be ineligible for the major offices of the Commune of Florence.

I replied that I liked the idea and that he should arrange it with the abbot; I did not wish to become involved in the matter. Then he said, "Tell your servant Santi to do what I tell him, and leave it to me." That evening at the first hour, Ser Giuliano said to the abbot: "Let us go to the home of Messer Giovanni di Ser Ristoro to ask him to help with your case." He instructed his brother Francesco to take the servant Santi and Messer Lapo da Ricasoli, a long-time enemy of Albertaccio and his associates who happened to be dining with us that evening, to go toward the home of Messer Giovanni. When the abbot and his monk passed by on their way back to my home, they were to fall on them, attack them without harming them, and then flee. They did so, and neither the abbot nor the monk nor the guard who had been assigned by the Seignory knew what had been planned, so they firmly believed that Albertaccio or someone acting on his behalf had intended to assault the abbot and do him great harm, but they hadn't carried out the deed on account of the presence of the guard. They went straight to the Public Palace to lodge a complaint with the Seignory. That very night, the Seignory issued a proclamation to the effect that whoever knew who had planned the attack and did not reveal his name within three days would be liable to penalties against his property and person, and that the perpetrator would be freely absolved if he gave himself up. On the following day, together with the members of the Colleges, they made the proclamation into an official decree.

When the real assailants returned to my home, followed by the abbot and his companions, I heard the story first from the assailants, who told me the truth; then I heard the version of the abbot and his companions, who added some lies, because they said that they had been battered and knocked about, and they claimed to have recognized Carlo da Ricasoli, who had returned from Rome. The next day, Carlo was summoned before the *podestà*; he obeyed the summons, knowing himself to be innocent. He was imprisoned in the chapel. And that same evening, Giuliano was arrested by the guards of the *podestà*, who had been prompted by Albertaccio and Papino di Messer Rinaldo, who suspected that Giuliano knew about the affair. But the *podestà* released Giuliano immediately after questioning him, saying: "Return to me tomorrow morning." Giuliano returned to my home and told me about his arrest, and having heard about the proclamation, I had Giuliano, Messer Lapo, Santi, and Francesco leave my house. I also sent Brando da Cachiano di Chianti to the Val di Pesa, for he knew about the disgraceful incident, even if he had not been there when it happened. The following day, the *podestà* summoned Giuliano, and then summoned me. I appeared before him, and

he told me that if I did not get Giuliano to appear before him, he would
prosecute me. I said that I did not know where Giuliano was. He sent
me away, and on the third day he sent for me again with the intention of
locking me up, as I later learned. I went to him and he questioned and
threatened me a great deal, and finally he sent me away, ordering me to
return the next day. On the fourth day, I decided to go before the Seignory and tell them all I knew, fearing that someone who knew the truth
might reveal it; I wanted to avoid having the new decree invoked against
me. So I did this, and when they had heard my revelation, the members
of the Seignory and the Colleges issued an order to the *podestà*, instructing him to begin proceedings against the men whom I had named, that
is, my servant Santo, Francesco dalla Cicogna the brother of the priest
Giuliano, and any other accomplices. They were all to be punished in
property and in person while I, if I had committed any blameworthy action, was to be pardoned. The *podestà* began proceedings against Santi,
the priest Giuliano and his brother, Messer Lapo da Ricasoli, Brando
da Cachiano di Chianti, and me. We were all summoned, but I was the
only one to appear, because the others were afraid that they would be
tortured. I was questioned and released upon paying a surety of 3,000
florins. The *podestà* fined Santi 800 florins, Messer Lapo, Francesco, the
priest, and Brando 500 florins each, and banished them from Florence
and its territory for three years. He pardoned me.[155]

Note that during the trial, Messer Michele Castellani, Papino Gianfigliazzi, and the others mentioned above did everything in their power,
publicly and in secret, to have me found guilty so that I would be banned
from holding public office. The whole band of evil conspirators worked
secretly against me, especially Niccolò Barbadoro. I heard about their
dealings, secret and open, from the *podestà* himself and from his subordinate, Messer Tommaso. Many relatives and friends came forth to support
me, including Giovanni Carducci, Migliore di Giunta Migliori, Rinaldo
da Messer Maso degli Albizzi, Piero di Luca degli Albizzi, Messer Cristofano degli Spini, Messer Francesco Machiavelli, Nofri Bischeri, Sando di
Vieri Altoviti, Currado Panciatichi, Guidetto Guidetti, Francesco Canigiani, and many other citizens including my trusted friend Ruberto de'
Rossi, who was extremely useful to me in getting the *podestà*'s subordinate

---

155 As Brucker points out, Bonaccorso's version conforms to the account of the case in
    the records of the Florentine criminal courts. Archivio di Stato di Firenze, *Atti del
    podestà*, 4272, 17 December 1412.

to look favourably on my case. The Seignory imposed a harsh punishment on account of the offence to their guard, who had been with the abbot. Messer Lapo paid his fine, as did my servant Santi, from my own funds; the others went into exile.

Now, I wished to recount this unfortunate case, and name those who acted against me and the chief persons who helped me, not so that you, our sons and descendants, would seek a vendetta against those who harmed us, but rather so that you should be grateful and acknowledge the descendants of those who helped us. As I wrote at the beginning of this episode – learn a lesson from this story, which came about because we attempted to vie with the great and the powerful, and got embroiled in things having to do with ecclesiastical benefices, dealing with priests. If you take care not to become involved with priests, you shall be wise.

On the 16th of May 1413, I began a term among the Eight Magistrates on Security[156] along with Simone Salviati, Marco di Goro degli Strozzi, and Giovanni di Bicci de' Medici. Riccardo di Niccolò di Nome, Giovanni di Francesco Caccini, Brando della Badessa, and Piero di Giovanni dal Palagio were already serving among the Eight; they left office on the first of June, and were replaced by Astore di Niccolò di Gherardino Gianni, Antonio di Vanni Manucci, Guccio da Sommaia, and Banco di Sandro.

That same year – an ill-fated one for me and my brothers – on the 24th of July, the vigil of the feast of St James at two o'clock in the morning, the Executor and Captain sent one of his officers to tell me that I must appear before him. I went, and was put into a chamber. At dawn the next morning they brought in my brother Bartolomeo, whom they had arrested in the Val di Pesa, and placed him in another chamber. At about 9:00 that same morning, the Executor came to the chamber where I was being held, and told me that Bartolomeo and I would be held until such time as our brother Luigi appeared before him. Luigi, who the Executor had heard had gone several days earlier to Naples or, to be more precise, to L'Aquila, had been served a summons at his home. The executor told me that if Luigi did not appear to clear himself of the accusation against him – to wit, that he had informed the ambassadors of King Ladislaus, who were in Florence at the time, about certain secret deliberations that

---

156 Bonaccorso had already served on this body, and would do so again. The Eight on Security became increasingly important during the course of the fifteenth century, assuming the powers of the Ten Magistrates of War and other magistracies. See Martines, *The Social World of the Florentine Humanists*, 146 ff.

had taken place in the Priors' Palace. The evidence was a letter that the
ambassadors had written to the King, which had fallen into the hands of
the Ten Magistrates of War. The Executor ordered me to write to Luigi
that if he did not return, harm would come to Bartolomeo and me. I
wrote the letter and sent it by my own courier, along with the summons
to appear.

My relatives and friends appealed to many prominent citizens, and
about two hundred of them assembled in San Piero Scheraggio, where
our nephew Neri di Piero asked for their advice and help. They resolved
to all appear before the Seignory to request our release; and this they did.
That same morning they all went before the Executor and warmly entreated him on our behalf. The spokesman to the Executor was Messser
Rinaldo Gianfigliazzi; at the Palace, Messer Filippo Corsini had spoken
before the Seignory. On the 31st of that month, all of our wives and children who were then in Florence went to the Palace to appear before the
Seignory and the Colleges and the Ten Magistrates of War, and implored
them to release us. They found that indeed we had been wronged, and
determined that we should be released. They sent for the Executor and
informed him of the vote they had taken in favour of our release; they
ordered him to release us, and it was done. Subsequently in Naples
Luigi received my letter and the summons to appear, and he immediately
begged leave of the King and set out for Florence. But when he reached
Perugia, he was told that he had been banished.[157] And indeed he had
been; to the sound of the trumpet, he had been summoned to appear
within three days, and then he was sentenced to a fine and banishment
for non-appearance, and we were unable to obtain any term for his banishment. At the urging of the band of conspirators who were our adversaries,[158] the Executor used his special powers to punish Luigi unjustly,
as we have recounted in this book. Luigi returned to L'Aquila, where
the King reappointed him to serve for another year as Captain; he had
already served for a year, with our brother Francesco as his lieutenant.
Then Luigi left Francesco in L'Aquila and went to Naples to renounce
the office, for war was about to break out between the King and the City
of Florence on account of the seduction of the evil conspirators who, at

---

157 Luigi's sentence to exile was identified by Gene Brucker in the Archivio di Stato di
    Firenze; the sentence was cancelled on 20 October 1414. See *Civic World of the Floren-
    tine Humanists*, 363.
158 Ricasoli, Castellani, Gianfigliazzi, et al.

the urging of the Pope, were leading our city to the brink of war. When Luigi had renounced the office, he received letters from the King telling him that the review that was normally held of outgoing office-holders would be waived for him and anyone whom he had brought with him to L'Aquila.[159] Three days before these letters reached L'Aquila, Francesco died, God rest his soul. We held his funeral here on the 9th of October of that wretched year.

I said that 1414 was an ill-fated year for us, but really we have experienced great adversity for almost 4 years as our adversaries have continuously sought to harm and bring shame upon us, on account of the peace treaty that Luigi brokered between King Ladislaus and Florence at the time he was a member of the Seignory – that is, in December of 1410. That faction, at the urging of the Pope and because they had had and hope to have benefices from him, have continuously shown that they are unhappy with the peace treaty, and have made every effort to undermine it, to the point that today, the 30th of October 1413, they are very close to achieving that goal. They have led the populace to believe that the King's capture of Rome[160] and of many other Church lands means that he intends to deprive us of our freedom, and they have generally created an atmosphere of fear and suspicion among our citizenry. I, in fact, am among those who are not completely certain that the King does not yearn to subject us, but if he does, it is on account of the villainous actions of those who have conspired against him since the peace treaty was signed against the Pope's wishes.

For the whole next year, 1411, the Pope and King Louis continued the war against King Ladislaus. Then in 1412, when King Louis had returned to France, the Pope out of fear made peace with King Ladislaus, who was approaching Rome with a large army. After that peace treaty was signed, the Pope began to try to persuade the Emperor[161] to come to Rome. King Ladislaus, suspecting that the Pope was doing this to gain an ally against him, sent a legation of special ambassadors to Florence to protest this; on several occasions they entreated the government of Florence to enter into a defensive alliance with them, or to promise King Ladislaus

---

159 This waiving of the normal review process for outgoing officials was a sign of the king's regard for Luigi Pitti.

160 Between 7 and 8 June 1413.

161 Sigismund of Luxembourg, who succeeded Rupert of Bavaria as emperor in 1410. The Roman pope was still John XXIII.

that the Pope would not bring the Emperor to Rome to make war against him. Both the alliance and the promise were refused. For this reason, King Ladislaus came to Rome with his powerful army and captured the city; he would have captured the Pope and his cardinals as well, if they had not fled to Florence. Here in Florence, the Pope has endeavoured to get us to enter into an alliance with him in order to wage war against King Ladislaus, and I think that he will achieve this because of all the benefices he has granted and continues to grant to our citizens. May it please God that things go better for our city than I hope, for I fear that the great cost of such a war cannot be sustained by our people. May God prevent such dire consequences for us, so that our freedom may be safeguarded.

[FOREIGN AFFAIRS AND INTERNAL POLITICS]

That same year, 1413, on the 8th of June, Pope John XXIII, who had fled Rome when it was taken by King Ladislaus, arrived at Sant'Antonio del Vescovo,[162] whither the Priors went to visit him and pay their respects. He stayed there until the [*text missing*] of November. His cardinals and courtiers were lodged here in Florence. During the time that he stayed at Sant'Antonio del Vescovo, he drew up and concluded the alliance with our government. Then he departed for Bologna.

In November of that year, the Captains of the Guelph party, Giovanni di Giannozzo Vettori, Niccolò di Nino Orlandi, Inghilese di Simone Baroncelli, Jacopo di Piero Gherardini, Piero di Giovanni Anselmi, Luca di Giovanni di Luca Pezzaio, Giraldo di Lorenzo Giraldi, Dingo di Guerriante Marignoli, and Andrea di Guiglielmino de' Pazzi, took counsel at great length with a large number of Guelphs, and also with the Council of One Hundred and the Council of Sixty. With their Colleges and with 96 Guelph adjutants, they undertook to reform the offices of the Guelph party with a new system of voting; they annulled and burnt all of the votes that had previously taken place. They were moved to do this because the party had been greatly vilified and had lost its accustomed honour and reputation. The Guelphs had fallen so much in the people's estimation that the Captains could hardly get any citizens to accompany them to go and make the offerings ordered by the party. This was because of the

---

162 A villa called the Palazzo dei Vescovi Fiorentini, on the hill of Montughi near Florence, destroyed in 1530. Known as the place where St Antonino Pierozzi, archbishop of Florence, died in 1459, it was used by bishops as a summer retreat.

disdain that the good and true Guelphs felt at seeing many Ghibellines and base parvenus holding offices in the Guelph party.

That same year, my name having been selected as *podestà* for Pieve Santo Stefano,[163] at first I thought that I should go, in order to distance myself from the evil conspirators who had sought my death. But after thinking it over for a while and getting some good advice, I decided to refuse the office. For in the meantime the Guelphs had had their voting, and it seemed that my adversaries were losing power, because all of the merchants and the people of Florence saw that, at the instigation of the Pope, the Guelphs were trying to lead us back into war, and were unhappy with them. I petitioned the Seignory and the Colleges to release me from the office, and the petition was granted by a large majority. The Guelph faction, hearing that I had been released from going to Pieve Santo Stefano and realizing that if I did not go there to assume the office of *podestà* I would inevitably be chosen as the next Standard-bearer of Justice at the beginning of July, saw to it that Barduccio Chierichini, who was Standard-bearer of Justice at that time, delayed calling the Council of the People until a new College of Twelve had been elected, which was due to happen in a fortnight. When the new College of Twelve was in place, I resubmitted my petition, and it was put to a vote several times, but it was not approved, on account of all the beseeching and canvassing that my adversaries carried out, both secretly and in the open. So in the end I was obliged to go as *podestà* to Pieve Santo Stefano, where I endured great suffering and aggravation. When I returned to Florence in mid-June of 1414, Messer Maso degli Albizzi was Standard-bearer of Justice. At the end of that month, a peace treaty was brokered with King Ladislaus, in defiance of the papal faction, who did everything they could to prevent it.[164] In the peace treaty, the King wanted to insert a clause stipulating that our brother Luigi should be recalled to Florence, alleging that he had been wrongfully banished. When I heard about this from Gabriello Brunelleschi,[165] Luigi's brother-in-law, who had been sent by the King to negotiate the peace treaty, I opposed it, doing everything in my power to prevent the clause from being included in the treaty. Because Luigi was

---

163 A small town in the province of Arezzo, about seventy kilometres east of Florence, which had come under Florentine rule in 1384.

164 On the conflicts and problems relating to this peace treaty, see Anthony Mohlo, *Florentine Public Finances in the Early Renaissance 1400–1433* (Cambridge, MA: Harvard University Press, 1971); and Brucker, *Civic World of the Florentine Humanists*, 364 ff.

165 Gabriello d'Alderotto Brunelleschi was one of Ladislaus's courtiers.

innocent, I did not wish him to be recalled as part of a treaty with the King. I had a very difficult time convincing Gabriello and many others of our relatives and friends who had heard about the King's proposal and advised us to ask for the clause to be added to the treaty, for they feared that we would not succeed in getting Luigi's banishment revoked if we ourselves petitioned for it.

In September of that same year, when Messer Vanni Castellani was Standard-bearer of Justice, we petitioned the Seignory and the Colleges to officially recall Luigi to Florence, and our request was granted. He came. We petitioned for his banishment to be rescinded, and our petition was granted, in spite of the papal faction, who had done everything they could to prevent it, both secretly and openly. Luigi's banishment was revoked and his full civil rights were restored that same year, 1414.

On 5 October 1414, I left Florence for Pisa, where I boarded one of the three galleys that had come from Provence to take Pope John to Avignon. I had them let me off at Fréjus, where I bought three pack-horses, to which I added a fourth at Avignon. At Tarascon I visited King Louis, who welcomed me warmly. On leaving him, I went to Paris by way of the Alps and Auvergne. In Paris, I tried to collect the balance of what the Count of Savoy owed me, and to claim the estate of Luigi di Bartolomeo Giovanni, who had named my nephews Neri and Giovanni as his heirs. I received letters from Florence telling me that my name had been drawn as Vicar of the Upper Arno Valley, so I left Paris on the 12th of January and went to Avignon, and thence to Arles to call on King Louis, and then through Provence to Marseilles, where I planned to board one of the galleys that the King was having readied to send to Naples. I found that the galleys wouldn't be ready to set sail for a fortnight, and fearing that I would arrive too late to take up my office, which was supposed to begin on the first of March, I decided to go overland via Nice and the Italian Riviera. When I was two leagues from Nice, I sent ahead for a safe-conduct pass, but was refused. I went to a hill-town called Cagne, of which Giorgino and Onorato de' Grimaldi are the lords.[166] They were delighted to see me and welcomed me grandly. I asked them to help me fit out a vessel at Antibes so that I could bypass Nice and go straight to

---

166 The Grimaldi had been made Florentine citizens around 1370. They were already lords, albeit contested, of Monaco and Menton.

Monaco or Menton, and to get my horses through Nice by passing them off as their own. They said that they would be happy to do this. As we were deciding about this, a relative of theirs arrived from Nice; hearing our plan, he told us that there was a small galley anchored near Nice, for what purpose nobody knew. This aroused my suspicions, also because I heard that there were armed men all over the Riviera and that travellers were being robbed and murdered. I decided to return to Marseilles and wait for the galleys, which set sail on the 14th of February; I boarded a small vessel that was with them. We had so much bad weather that it took us 17 days before we reached Porto Pisano, and at one point it looked as if we were going to end up being blown all the way to the Barbary Coast. On account of the storm, the vessel in which I was travelling got separated from the three galleys during the night. Yet by the grace of God we reached Porto Pisano on the 2nd of March. On top of the great discomfort of being packed onto that vessel with the captain weeping and saying: "We'll get blown to Barbary and be sold as slaves," you can imagine how I suffered and worried that our enemies would prevent my brothers from deferring the start of my term in office, so that I would arrive too late and be banned from holding office for two years.[167] I reached Pisa and heard from Filippo del Toccio that I had been granted an extension until the end of March. I came back to Florence, and was at my post on March 6, and, by the grace of God, I spent a very pleasant time there and did a good job, and returned thence with honour.

On December 15, 1415, I entered the harbour tax office for two months, taking the place of a man who was a member of the Twelve Good Men. My fellow officers were Piero di Sandro Masini, Filippo Giugni, Antonio di Francesco Bartolini, Andrea di Rinaldo Rondinelli, Bartolomeo di Taldo, and Antonio di Durante.

In 1416, I went as commissioner and ambassador to Foligno. I left Florence on the 5th of May, and remained in Foligno until the 20th of September. During the time that I was there, on the 10th of July, Ugolino de' Trinci was born.[168] He was the son of Corrado de' Trinci and his

---

167 This was the punishment at the time for anyone who did not take up an office designated for him without making a formal refusal or resigning within the allotted time.

168 Ugolino de' Trinci's father, Corrado, who was the last lord of Foligno, was killed in 1439. Ugolino himself was subsequently imprisoned, and was beheaded on 14 June 1441.

wife Madonna Tancia, the sister of Orso da Monte Ritondo degli Orsini. I attended Ugolino's baptism and acted as his godfather on my own behalf as well as on behalf of Messer Matteo Castellani, Messer Palla degli Strozzi,[169] and Agnolo d'Isau Martellini. We gave a piece of figured green velvet and many other gifts, which cost 100 new florins.

During the time that I was in Foligno, on Sunday, July 12, Braccio dal Montone and Tartaglia da Lavello with their armed brigades attacked and defeated Signor Carlo Malatesta.[170] Carlo and Galeazzo Malatesta and Cieccolino and Guidone de' Michelotti and most of the best soldiers they had were captured, and many were killed or badly injured. Then on the 19th of that month, Braccio entered Perugia and was made lord of that city; he reinstated all of the men who had been exiled.

Then on the 5th of August, Braccio and Tartaglia went with their forces to the Marches. They had made an agreement with Paolo Orsini that Paolo would come with his forces, but he arrived two days after the defeat of the Malatesta and Michelotti. Orsini made camp at Colle Fiorito, and once he had settled in and was unarmed, Tartaglia arrived and had him killed by a bastard son of the Colonesi, and then they robbed everyone in Paolo's company. Braccio said that the reason why he had consented to have Paolo killed was because he had failed to keep his promise and arrive in time for the battle against Carlo Malatesta.

In 1419, Antonio di Giovanni di Messer Zanobi da Mezzola was arrested in Siena, because he had been condemned to the gallows in absentia for having run off with a woman. When he was set to be hanged, his relatives entreated one of our ambassadors to beseech the Seignory and the government of Siena on behalf of the Florentine Seignory to release Antonio. The ambassador's request was granted, and he brought Antonio back with him to Florence.

At that time, I was *podestà* at Montepulciano, and I levied a fine of 600 florins on Andrea di Salimbene degli Scotti of Siena, who was living there, for having traded grain against the orders and statutes of the

---

169 Palla di Onorio Strozzi (1372–1462) was a noted scholar and statesman who played
     a leading role in Florence in the early fifteenth century. Banished to Padua by the
     Medici in 1431, he led a lively circle of humanists, devoting himself to the study of
     Greek. See Martines, *The Social World of the Florentine Humanists*, 316 ff.

170 Carlo Malatesta, like his brother Galeazzo, was a *condottiere*, first in the service of the
     Visconti and later of the pope. He carried Gregory XII's resignation to the Council
     of Constance. The encounter of July 1416, known as the Battle of Sant'Egidio, was
     depicted in a famous painting by Paolo Uccello now in the Uffizi Gallery.

government of Montepulciano. I gave Andrea a period of 20 days to pay the fine, in accordance with the statute, and I released him on bail. He went to Siena and petitioned an ambassador of the Sienese Seignory to go to Florence and entreat our Seignory to cancel the sentence against him. When the government of Montepulciano found out about this, they sent two ambassadors of their own to Florence to entreat the Seignory and the Colleges not to break their laws. Both sides' arguments were heard, the question was put to a vote, and the decision was that the Priors and Council of Montepulciano could do what they wished about the sentence. They did this because the government of Montepulciano cannot pardon any fine of more than 500 Cortonese *lire*, equivalent to about 400 Florentine *lire*, and all fines belong to the government of Montepulciano; also the Seignory cannot pass decisions relating to Montepulciano without the participation of the Colleges. The ambassadors from Montepulciano protested this decision, because they distrusted what their own Seignory might do. The question was put to a vote 46 times in two days, and finally, thanks to the importunity and aggressiveness of Giovanni Minerbetti, who was at that time Standard-bearer of Justice, along with Antonio di Piero di Fronte and Giovanni Luigi Mannini (who, at the urging of the Ricasoli faction, were on Andrea's side, to please him and to thwart me, as they did on other occasions), the decision was made in Andrea's favour. So the Florentine Seignory wrote to the government of Montepulciano that the sentence against Andrea should be revoked. And they wrote to me as well, harshly ordering me to carry out the decision, and stating that Andrea was not liable to pay any fees, neither to myself, nor to the prosecutor, nor for the cancellation tax nor for any other reason.

I called a meeting of the Council, and when they had read the letter of the Seignory and my own, they resolved to send another two ambassadors to the Florentine Seignory and the Colleges, to entreat them that if Andrea was to be pardoned, he should at least pay 10 per cent of the fine, as stipulated in their statutes. Otherwise, they could not pardon him without great detriment to themselves, and the pardon would not be valid. The ambassadors were instructed by the Council of Montepulciano not to present their petition to the Seignory unless the Colleges were also present.

In the meantime, Andrea went to Siena, and again got the ambassador to go with him to Florence. It happened that while both parties were waiting in the hall for the audience with the Seignory and the Colleges, Pandolfo da Ricasoli, who had heard that the party from Montepulciano wished to speak to the members of the Seignory in the presence of the Colleges, sent in a relative of his, who was a member of one of the Colleges, to inform the members of the Seignory of this; they immediately summoned the Montepulciano party, who said that they had been instructed to speak to those to whom the letter of credence was addressed. They were asked to produce the letter, and were ordered to state their business; they obeyed. The answer given to them was that they should return immediately to Montepulciano and report that the Florentine Seignory wished to be obeyed. And the Seignory wrote to me again, ordering me to pardon Andrea. Since I had received very alarming letters from my son and from Filippo Machiavelli, telling me that I would be ruined and disgraced if I did not obey, I resolved not to follow my own impulse, which was to wait until they sentenced me to banishment rather than obey unjust orders. I summoned the Council and got them to resolve to pardon Andrea and to release him from having to pay anything to me or to anyone else. Fearing that this irregular decision on the part of the Council might cause him trouble in the future, Andrea went to Florence and returned with a letter to me from the members of the Seignory, a copy of which is written out here:

Priors of the Guilds and Standard-Bearer of Justice of the People and Commune of Florence

We have written to you twice before to the effect that you should see to it that the sentence passed by you on Andrea Lancianti be lifted and completely annulled, and that he should not have to make payments of any kind for any reason. We believed that you had the proper reverence for this Seignory, which is due from good citizens. If you had had it, Andrea would have been absolved and our orders would have been followed, and we would not have had to write to you again or taken any other action regarding this matter. Now we have learned that Andrea has not been exonerated, nor has the sentence against him been cancelled, since certain citizens have been given the authority to take action with regard to it. These things astonish us. We understand very well what these actions of yours mean, and what their intent is, and we are greatly displeased with you for not carrying out the orders of our Seignory. Wherefore we wish and command you, upon receipt of this letter, to see to it that Andrea be fully exonerated and absolved from the charges against him, on the part of the Commune, yourself, and the prosecutor, and that he be absolved of any other charges or judgment that might derive from the charges in any way, and that he should not be required to pay anything. We are notifying you that you must not delay any longer regarding this matter about which we are writing to you. And so that you shall see that we wish to be obeyed, we have imposed upon you a fine of a thousand gold florins, to be paid to the Treasury of our Commune, if by the 15th of the present month of April Andrea and his guarantors have not been fully absolved according to the usages of local law, and not required to make any payments, as stated above. If you have complied with our orders by the aforementioned date, your fine will be cancelled, subject to the approval of the Seignory. Furthermore, if what we have written is not carried out, we order your judge, police official, and notary to appear before our Seignory on the 16th of the current month of April. We shall accept the word of the bearer of this letter that he has delivered it to you. Florence, VI April 1420.

At the top was written

*To the nobleman Bonaccorso son of Neri dei Pitti
Podestà of Montepulciano and Citizen of Florence.*

After I had received this letter, I quickly summoned the Council of Fifty and then the General Council and had them exonerate Andrea, who wrote to the Seignory in Florence to say that he was happy with what had been done. The Priors of Montepulciano and I also wrote to the Florentine Seignory to tell them what had been done. On account of the letters from Andrea and those from the Priors and myself, the Seignory cancelled the thousand-florin fine against me. My son Luca paid the bill for my exoneration and the cancellation tax to the notary of the Treasury of the Seignory.

This is the end of my account of the wrong that the Seignory did to me at the urging of the Ricasoli faction, on the pretext of showing gratitude to the Sienese for their clemency toward Giovanni di Messer Zanobi da Mezzola.

On the 14th of June 1420 while Agnolo di Filippo di Ser Giovanni Pandolfini was Standard-bearer of Justice, and the Priors were Messer Ruberto Acciaiuoli, my brother Bartolomeo, Ridolfo Peruzzi, Ubertino Risaliti, Niccolò di Francesco Falconi, and Neri di Ser Viviano, the appropriate councils determined that I should be reinstated in the voting for Standard-bearer of Justice.

On the 15th of October, I began to serve as one of the officials of the wine tax; my colleagues were Benino di Francesco, Giovanni di Messer Forese, Antonio di Messer Niccolò da Rabatta, Salimbene Bartolini, Niccolò di Bartolomeo Valori, and Giovanni di Francesco Arrigi.

Pope Martin V departed from Florence for Rome on the 9th of September 1420.

I became Standard-bearer of the Magistracy of the Shell on 8 January 1420, along with Arrigo di Giovanni Sassolini, who was Standard-bearer for the Magistracy of the Ladder; Niccola di Giuliano di Cola di Nerino, the Sail; Niccolò di Ser Francesco Masini, the Dragon; Masino di Piero di Masino dell'Antella, the Cart; Domenico di Piero Guidi, the Ox; Niccolò di Giovanni del Belaccio, the Black Lion; Andrea di Zanobi Borgognoni, the Wheels; the Snake, Cille di Neri Viviani; Unicorn, Lapo di Biagio Vespucci; Red Lion, Giovanni d'Andrea Minerbetti; White Lion, Filippo di Niccolò Popoleschi; Dragon in the quarter of San Giovanni, Andrea di Noferi the latten-maker; Gold Lion, Giuliano di Ser Francesco Ciai; Keys, Niccolò di Bardo Rittafè; Squirrel, Giovanni di Nofri Bischeri.[171]

We took a vote on all of the external and internal offices, except the three chief ones,[172] and then in March and April of 1421 we voted for the Priors and the members of the Colleges.

I took office as the *podestà* of Tizzana[173] on the 26th of June 1421.

In the aforementioned voting, I nominated Filippo Machiavelli and Bartolomeo d'Andrea del Benino as adjutants to the magistracies. Filippo was not elected, and I did not put forward any other names.

Guido Guerra da Battifolle, Count of Monciona, was killed on the 10th of May 1421. The Fibindacci[174] had him killed.

Leghorn was bought in 1421; it cost 100,000 florins.[175]

Genoa went into the hands of the Duke of Milan that same year, in the month of November.

My son Luca entered office as *podestà* of Chiusi and Verghereto on the 29th of October of the same year.

---

171 The *gonfaloni* (gonfalons) were the sixteen standards that represented the four quarters of the city of Florence, named for the four main churches (Santo Spirito, Santa Croce, Santa Maria Novella, San Giovanni). See Henry E. Napier, *Florentine History from the Earliest Authentic Records to the Accession of Ferdinand the Third, Grand Duke of Tuscany*, vol. 4 (London: Edward Moxon, 1847), 316.

172 That is, the Priors (members of the Seignory), the Ten Good Men, and the sixteen Standard-bearers of the gonfalons.

173 A town in the Ombrone Valley, in the province of Pistoia.

174 Fibindacci was the name taken by the Ricasoli family in 1380, when they became *popolani*, so that they could hold public office. According to the norms, they had to take a different name from their noble family name; the name Fibindacci was derived from the name of their ancestral castle in the upper Arno Valley.

175 Genoa, which had taken over the rule of Leghorn after it had been under Milanese domination for many years, sold it to Florence in June of 1421.

I became a member of the council of the cathedral of Santa Maria del Fiore at the beginning of January 1421.

I went as ambassador to Venice on the 4th of February 1421. I returned to Florence on the 28th of February. I found that the Countess Caterina, the widow of the Count of Monciona and my niece, had died; for she never recovered after seeing her husband killed, but mourned continually. I believe that she died of sorrow.

On the first of May I became a member of the Council of the Wool Guild; my colleagues were Antonio Velluti, Messer Rinaldo degli Albizzi, Bernardo di Jacopo Arrighi, Agnolo di Bindo Vernaccia, Francesco di Messer Palla degli Strozzi, Antonio di Piero di Fronte, and Piero di Giovanni dal Palagio.

On the 25th of June 1422, my nephew Nerozzo went to Athens, Greece, to meet with Signor Antonio degli Acciauoli, to conclude the negotiations for his marriage to Laudomina, daughter of the late Franco di Messer Donato Acciaiuoli. The contract was drawn up by Ser Domenico di Arrigo di Ser Piero Mucini. Rinaldo di Bernardo da Mezzola was the representative for the bride; the dowry promised is 2,000 gold florins.

On the first of July 1422, I became Standard-bearer of Justice. The Priors who were my colleagues were the brassworker Bonaccorso di Paolo Corsellini, the belt-maker Baldo di Nofri di Baldo, Bernardo di Bartolomeo Gherardi, Seimo di Lapo di Francesco Corsi, Domenico di Bartolo Ottavanti, Manno di Giovanni di Temperano Manni, Paolo di Berto Carnesecchi, and Antonio di Tommaso di Guccio Martini.

I recall that while we served together, we sent an ambassador to Rome. We received under our protection Messer Tommaso da Campo Fregoso, the Lord of Sarzano.[176] We hired Braccio da Montone, the Lord of Perugia, with 1000 lancers and 300 foot soldiers at the ready. We entered a five-year alliance with the Lord of Lucca. We sent ambassadors to the Duke of Milan. We elected an ambassador to the Duke of Savoy, and we did many other things that were beneficial to our Republic. We sent an ambassador to Venice. Our notary was Ser Antonio di Ser Michele da Ricavo. We launched several large galleys.[177]

---

176 A town in the province of La Spezia, in Liguria.

177 Gene Brucker points out that Florence sent these ships to the Levant and to the North Sea in hopes of establishing itself as a maritime power and to strengthen its position as a commercial centre.

On the 20th of September 1422, I resolved to pardon all of the injustices that had been done to me, especially on the part of the Fibindacci and Ricasoli factions. In the Public Palace, I made peace with Pandolfo Ricasoli in the presence of the members of the Seignory, through the mediation of Guidaccio Pecori. Pandolfo promised on behalf of himself and all of his brothers, sons, grandsons, and consorts to treat me and my brother, sons, and grandsons as good friends. Likewise I promised in the name of my brother and sons and grandsons to treat him and his family as friends should be treated. I record this here so that you brothers and grandsons will obey my wishes; and I command you to do so.

On the first of September of that year I entered the magistracy of the Grascia.[178]

On the 30th of May, my daughter Maddalena received a ring from Rosso di Giovanni di Niccolò de' Medici. The marriage contract was drawn up by Ser Niccolaio di Berto from San Gimignano. She was wed on the 30th day of May. I gave her a dowry of 400 gold florins in cash and 150 florins promised. The guarantor for the dowry was … [*text missing*].

On the 9th of May 1423, Giovanozzo di Francesco de' Pitti gave a ring to Francesca, the daughter of Bartolomeo di Tommaso Corbinelli[179] and took her to wife the same day. She got a dowry of 1,000 gold florins in cash and promised gifts of 100 and 300 florins. [*text missing*] … a piece of land that shall be purchased in Francesca's name. The guarantor for the dowry was … [*text missing*]

On [*text missing*] Lena, the daughter of my brother Bartolomeo, was wed to Nofri d'Antonio di Moccio. She got a dowry of [*text missing*]. The contract was drawn up by [*text missing*].

Here below I shall make a copy of a passage written in a book of Bonaccorso di Maffeo de' Pitti on June 29 in the year 1318, on page c.xlv:

This is a record that I, Bonaccorso Pitti, purchased a house and land bordering the Arno River in the neighbourhood of Santa Maria a Verzaia from Ser Andrea Masi, the notary of San Brocolo, for a price of ninety-three gold

---

178 This magistracy supervised the provision of foodstuffs and regulated the markets, prices, and quality of foods.

179 Evidently a brother of Angelo and Antonio Corbinelli, both leading figures in the cultural and political life of Florence in the first two decades of the fifteenth century. See Martines, *The Social World of the Florentine Humanists*, 319–20.

florins, to build a church with a monastery for the nuns of St Anne. The bishop gave us his word and allowed us to consecrate it and gave us a letter authorizing it as a charitable organization, and did every other necessary thing for this. He set us up at Santa Maria a Verzaia; and every year we must light a candle to St Anne for him. Ser Stefano Fighini drew up the contract for the sale. We had Ser Neri put down as half owner, as security for me, but I, Bonaccorso, was the one who paid ninety-three florins, which is what the property cost, to Ser Andrea Masi on the 18th of June in the year one thousand three hundred eighteen.

I wrote this copy because the book is very old and hasn't been well preserved; it is very torn and tattered.

We arranged for Bartolomea, the daughter of my late brother Francesco and widow of Bartolomeo di Ghirigoro di Fetto Ubertini, to marry Filippo d'Otto Sapiti. She got a dowry of 600 gold florins. The marriage contract was drawn up by [*text missing*]. She was wed on the 20th of May 1423.

I refused the captaincy of Leghorn in July 1423 on account of the great pestilence that was there at the time. And I did not have to pay 25 florins because I gave up the post.

I became a member of the Eight Magistrates on Security on the 15th of September 1423; entering with me were Giuliano Giuntirsi, Francesco di Francesco della Luna, and Francesco d' Antonio Palmieri. Antonio di Tommaso Corbinelli, Nofri di Bondi del Caccia, Betto di Giovanni Rustichi, and Zanobi di [*text missing*] ...vaiaio were already in office. Later, on the first of October, our colleagues Gherardo Machiavelli, Giovanni di Francesco Biffoli, Carlo di Tommaso Bartoli, and Jacopo Bucherelli took office, and the four who had been in office when we arrived left office that day.

On the 19th of November 1423, I gave my son Luca my power of attorney. The document was drawn up by Ser Niccolaio di Berto da San Gimignano.

On the 30th of November 1423, the feast day of St Andrew, I took office as Captain of Castrocaro.[180] The following February, I discovered a conspiracy of seven inhabitants of Castrocaro, all of them Ghibellines from Forlì, who had had keys made by one of them who was a smith. Their intention was, on the night of Carnival, to let the Duke

---

180 A spa town in the province of Forlì.

of Milan's men into the town. Of the seven involved in the plot, I arrested five and two got away. The ones whom I arrested, I had decapitated. Note that in the town of Castrocaro and its surroundings there are more Ghibellines than Guelphs. Evidently about 36 years ago, the Ghibellines of this area killed all of the Guelphs they could lay their hands on, including children and pregnant women, with great wickedness and cruelty.

During that year while I was in Castrocaro, and the plague having begun at Corno di Valdipesa, I wrote to my son Luca, who was there with his children and Fioretta, telling him that he should leave immediately with all of his household and go to some place where the plague had already been and gone. He took himself off to Pescia, where he rented a house for 4 gold florins per month that was pretty well fitted out. Then I sent some of my children from Castrocaro to him at Pescia. Later, after I had returned to Florence, I sent him the rest of our children. Monna Francesca and I left Florence and arrived in Pescia on the last day of June. And because the house in Pescia was small and our family was large, with 16 mouths to feed, not counting the guests who often showed up, I rented a furnished room next to the house for three *lire* per month.

During that same year, in the month of June, Braccio da Montone was defeated and killed by the Pope's men.

On the 21st of July, our soldiers were defeated in Romagna by the Duke of Milan's troops.[181] Signor Carlo Malatesta and several other leaders were captured, and many were killed. Lodovico degli Obizi, who was always so faithful to our city, was killed. His body was accorded solemn rites and great honour in Florence.

I entered office as Captain of the citadel of Pisa on August 20, 1424.

Filippo d'Otto Sapiti died in 1423.

I entered office as Consul of the Wool Guild on the first of January of the same year; my colleagues were Bartolomeo di Iacopo Ridolfi, Filippo del Bugliaffa, Giovanni di Francesco Arrighi, Biagio di Jacopo Guasconi, Antonio di Luca da Filicaia, Francesco d' Ugolino Rucellai, and Tommaso d'Andrea Minerbetti.

We arranged for Bartolomea, the daughter of my late brother Francesco, to marry Antonio di Scarlatto Scarlatini. She was betrothed on the

---

181 This was the famous battle of Zagonara, which followed Braccio da Montone's defeat
     and death near L'Aquila. This was a dire moment for the Florentine Republic.

17th of January 1424; the document was drawn up by Ser Niccolò di Ser Verdiano.

Madonna Margherita, the widow of Franco Acciaiuoli and mother of Laudomine, the wife of my grandson Nerozzo, came to Florence in May 1424, bringing with her Laudomine and Neri Donato, Franco's son, and Nerozzo and Rinaldo da Mezzola, and many of her servants and maids. Madonna Margherita stayed with her family in our home until 9 May 1425, when she departed, taking with her Nerozzo, Laudomine, Neri Donato, and a daughter of Nerozzo's to whom Laudomine had given birth while they were in Florence, whom they named Biondella; she also took Caterina, Nerozzo's sister.

Here below I shall copy a text about the things that Nerozzo took with him; we have entrusted the original document to my wife, Monna Francesca, in the event that the dowry of Laudomine should have to be returned, so that those things and possessions could be deducted and taken into account in returning the dowry, which was promised to Nerozzo – that is, 2,000 florins, of which Nerozzo admits he has received 1,400, which his brother Doffo promised and ensured as written above.

Nerozzo	A green and black satin cloak lined with miniver fur, valued at a hundred florins.
	A rose-coloured cape lined with granat taffeta, valued at 45 gold florins.
	A crimson satin cloak, lined with green taffeta, valued at 20 gold florins.
	A double rose-coloured cloak, valued at 18 gold florins.
	A black satin cloak, valued at 10 florins.
	A dark reddish brown cloak, lined with fur, 15 florins.
	A black mantle, 8 gold florins.
	Several rose-coloured cowls and satin doublets, valued at 16 gold florins.
Laudomine	A cloak of worked satin, valued at 75 gold florins.
	A rose-coloured cape, lined in taffeta, 60 gold florins.
	Three silver belts, valued at 31 florins.
	An emerald, a diamond, and a silver necklace, a small bone casket, valued in all at 50 gold florins.

I entered the Dye Office[182] on the first of July. My colleagues were Messer Rinaldo degl' Albizzi, Giovanni Ricialbani, Giovanni Binerbetti, Nerone di Nigi, and Piero di Lionardo degli Strozzi.

Member of the board of Florence Cathedral.

On the first of November 1425, I became a member of the board of Santa Maria del Fiore along with Biagio Guasconi. Lapo Niccolini, Agnolo di Bindo Vernaccia, Tommaso Corbinelli, and Agostino di Gino Capponi were already board members.

On the 18th of November of the same year, I made my will. It was drawn up by Ser Niccolaio di Berto from San Gimignano. I annulled every other will that I had made in the past.

On the 4th of December of the same year the treaty with the Venetians was concluded, and on the 17th of January it was proclaimed in Florence.[183]

I took office as the Vicar of Mugello on the first of March 1425.

My son Ruberto took to wife Giovanna, the daughter of Salvestro di Simone de' Gondi and his wife Monna Alessandra, the daughter of the late Filippo di Tadeo. He wed her on the 22nd of October in the year 1426. She brought a dowry of 1,500 gold florins. The dowry was ensured by me, my son Luca, and my nephew Giovanozzo di Francesco. The contract was drawn up by [*name missing in the original manuscript*].

Today there are four brothers – Simone, Filippo, Carlo, and Mariotto, and four sisters; one sister, named Lena, is the wife of Amerigo di Matteo dello Scielto; the others are unmarried.

I entered office as an official of the Company of Santa Maria del Bigallo[184] on the first of November along with Angiolino di Guglielmo d' Angiolino, Niccolò del Belacio, Niccolò di Domenico Giugni, Antonio di Piero di Lapozzo, Giovanni di Ser Nigi, Alessandro d'Ugo degl'Alessandri, and Marco di Antonio Palmieri. Later Angiolino e Niccolò Giugni, Giovanni di Ser Nigi, and Alessandro d'Ugo left office, and were replaced by Gherardo Machiavelli, Filippo Fagni, Gianozzo Gianfigliazzi, and Giovanni di Bicci de' Medici.

---

182 The *Ufficio della Tinta* was the magistracy that oversaw everything having to do with the dye industry, an extremely important trade in Florence.

183 On the significance of this alliance between Venice, Florence, Ferrara, Mantua, the Savoy family, and the king of Aragon against the duke of Milan, see Brucker, *Civic World of the Florentine Humanists*, 468 ff.

184 An organization that cared for pilgrims and travellers.

My son Luca left to become the captain of a ship. He departed from Leghorn on the 11th of May 1427.

On the 25th of May 1427, my daughter Primavera wed Stefano di Nello di Ser Bartolomeo Serenelli.

I took office as *podestà* of Prato on 27 June 1427.

That same year, on the 12th of October, the troops of the Duke of Milan were defeated by the troops of our league in Lombardy.[185]

Luca returned from Bruges on the 11th of February, Fat Thursday; he came by land. He went to Pisa on the 16th of that month. He waited for his ships, and returned to Florence on the 15th of March 1427. He decided not to return to sea, because he was ill, and suffered greatly at sea. He had left Doffo di Luigi Pitti ill at Bruges, with a good servant to take care of him. Luca returned by land at a loss of about 500 florins, between giving Jacopo Benizzi 150 florins and a horse, which he gave to him to take over his ship, and he left 110 florins for Doffo, and incurred many other expenses. I was very glad that Luca returned, knowing that his life was in danger; and I praise and thank God for everything.

On the 16th of May, the peace treaty between the league and the Duke of Milan was decreed.[186]

My son Francesco departed for Valencia on the [*date missing*] of May of that year.

Rosso di Giovanni de' Medici[187] died on the 31st of July 1429.

My brother Bartolomeo died on the 8th of August 1430.

THE END

---

185 This was the famous Battle of Maclodio, where Francesco Bussone da Carmagnola, the leader of the league, defeated the Milanese under Carlo I Malatesta. Because he did not take advantage of that victory and even received messengers from the Milanese, who were trying to get him to switch his allegiance to them, Carmagnola was later accused of treason by the Venetians and beheaded. This was the episode that inspired Manzoni's first historical tragedy, *Il Conte di Carmagnola* (1826).

186 The peace treaty was signed on 18 April in Ferrara, and announced in Florence in May, with very little enthusiasm.

187 Bonaccorso's son-in-law, the husband of his daughter Maddalena.

Mirror of Humanity

Domenico Lenzi the Grain Merchant

I. [PREMISE OF THE PRESENT BOOK]

As is truly manifested in many and various books by diverse authors who have gone before, the ancients bequeathed to us for our virtuous living examples of their true behaviour, because at that time it was rare to act against divine power; they always, both in their private affairs but also in civic life, practised orderly virtues, for they abhorred evil vices as a horrible thing – vices which in our day are blindly believed to be well done. One might say that the ancient way of good behaviour has been turned around in favour of a perverse way of living.

Therefore the ancients were not punished by God for evil deeds, because, as we have said, they rarely committed them. Their families always had an abundance of victuals, so we have no written records of great shortages of food or periods of famine. But who today or in the future would be reproached for leaving for those who will come after us a written record, as poorly as an uneducated man like me might put it down, of these vicissitudes, these catastrophes that continuously crash down upon us? I mean to say, the way in which since June of 1320, the price of fodder and grain has gone up and down, which is without a doubt God's punishment for our perversities, which I shall recount in this little book. I shall show the wretchedness of men and the power of God their creator, hallowed be his name, and of his glorious mother and of St John the Baptist, the excellent defender of the most beautiful and most famous daughter of Rome – Florence, in whose bosom I was born and raised. I dedicate this humble work of mine to these saints, and devoutly entreat them in their mercy and compassion to give me aid and courage in the writing of this little book entitled "Mirror of Humanity." In this book I shall recount the year and the month and the day when grain and other fodder was sold in the market square of Orsanmichele,[1] and of the cruel famine that was felt in the place of my birth and in all the surrounding towns and in other diverse places. I shall also write of the horribly vile acts that were committed against Florence by the city or rather by the lords of Colle di Valdelsa, and other diverse heinous, ultra-diabolical acts perpetrated by the city of Siena, showing how best to portray the delights of abundance, what it is and whence it originates, and the illness and discomfort that man experiences during periods of great abundance, and the cruel, damnable, heavy famine, and how God lets this happen, and other things that I, Domenico Lenzi, a grain merchant, the crude, ignorant author of this book, will attempt to describe as best I can.

And let this little book not be despised because it is written in the vernacular mother tongue, for I never learned the Latin language. I humbly beseech my readers, if they find anything ill expressed or not well written, to impute this to my scant knowledge and poor facility in writing, and to graciously correct any such errors. And if it should appear anywhere in this book that I have failed in my Catholic faith or strayed from the holy Christian religion, the book should be subjected to correction by the militant Church of God, or destroyed by fire without respect or memory.

II. [PROVIDENTIAL SONNET]

The celestial messenger carries to earth
news full of happiness and joy
moved by the power of the great place
whose righteous will never errs,
shouting: Enjoy life, stay, avoid war,
give thanks to Him who gives you so much.
Do not await the disdainful, weak horn that pours out cruelty.[2]
Every true fruit comes from God.
Yet you, man, take delight from that evil horn,
scorning the poor man, and bitterly resenting the rich man.
Your heart is always hardened against praising God,
And the fact that you don't observe his sacred counsel

---

1 A loggia was built circa 1284 in the square of Orsanmichele as the headquarters of the public grain market. The name Orsanmichele derives from the church of San Michele in Orto that had formerly occupied the site.

2 The horn may be an allusion to the devil, or perhaps to the cornucopia as a pagan symbol of good fortune.

shall cause you to fall precipitously from a threshold you never
   imagined.[3]
The first story seen here below
shows the good that comes in times of abundance.[4]

III. [FAMINE AND DISORDER IN FLORENCE IN 1329]

April 1329. Grain and fodder.

   On Saturday the 8th day of the said month of April, the Council of
Six,[5] seeing that there was little grain in the market square of Orsanmichele, and that a great multitude of people from various places, both
farmers and city dwellers, were coming to buy and that barely a third of
the people could be served, for fear of trouble they sent for the captain
of the *podestà* and his men.[6] When the men arrived, armed as if for a
battle or attack, an edict was declared on the part of the officials and the
chief magistrate that no merchant or any other person who had grain to
sell could charge more than 30 *soldi* per bushel. The moment the edict
was declared, the armed men went around the square to make sure that
anyone who had good grain from Calvello or Sicily to sell was compensated at the expense of the state for as much as 12 *soldi* per bushel.

   There were so many people who wanted to buy grain that there wasn't
enough for each to get even half a bushel, so they began to grumble and
to complain, "These merchants are the ones who are causing the famine –
they should all be killed, and their goods taken away." The said officials were
on a bench beside the pilaster of the loggia.[7] When they heard this murmuring, they feared that worse might ensue, so they quickly ordered several guards to protect and assist the grain vendors, to ensure that no harm
would come to them. Anyone who threatened or attempted to steal from

---

3 I.e., to fall into Hell.

4 The last two lines of the sonnet refer to a miniature on folio 7 recto of the manuscript,
   which depicts the square of Orsanmichele (originally built as a grain market) during a
   time of abundance.

5 Starting in the last decades of the thirteenth century, the six "Grain Officials" were
   responsible for the distribution of foodstuffs in the city of Florence.

6 The *cavaliere* or captain of the *podestà* at this time was Ser Villano, a hired henchman
   and the protagonist of a great deal of Lenzi's narrative. The *podestà* was the chief magistrate of the city-state of Florence.

7 The loggia of Orsanmichele appears in several miniatures in the manuscript. On one
   of the pilasters there hung an image of the Virgin Mary that was an object of particular
   veneration in Florence.

any of the vendors was immediately seized and brought before the officials. At this point the bushel baskets were brought forth, and there was a great uproar on the part of the buyers, who wept and sighed and screamed and carried on. Everything was sold very quickly, and that day two-thirds of the buyers went away empty-handed, cursing and weeping in a terrible manner.

More grain would have been sold that day if the officials hadn't acted as they did.

On Sunday, the 9th day of April, no market was held.

On Monday, the 10th, the Council of Six ordered certain wealthy men of the city who had grain and fodder to make it available in the square of Orsanmichele at the price that they had fixed. This day, there was plenty of grain and fodder in the market square. Shortly after the ninth hour had sounded, and the Council of Six had come to sit on the bench under the loggia and saw that the market was full of buyers, they suddenly sent for the captain of the chief magistrate, whose name was Ser Villano from Gubbio, along with his men; and they arrived in a short time, well armed. The Council of Six then issued an edict that no one should sell grain at more than 30 *soldi* per bushel under any circumstances. And then they had the armed men watch over the vendors as on the previous occasion, for fear of what might ensue. Then they had the bushels of grain brought out. There were many buyers, their numbers always growing, and there wasn't enough grain to go around.

On this day, a good third of the buyers went away empty-handed, weeping and lamenting loudly. And if the officials hadn't issued the edict, the grain would have sold for 2 *soldi* more per bushel.

How the Council of Six commanded that grain be sold: April 1329.

On Tuesday, the 11th day of this month, grain was sold at the price indicated. On Wednesday, the 12th day of the month of April, the Council of Six issued an edict to the city on behalf of the chief magistrate, to the effect that whoever had more grain or fodder than was necessary for their own sustenance should, from this day until the calends of July, bring a written account of how much they had to the Council of Six within five days for those in the city and within ten days for those in the country, or it would be confiscated from them.

The second day after the edict was issued, the Council of Six sent for the men who reported to the chief magistrate, the captain, the assessor, and the head of the foot soldiers, and for messengers and guards armed with pikestaffs. And they had many axes brought and sent a party of the armed men along with the messengers and guards with the axes on their shoulders to roam around the city. Another party of armed men was sent into the country, breaking down locked gates and doors if they were not immediately opened to them, searching cellars and rooms and in bedchambers under the beds and in the bedsteads, and in chests and trunks and many other places where they thought they might find grain or fodder. They made a record of the grain and fodder that they found throughout the city and then sent it to the Council of Six, and they in turn had it stored in city warehouses, and sold it for 30 *soldi* per bushel. The grain and fodder that the vendors had was taken away from them and stored in city warehouses. And no one dared to sell grain in the market square unless it were for fodder.

April 1329. Grain for the city.

From the 12th to the 18th day of this month, good grain mixed with one-quarter barley was sold for 29 *soldi*, which comes to about 30 *soldi* 18 *denari* per bushel. The Six did this for the city. That day, the chief magistrate's men were in the market square, armed, in order to ensure that no one started any brawling or tried to overpower anybody else. The Six feared that the buyers might try to steal grain, because the buyers were so furious and their numbers were so great that the market square could barely hold them all. On this day, no more than one bushel was allotted per person,[8] and even so the grain ran out, and no more than a third of the buyers were able to get any grain. And they went about crying and lamenting and loudly cursing themselves and the divine power, saying: "These thieves want us to die of hunger!"

April 1329. Grain for the city.

On the 18th day of April, the Six had 89 bushels of grain, mixed with a quarter of barley, brought to Orsanmichele and sold for 28 *soldi* per bushel; this is equivalent to 31 *soldi* per bushel.

Having done this, they immediately sent for the captain of the chief magistrate, Ser Villano, a valorous man from Gubbio, and he came with many armed men to the market square. And they had a chopping block and an executioner's axe brought to Orsanmichele and two policemen to stand guard and to cut off the feet or hands of anyone who tried to

---

8 A bushel was equivalent to seventeen or eighteen kilos of bread, considered sufficient for about a month.

start a brawl or steal grain. And they did this on account of the extremely large crowd of people who wanted to buy grain. All of the men were murmuring to one another, saying: "We ought to go to the homes of these thieves who have grain and are making us die of hunger and kill every one of them." If such good provision of grain and such a good guard had not been assigned that day, a big tumult might have broken out, with a great deal of violence and killing and robbing. Thus the city sold grain from the 18th day of the month of April until the 3rd day of June of that year. In this way, no one else except those authorized by the city officials was able to sell grain in the market square.

April 1329.

On Thursday, the 20th day of the month of April, the Six had 86 bushels of grain brought into the market square, mixed with a third of barley. They gave it for 28 *soldi* per bushel, a net of 32 *soldi*.

Having done this, they sent for Ser Villano, a man whom the people greatly feared. And he arrived in the market square with many men, well armed with lances and shields. He immediately had the chopping block and axe brought into the square of Orsanmichele with two hired executioners to punish anyone who started to brawl or tried to steal or otherwise cause trouble, as on other occasions. And the proclamation went forth that whoever caused disorder of any kind would have his foot cut off there and then, without the possibility of paying a fine in lieu of the punishment.

This proclamation was made because the crowd of people who were there to buy grain was so great that both inside and outside the loggia it was full of people. And still many people kept arriving, and they were all furious because no one could get any grain unless he was very strong and could wade into the dense crowd. And both men and women were so badly jostled that day in the crowd that they felt the effects for a month afterward, and some even longer. Some had their purses emptied, some had their purses slashed, or their clothes torn to tatters; some lost their cloaks and some their vests or head coverings. On this day, there were many people who obtained no grain, and they went away very sad, loudly complaining along with those who had been injured some in one way and some in another, calling upon Death to take them away.

April 1329.

On the 21st day of this month, Holy Friday, there was no market held in the square. On Holy Saturday, the 22nd day of April, the Six along with other city officials had 54 *moggia*[9] and 12 bushels of grain brought. And a mixed bushel sold for 28 *soldi*, which comes to a net 32 *soldi*.

On this day there were so many buyers that the grain wasn't sufficient, and the bushels were put away. And the wretches who were in the market square and couldn't get any grain were sobbing their hearts out and shouting at the Six: "Mercy! Have pity on us so that we shall not die of hunger on this holy Easter! Console us, help us for the love of Jesus Christ." This incited compassion in the Six, who quickly had it proclaimed that these buyers should wait a little and they would each be allowed to buy a basket of grain. Thus the Six let each person have one basket. These additional baskets amounted to 30 *moggia* and 12 bushels of grain.

April 1329.

Sunday the 23rd day of the month of the aforementioned year was Easter, the feast of the Resurrection; there was no market held in the square. On Monday the 24th and Tuesday the 25th, no market was held. The 26th was the Bright Wednesday,[10] and no market was held.

April 1329.

On Tuesday the 25th day of the month of April, the Six sent buyers for the city to Figline and also to other markets, which I will not take into account in order not to go on too long.[11] Also, I don't want to give erroneous information by mentioning other towns of which I am not sure, so I will only speak about the market at Figline. When the buyers from Florence arrived at the said market, they had it proclaimed throughout Figline that no grain or fodder vendor or other merchant should go into the market to buy grain or fodder, under pain of a fine of 25 *lire* and losing whatever grain or fodder he might have bought.

That same day, they purchased 30 loads of good grain. The cost per bushel was 36 *soldi*, plus the costs for transportation and fees to get the

---

9   A *moggio* (plural: *moggia*) was a unit of measurement for dry goods, in use before the metric system was adopted; the amount varied from region to region.

10 The Wednesday of Easter Week (the week after Easter Sunday), not to be confused with Holy Week (the week before Easter Sunday).

11 There was an important market in the town of Figline di Valdarno, held on Tuesday and Thursday. Other important markets in the vicinity, to which Florence could turn for additional grain, were at Poggibonsi, Empoli, Montelupo, San Giovanni, and Borgo San Lorenzo.

grain to Florence, 2 *soldi*. They sent almost all of this grain to Florence, and they sold some of it in the market at Figline. The grain that was sent to Florence was taken to the market at Orsanmichele, as you shall hear below.

April 1329.

On Thursday the 27th day of this month, the Six had 61 *moggia* of good local grain, mixed with a third of spelt, for 28 *soldi* the bushel. That comes to a net of 34 *soldi*.

And when they had supplied the market square of Orsanmichele with grain, they sent all the buyers to the courtyard of the Macci,[12] which is right across from the market square. There was a man there who gave a voucher to each person who wanted to buy grain. And the square was so full of buyers, who kept arriving, that they were one on top of the other and so crowded together that a pretty young girl who had fainted was carried out and taken to the shop of the guild of Orsanmichele; and her money purse had been slashed open. That day, many men and women had their purses slashed, and some people lost their cloaks and some their vests and some their head coverings; some had their clothing torn because of the jostling crowds; and there were some who were sore for more than a month afterward.

Whoever managed to get a voucher went to the loggia to get their grain. They gave no more than one basket to each person, and two-thirds of the buyers got nothing. There was a great deal of complaining and weeping from both men and women. In order to console those who had not gotten any grain, after the square was cleared, the Six gave one basket to each person who gave money.

April 1329.

On Friday, the 28th day of the month, the Six had 93 *moggia* of good local grain taken to the market square, mixed with a third of spelt, for 28 *soldi* per bushel, for a net of 34 *soldi*. And when the grain and been brought into the square and the multitudes of buyers arrived, when the ninth hour sounded and the baskets were brought out, the buyers began to shout and jostle one another in their anger, in order to reach the containers of grain, for there wasn't enough to go around. The grain

---

12 The courtyard of the Macci was where the Council of Six resided, and where vouchers
    for grain were issued.

was all sold in a very short time, and those who remained and who had not gotten any wept and complained loudly, saying: "This is a poorly run city, where we cannot get any grain! We should go to the homes of these thieves who do have grain, and set fire to their houses and burn them inside, because they are keeping us hungry." And thus they went on saying one thing and another, and they wouldn't leave the market square.

The city officials were moved to pity by this great and piteous lamentation on the part of the buyers. They quickly ordered one basket of grain, mixed in the usual way, to be given to each person to pacify them.

IV. ["SIENA THE PERVERSE ACTS AGAINST THE POOR" DURING THE FAMINE OF 1329]

How there was a great famine in Florence and in other parts of the world, and how the Sienese expelled all the poor people from their city, and the Florentines gave them refuge.

Such a cruel famine and shortage of food went on here in Florence[13] that you who read this account surely must know that other parts of the world were affected as well. According to reliable eyewitnesses, it was felt so cruelly and harshly that the poor had nothing to eat but plant roots and fruits of trees, and meats disgusting not only to the mouth but to the nose as well. Italy, and especially Tuscany, was more overwhelmed by this pestilence than any other place. But I can say that during this time of famine my fatherland, Florence – whose countryside does not produce enough grain to support it for 5 months, and where victuals are always more expensive than in any other part of Italy – by itself supported half of the poor of Tuscany through the providence and aid of the good rich people and their money.[14] Thus it might be said, and indeed is true, that the poor, having been expelled from the grain-rich surrounding lands for fear they might seize them, and having been deprived of the remedies offered to assist them, could only turn to Florence as a trusted port of consolation. During the aforementioned famine Florence not once but many times graciously sustained the poor and others, each in his own degree.

---

13 From 1328 to 1330. The uprising described below erupted in Siena in April 1329 (not May, as Lenzi writes). It appears that Lenzi was writing about these events at a distance of several years, based on what he himself remembered or had recorded, and with unrelenting animosity toward the city of Siena.

14 Probably an allusion to the *prestanze* (forced or voluntary loans) to which the Florentine government had recourse during times of sudden necessity.

Now, I certainly would prefer to remain silent about such events as now occur to my mind; but I cannot suffer that such cruel insolence and miscarriage of mercy as that which the decadent, perverse, cruel, insane city of Siena showed during this famine should go untold. For Siena was so insolent and presumptuous as to act blindly against the disinherited poor when they were all cruelly bereft of benevolent mercy, giving full rein to her impious cruelty. And would that those perfidious citizens of the city of the she-wolf[15] had not been borne and suckled by their mother, who not only devours flesh, but swallows up even the earth, and viciously assails the winds with all her cruel forces.

But, sirs, I know not whether to prove that they are made of different stuff, or to bring down greater and more cruel judgment of their evils by the One who is the height of compassion, in the early days of the famine there was someone in Siena, the minister of the Hospice of Santa Maria della Scala,[16] who was willing to give so many alms to the poor that it seemed that all of God's power were intervening. Everyone – women, men, children, and adults – was given a loaf of bread weighing 14 *once*;[17] if a woman was with child, she was given two loaves. Such great and open charity attracted the poor, who came from near and far. But the alms did not run out even though the number of hungry people increased, for a way was found to replenish them by having everyone contribute to such a good cause. Thus, as can be seen in the painting on the next pages,[18] this was how it was organized: alms were distributed three days of the week – that is, Monday, Wednesday, and Friday – to as many poor as came to the Hospice of la Scala for that reason. All of the poor people would enter, and then three doors were left open through which they left the building; one was for men, the other was used by the women, and the third was for little children, who streamed out continuously. At each of the doors were positioned two very worthy members of the Hospice, who distributed the alms to the people as they emerged.

Oh! Great God, you should grant your grace directly to that house! But we know that only from you, O Lord, does good proceed, and that whoever out of love for you imparts his goods to your ambassadors the

---

15 A symbol of Siena, and also the name of one of the city's *contrade* or districts.

16 Giovanni di Tese dei Tolomei was rector of the Hospice of Santa Maria della Scala from 1314 to 1339.

17 An *oncia* (plural: *once*) was equivalent to a little less than thirty grams.

18 There is no miniature corresponding to this passage in the original manuscript, either because it was never painted or inserted, or because it was later removed.

poor, by your virtue and power that good will abound in his house without discord.

But, dear readers, regard this "Mirror" entitled "Mirror of Humanity," which recounts such godless behaviour, heeding God who gave himself to so much goodness. The city of Siena became envious, and in her insane iniquity clandestinely opposed what Messer Giovanni was doing. The Council of Nine[19] sent for Messer Giovanni; when he came into their presence, he asked what they wished of him. O prideful Siena, let the whole world hear what you are! They replied that under pain of death by fire this almsgiving should not continue thenceforward. Take heed, all men! These people were not only ordering that an injury be done to God; but that all those to whom God alone is a brother should be allowed to die of hunger, in a prosperous city that had plenty of food. For I say, sirs, that these men were well brought up and trained by their mother the she-wolf; let this argument alone be brought against them, without any other syllogisms. But even if this helps no one else, listen to how this evil went forward; now I shall recount how they went on. Having given this grim order, the city of Siena continued thus:

The next day the poor returned to the Hospice, their accustomed refuge, believing that they would receive the usual charity and relief, and that when they heard the word "Enter," they would all be comforted. But that sweet greeting became an ill-fortuned dismissal, for this is what they heard instead: "Go away, you hungry beggars, to perish along with your needs, for the lords of this city have ordered that you be left to perish in your misery; otherwise both we and our houses and possessions will be consumed by fire. We have no more charity in us."

At this cruel, arrogant reply, there arose infinite cries and sounds of hands striking, shouts and crying, and people clawing their faces so deeply that they seemed to bear the marks of rivets or nails. The voices of people crying for someone in their family who had died were heard throughout the entire city, countryside, castles, and fortresses. And thus the poor ran desperately in infinite numbers toward the public palace whence those orders had emanated, crying out "Have mercy!" or "Fire!" or "Die!" All this noise brought the people of the city running, armed with whatever they could find. Armed guards emerged from the public palace to put down the uprising, but to little avail; for the poor, striking

---

19 The highest magistrates of Siena.

with stones and sticks, stormed the palace, driving back the guards, who were fearful of greater injury.

At this, Guido Ricci da Reggio,[20] the captain of the army of that city, came running into the fray. One of the guards, carrying a staff and caring nothing for death, came up and struck Guido a blow on the lower back, knocking him off his feet; and if it hadn't been for the strong armour he was wearing, he might have died. There was great confusion, and many people were gravely wounded on all sides. If it hadn't been that God did not wish it, that day Siena might have been properly paid back for her thieving, evil ways, providing a fearful reminder for all ages.

Several days after the uprising had quieted down, there began an intense search for whoever had incited or consented to so much violence and turmoil. In one night, no fewer than 60 men were taken from their beds, and as many were tortured as were executed by hanging, including the man who had felled the captain. And there may have been men among those who were hanged who had never even heard about the uprising. More than a hundred men were exiled at that time; but that's the way that city is! The others remained in prison for several days.

But this did not end the cruel assaults of fiery Siena; for at a public council it was voted at last that the poor should be driven out of Siena and that no further succour for the love of God was to be given them.

Oh! Cruel earth, why did you not open up?[21]

There came the blare of a trumpet and then a human voice declared that under pain of death, every poor foreigner must leave the city within three days' time. Police squadrons went around with clubs and stones, cruelly driving people out of the city gates, caring not if they were children or adults, men or women, with child or not. Those who had been driven out of Siena turned to Florence as their certain source of relief and mercy; they were well received and well treated there. And giving thanks to God, they devoutly prayed that he would keep Florence in his blessed peace and that she and her citizens be worthily praised.

---

20 Guidoriccio da Fogliano, the *condottiere* (mercenary captain) depicted by Simone Martini in a famous fresco of 1328 in the public palace at Siena.

21 A quotation from Dante's *Inferno* (XXXIII, 66), powerfully dramatic in its allusion to the desperate plight of Count Ugolino and his sons and grandsons.

V. [MESSER VILLANO TORTURES MERCHANTS SUSPECTED OF
HOARDING GRAIN]

When the Council of Six Called the Grain Merchants before Them

September 1329.

On the 18th of this month, the Grain Council called before them 60
grain and feed merchants. They quickly appeared before the Council,
saying: "We are all here at your request. What do you command of us?"
The magistrates conferred together and said: "We cannot be with you
nor confer with you now, for there is no time; but, in brief, we would like
to ask your advice on whether there is any way to get the price of grain to
come down. We know you will give us good advice, with the help of God,
since you know all about these things. Go now, and return early tomorrow and we shall see to it that our officer Messer Villano meets with you;
and we pray you to confer well with him and to advise him on what you
think is the best course to take." Then they were given leave to go.

The next day, that is, Tuesday morning, they all gathered in the square
of Orsanmichele as they had been told to do. Around the third hour, they
appeared before the Grain Council. "Go to our officer Messer Villano, and
advise him as best you can about what we told you," said the Six. They all
went before Messer Villano and said: "We are here before you; what do you
want us to do or say?" Messer Villano replied: "Let us go inside, where we
shall be more comfortable." So they all went in, and when they were inside
the building where the Six met for their councils, Messer Villano had the
doors locked, and had the merchants come forward one by one; he called
them and wrote down their names and then sent them into another room,
which was sealed off. When he had written all their names and sent them all
into the sealed room, he went off with two guards of the chief magistrate,
for he was to dine with him at the palace. After a little while four policemen
arrived and took two of the men away to the Stinche.[22] Little by little the palace guards began to arrive, and took three more men away to prison. Thus
by twos and threes they were all taken to prison; in all 36 were arrested. The
Grain Council ordered each of them to stand surety for five hundred pounds
of grain, and they were carefully watched. This was an excellent thing.[23]

---

22 The Stinche was the name of the chief prison in Florence for debtors or people con-
    demned to life imprisonment.

23 It might seem surprising that Lenzi, a grain merchant himself, should approve the
    arrest of thirty-six of his fellow merchants. But this is merely a particularly forceful ex-
    ample of the exaltation of the officials of the Florentine state (and hence of Florence
    herself) that is one of Lenzi's main themes.

They stayed in prison until Wednesday night; and at the first watch, several palace guards arrived and took four of the grain merchants to the place where the Grain Council met, where they were detained by Messer Villano; these four men were detained in separate places. Then Messer Villano called one of the four men, Dolce Guidicci, and began to torture him with a *colla*[24] without even questioning him first; and he tortured him mercilessly. Dolce cried out, "Sir, why do you torture me? What are you doing to me? What do you want of me? What have I done that you torture me so?" Messer Villano never ceased tugging on the rope; and the other three men, who were nearby, could hear the man screaming and crying, and were so afraid that they shook like leaves, even though they had committed no irregularities; for they knew that the same thing was going to happen to them.

When Dolce Guidicci had been tortured for quite a while and had screamed a good bit, Messer Villano had him lowered to the ground, and asked him: "Tell me how much grain or fodder each merchant has in his shop or house, who has bought grain in Florence in order to hoard it, and which grain merchants in Florence have been consorting with anyone who has been hoarding grain. All this I want to know. And you had better tell me, if you don't want to stay hanging by your arms and the torture to continue." Dolce answered fearfully and with humble words, saying: "May God help me if I don't tell you truthfully everything I know about what you've asked me." And he told the truth of what he knew, moaning and groaning all the while.

Then Messer Villano called the other three men before him one by one and interrogated them in the same way. They told whatever they knew, and he kept them until Thursday at the first watch, when he sent them back to prison, and had four more men brought to him. These he tortured and interrogated as you have heard above, and sent them back to the prison in the same way.

The grain and fodder merchants sought the intercession of many of their friends; these were important men in Florence, who appeared before the Council of Six and asked why the merchants were being kept in prison. After much pleading, finally on Friday morning they were ordered to appear on Saturday, and each one was made to stand surety for five hundred *lire,* and they were told that they could not buy grain or fodder in the city or countryside of Florence, nor sell it, nor barter for it. So they were released under the condition that they would neither buy nor sell grain until Thursday, 15 October.

---

24 A rope run through a pulley, which when pulled lifted a suspect off the ground by his arms, which were tied behind his back.

Memoirs

Donato Velluti

I. ["OUR FAMILY AND EARLY HISTORY"]

December MCCCLXVII

Man desires to know about his brith, his past, what his ancestosr were like, and the wealth they acquired; and many times this helps to avoid much mischief and prevents many errors. Therefore I, Donato, a judge, son of Lamberto di Filippo di Bonaccorso di Piero di Berto de' Velluti, finding myself to be the oldest member of our family, for the perpetual memory of my descendants, and others of the Velluti family and everyone else, have decided to make a record of what I heard from my father and others older than myself, and of what I have read in letters, books, or other writings, as few as they may be, and what I have seen or learned myself; also because every man is mortal, and I am especially, as I suffer greatly with gout. I shall begin in the name of Our Lord Jesus Christ and his most holy and precious Mother, the Blessed Virgin Mary, his blessed apostles, and the precious confessor St Nicholas and the precious virgin St Catherine and all the other saints in heaven, on the first day of December, 1367.

I shall commence with our beginnings and early history and our forefathers, writing of their goodness and their actions, mixing in with this their family relations. Then I shall say something about our property.

I found, from what I heard from my father and others older than I, who heard it from their elders – not in any documents – that our ancestors were originally from Simifonte di Val d'Elsa.[1] This was very rich land,

---

1 Dante, *Paradise* XVI, 60–3, alludes to Lippo Velluti, one of Donato's ancestors from
  Simifonte or Semifonte in the Val d'Elsa.

and there were great, honourable families there, and many gentlemen with golden spurs. Simifonte had a big war with Florence; in the end, it was razed to the ground by the Florentines, who decreed that it could never again be encircled by a wall nor could houses be built there. The Florentine government kept the hill there from that time on, except for perhaps two or three years when the Florentine officials, who were deputed to be able to dispose of the property of the state, leased the hill and land to Filippo di Vanni da Petrognano. I know not whether our ancestors came thence to live in Florence before or after the place was destroyed. Whether we were originally from there or not, I do not give as certain, but only as hearsay. Not so long ago, some of our ancestors found people living there who bore our same coat of arms; and for this reason it was believed that both we and they had belonged to the same family.

What I found in authentic documents about my nearest ancestors (for I haven't found or heard anything about those who came before them) was in a document from 1244 or thereabouts, which stated that Donato, Bonaccorso, Cristiano, and Jacopo, the sons of Pero di Berto, entered into a certain agreement. I have found nothing from before the time of Berto, so I shall start from Donato, Bonaccorso, Cristiano, and Jacopo, from whom all of us in our family descended. They all lived together, and theirs was the tower that is in the street of the Canto de' Quattro Paoni[2] (the second house on the right going toward the piazza where the Guicciardini family lives now). They did some trading and had several warehouses in Borgo San Jacopo. At that time there were no houses in the Via Maggio – just orchards – and it was called Casellina. But as time went on and their numbers and property increased, as I shall write at greater length, they began to build and live in the area where we live now. Since they began to build during the time of their children, first I shall write about their descendants and children. Since it appears that Jacopo died quite young, without marrying or having children, I shall not mention him at all, but shall begin with Donato, who, I find, was the eldest.

Donato had five sons: Mico, Ghino, Dietaiuti, Gherardino, and Lapo. Who his wife was, I can neither find nor ever heard; I think she was a sister or an aunt of Cino di Messer Dietisalvi Bonamichi.

I find that Bonaccorso, who was sometimes called Corso, from whom our side of the family descended, had only one son, who was sometimes called Lippo. I neither know nor can find who his wife was.

---

2 That is, the Via Tanfura. The Canto de' Quattro Paoni is now called the Canto ai
   Quattro Leoni, which is at the corner of the Via Toscanella and the Via dei Velluti.

Cristiano had one son, who was named Velluto. I can neither find nor know who his wife was.

Some time passed, and Donato, Jacopo, Cristiano, and Ghino di Donato all died, and Velluto went off on his own, increasing his wealth and the size of his family. Bonaccorso, along with Donato's sons, decided they wanted to live in a grander style, and to build their warehouses elsewhere. So they bought the land where the palazzo in the Via Maggio is today. This palazzo belongs to the sons of Piero and Matteo, and the land behind it, where my houses are, belonged to Lapo's sons. The land didn't cost much, because it was all orchards then; the area was called Casellina because of a little house that was nearby,[3] outside the city walls. The second circle of walls[4] behind which were the houses on this side of the Arno River – that is, the houses that used to belong to Cino Cerchi and today belong to Michele di Vanni di Messer Lotto and the houses that used to belong to Lotto dell'Abraccia and today belong to the cloth cutter Francesco di Guidalotto, whom they call Rosso, on the back side. At that time, our ancestors were mocked, thus: "Look where the Velluti have gone to make their home!" For then it was held to be a beautiful, honourable palazzo, in an out-of-the-way location, almost as if it were in the country. When this palazzo and the houses behind it had been built, and Bonaccorso had gone to live there with his nephews and they brought their warehouses to that place, they created a new company, as I have mentioned earlier in this book. Little by little, this company began to trade in Bologna, Venice, Milan, Pisa, Genoa, Rome, Paris, France, and England. It was deemed unseemly that the letters that came from outside of Florence should be addressed to *Bonaccorso Velluti and Company, Casellina*; so, since the Via Maggio had been made wider and longer, and more houses had been built there, my great-grandfather Bonaccorso had his agents address letters to him thus: *Bonaccorso Velluti and Company, Via Maggiore*. That is how this street got its name, and it was called thus ever after; but because it later happened that with the passage of time, in spoken language all the names of people and things were shortened – Bonaccorso was called Corso, Filippo was called Lippo, Dietaiuti was called Duti, Gherardino was called Dino – the name of the street was shortened as well. Where it had been called Via Maggiore, it now came to be called Via Maggio.

---

3 The word *casellina* means "little house."

4 These walls had one gate facing toward Pisa (from Borgo San Jacopo) and another toward Siena (from San Felice), between which the Velluti houses were located.

II. [MADONNA DIANA AND HER TURBAN]

Madonna Diana, the sister of Donato and daughter of the late Mico, was the wife of Guerrucciolo de' Rossi. She had two sons, Tribaldo and Binguccio. Tribaldo's descendants today are Guerrieri and his children. Binguccio's descendants today are Amerigo, Bartolommeo, Pieraccino, and their children, as well as Madonna Filippa, the wife of Piero di Neri del Zanca. Their descendants were Binguccio, Pescaia, and Neri. Madonna Diana was a very good woman, and was very fond of me, for love of her brother; she kept me much with her at Boboli[5] when I was a boy. She always wore a massive turban on her head. So on one occasion when she was at the old palazzo of the Rossi family across from the church of Santa Felicita, where the inn is today, a large stone fell from the top of the palazzo and hit her on the head. To Madonna Diana, it felt like dust that had been scratched up by chickens; so she said, "chick chick chick." It did her no other harm, on account of all the cloth she had on her head.

III. [BONACCORSO DI PIETRO: "A BOLD, STRONG, WELL-BUILT MAN"]

Bonaccorso di Pietro was a bold, strong, well-built man, and very able in the use of arms. He accomplished great feats of valour and gallantry, both in Florence and in other places. He had received so many wounds in battles and skirmishes that he had been stitched up all over his body. Bonaccorso was a great opponent of the Paterins[6] and heretics, when they were openly fighting about this type of thing in Florence, as I heard, at the time of St Peter Martyr.[7]

Bonaccorso was tall in stature, with strong limbs, and well put together. He lived a full 120 years,[8] but he was blind for the last 20 years of his life. He was called Corso; and I heard that when he was very old, he had become so stiff that he couldn't bend his body; and it would have taken a youth even more solid of build than himself sitting on his shoulders to make him bend. He was also an experienced, honest merchant. He enjoyed such a good reputation that when a shipment of Milanese cloth

---

5 Where later the Pitti Palace and Boboli Gardens were built.

6 "Patarin" or "Paterin" was a term applied to Albigenses and other heretics.

7 St Peter Martyr, also known as St Peter of Verona or Fra Pietro da Verona, was a Dominican friar whom Pope Gregory IX made general inquisitor. Peter was called to Florence by the Inquisition in 1243, and promoted a citizens' crusade against the Paterins. Pope Innocent IV canonized him in 1253.

8 A typical exaggeration in this kind of family history.

arrived in Florence (for he ordered a great deal of cloth from Milan), he would sell out of it even before the bales were untied. He had a great deal of the cloth dyed here in Florence; and I heard that a certain Giovanni del Volpe, who was a buyer of theirs, seeing that Bonaccorso was selling such a great quantity of this cloth, got the idea of making more profits for the company by having it dyed with weaker dyes at a lower cost. After some time had passed, the cloth didn't have the same durability as usual; seeking the reason why, they found that it was due to this Giovanni's sly trick, and Corso, because he was so honest, wanted to kill Giovanni for it.

After he lost his eyesight, Bonaccorso stayed at home most of the time. He had the back part of the palazzo in the Via Maggio before it was divided up between him and his nephews. There was a balcony along the length of the palazzo, which had three bedchambers on the back side. He would walk back and forth there every morning until he reckoned he had walked three or four miles. After his walk, he breakfasted, and his breakfast wasn't just two bread rolls. Then at midday he ate copiously, for he was a great eater. And thus he passed his days.

Now I want to tell you how he died. My father told me that one day Bonaccorso decided he wanted to go to the warming room;[9] while there, he struck his foot on something. When he returned and saw that on account of this injury he was unable to take his usual exercise, he immediately believed that he was going to die. It happened that at this time his son Filippo, who was my grandfather, was about to marry his second wife, Madonna Gemma de' Pulci. That day, Bonaccorso had jested a great deal, saying: "I, not my son, am the one who needs to take a wife," and many other witticisms. Lying on his bed, he decided to have himself carried to his lounging chair; so he called his kinsmen – that is, my father and my uncle Gherardo – and leaning his hands and arms on their shoulders, suddenly the life went out of him on account of his great age, and he died; that was in 1296.

IV. [DONATO'S BROTHER LOTTIERI, THE AUGUSTINIAN FRIAR]

After Friar Lottieri[10] returned from Paris,[11] he lived in Florence most of the time. He was prior or provincial[12] several times, and very beloved

---

9 A *stufa secca*, a room warmed by hot air coming from below or the sides.
10 Born in 1314, Lottieri entered the order of Augustinian friars at Santo Spirito in Florence around 1329–30.
11 Following the plague of 1348.
12 A monastic superior who has the direction of all the religious houses in a given province or district.

and revered in the monastery, and was a great consolation to me and others. He was kind, friendly, and honest, without a bit of malice in him. He was stout, of average height, brawny, and full-figured. He had great illnesses, and several times we feared for his life. He was a great eater and drinker; indeed, he had an enormous appetite. He suffered from colic and gout. Finally, it pleased God to suddenly call my brother to him. On the 27th of March, 1367, Lottieri was in the second cloister, while the brothers were at vespers. He was at the foot of a pine tree in the cloister; there were no other friars around. He had a stick in his hand and was striking the tree to knock down the pine cones. He fell to the ground; when the friars returned from vespers, one of them saw him lying on the grass. Not recognizing Lottieri, the friar went up to him; realizing who it was, he immediately called the other friars. They carried him to his cell, where, on the doctor's advice, they rubbed him down and took other appropriate measures. But in spite of everything they did, he never spoke or showed any sign of consciousness. According to what was said by Master Jacopo of Bologna, a most worthy physician, the infirmity that befell him is called apoplexy, which so alters a man that few survive it. He remained in that afflicted state until midnight, and then passed from this life; God keep his soul. This was a great blow and loss for me, and likewise for the monastery.[13] He was born on the feast of Our Lady[14] in August 1314, and passed from this life on the 27th of March, 1367, at fifty-three years of age.

V. [DONATO'S ADVENTURES AS A BOY, AND LATER AS A YOUNG JUDGE AT THE TIME OF THE DUKE OF ATHENS]

The time has now come for me to write about myself, Donato, a judge, the son of the late Lamberto Velluti, and about the descendants and relatives I acquired through my wife and children. It would be more seemly for someone else to write about me, rather than that I myself should do so; but my children are quite young, and know little about my affairs. So, since no one else knows my story, I have decided to write about a few things, politely passing over events that might lead too much to my praises or virtues. And if I should trespass in anything, I shall not do so

---

13 The monastery of Santo Spirito was hoping to make Lottieri a bishop. In 1351, the Florentine government recommended to the pope that Lottieri be promoted to this rank.

14 The principal feast day of the Blessed Virgin Mary is 15 August.

to praise myself, but to record things that have occurred, since I believe that it will please my readers to know about them, and especially how and why they happened.

I was born on July 6, 1313, and was raised and educated mainly by my mother and my brother Filippo. I am of average height, with a fresh, rosy face, white complexion, and small limbs. When I was young and before I took a wife, I was very healthy, and didn't suffer any fever or other illness; I weighed very little, being quite thin. After I took a wife, for 7 or 8 years I suffered from stomach ailments and colic; then the humours that were creating these problems changed into gout, which has given me a great deal of discomfort; it began around 1347, when I was 34 or 35 years old, and causes me to have a little fever sometimes. God be praised, up to now He has spared me from illnesses with continuous fevers; in future, let Him do what He will.

It is true that when I was a boy of about ten or so, late one evening I was enticed by a citizen of Florence into going with him to carry some arms outside the Ognissanti Gate along the banks of the Mugnone River.[15] First he took me to the Carraia bridge; then, pretending to be afraid of the police, he took me all the way to the Prato Gate and from thence to the Ognissanti Gate, and thence along the Mugnone. Being foolish and eager to please, I let myself get caught in a trap. While we were going along the Mugnone in the direction of Faenza, suddenly three men emerged from the fields. With knives drawn, they and the man who had enticed me there seized and gagged me, and kept me concealed in the Mugnone river-bed, for the city gate was closed. They led me on foot or carried me on their backs, all night long. Around dawn, we arrived near the town of Pistoia. From thence we travelled until dinnertime to Borgo di Buggiano,[16] leading me to believe that we were in Peretola on the way to Florence; and they acted very kind and solicitous to me. We stopped at an inn in Borgo di Buggiano, and the innkeeper realized that I had been entrapped and reported it to the chief magistrate of the place,[17] who immediately took me away from my captors and put me in the care of the leading farmer in the area, and put them in jail while he waited for a reply from Castruccio[18] about what he should do with me and the men

---

15 A tributary of the Arno River.
16 In the province of Pistoia.
17 The *podestà* or chief magistrate was elected annually in medieval Italian towns and republics; the position had judicial functions and almost unlimited powers.
18 Castruccio Castracani, who ruled Lucca between 1308 and 1328.

who had kidnapped me, which I was not happy about. But when I was informed why I had been taken – that is, to demand ransom for my release – and how they would have mistreated me, taking me to Carafagnana, I was duly alarmed, and was therefore content that they had been put in jail. The reply came from Castruccio that the men should be released and that I should be taken to him at Lucca; the men also came to give their side of the story. Castruccio questioned me personally about my background and how I had been taken and many other things, and then sent me to stay with his wife and children. After I had been there for several days, he sent for me again and asked me if I wanted to stay with him. I said that I would be happy to do as he pleased and to follow his orders, but I begged His Lordship to let me return to Florence to console my mother and brothers. He agreed, and immediately called for two horses and a servant to take me back to Florence. We wanted to give the servant some cloth to make clothes for himself, but he wouldn't take it, because Castruccio had told him not to accept any gifts. My brother Filippo accompanied Castruccio's servant as far as Santa Gonda, and wanted to give him 25 florins, but he wouldn't take them. My friends and relatives were overjoyed at my return, and Castruccio was greatly praised and esteemed by everyone. We had the knaves banished from Florence.

After my return, I began to study grammar and then logic. I lived in Bologna, beginning in 1329, for eight or nine years, while pursuing my studies, and had many discomforts there. I stayed on at the University of Bologna, except that one year I returned to Florence on account of the unrest when the Cardinal of Ostia, who was lord of Bologna and the Romagna, was expelled by the Church and the Cardinal Legate. I stayed in Florence for about six months, and then returned to Bologna, where I remained until May of 1338. Then I left, because Bologna and the University had been placed under interdict.[19] I went to Careggi, outside the city walls of Florence, to the home of Gherardo Manetti, where with Ugo di Piero, the son of Messer Oddo Altoviti, I studied the book that we had been reading that year in Bologna, which is called "The Old Digest."[20] If it hadn't been for the fact that I couldn't continue studying in Bologna – for it was my last year of study – I would have taken my doctorate in a public ceremony, although I had already paid the fee of 40 florins, which my father had sent me, to take the private examination. But seeing that

---

19 In 1338 the city and the University of Bologna were placed under interdict by Pope Benedict XII on account of the uprising against the cardinal legate.
20 Probably Justinian's *Pandects*, a digest of Roman law.

most of the students had already departed, and since the public examination for the doctorate is a mere formality, I didn't take it.

We stayed at Careggi until October, when we left. Since the University
of Bologna had not been reinstated, Messer Ugo went to Pisa to finish
his studies, because a great legal scholar, Rinieri da Forlì,[21] was there,
with many students. I returned in secret to Florence, and stayed shut up
in the house unbeknownst to anyone. I studied all winter and emerged
publicly in the summer.

It happened that Piero Velluti[22] was going to take up the duties of
captain of the guard at Colle[23] in November; at the last minute the judge
who was supposed to go with him backed out, and Piero couldn't find
another judge. So Piero hounded my father until he told him where I
was. Piero came to speak to me and asked me to serve for two weeks or a
month, until he could find another judge. I went, and I liked my chambers, and the office wasn't so onerous that I couldn't continue to study;
so I decided to stay there for the whole duration of the office. In the
meantime, I studied law with several knowledgeable local notaries. After
the office terminated, on the calends of May we returned to Florence;
and it happened that I entered the city late in the evening. I remained in
the house, without going out, until the feast of the Ascension,[24] in May
of 1339, with no pomp. The next day I went to the Public Palace, where
I was seen and honoured by judges and notaries alike; and practising
the law between the Public Palace and at the Seignory, I was in great
demand. My father wanted to give me a wife; but wishing to honour my
brothers, who were older than I and were not in Florence at the time, I
did not obey him. I still regret this, for though my father was very happy
with me, I wish I could have given him that consolation while he was
alive. The plague of 1340 arrived, and he passed from this life and I
was left alone in the house, with no woman to help me. The following
November, Piccio[25] returned, and I wanted him to take a wife; but since
he hadn't yet made a start in a profession, he did not wish to marry. So
I, encouraged by friends and relatives, made up my mind to take a wife,
and the following January I took as my lady and wife Madonna Bice, the
daughter of the late Messer Covone de' Covini – a dear, wise, very good

---

21 The famous jurist Ranieri degli Arsendi da Forlì.
22 Pietro di Gherardino di Donato, a second cousin of the writer's father.
23 Colle di Val d'Elsa, a town in the province of Siena.
24 24 May.
25 One of Velluti's brothers.

woman, though not a beautiful one. I was very happy with her, and while she lived every good befell me, both in terms of my family and my advancement in the world.

On the feast of All Saints in November of that year, the Bardi and the Frescobaldi families were driven out by the fury of the populace, because those families wished to overturn the popular government. For this reason, a body of 40 good men was created, and they were given a great amount of power. I was one of this group, and succeeded to many other public offices, such as the Council of Twelve of Pistoia and Arezzo, and many others.[26] I was honoured more than was seemly, considering my youth and lack of judgment.

After the affair of the purchase of Lucca by Messer Mastino,[27] and the subsequent war with Pisa, and our defeat by Lucca and loss of that city, Florence was in a bad state. On the feast day of Our Lady in September, the Duke of Athens[28] was made lord, or rather tyrant, of Florence. He made me one of the first Priors, although I was very worried about it; when he sent for me, I was very afraid. I got very much into his good graces, both because he found me to be honest and loyal and because once peace had been made with Pisa, Duke Guarnieri[29] formed a large company of soldiers with men who had been discharged after that war. In order to prevent Guarnieri from doing damage in the countryside, the Duke gave him money, although he himself was quite short of funds. Since I had about 400 florins, without the Duke asking me I offered them to him, and he accepted the money and then immediately had it returned to me without asking for it again. For this reason and others, he made me Advocate of the Poor;[30] and when my office as Prior ended,

---

26 Velluti was Prior from 14 October to 14 December 1341; he was elected *podestà* with two other lawyers against Gherardo Vecchio on 29 December 1341; he went as ambassador to Prato on 4 February 1342; he went with other Florentines to elect the new *podestà* on 6 March 1342; and was one of the Twelve Good Men appointed in April 1342 to oversee Pistoia for three months.

27 Mastino II della Scala, lord of Verona, a member of the famous Scaliger family. Mastino purchased the city-state of Lucca from the Rossi of Parma in 1335, and subsequently sold it to the Florentines in 1341 for 100,000 florins.

28 The "Duke of Athens" was Gualtieri di Brienne (Walter of Brienne), who died in 1356. His father, with the aid of knights of the Fourth Crusade, had been lord of the so-called Duchy of Athens (in Byzantine territory), but was killed in battle and lost the duchy. Walter claimed the empty title.

29 Werner or Warner, duke of Urslingen, a German soldier of fortune.

30 This seems to have been an institution created by the duke of Athens in an attempt to curry favour with the underclasses.

he ordered all of his doorkeepers and servants to give me access to his
private apartments. When people saw how much I was in favour, I became in great demand; if I had been interested in money, I could have
gained a great deal. But I did a lot of favours for many people, and bestowed many honours on the citizens of Florence, always remembering
the common people as well. The Duke's advisers were greatly displeased
at this, for they wanted neither equals nor colleagues. It was on account
of their bad counsel that the Duke ended badly, for they advised him to
be a tyrant rather than a ruler, and to make himself rich rather than to
govern, and they led him to do evil deeds. Seeing this, and realizing that
the Duke was becoming very unpopular with the citizens of Florence, I
slowly began to distance myself from him, but not totally. I asked him
for nothing, I never went to the Public Palace except to hear mass[31] on
feast days, and on rare occasions for festivities, when I would pay my respects to him and then leave. Continuing his evil operations, the Duke
was driven from power; the uprising began on the feast day of St Anne[32]
in July 1343. After he was expelled, the office of the Fourteen[33] was created, and they were given full powers.

---

31 Evidently in the chapel of the Signori in the Palazzo Vecchio.
32 26 July.
33 In August 1343, fourteen *Riformatori* under the leadership of the bishop of Florence
     began a re-districting of the city of Florence.

Secret Book

Goro Dati

I. [COMPANY TROUBLES, ESPECIALLY IN SPAIN]

Making a rough estimate of my assets, I find that when Michele left the company on the first of January 1392, and I remained, I was left with a net amount of about 800 florins that would have been mine if I had left the company.[1] In fact, I had made no profit, but rather would have had to make good on a portion of the debts amounting to about 950 florins that were owed to the company in Catalonia and elsewhere, which were not recoverable at that time. We discovered this later when on account of Antonio di Segna's treachery we decided that we should ascertain what we really had in cash assets in the company. This was why I resolved to endure everything for these last 2 years, and to stay with the company and put up with Antonio di Segna and everything else, for I felt myself to be too short of money to be able to do things my own way should there have been a need of it. And I've been hoping that Matteo would help me, and that I would be able to send Simone to Valencia so that he could help me with my affairs here.[2] I pray God to grant that it should be so.

After that, in 1393 I received my wife's[3] dowry, which was 800 florins, and had profits of 162 florins, and this year I made 325 florins in profits, which comes to 1,287 florins. On the other hand, I made two payments totalling 1,425 florins as appears under Expenditures on page 3. This includes my losses when 250 florins were stolen from me on the Riviera,

---

1 Dati had gone into business with Michele di Ser Parente on 1 October 1384.

2 Matteo and Simone were employees of Dati's in Spain.

3 Dati's second wife, Betta di Mari di Lorenzo Villanuzzi.

and the purchase of the farm for 275 florins, and the 100 florins I lent to Michele's heir. Thus, while in 1392 I was owed 950 florins and owed about 150 florins, since then I find my debits exceeding my credits by about 140, for a total debit of 390 florins. I estimate that in the last eight months that I have been in business on my own, I have made good my losses and wiped out the debt, or at least I will have when the ventures I have embarked upon have been concluded. So I have preserved my capital. Would to God and the Virgin Mary that I were certain of retaining my capital in cash on the first of January 1395 – that is, that my debits would not exceed my credits since the time I went into partnership with Michele. But God will grant us his grace as he has always done. I am not counting the 950 florins and 25 *soldi* owed to me by debtors, which I mention on page 6, because I cannot use them.

After that year, by the grace of God I did better than I had anticipated, because the business in Valencia turned out well for me. And I find that I have been able to transfer 200 florins from the credit side and deduct them from the debits, as appears under Expenditures on page 3.

The new company is recorded on page 6.

II. [CONFESSIONS AND RESOLUTIONS]

1403, January 1[4]

Because in this wretched life our sinfulness subjects us to many tribulations of the soul and passions of the body, if it weren't for the grace of God, who deigns to assist our weakness with his mercy by revealing to our mind what we should do and by sustaining us, we would perish daily. I realize that I have already passed the age of 40 with little obedience to God's commandments; not trusting in my own powers of getting on the right path, but hoping to advance by degrees along that path, I resolve from this day to refrain forever from going to the shop on solemn feast days declared by the holy Church. Nor will I conduct any business, nor allow others to work for me for temporal gain, with this exception: in cases of extreme necessity, each time I transgress I shall distribute alms of one gold florin to God's poor on the following day. I have written this down so that I may keep this resolution in mind, and to shame myself if I should break it.

---

4 Dati uses the Florentine style date, which corresponds to 1404 in the Gregorian calendar.

Also, in memory of the Passion of Our Lord Jesus Christ by whose merits we are freed and saved, that he may forever save us from every evil passion by his mercy and grace, from this day I resolve in my heart to keep Friday as a day of chastity in perpetuity – by Friday I also mean Friday night – and to abstain from any act of carnal pleasure on that day of the week. May our Lord grant me the grace to do so; and if it should happen that I should fall, either through inattention or forgetfulness, I pledge to give twenty *soldi* the next day to God's poor for each time that I err, and to say the Our Father and the Hail Mary 20 times.

I also resolve this day to do a third thing while I am healthy and able to, remembering that we need Almighty God to take care of us every day. Each day I wish to honour God by giving some alms or saying some prayers, or some other pious act. And if by an oversight I should fail to do so, as soon as I realize it, that same day or the next I must give alms of at least five *soldi* to God's poor.

These, however, are not vows;[5] rather, I am doing this to help myself keep these resolutions to the best of my ability.

May 3rd of the year of our Lord 1412. On 28 April my name was drawn as Standard-bearer of my Company.[6] Until that time, I had not been sure whether my name was in the rolls of the College, and yet I desired it both for my own honour and that of those who shall remain after me. I remember that Stagio, my father, held many offices in his lifetime, and was several times a magistrate of the Guild of Porta Santa Maria, and of the Merchants' Council of Five, and a tax official and a chamberlain; but his name was never drawn for any of the Colleges in his life, though shortly after his death his name was drawn as a Prior. And I remember that eight years ago I underwent many adversities on account of my business in Catalonia, and that last year I had to take care not to be arrested for debt to the City of Florence. On the very day that I was chosen for this office, a quarter of an hour before, I had finished paying my debt to the city thanks to a reprieve, which was an inspiration from God, may he always be praised and blessed. Now that I can secure other offices, it seems to me that I have received a great blessing, and I should be content with being able to say that I have sat once in the Colleges and

---

5 That is, solemn promises to God, the breaking of which implied a mortal sin.

6 In the constitution of 1250, the people of Florence were divided up into twenty "companies"; these were reduced to nineteen in 1306. Dati's *gonfalone* or district was Ferze, in the Santo Spirito quarter.

should aspire no further. So, lest I be ungrateful or become too hungry for power (for the more men have, the more they want), I have decided and resolved that henceforth I shall never ask anyone to help me obtain whatever public offices there might be up for selection or voting, but rather I shall let those who are in charge of such things do their job, and abide by God's will. I shall accept whatever public or guild office for which I might be chosen, not refusing the work but obeying the call, and I shall do whatever good I can. In this way I shall avoid the vice of ambition and presumptuousness, and shall live in freedom without having to demean myself by begging for favours. And if I should depart from this resolve, each time I do so I condemn myself to give two gold florins in alms within a month. I have made this resolution in my fiftieth year.

This same day, for the good and security of my conscience, knowing myself to be weak in the face of sin, I resolve never to accept any office, should my name be drawn, in which I would have the power to exercise the death penalty. And if I should depart from this resolution, I condemn myself to give twenty-five gold florins to the poor within three months of accepting such an office. And I shall in no wise attempt to influence those who make the selections for such offices, either by asking them to put forth or not to put forth my name, but shall let them do as they see fit. And every time I might fail to do so, I condemn myself to donate a gold florin.

III. [THE COMPANY IN DANGER OF FAILING]

Company with Piero Lana. 1408

The accounts for the shop and for the last company are written above, on page 8.

Because things went badly for us in Barcelona, and on account of the lawsuit here that followed, and the suspicions about what Simone was doing, and the evil rumours that many people were spreading, we couldn't get any credit. So we were forced to withdraw from business in order to pay all our creditors, and we got money from friends and by using every ploy we could, suffering losses, paying interest, and incurring other expenses in order to avoid bankruptcy and shame. And although my partner[7] would have preferred to go bankrupt in order to avoid some

---

7 Piero Lana.

losses and expenditures, I decided that I would rather lose all my money than lose my honour. With great effort, I held on until we paid everyone off, and I had only my partners left to deal with. May the Lord be praised and blessed for it.

I truly believe that if I had been able to send Simone the silk and gold cloth that he was supposed to sell to the King, he would have succeeded in bringing his business to a successful conclusion. But I was unable to do so – indeed, I had to refrain from business activity until the year 1405 – for the disputes and lawsuits began, and I had to sell what I had here in order to pay my debts. Thus I could not send him the things he was expecting from me, which he had promised to the King, and his business began to falter and to encounter great difficulties, so there was never any way to make it right again, and things went from bad to worse.

Since Simone's affairs in Spain were going badly, he could not fill our orders and remittances, and my partner became impatient and began to complain loudly and to behave in a way that was contrary to our business interests. Proceedings were taken against him by Antonio di Messire Bartolomeo and two other powerful companies for an earlier transaction they had had with me, and there was a dispute and lawsuit about that transaction. I had gone to Spain; Piero defended our interests badly, did not produce our accounts as evidence, and merely tried to show that he was not liable. The judgment went against him, and he had to pay up. Of the 500 florins we owed, I had already repaid 300 florins to their agents in Spain, so we only owed them 200 more florins; but they were awarded two thousand two hundred florins. I do not think that such a thing was ever heard of, and I hope it may bring them bad luck. Yet we are the ones who suffer from it, and the fault lies with my partner and his contrary ways.

I decided to go to Spain to see if there was some way to prevent us losing everything there; and I left Florence with Paolo Mei[8] on the 12th of November 1408. Paolo had decided to go some time before, and when he told me this, I decided to go as well. We travelled by land, and had a very wearisome journey in harsh winter weather, arriving in Murcia on December 30th. We found Simone there, and we all had high hopes for his business. But it didn't turn out well for us, on account of the falsity of the Spaniards; it certainly was through no fault of his, but because he

---

8 A friend and business associate whom Dati mentions several times.

was treated unfairly. I was back safe and sound in Florence by March 15, 1410, but all I had acquired on my trip was toil and misfortune.

It then transpired that my partner Piero Lana kept pursuing me in every way he could, and he accused me before the Merchant's Court as a bankrupt and had me publicly denounced by their herald. But he didn't succeed in getting a judgment against me, which would have been a great iniquity, for I had not gone bankrupt but had returned from abroad to settle my accounts with him and to do whatever I could to remedy things. He died of the plague in July 1411, while the lawsuit was going on.

Later I came to an agreement with Piero's brother Papi, in his name and the name of Piero's children. I have recorded this on page 15 of my long account book.

Last Will and Testament

Francesco Datini

[FOUNDATION OF THE HOSPICE FOR THE POOR][1]

The Testator, Francesco, for the love of God and so that God's poor would be given what he himself had received as a gift and blessing from God, wished and ordered that his chief residence in Prato, with its garden and the house opposite, loggias, rooms, and furnishings, should always belong to the poor as a private hospice, granary, and home, in no way subject to the Church or to ecclesiastical authority or Church prelates or other people of the Church; and that it should in no wise ever become the property of the Church, but that it should always belong to the poor, for the perpetual use of the poor of Jesus Christ, for their everlasting nourishment and emolument. Francesco left, destined, and ordered that his home be used in every best way and for every best reason; with the ways, order, agreements, and conditions in the present testament set forth below. To distinguish this house from the other hospices for the poor in the city of Prato, it shall be called *The Hospice of the Poor of Francesco di Marco.*

For this House, Granary, or Hospice of the Poor, Francesco ordered that land and buildings be purchased with any monies that derive from the estate of the said Francesco by the undersigned Executors or Governors of the House, who shall be listed below. The said testator Francesco

---

1 This is the second part of the last will and testament of Francesco di Marco Datini, dictated by him on 31 July 1410 to Lapo Mazzei, his notary, friend, and assiduous correspondent. The official text was in Latin but Lapo attached this version in Italian, which probably retains dispositions dictated to him orally by Francesco. The hospice is still operating today.

gave, consigned, left, and adapted for the love of God, to the said House or Hospice, which is his sole beneficiary, all of his property and buildings wherever they may be, both present and future. He forbade the sale, cession, or long-term lease of the said real property, so that their fruits might feed God's poor in perpetuity. And if, contrary to said prohibition, any of his property should be given away or leased, then Francesco ordered that said property should be given to the Guild of Orsanmichele. It was his wish that said property and lands and whatever they produced should be given to, spent for, and distributed to the poor of Jesus Christ, both the poor who are publicly known and those who keep their poverty secret out of shame, as is done at the other hospice of the poor in Prato. This shall be executed by four of the best and most honest citizens of Prato, who should be elected or named in the general council of that city every year, as shall be related below. Each year the city council of Prato shall select the appropriate directors of the foundation, and determine their removal. Francesco decreed that this election should be done with the full mandate and authority, and in accordance with the wishes of the said city of Prato; always excepting the things that are contained in the present last will and testament.

Since he has great confidence in the city of Prato and its leaders, Francesco left the maintenance, protection, governance, and rule of the Hospice to the said city, at the expense of the foundation. He put the rule, governance, and administration of the Hospice entirely and in perpetuity in the hands of the city of Prato, including the collection of his debts and accounts, just as he would have done during his life. This he did so that, for the love that he bears the city of Prato and her citizens, the proper things should be done for the Hospice, and so that what has been set forth above and below might be duly carried out. With the assistance of the city of Prato, the Hospice should be protected from any powerful person or magnate who might wish in any way to take it over in some secular or ecclesiastical guise. Francesco entreated and admonished the city of Prato to protect his sole heir, the Hospice, from any damages resulting from payments or promises made by him, the Testator; and that the sums paid and received and the amounts promised should be duly settled within the proper amount of time.

The Testator wished and declared that at the time of the annual appointment of the four directors who are to administer the foundation to the best of their abilities and according to the dictates of their conscience, in the general council of the city of Prato, the following persons should be present in order to vote or to speak during the deliberations: Chiarito di Matteo Chiariti, Lionardo di Ser Tommaso di Giunta, Barzalone di Spedalieri, Ser Amelio di Messire Lapo, Messire Piero Rinaldeschi, Giovanni di Bartolomeo, Stefano di Ser Piero, Messire Torrello di Messire Niccolò, Messire Bonaccorso di Messire Niccolò, Martino di Niccolò Martini, Bartolomeo di Matteo Convenevoli, and Biagio di Bartolo, all from Prato; in their absence, their descendants in the male line should attend, but not more than one per family, and they must be of legal age. Francesco named the aforementioned men and their descendants as continual protectors, watchful guardians, and loving defenders of the Hospice and of his last wishes. Nothing should be done outside of the general council of the city of Prato or against the wishes of the four directors. Nevertheless, when their term of office comes to an end, the aforementioned four directors must render to the city of Prato an accounting of what they have done.

As a precaution, and to expedite assistance to the poor of the Hospice as well as the management thereof as mentioned above, Francesco ordered that whoever should become the four directors of the foundation after his death should review and calculate and settle all of his accounts and collect from the city of Florence and its administrators the payments, gifts, and interest on Francesco's credits in any of the public funds of Florence, present and future; even those monies that are held as taxes or duties, and negotiable titles.[2] They should properly settle these and any other debts or obligations so that Francesco's name is no longer associated with them and so that no one else is affected by the aforementioned loans. He prays the four directors of the foundation to act benevolently toward his poor friends, who are well known to Madonna Margherita, Luca, Barzalone, and Lionardo.[3]

So that the doors of the Hospice might always be open to receive people coming and going, and to keep an eye and ear on things useful to the foundation, he stipulated that the city of Prato should find a caretaker, be it a married man or single, of good standing and reputation, whose sole care should be the Hospice. This guardian should be given a residence somewhere in the Hospice, and some kind of stipend for his living

---

2 *Accattoni* were negotiable titles for the reimbursement of forced loans; the *Monte dei Prestanzoni* was a public fund that returned 6 per cent interest.

3 Francesco's four executors were his wife, Madonna Margherita; his partner, Luca del Sera; his son-in-law, Lionardo di Ser Tommaso di Giunta; and his partner and steward in Prato, Barzalone di Spedalieri.

expenses; the amount and schedule of payments shall be determined by the city of Prato.

Francesco ordered that the aforementioned Madonna Margherita, along with Luca, Barzalone, and Lionardo, and those who should survive them, be the executors and agents of the aforementioned matters, that debts be paid and that goods be purchased with the monies that shall be derived from the said payments, gifts, interest, and credits, and that his last will and testament as herein written be executed in its entirety; for these four persons are fully informed of Francesco's wishes in almost everything. He requests that the city of Prato confer with them and with those who survive them about any of the things to be done in his name that may be of particular weight or importance. And he wishes that, if those things should not be done, the four aforementioned persons should be able to lodge a complaint, wherever necessary, and, should they deem it essential, even to execute the present last will and testament themselves. This in the event that the will should not be duly executed and that the things that Francesco ordered should not be done with the diligence and in the way and form ordered by him. In such a case, these four persons and their survivors may collect debts, finish making payments to the Public Fund, and handle Francesco's credits, loans, negotiable titles, monies, and capital. They should do all of the things that the testator, had he lived, would do: pay off Francesco's loans with the money as long as it lasts, or put it at the disposition of the Hospice in order to execute his will. In such cases, these four persons and their survivors will act as executors after the death of the trustor, make the said payments to the Public Fund, and do the other things that are granted to the city of Prato or to the four to be selected by the said city to do. They can also name another executor as they see fit, and they can remove the substitutes and appoint others.

For all his other goods and property, accounts, and holdings present and future, for the love of God Francesco named the said Hospice as his sole heir, which as above is designated in perpetuity, for the future use and needs of the poor of Jesus Christ, and the said poor as ordered above in the section that begins "The testator, Francesco," etc. Francesco declared that it was his wish and intention that the Hospice be completely private and not related to the Church, and that it in no way and for no reason should it be called ecclesiastical but rather designated as secular, for the love of God, for the aforementioned use in perpetuity; nor should it be subject in any way to the Church or the clergy. Francesco desired that his last will and testament be kept on public view at the Hospice, in book form, attached by a chain, so that his wishes would be known to everyone, and that it should not be easily removable from thence. He also desired that every year the names of the aforementioned four appointed directors should be written in this book, as well as other things of which it shall please the city of Prato to keep a record in the future.

It was Francesco's desire that the general fideicommissaries of this his last will and testament be, for a period of no more than three years, the Consuls of the Guild of the Cloth Merchants of the city of Florence, honourable citizens and faithful in the matters entrusted to them.

Finally, as on another occasion he said he had taken counsel about this, the aforementioned testator entreats the magistrates, the city of Prato, and the four men who shall be elected directors of the foundation, and all his other aforementioned executors, to be very careful not to raise any altar in the Hospice, nor to turn it into an oratory or any type of ecclesiastical place, nor do anything else by which the Hospice might be construed as an ecclesiastical place. Nor should any evil people, under the title of benefice, enter or occupy the said Hospice, which is entirely contrary to the testator's wishes. If any impediment to this should arise (God forbid), Francesco's desire was that every effort and expenditure be made from his estate to prevent this from occurring.

This is the last will and testament of Francesco di Marco Datini.

Book of Family Affairs

Lapo di Giovanni Niccolini de' Sirigatti

I. [RUZZA'S REVENGE]

Here I shall write about our ancestors, the ones I know about from the beginning of our family history all the way down to myself, Lapo. And I shall begin with the man who was the founder of our side of the family: Ruzza d'Arrigo di Luchese di Bonavia de' Sirigatti.[1] Ruzza had two brothers, one of whom was the prior of San Pietro a Scheraggio and rector of Antella. His name was Messire Bonavia, and the other brother's name was Luchese. When their father Arrigo died, they divided up his estate. The prior gave his portion to Luchese, either because he liked him better, or because Luchese had a greater need of it, for he had no fewer than seven sons, and many daughters. At that time, the Guelphs were exiled from Florence for the first time,[2] and the prior was sent away from his church by the Cavigniano family. Later, when the Guelphs returned, the Siminetti family and our own ancestors restored him to his church, where he stayed until the end of his life. Luchese and his sons had many descendants, many of whom are still here today; but since they don't have anything to do with our affairs, I shall skip over them and return to Ruzza, the founder of my side of the family. He was a big man, handsome

---

1 According to the nineteenth-century genealogist Luigi Passerini in *Famiglie celebri italiane* (1866), Ruzza de' Sirigatti lived between 1253 and 1293; the seventeenth-century historian Eugenio Gamurrini (*Istoria genealogica delle famiglie nobili toscane, et vmbre*, published in five volumes between 1668 and 1685), believed that Ruzza lived somewhat earlier.

2 Probably after the defeat of the Florentine Guelphs near Siena at Montaperti, "the hill of death," on 4 September 1260.

and strong, and lived about a hundred and thirty years.[3] I know this from Giovanni my father, who saw Ruzza at the time when he was completely bedridden. Ruzza had a son named Niccolino, whom he married to a daughter of the Scolari family in order to make peace with that family.

The reason is this: It seems that one of the Scolari family was out hunting, and so was one of Ruzza's kinsmen. A dispute arose about some prey, for both had let their dogs loose, and they had come from opposite sides. The argument grew heated; the man from the Scolari family, who was carrying a spear, struck the other man with it and killed him. Then to mock them he sent to Ruzza's family to ask for the spear back, for he had left it in the body of the dead man. Ruzza did not rest until he and his men killed the man who had killed his kinsman, at the foot of Passigniano in a stream called il Rimaggio. Then he sent a message of his own to the Scolari family, telling them to go to il Rimaggio and they would find their spear, for Ruzza killed the man with the same spear with which that man had killed his kinsman. The Scolari were outraged, for they were a powerful family at that time, and if the Buondelmonti family hadn't come to our family's aid, they would have been undone. But they made peace between the two families, and Ruzza married his young son Niccolino to the sister of the Scolari who had been killed, and peace was made between them.

II. [PROPERTY TRANSACTIONS]

And then in 1417 Monna Antonia, the daughter of the late Ser Giovanni di Ser Piero Gucci de' Sirigatti and of Monna Ghita, took over the estate of Ser Francesco, her brother, who had died intestate, not having made his will. Monna Antonia then took action against me over a house that I had bought from Ser Francesco; the purchase of this house is recorded on page 47 of this book. Monna Antonia was very wrong to sue me for this house, to the detriment of her soul; because after Ser Francesco had sold it to me, he returned the money that I had given him as part of the payment for the house, as we had agreed between us, and I insisted that I wanted to return the deeds of the house to him. Ser Francesco replied: "Lapo, you can see that there is going to be a plague in this year 1417. If I die, I trust you and want you to give this house, which my father built, to Francesco di Ser Niccolò di Ser Piero Gucci Sirigatti, my cousin; and

---

3 This kind of exaggeration is not unusual in accounts from this time.

have papers drawn up for this. And if Francesco should die without any legitimate male heirs, I want the house to go to you and to your children and heirs. So I in no wise want the deeds back, because I trust you." And he was right to trust me, for I would have followed all his instructions to the letter. Monna Antonia filed suit against me four times, and I was forced to come to an agreement with her. This was during the time that Niccolò da Uzzano was chief magistrate in Florence.

III. [LAPO'S SON, "A GREAT WASTER OF HIS OWN AND OTHERS' MONEY"]

Almighty God called my son Niccolaio to him on Saint Lucy's day, 13 December 1417. May God grant great pardon to his soul, with His blessing and mine. Niccolaio was born on 29 March 1386, as appears on page 19 of this book. He lived in this world for 31 years, 8 months, and 14 days. He had neither wife nor children, nor did he make a will, although I had made him independent, for he had nothing of his own and he had dissipated and squandered more of my money than was his fair share. I have written in some of my books part of what he squandered, for although he was a man of understanding, and very talented, he was a great waster of his own and others' money. For he cared little for anything except following his own appetites and desires, and gave me a great deal of trouble while he lived in this wretched world.

Memoirs

Bernardo Machiavelli

I. [AN AFFAIR WITH A SERVANT GIRL]

I record on this 17th day of November 1475 that on Wednesday the 25th of last month, when I returned in the morning from Santo Andrea,[1] my wife[2] told me that because of certain signs that she had seen, she thought that Lorenza, a servant in our house whom we call Nencia di Lazerino, had acted dishonourably, for she believed her to be pregnant. My wife described the signs to me, and I told her to question the girl, and in one way or another, by threats or blandishments, to find out the truth. I went out, and when I returned at about the hour of vespers, my wife told me that she had called the girl into her room and between soft words and threats she had got it out of her that it was true that she was with child, and that the father was Niccolò d'Alessandro Machiavelli.[3] When my wife asked her how the thing had come about, the girl told her that after we returned from the country last year on 8 November, she had gone out at night many times through the window onto the roof or through the little window near the fireplace in the kitchen to Niccolò's house to be with him, especially during the time that my wife had been big with child, and

---

1 Sant'Andrea in Percussina, about eleven kilometres from Florence (near San Casciano), where the Machiavelli family owned land and where Bernardo's famous son Niccolò was in the habit of retreating for long periods of time, writing extensively.
2 Bartolomea Nelli, who wrote prose and poetry. Bartolomea died in 1496, four years before her husband.
3 A cousin of Bernardo (Bernardo's grandfather and Niccolò's great-grandfather were brothers), then twenty-six years old.

after she gave birth; and that last May and June, when Niccolò's wife had been ill, Niccolò had come in many times through the little window and had his way with her on the hearth in the kitchen.

When I heard this, I went out to find Giovanni Nelli, my wife's brother, and it so happened that his brother Carlo was in Florence, having come to visit from Pisa. I told them the story and asked them to come the next day to dine with me to discuss the matter and to take whatever action they thought best. I did this because Giovanni had found the girl and had asked her father, who was a friend of his, to send her to me. The next day they came and dined with me; after we had eaten, I called Nencia into my room with the two of them and my wife and questioned her. She made the same reply as she had to my wife, and although Giovanni and Carlo and I warned her many times to take care about what she said and that it didn't seem likely to us that Niccolò, who had a young, pretty wife, would have gone after her, she made the same reply. She also said that when Niccolò's household was in the country (for most of the time they stay at Colombaia),[4] he would climb up on the balcony and call to her through the iron bars of the window in her bedchamber, and that they were together 2 or 3 times every week, and that the truth was that she was pregnant by Niccolò and that he had promised to give her a coat and a wool dress. I sent Nencia out of the room and Giovanni and Carlo told me that I should go to Niccolò and tell him the state of affairs and what the girl was saying, and then I should tell them what he said, after which Giovanni wanted to talk to Niccolò himself. I agreed, but I told them that I absolutely did not want the girl in my house any longer, and that we should inform her mother, who is a member of Giovanni's household, and also her father, and that they should come and fetch her. They replied that I should talk to Niccolò first and then we would do whatever was necessary.

So on Saturday the 28th, the evening of St Simon's day, around 4 in the afternoon, I went out; as I was walking toward the Ponte Vecchio I ran into Niccolò coming toward me in the square of Santa Felicita. I told him that I wanted to speak to him about Nencia and what she had said. He replied that he had wanted to tell me about this for more than six months and he himself didn't know why he hadn't done so. But the reason was that more than six months earlier, Francesco Renzi, whom they call Agata, a nephew of the doctor Maestro Raffaello da Terranuova, had

---

4 Not far from Sant'Andrea in Percussina.

asked Niccolò to leave him alone with Nencia in his house in Florence while his family was in the country (and he often left him alone there, for they were fast friends) and that Nencia would go out over the roof of our house into Niccolò's house to be with Francesco. This had happened many times since I had returned from the country, and the truth was, Niccolò said, that he had never had anything to do with the girl, but that Francesco had, and that his only fault in the business was not having told me about it. I was very upset, and told him that he had done me a great injury, great in any case but more so in a next-door neighbour and a close relative, and that I had never done such a thing to him or to his father, and that I didn't understand how he could have so little regard for me. For if it were true that it had been Francesco, who was often with me both here in Florence and in the country, he had never given me to understand it, so that I could take measures so that my house wouldn't be used as a bordello. I told him that he should think hard about this affair, for this girl wasn't from Mugello[5] but from Pistoia, of good but poor people; that her father and brothers might want to avenge her; that I absolutely didn't want her in my house any longer; and that the best thing for me to do was to tell Giovanni Nelli, who had placed her in my household, or to have her father and mother come and take her away. I said that I didn't know what the father would do when he heard the girl's story, for she said that Niccolò was the father; and that he should think it over. Niccolò replied that he realized he had done me an injury, but that the truth was that it had been Francesco who had sinned with the girl, and that he, Niccolò, had only erred in not telling me about it, and that it wasn't his responsibility, for he had a wife and sisters. He said he would think about it and would see me again. The 24th hour had already rung, and he didn't want to stay inside the city,[6] so he left, returning to Colombaia, where he said his family was staying.

On Monday the 30th of October I went to Giovanni Nelli and told him that I had spoken to Niccolò and related everything he had answered to me. Giovanni said I should be patient, that he wanted to speak to Niccolò himself. On the morning of the 31st, walking toward the Ponte Vecchio

---

5 In Bernardo's day, the area of Mugello (in the countryside north of Florence, between the Apennine ridge and the Arno Valley) was known as a place of women of easy virtue. Giovanni di Paolo Morelli paints a very different picture in his panegyric of this area of the Tuscan countryside.

6 The city gates of Florence were locked each evening.

I met Niccolò outside the palazzo of Mariotto de' Rossi. He said to me: "I hadn't seen you again, but now I want to tell you why I never told you about Nencia and Agata. As you know, Francesco Agata lives in the same house with Doctor Raffaello; please don't say anything about what I'm going to tell you to the doctor. Francesco had a pretty girl in his household whom I wanted for my own pleasure, and Francesco acted as go-between for me. So since he had done me that favour, I went along with what he was doing with Nencia." He said that later the thing had come out and that there had been the devil of a fuss, but that he had extricated himself. "So," he told me, "you see the reason for the injury I did you, which I know is a great one." I replied that this was a nice alibi, and that the girl was telling a different story – that he himself was the father; and that if things were really as he said they were, I was even more offended, for he had dared to act as pimp for Agata with my maidservants and to turn my house into a bordello with people coming and going at all hours of the night. I told him that I had told Giovanni Nelli about the affair, and that I wanted Giovanni to send for the girl's father and give her back to him, for I didn't want her any more; and that Giovanni had told me he wanted to speak to Niccolò before he told the girl's father, to see if a scandal could be avoided. And I added that he should think it over and take care to find some kind of a solution with Giovanni, for I didn't want the girl in my house under any circumstances. Having said this, I left him.

Then on Friday the 3rd of the present month Giovanni came to supper and to spend the night at my home, and told me that that evening he had been in the New Market with Niccolò, and that Niccolò had told him the same story he had told me on the 29th and 31st of last month. Moreover, Giovanni said that he had told Niccolò that he thought in order to avoid a big scandal, which might come out if the girl's father found out, they should find a woman whom she could stay with until she gave birth and see to it that the girl had 25 florins to marry on right after the baby was born, in order to save Giovanni's honour, for he was the one who had placed the girl in my household. Niccolò said he liked the idea; still insisting that he hadn't been the one to get the girl pregnant, but that it had been Francesco Agata, he said that he wanted to talk to Francesco and see if he could convince him to do what Giovanni said, and that he would let Giovanni know in a few days; so that's how they left things.

Then on Monday the 6th of this month, while I was in the country, Niccolò came to see me at my country home, where I was consigning some apples to a reseller who had bought them from me. Niccolò told me that Giovanni had spoken to him and that they had agreed that he would talk to Francesco Agata and make him do what he had agreed with Giovanni, but that later he had had second thoughts. He decided not to say anything to Agata, because he knew that he was hare-brained and that it would have been a waste of time to say anything to him. So Niccolò had decided that he would rather bear the brunt himself, since he had done so wrong never to have told me about the sin that Nencia and Francesco Agata were committing together. He said that now he wanted to do what Giovanni Nelli and I told him to do, and begged me to tell my wife not to say anything to his wife about it. I told him that in two days he would see Giovanni in Florence and that I thought that we should try to avoid a scandal at all costs.

Then on the 12th of this month Giovanni, Niccolò, and I met in Giovanni's shop and agreed that Niccolò would promise in writing to pay Giovanni this coming March one hundred *lire* so that Nencia could get married; and that he should make him his creditor in a bank under the following terms: that when the girl would be given to her husband, Niccolò would cash the dowry that is under Nencia's name in the Monte.[7] I had opened this account for her in May 1471 for 12½ years, spending 4 florins, 3 *lire*, and 12 *soldi*. And when he removed all or part of her dowry from the Monte, Niccolò was obliged to repay me the 4 florins, 3 *lire*, and 12 *soldi*. And since the next morning Giovanni wanted to go to Mugello, we agreed that in the meantime I would draw up a document containing what is said above, and that they would sign it without any other witnesses so that the affair wouldn't become known. So right there in Niccolò's shop I made three copies in my own hand of a document of the same tenor as above, with all of the pledges and agreements. I wrote down the day, that is the 17th of November 1475, and each of them signed all three copies, of which Niccolò kept one, Giovanni the second, and I the third.

I hereby record that yesterday, which was Saturday the 18th of the present month of November 1475, in the evening Giovanni Nelli came to me and told me that that same evening he and Niccolò Macchiavelli had been to see Monna Lisa, the midwife who lives at the Croce a Trebbio[8] in Florence, and that they had arranged to take Lorenza, otherwise known as Nencia di Lazarino, the girl who serves in my house, to her this morning, and that Monna Lisa had promised them that she would keep her until she gives birth. Niccolò had promised to give her five *lire* every

---

7 That is, the Monte delle Doti (Dowry Bank), a Florentine institution where money was deposited periodically to build up dowries for marriageable young women.

8 A small piazza not far from the church of Santa Maria Novella.

month, and he had given her a florin in advance. So this morning, a little
before the 14th hour, Giovanni took Nencia to Monna Lisa's house and
my wife let Nencia take all her shifts, handkerchiefs, and other linen.
So Nencia left my house and went with Giovanni this morning, the 19th
of November. Later Giovanni dined with me and told me that he had
taken Nencia and left her with Monna Lisa. And for clarity's sake I have
recorded it on this 19th day of November.

II. [NICCOLÒ AS PUPIL AND APPRENTICE; BERNARDO BUYS SEVERAL
BOOKS AND HAS THEM BOUND]

I record that on this 6th day of May 1476, my son Niccolò[9] began to
go to Maestro Matteo, the grammar master who lives at the foot of this
side of the Santa Trinita bridge, to learn to read the Donatello.[10] And
to pay for this teaching I must give him 5 *soldi* per month, plus twenty
at Eastertide.

I record that on this 8th day of May my son Niccolò brought 5 *soldi* to
Maestro Matteo who teaches him, as his salary for this month.

I record that on this fifth day of July 1476 I brought to Maestro Niccolò
Tedesco, the priest and astrologer, twelve *quinterni*[11] of quarto size, on
which I had written all of the cities and provinces, islands, and mountains that are mentioned in Livy's *Decades*, with their addenda according
to the books of each of the *Decades* in which Livy mentions them. And
he wrote them out for me in Latin, for which he declared himself to be
content and satisfied. I had purchased the 3 *Decades* in print from the
stationer Zanobi, as we had agreed and as I recorded on page 4 of this
same book, and we also agreed that as a reward for my labours he would
bind them for me.

I record that on 20 March 1476 my son Niccolò began to go to Ser Battista di Filippo da Poppi to learn the Donatello. Ser Battista gives lessons
in the church of San Benedetto in the area of San Giovanni.

I record that on this 3rd day of November 1477 I purchased from Francesco Bartoli and company, cloth cutters, 5½ *braccia*[12] of reddish-brown

---

9 Then six years old.

10 The *Ars grammatica* of Elio Donato, a canonical, widely used work during the Middle
    Ages; the diminutive form "Donatello" indicated the abridged edition that was used
    in schools.

11 A *quinterno* (plural *quinterni*) is a group of five sheets of paper.

12 A *braccio* (plural *braccia*) is a unit of measurement roughly equal to sixty centimetres.

dyed wool cloth to make a little tunic and cloak for Niccolò. It came to 10 *lire* and 15 *soldi*. I gave them nine *lire* in cash: 15 *soldi* in a Sienese half florin and 6 *lire* and 18 *soldi* in small change. I still owe them 20 *soldi*. Their boy took the cloth to Leonardo the cloth cutter to have it cut, and left it with his son-in-law Girolamo. He promised me that I could have it back next Thursday morning.

Later I gave them the remaining 20 *soldi*.

I record that on this 3rd day of January 1479 I put my son Niccolò to board with Piero Maria, the master of arithmetic and bookkeeping, and we agreed that I would pay him for all this teaching as follows: a half florin when Niccolò begins to study the rudiments of arithmetic, and another later on in the teaching.

On the same day I set Totto[13] to learning the alphabet. I record that on the 5th day of November 1481 my sons Niccolò and Totto began to study with Maestro Pagolo da Ronciglione, the grammar master. Niccolò is doing the Latin classics, and Totto is learning Donato; I don't yet have an agreement with Maestro Pagolo about the payment.

I record that on this 21st day of June 1486 I gave to Francesco d'Andrea di Bartolomeo, the stationer at San Giorgio in Florence, a printed version of a *Reading* of the abbot of Sicily[14] on the 4th and 5th *Decretals*, in folio, as well as the three *Decades* with the epitome of the 140 books of Livy, printed, also in folio. He is going to bind them well for me, with half-leather boards and two clasps each, and I have agreed to give him four *lire* and 5 *soldi* for binding both volumes. I also agreed to sell him some red wine that he tasted for 50 *soldi* per barrel. He took the books away with him, and promised to bring them back within eight days.

On the same day, in the evening after the 24th hour he came with a porter and took away a barrel of red wine for 50 *soldi*, as we had agreed above.

On the 27th of June I gave him Giovanni d'Andrea's gloss on the sixth *Decretal*[15] to bind; I bought this from Bartolo di Fruosino, a bookseller in the Garbo,[16] and then Francesco d'Andrea took it to bind it along with

---

13 Another of Bernardo's sons, born in 1475.

14 *Nicolaus de Tudeschis, abbas Siculus, Lectura super quarto et quinto Decretalium*, perhaps the edition published in Pavia in 1482. Nicolò de' Tedeschi (1386–1445) was archbishop of Palermo.

15 *Johannes Andreae, Novella super sexto decretalium*, probably the edition published in Pavia in 1483. Giovanni d'Andrea (circa 1270–1348), a canonist born at Mugello near Florence, was well known for his commentaries on the *Decretals* of Pope Gregory IX.

16 The modern Via della Condotta.

the *Mercuriali*,[17] for which he promised to come here this evening when he leaves his shop.

On the same day, at the hour of the Ave Maria, Francesco came here, and I gave him Giovanni Andrea's *Mercuriali* to bind, and we agreed that he would bind them together with the *Novellina* in a single volume with half-leather boards and 2 clasps, for 40 *soldi*. I agreed to give him wine at 50 *soldi* per barrel as above.

I record that on the first of July my son Niccolò gave the stationer Francesco d'Andrea, to whom I had given these books to bind, as is recorded in the preceding page, a barrel of red wine for 50 *soldi*.

On the 4th he gave him 20 *soldi* in cash; for Francesco had said that he couldn't bind the books without 20 *soldi* to buy the leather.

On the 8th of July Niccolò gave Francesco d'Andrea 3 flasks of red wine and a flask of vinegar, which he came to pick up. So he no longer owed him 5 *soldi*. On the same day, Francesco delivered the bound books. One, the Abbot's reading of the sixth *Decretals*, was well bound, as we had agreed; the other two were poorly bound and didn't live up to our agreement. And he did this while I was away in the country.

---

17 *Johannes Andreae aureum comentum super regulis iuris quod nuncupatur mercuriales*, probably also from the 1483 edition published in Pavia.

Appendix: A Portrait of Vittore Branca

Cesare De Michelis

Vittore Branca was born on 9 July 1913 in the city of Savona on the coast of Liguria, where his family had moved after his father was hired as director of research at the ILVA ironworks there. Vittore, however, never truly considered himself a Ligurian, but rather a Lombard or a Piedmontese, in homage to his family, which hailed from the town of Lesa on the western shore of Lake Maggiore. In fact, it was Branca's wish that Lesa be his final resting place, and after his death in Venice on 28 March 2004, he was buried there. He was especially proud of the place's strong literary tradition – Antonio Stoppani, to whom Branca was distantly related, had lived in Lesa, and Alessandro Manzoni had long resided there at the house of his second wife, Teresa Borri. Antonio Rosmini often visited Manzoni at his home, as did Giulio Carcano, Cesare Correnti, and even Antonio Fogazzaro. All of these writers exemplified the intersection of the writing experience with religious tension and a fervid search for inner truth – a confluence that would be central to Branca's own life and work.

It is not an easy task to give a sense of the extraordinary existential commitment of Branca the man and the scholar on the basis of a detailed reconstruction of his life, in which interests and passions that seemed to be so diverse were mingled; he always maintained a rigorous, coherent approach, centred on an enduring Christian activism. But Branca's religious beliefs did not distract him from his deep commitment to scholarship and journalism; on the contrary, he approached all of his many journalistic and publishing endeavours with an energetic enthusiasm. Starting in the early 1950s, Branca was involved in the founding and organization of the Giorgio Cini Foundation in Venice. Rich in collections, research projects, and cultural initiatives, the Cini Foundation is dedicated to protecting and restoring the island of San Giorgio Maggiore and the magnificent former Benedictine monastery located there.

Branca was a young boy when his father died, so from an early age he developed a strong sense of responsibility that drove him to excel in his studies. At eighteen years of age, he finished the *liceo classico* in Savona, where he had been inspired by a pivotal lecture on literature as the "food of life" (despite the fact that the lecturer was a notoriously cantankerous professor). Almost immediately upon graduating, in the autumn of 1931 he took the admission exam for the prestigious Scuola Normale Superiore of Pisa. He passed with flying colours, despite the fact that he flaunted, in open protest, the badge of the Italian Catholic Youth Society, which had been banned by the Fascist regime.

The admissions board was composed of the Scuola Normale's president, Giovanni Gentile, as well as two men with whom Branca would form and maintain very close friendships – his professors of history, literary criticism, and philology, Attilio Momigliano and Giorgio Pasquali. From the very beginning, Momigliano and Pasquali witnessed another key aspect of Branca's character – his tenacious loyalty to both people and ideas. This determination would characterize his behaviour in both good times and bad. Branca was so independent in his thinking that throughout his life, even – and often – in the face of adversity, he never allowed himself to be fettered by pre-established notions.

In that same year, as the controversy between the Catholic Youth and the Fascists was being rekindled, Branca joined the Italian Catholic Federation of University Students (FUCI). He soon met another important teacher and lifelong friend, Don Giovanni Battista Montini, the future Pope Paul VI. Montini instantly recognized Branca's talent, and presented his student with the opportunity to contribute to the journal *Studium.* Apart from his early articles in the Savona newspaper *Il Letimbro,* it was at *Studium,* in 1933, that Branca began his work as a critic and scholar, writing a substantial number of reviews as well as a brief study of the poetry of Giuseppe Ungaretti.

Branca's university years were divided between passionate activism and an equally unrestrained and persistent commitment to his studies. He was selected as leader of FUCI, and in 1933 was almost expelled from the Scuola Normale when, in a gesture of intolerance toward the Fascist regime, he mockingly wore a dirty shirt instead of the characteristic black shirt. (The irony of Branca's actions rests on the double meaning of *nero* in Italian: *black* or *dirty*. The Blackshirts, or *camicie nere,* were Fascist paramilitary squads operating in Italy under Mussolini.) His expulsion was postponed and then rescinded, due to Giovanni Gentile's direct intervention. The president of the Scuola Normale had taken a great liking to Branca, despite – or perhaps precisely because of – the student's youthful impulsiveness and the profound difference between his ideas and Gentile's own. Branca graduated in 1935 with a thesis on the history of Boccaccio criticism, which passed with highest honours and was awarded right of publication. Still, his first book, which would be published in the following year, would be a much more specific and accurate study of the fourteenth-century *cantare* and Boccaccio, entitled *Il cantare trecentesco e il Boccaccio del Filostrato e del Teseida*. This work lead Branca to related research that appeared in the series *Studi di lettere storia e filosofia pubblicati dalla R. Scuola Normale Superiore di Pisa* (published by Sansoni). Later, Branca reworked his thesis and published it with the title *Linee di una storia della critica al "Decameron"* in 1939.

While pursing grant-funded postgraduate research, Branca took the examination for qualification as a teacher, and received the highest score; he moved to Florence in 1937 and immediately began teaching. At the same time, he was working for the Accademia della Crusca on a critical edition of Boccaccio's works, for which he prepared an edition of the *Amorosa visione* (published by Sansoni in 1944). Meanwhile, he edited a volume for the *Scrittori d'Italia* series directed by Benedetto Croce, which included Boccaccio's *Rime, Amorosa visione,* and *La caccia di Diana* (published by Laterza in 1939). He subsequently edited the collections *Mistici: Fioretti di San Francesco* and *Lettere di Santa Caterina* (both published by the Dante Alighieri Society in 1941). He then edited the critical edition of *Epistolae et Orationes Carmina* by the Venetian humanist Ermolao Barbaro (published by Libreria Bibliopolis in 1943).

During these years, Branca married fellow FUCI member Olga Montagner and their daughters were born. The year 1942 marked a milestone in Branca's scholarly career – he passed the state exam and received his habilitation (the highest academic qualification) in Italian literature. It was also a significant year in his life as an activist. Branca had continued to engage in clandestine activities as the Fascist regime increasingly showed signs of instability. Then, on 25 July 1943, Mussolini was finally overthrown. In those convulsive moments, Branca participated in the drafting of the Codice di Camaldoli, a pragmatic manifesto of Catholic anti-Fascism. He came into contact with Alcide De Gasperi, the acknowledged leader of the Christian Democrats, who entrusted him with the responsibility of the Tuscan branch of the National Liberation Committee

(CLN) alongside distinguished representatives of the other anti-Fascist parties, including Piero Calamandrei and Eugenio Montale.

The early 1940s were terrible for Branca for many reasons: on a personal level, he had to help his family survive in times of extreme poverty, and, on a professional level, the oppressive threat of the Republic of Salò – the final incarnation of the Italian Fascist state – was looming. In the ongoing political struggle, the situation became more and more complex and dangerous each day, putting Branca's ideological and moral consistency severely to the test.

Branca resolutely resisted pressure from Gentile, who asked him to agree, "for love of country and culture," and "for solidarity in research," to cooperate with the Fascist state's institutions and media outlets. This allegiance to Fascism would ultimately lead to Gentile's demise; on 15 April 1944, he was murdered by a group of communist partisans.

Then, on 11 August 1944, came the day of Florence's liberation. It was the end of a nightmare that had lasted almost a year. Branca remembered the day the Germans surrendered to Allied forces with an emotion that remained unchanged up to the last days of his life. While CLN representatives were preparing to sign the treaty, the Florentine patriot Giorgio La Pira suggested that they read the famous *Canticle of the Sun* by St Francis together as a prayer of thanksgiving (Branca, in fact, would later edit critical editions of the *Canticle* in 1948 and 1950). La Pira asked the German commander of the Wehrmacht, who was by then defeated and stripped of his weapons, to join in as well. Thus a "new life" began with some of the greatest words of love and peace from the one of the most radiant poems and prayers ever written.

That same day, Branca, together with Carlo Levi and Ranuccio Bianchi Bandinelli, founded the first post-Fascist daily Florentine newspaper, *La Nazione del popolo*, for which he wrote the first editorial. After the Liberation of Italy, Branca's political activism would manifest itself in an extraordinary level of journalistic activity. Besides working for *La Nazione del popolo*, for which he produced fifty-four articles in 1945 alone, Branca was a founding member of Pietro Calamandrei's *Il Ponte*, for which he wrote twenty-two articles during that same year. In 1947, he was also involved in the creation of a new Christian-oriented newspaper, *Il Mattino dell'Italia centrale*.

Already during the early 1940s, when his publishing career was in its infancy, Branca effortlessly mingled his literary interests with his political fervour and the moral values that formed its basis. He inaugurated a series entitled *Collezione in venitquattresimo* ("twenty-four" refers to the trim size of the books in the series) with a new edition of *Dei delitti e delle pene* by Cesare Beccaria, with an introduction by Calamandrei (1941). Shortly afterward, he began directing the *Biblioteca Nazionale* series (published by Le Monnier), publishing Giuseppe Mazzini's *Note autobiografiche* (1943). In those dramatic circumstances, Mazzini's work was presented as an energetic appeal to Risorgimento-style patriotism.

During those same years, Branca met another very important figure, the priest and publisher Giuseppe De Luca – to whom he dedicated his critical edition of Boccaccio's *Amorosa visione*. After a number of failed attempts in the 1930s, De Luca succeeded in launching the *Edizioni di storia e letteratura* shortly after the end of the war. Branca, along with other colleagues and friends, made a significant contribution to this venture, especially to the *Archivio italiano per la storia della pietà*, a gargantuan project that followed the methods of the eighteenth-century historian Ludovico Antonio Muratori, the father of Italian historiography. A year after De Luca's death, Branca edited a collection of his writings, *Letteratura di pietà a Venezia dal '300 al '600* (published by Olschki in 1963).

Branca deliberately kept his distance from active politics, the intrigues of the Christian Democratic Party, and electoral campaigns. He firmly believed that he was meant to heed another vocation – an academic and literary one – to which he intended to remain resolutely faithful. On the other hand, it is no coincidence that one of his first contributions to *Il Ponte* was entitled "Carità di patria e storia letteraria" (Charity for the Fatherland and Literary History). Branca was relentless in his activity both as an editor and as a critic, and his research focused on the most important texts of the new postwar literature, from Eugenio Montale to Alberto Moravia, and from Rocco Sinisgalli to Carlo Levi.

In 1944 Branca also began his university teaching career. He taught Italian literature at the University of Florence and, shortly afterwards, at the Magisterium "Maria Assunta" in Rome, until, in 1949, he earned a full professorship. During the academic year 1950–1 he taught at the University of Catania and also joined the directorate of the Division of Arts and Letters of UNESCO in Paris. In 1953 he began teaching at the University of Padua. The following year he became secretary general of the Giorgio Cini Foundation in Venice.

Branca's critical and philological achievements in that hectic but highly stimulating postwar period were equally impressive. He wrote books about Emilio De Marchi (1946) and Vittorio Alfieri (1947–8), and edited several critical editions apart from those already mentioned, including Ippolito Nievo's *Varmo* (1945), three volumes of the Risorgimento-era scientific and literary journal *Il Conciliatore* (1948–54), and a critical edition of Boccaccio's *Decameron* in two volumes (1950–1). Branca was tireless, always active, present everywhere, and curious about everything. He developed new research methods, historical perspectives, theoretical tensions, and intellectual connections with scholars in every part of the world – so much so that it would be easy for him in the following years to promote and direct, along with Umberto Bosco, the International Association for the Study of Italian Language and Literature (AISLLI).

Branca, by now in his forties and at the height of his moral and intellectual strength, finally stopped to catch his breath after years of living with what he liked to remember as an "anguished and anxious" passion. He was content with how much he had achieved and wanted to develop a research agenda that would define his future goals without sacrificing any of his interests, but rather recomposing them into a program of work that was even grander, more integrated, and more coherent. In 1954, along with Giovanni Getto, he founded the journal *Lettere italiane*, which would become an obligatory point of reference in Italian studies.

In 1956, Branca published what is considered his greatest book, *Boccaccio medievale* (published by Sansoni), which provocatively overturned the traditional image of the author of the *Decameron*, and shed a surprising light on the "autumn of the Middle Ages." In 1958 he introduced the first volume of the highly erudite *Tradizione delle opere di Giovanni Boccaccio*, entitled *Un primo elenco di codici e tre studi* (published by Edizioni di Storia e Letteratura). From that moment on, it would be impossible to speak about Boccaccio without mentioning Vittore Branca – he had introduced a perspective to Boccaccio studies that continues to this day. Philology would no longer be limited to examining what Branca called the *tradizione caratterizzata* (characterized tradition); instead, he championed the reconstruction of a *tradizione attiva e caratterizzante* (active and characterizing tradition), which allowed "for a long and arduous, but sure journey – one open to fascinating landscapes … a real philological understanding of the works that we study … set in the style, the culture, and the spiritual and social life in which the author participated and to which he responded." At the same time, as secretary general of the Cini Foundation, Branca redoubled his efforts, organizing a rigorous program of collecting, research, seminars and conferences, and publishing projects of all kinds.

The centre of Branca's critical reflection remains his *Boccaccio medievale* (the latest edition was published by BUR in 2010), along with his annotated edition of the *Decameron* (published by Einaudi). *Boccaccio medievale* has been an extremely successful work, not only reprinted eleven times and translated into six languages but also continuously enriched and revised for more than half a century, ultimately doubling its original length (the 2010 edition, with an introduction by Franco Cardini, is 550 pages long). In spite of what was perceived as an overtly polemical and even intentionally provocative tone, especially in the first edition, *Boccaccio medievale* presented a new picture of the transition from the Christian tradition of the society of the city-states of the Middle Ages to full-fledged humanism. Branca identified the existence of a deep underlying continuity in this shift from the Christian to the humanistic perspective, which was prompted by a dramatic mid-fourteenth-century crisis, the Black Death. He demonstrated how this deadly plague forced everyone in the society of the times to measure themselves against the background of sudden change.

It might seem surprising that a scholar who was so proudly Catholic would concentrate his critical activities on the most raucous work in Italian literature and on the most libertine and worldly of Italian writers. However, the study of Boccaccio – more than Dante and Petrarch, whose lives were tormented by moral issues – allowed Branca to avoid any ideological manipulation of the text, and forced him to confront the experience of civic history, the fascination of literary invention, and the vitality of men and women destined to live in the secular world.

Boccaccio recounted the deeds of men destined to sin and repent, to travel the length and breadth of Europe engaging in trade and business of every kind, to love and to desire, to mourn and to rejoice. These men lived by no other moral code than that of the individual – a code that did not know perfection and purity, but embraced all possible feelings. Thus, rather than demanding his readers' loyalty and confidence, Boccaccio's work introduced problems and questions that, in order to be solved, had to be investigated with the tools of a completely human and secular wisdom.

As a historian and a Christian, Branca might have chosen to rely solely on erudition and philology in order to avoid doubts that might have compromised his faith and ideology. Instead, he embraced doubt, and allowed it to guide his research. He was intrigued by the uniqueness of Boccaccio, and, by choosing that author as a main focus of his research from the time he was a very young man, Branca kept his scholarship and his inner spiritual life strictly separate. He jealously defended his spiritual life from any indiscretion, "intimately abhorring uncontrolled inhibitions, showy displays of intimacy, and immodest floods of feelings," to use the words of his colleague at the University of Padua, Professor Manilo Pastore Stocchi. Branca remained doggedly faithful to this separation of his scholarship and his spirituality throughout his life, as evidenced by the freedom with which he selected and associated with his students. He was indifferent to their ideologies and uncompromising on the quantity and quality of their studies, as well as on the rigour of their research.

Branca was the opposite of an accommodating man who is easily prone to compromise; rather, he was absolutely resolute in what he wanted to do, could even be scathing in his judgments, and inflexible in his choices. Yet at the same time he was inexhaustibly curious, open to discussion and dialogue, attentive to any suggestion.

There was a space in Branca's life to bear witness to his faith without subordinating free intellectual commitment, and *Boccaccio medievale* demonstrated the extraordinary independence of its author and the unpredictable results that philology was capable of producing. Boccaccio did not predict the future, nor – despite his devotion to Petrarch – did he aspire to be the ideologue of a new culture. It was enough for him to write of the world in which he grew up and lived by creating a fresco of it as wholly alive, true, real, rich, and varied. Boccaccio investigated the deep-rooted causes of the crisis that affected him, a crisis that was first of all moral, but also economic and social, cultural and artistic – heralded by a monstrous and terrible epidemic that seemed impossible to escape.

In the 1960s, Branca's work on Boccaccio was enriched by two new initiatives. One was the 1963 publication of *Studi sul Boccaccio*, indispensable annals of the international community developed by their founder and kept alive by the work of his followers. The following year, Branca edited the Mondadori Classics edition of Boccaccio's works. (This last endeavour would take thirty-five years to finish – at one point, in fact, the publisher became exasperated and cancelled the project, only to restart it and finally oversee its completion in 1998.) Both of these accomplishments were preceded by Branca's exceptional 1962 discovery of a late holograph manuscript of the *Decameron* – the so-called Manuscript Hamilton 90, preserved in the Staatsbibliothek Preussischer Kulturbesitz, published in a facsimile edition by Alinari in 1975 and in a critical edition by the Accademia della Crusca in 1976. With this manuscript as evidence, Branca succeeded in proving that Boccaccio's supposed renunciation of his masterpiece in his old age was nothing more than a legend.

I still remember my former professor's satisfaction when he identified via infrared photography the corrections that were not in Boccaccio's hand in the Hamilton manuscript, thus solving the mystery of the inexplicable presence of unjustifiable errors in this holograph work. I remember Branca experiencing this same satisfaction many years later, when he completed the last two volumes of the ten-volume *Tutte le Opere* series, *Genealogie* and *De montibus*, which he prefaced with some brief but very meaningful words of thanks and dedication. He was truly proud to have succeeded in an enterprise that had been attempted over the centuries and had never been achieved until then.

Branca came to Venice in the beginning of 1953, at the same time that the newly appointed Patriarch Angelo Roncalli arrived there from Paris. Branca's relationship with the future Pope John XXIII – who became a leading figure in the life of Venice – was fruitful in both collaboration and solidarity. Their friendship would last even after Roncalli's move to Rome, and up to the time of his election as pope and his death. Branca's relationships with leading figures in the Catholic Church continued and grew even richer with John XXIII's successors, Paul VI, who had been Branca's guide during the years of FUCI, and John Paul I, who was also a patriarch of Venice before becoming pope. These relationships brought Branca the scholar's civic passion, as well as his social commitment as a Christian believer, to new heights.

The strength and determination of Branca's faith were rooted in the certainty that truth would always give glory to God, and that beauty would never contradict goodness. This perfect circularity, however, had to be put into action anew every day with the momentum of enthusiasm that, for him, corresponded with the most sincere and fervent of prayers.

The 1960s, the very years in which I was closest to Vittore Branca – first as a student and later as an unruly apprentice – were exceptional ones. They opened with the 1961 discovery of the unpublished and unfinished second *centuria* of Angelo Poliziano's *Miscellanea*, purchased by the Cini Foundation and which Branca, together with Pastore Stocchi, would later publish (first by Alinari in 1972 and then by Olschki in 1978). Branca was an exceptional interpreter of the works of authors from past epochs; he collected the abundant fruits of two decades of study and research in the volume *Poliziano e l'umanesimo della parola* (published by Einaudi in 1983). This study was supported by his research on humanism in Venice, which he conducted for more than a half a century and collected in the volume *La sapienza civile* (published by Olschki in 1998).

It was in the mid-1960s when Branca began again to write regularly for newspapers, starting in 1965 with the *Corriere della Sera,* for which he wrote increasingly numerous articles over a period of more than twenty years, until 1987. He progressively expanded his topics well beyond the usual ones, as is clearly shown in a collection of his articles published in 2013 that focuses entirely on twentieth-century literature, edited by myself and Gilberto Pizzamiglio. Branca later wrote for the newspapers *Il Messaggero* (1985–95) and *Il Sole 24 ore* (1988–2004).

Branca's editorial work was no less intense. He loved not only the authority to make decisions and the power of managing editorial projects but also, above all, the practice of collaboration. He enjoyed working with others, patiently supervising and offering generous assistance in the dissemination and promotion of the works he oversaw. He was a true teacher – he managed his students and collaborators with great attention and strictness. His approach stimulated their activity, and always ensured results.

Branca oversaw the compilation of the great encyclopedias published by the Cini Foundation on the performing arts, art, and philosophy, as well as the *Dizionario critico della letteratura italiana* (published by UTET in 1973 and 1986). When he was in his eighties, Branca oversaw the ambitious *Storia di Venezia,* published by the Enciclopedia Italiana (beginning in 1991), which is still unfinished today. He was editor of the series *Scuola aperta,* published by Sansoni. He also oversaw the series *Classici italiani per l'uomo del nostro tempo,* published by Rusconi, which projected the presence of the classics of Italian literature into the future, looking "at the reactions and efforts that these texts have stimulated, the ideas and the expressions that they have prompted ... even in modern life." At the Cini Foundation on the Island of San Giorgio Maggiore in Venice, Branca tirelessly promoted the lecture series *Corsi d'alta cultura,* which dealt with the most pressing issues, discussed by the most stimulating and provocative figures of the day, as is demonstrated in his foreword to a book entitled *La critica, forma caratteristica della civiltà moderna* (published by Sansoni), and in the 1970 collection of lectures by Theodor Adorno, Maria Corti, Max Horkheimer, Jean Starobinski, and Elémire Zolla. Here Branca identified, "in the rejection of judgments of value," the signalling of a widespread tendency "to discard permanent values; that is, those above and beyond history." He then reiterated that criticism "is not and cannot be a science because it is in all cases and above all the insight and action of an individual." This, he maintained, was especially true "in today's world, which is ever more threatened by ideological anathemas and witch-hunts" and requires moral choices and meanings; that is, "a permanent school of freedom."

At last the time came for Branca to retire, and with it came the opportunity for him to look back at his life and career, and to return to subjects that summarized critical itineraries that were only seemingly minor – such as the merchant writings that Branca had begun to publish as early as 1956, beginning with the *Ricordi* (Memoirs) of Giovanni di Paolo Morelli (published by Le Monnier). Three decades later, in 1986, Rusconi Libri published Branca's seminal anthology *Mercanti scrittori: ricordi nella Firenze tra Medioevo e Rinascimento*, of which the University of Toronto Press is now publishing a full English translation. Branca returned again to the writings of merchants from the medieval and Renaissance periods in his *Con amore volere: narrar di mercanti fra Boccaccio e Machiavelli* (published by Marsilio Editori in 1996), in which he included the most famous of all merchant writers, Boccaccio, to whom Branca also devoted a substantial second volume of *Tradizione delle opere* (published by Edizioni di Storia e Letteratura in 1991) and the three monumental volumes of *Boccaccio visualizzato: Narrare per parole e per immagini fra Medioevo e Rinascimento* (published by Einaudi in 1999). Branca's final philological undertaking took as its focus an older manuscript, an acknowledged copy of the first draft of the *Decameron*, the Paris Italian Manuscript 482; this was *Variazioni stilistiche e narrative*, the second volume of *Capolavori del Boccaccio*, published in 2002 by the Veneto Institute of Science, Letters and Art over which Branca had presided from 1979 to 1985. The first volume, *Riscrittura del Decameron*, on which Branca collaborated with Maurizio Vitale, focused on linguistic changes in Boccaccio's text.

In conclusion, I cannot fail to mention *Ponte Santa Trinità: per amore di libertà, per amore di verità* (published by Marsilio in 1987) and *Protagonisti nel Novecento: incontri, ritratti da vicino, aneddoti* (published by Aragno in 2004), in which Branca revealed himself to be a true memorialist – completely unselfish and as reluctant to make any type of personal confession as he was generous in sharing vivid and exciting memories. Here we find further proof that Branca was never distant or distracted from the events that unfolded during this lifetime, but was, on the contrary, a leading figure. He was capable at times of a furious impatience, but also of anguished insecurities and a vulnerable melancholy. His life is a testimony to the concept of "freedom as a pre-condition of morality," as he himself remembered when he was awarded honorary Florentine citizenship at the Palazzo Vecchio on 7 October 2002.

Index